D0844334

Clinical Social Work | Knowledge and Skills

Clinical Social Work | Knowledge and Skills

Helen Northen

Second Edition

New York | Columbia University Press

Columbia University Press
New York   Chichester, West Sussek
Copyright © 1995 Columbia University Press
All right reserved

Library of Congress Cataloging-in-Publication Data
Northen, Helen.
Clinical social work : knowledge and skills / by Helen Northen. —2d ed.
p.   cm
Includes bibliographical references and index.
ISBN 0–231–10110-4
1. Social service. 2. Social case work. 3. Medical social work.
I. Title.
HV31.N67   1994
361.3'2—dc20   94–11067
                                                                    CIP

Casebound editions of Columbia University Press books are printed on
permanent and durable acid-free paper.

Printed in the United States Of America
c 10 9 8 7 6 5 4 3

This book is dedicated to my sister, Ethel,
and Henry Winje who have
enriched my life in many, many ways.

Contents |

Preface |

Social work is a multifaceted profession. Its practitioners have assumed responsibility for a range of services to deal with problems arising from the interaction between people and their environments. They practice in varied settings, with diverse populations, and perform numerous roles. Within the broad domain of the profession, clinical social work consists of direct services to individuals, families, and other groups to help them prevent or resolve problems in psychosocial functioning. It includes work in the environment in behalf of clients as an integral part of practice. It is intended that this thoroughly revised and expanded edition will provide a comprehensive foundation of the values, knowledge, and skills essential for the effective practice of clinical social work.

The literature on clinical social work practice has expanded during the past two decades, and I have used in this text some of the exciting ideas found there. But there are many highly relevant contributions from earlier days that have been retained in the new edition. The theories that underlie particular skills are explicated: it is assumed that, to practice effectively, practitioners need to understand why they act in a particular way as well as what they do and how they do it.

A biopsychosocial systems perspective on people in their social contexts undergirds the description of values, knowledge, skills, and processes. Within this broad viewpoint, the social worker uses that knowledge from multiple scientific and experiential sources that contributes to understanding the interdependence of biological, psychological, social, and cultural forces that influence the behavior and well-being of clients, the dynamic processes of families and other groups, and environmental forces. Although much more is still needed, there is a growing body of research on practice that has been integrated into the book's content. Throughout the book vignettes of process are presented to illustrate how generic concepts and principles are applied in a variety of specific situations.

The book is designed for practitioners, educators, and supervisors who desire to update their knowledge, and for students in practice classes. Its purpose is to prepare practitioners for the informed and flexible use of family, individual, group, and community modalities of practice in direct services to people. In addition to its use in generic or integrated classes, it can be used in casework or group work classes or in concentrations by field of practice or type of problem, supplemented by the use of more specialized readings and illustrations. If the book contributes to enhancing the quality of clinical social work practice, it will have fulfilled its purpose.

A large network of colleagues and friends, including former students, has contributed greatly to my knowledge about practice theory. I continue to owe much to my membership in a group of present and former faculty at the University of Southern California who are committed to preparing students for effective practice and who have stimulated, supported, and collaborated with me in my teaching and writing. It is hard to single out those who have been most influential, but, for this book, June Brown, Sylvia Faulkner, Alan Levy, Barbara Solomon, and Marie Weil certainly merit my heartfelt thanks. Numerous social workers throughout the country have also been helpful in providing records of practice and consultation: they include Marilyn Biggerstaff, the late Thomas Carlton, Phyllis Caroff, George Getzel, Skip Hinchman, Roselle Kurland, Ben Orcutt, and June Simmons. Mary Kay Houston gave generously of her time and talents in reviewing the manuscript and providing case material and consultation.

My appointment to two terms on the National Council on the Practice of Clinical Social Work of NASW provided opportunities to learn about practice in many settings and in many parts of the country. Leila Whiting and Vivian Jackson gave excellent staff service to the Council, which included giving information about the latest trends and issues. Meeting with many groups of students and practitioners has given me further opportunities to test out my perspective on clinical social work and its applicability to specific situations.

The book could not have been completed without the aid of Jeanne Smith in preparing the final manuscript. Nor could it have been completed without the dedicated, friendly, and splendid help of Ruth Britton, librarian of the Arlien Johnson Library at the School of Social Work, University of Southern California. Gioia Stevens and Joan McQuary of Columbia University Press have guided me through the publication process. My sincere thanks to all of these wonderful people.

Clinical Social Work | Knowledge and Skills

One | Evolution of Clinical Social Work

Clinical social work is a term that now has wide acceptance among many practitioners, social agencies, licensing bodies, government programs, and the public. Some practitioners avoid the term, however, holding on to myths about it. For example, they believe that clinicians work only in private practice; do only psychoanalytically oriented psychotherapy; are not concerned about the clients' needs for practical resources and social networks; and foster a medical rather than a social model of practice. None of these assertions are characteristics of clinical social work today.

The term "clinical social work" clearly has its original roots in medicine, where it is defined simply as practice based on actual observation and treatment of patients, as distinguished from experimental or laboratory study.[1] A medical clinician is one who engages in hands-on practice. In psychology, the term is used to distinguish direct service practice from experimental and other specializations. It also serves a political purpose in differentiating psychologists with doctoral degrees from those not having that qualification. The term is now also used in Schools of Law where "clinical legal education emphasizes training in lawyering skills such as interviewing, negotiating, counseling, and advising."[2] Thus, the term has come to mean competence in the direct practice of a profession.

Early Developments

It is not clear when the term "clinical" was first used as an adjective for casework, group work, or social work practice. Eisenbuth reports that clinical social work was first used in a 1931 address by Edith Abbott, a professor of social work at the University of Chicago. Carlton stated that the term was coined in federal hospitals and clinics to describe the practice of social workers with and on behalf of patients. Lustman reported that the Veterans Administration initiated use of the term in the late 1940s as a unifying force in joining casework and group work and medical and psychiatric social work. Stewart pointed out that the term didn't really come into its own until the 1960s, primarily owing to events in the profession and political considerations. He noted that the early clinical social work literature tended to emphasize psychotherapy in private practice.[3] The National Association of Social Workers, through task forces and councils, has sought widespread acceptance of a broader view of clinical social work.

Any consideration of the evolution of clinical social work fits within the much broader history of social work practice. One major theme was the development of social casework, social group work, and social community organization work and, later, family treatment, which were the antecedents to clinical social work.[4] For a long time, these were viewed as separate and highly specialized methods of practice. Schools of social work offered majors in one or more of these forms of practice.

A second theme was the division of practice into specialties by fields, particularly child welfare, medical social work, psychiatric social work, and school social work. Specialized organizations were organized to further the interests of social workers in the first three of these fields: the American Association of Medical Social Workers in 1918, the American Association of School Social Workers in 1919, the American Association of Psychiatric Social Workers in 1926. Althoough not a professional organization, the Child Welfare League of America represented the interests of child welfare workers. Later, the American Association of Group Workers and the Association for the Study of Community Organization were founded in 1946 and, finally, the Social Work Research Group in 1948. A growing conviction about the common base of social work led to the merger of the seven professional organizations into the National Association of Social Workers (NASW) in 1955.

A third division of practice occurred around the emergence of different theories of practice, beginning with the debate about the similarities and differences between diagnostic casework, which used Freudian psychoanalytic theory as a base for understanding personality, and functional casework, which used Rankian psychoanalytic theory as its base.[5]

A Generic Base for Practice

By the mid 1960s, both casework and group work were practiced in all fields: both had defined their methods within a classic working definition of practice prepared by NASW and one prepared by Boehm for the Council on Social Work Education (CSWE).[6] The essence of these definitions is that social work practice seeks to enhance the social functioning of people—ndividually and in groups—through the use of interventions focused on the interaction between people and their environments. That focus has remained with us and been further elaborated on up to this very day. Systems theory became a useful framework for organizing the person-situation focus.[7] The search for unity in practice was emerging.

Simultaneous with the emphasis on different methods, fields, and theoretical approaches was a countervailing trend toward unification as definitions of social work practice set forth a common purpose, values, knowledge, and methodology for practice. This trend in practice was concurrent with developments in the behavioral and social sciences. The profession expanded its use of knowledge from the social sciences concerning such concepts as role, communication, family and group process, group development, and interpersonal and intergroup relationships. Selective use of concepts from systems theory became ubiquitous, moving the profession toward the integration of work with individuals, families, small groups, and social networks. As models of practice were developed, they influenced each other and became more eclectic in their use of knowledge from other disciplines and professions. The emergence of literature on generic or integrated practice occurred rapidly in the 1960s and 1970s.[8]

The increasing acceptance of system and ecological frameworks for practice hastened the shift away from linear cause-effect relationships between personal and environmental problems to recognition of the multiple influences of diverse people interacting with diverse environments, often referred to as an ecosystem or ecological systems perspective. During the first half of the 1960s, work on theory and practice was supported by councils and commissions within NASW. There was a burgeoning of literature, including studies that identified a strong common or generic base for direct service practice.[9] Many writers and educators came to the conclusion that individual, family, and group methods supplement and complement each other and that social workers should be able to serve people individually or as members of families and groups. More and more agencies expected their workers to be able to swing from one modality to another, as indicated by assessing client need and social problem. NASW and CSWE gave strong support to these efforts. More practitioners came to identify themselves as clinical social workers. But then, conditions changed quickly.

Chaos Within the Profession

The late 1960s and 1970s were chaotic times for the profession. Several events within society and the professional organizations have been cited as detracting from the advancement of direct practice in social work. These were the exciting days of the war on poverty and the civil rights movement. These events stimulated innovations in practice, with a major focus on urban communities, national policies, broad societal problems, and political approaches to poverty-stricken populations.[10] As a response, NASW lessened its attention to direct practice in favor of using its resources to support lobbying, political action, and grassroots community work. The study of casework, group work, and the common base of practice was no longer an activity of the professional organization. Within the profession, some leaders even questioned the relevance of direct practice. Conflict between direct service (micropractice) and macropractice was at a peak. Protagonists for macropractice argued that the profession should be transformed into a broadly based social movement. They criticized extant models of direct service practice as being ineffective, particularly in serving the poor and ethnic minorities. Fischer, a behaviorist, was vociferous in challenging what he perceived to be overemphasis on psychoanalytic theory.[11]

These social workers believed it was useless to help particular persons when the basic causes of problems resided in society's policies. The denigration of direct work with clients was so strong that Helen Harris Perlman wrote an article entitled "Casework Is Dead," describing the situation and making a plea for the preservation of individualized services to people, as well as macrolevel practice. She insisted that both were necessary. So did most social workers. Several national organizations expressed concern about what they thought was inadequate preparation of students for competent direct service practice; these included the Society of Hospital Social Work Directors, Family Service Association of America, and the Veterans Administration. Many schools had given priority to education for planning, grassroots community organization, policy, and administration over direct service practice. The time was ripe for action.

Simultaneous with the battle against direct practice, many experienced social workers were concerned about the quality of practice. By the middle of the 1970s, they had literally revolutionized the nature of the practice by shifting the conceptual base from specialized skill in a single method to expertise in multiple interventive modalities. By this time, many of them were using the title "clinical social worker." They rose to the challenge of securing recognition for direct service practice at the graduate level. They objected to the fact that both NASW and CSWE had reduced the criteria for membership by voting to admit persons with undergraduate degrees into the profession. They rose to the challenge by organizing the first Society of Clinical Social Workers.

Social workers in California received a severe setback to their efforts in 1966 by an opinion of the Attorney General which denied them the right to practice psychotherapy.[12] That action became the rallying point for a chain of events, leading to passage of a licensing law for clinical social workers that required two years of post-master degree education and passing written and oral examinations. The essence of that legal definition is "the use of psychosocial methods within a professional relationship." Services to families and groups, as well as individual clients, were specifically included. The term clinical was used to designate responsible practice focused on clients' needs, rather than on setting or modality. The legislation states:

> The practice of clinical social work is defined as a service in which a special knowledge of social resources, human capabilities, and the part that unconscious motivation plays in determining behavior is directed at helping people to achieve more adequate, satisfying, and productive social adjustments. The application of social work principles and methods includes, but is not restricted to, counseling and using applied psychotherapy of a nonmedical nature with individuals, families, and groups, providing information and referral services, providing or arranging for the provision of social services, explaining and interpreting the psychosocial aspects in the situations of individuals, families, or groups, helping communities to organize to provide or improve social and health services, and doing research related to social work.
>
> Psychotherapy, within the meaning of this chapter, is the use of psychosocial methods within a professional relationship, to assist the person or persons to achieve a better psychosocial adaptation, to acquire greater human realization of psychosocial potential and adaptation, to modify internal and external conditions which affect individuals, groups, or communities in respect to their intrapersonal and interpersonal processes.[13]

Jackson interpreted the law as defining clinical social work as indistinguishable from social work practice as often described. The intent of legislation was to protect the public and secure social sanction of what was a reality.[14] It is not a new category of practice, but is viewed as the core of competent practice.

The movement caught on quickly. Societies were set up in many states and in 1971 the National Federation of Societies for Clinical Social Work was founded. By 1973, the federation had founded the *Journal of Clinical Social Work*. These events developed out of concern for high standards, a commitment to the graduate level of education as a base for competent practice, and recognition of social work as a learned profession. These events developed also out of political concerns, such as achieving higher status among other professions and becoming eligible for third party payments. Perlman, reporting on her own, changed ideas about social work practice, concluded that "But I have come to believe that this banding together of clinical social workers may be a `saving remnant,' may lead to a salvaging and solidification of the professional core of social work."[15] Many social workers applauded her point of view.

Defining Clinical Social Work

What, then, is clinical social work? In addition to the definition of the California law, it has been defined in different ways, at different times, by different people. A detailed statement was presented by a committee of the National Federation of Societies of Clinical Social Work in 1977. The federation was interested in setting forth standards of education for clinical social work.

The introduction to the report stated that "some way must be found to define the parameters of clinical social work so that practitioners have an identity rooted in knowledge, values, and skills visible both within and without the profession."[16] The definition states that:

> Clinical social work integrates significant social work concepts with knowledge of human behavior and needs within an environmental context. The clinical social worker is a health care provider for individuals alone, in families and in groups where there are problems in biopsychosocial functioning. The objectives of the clinical social worker are both preventive and remedial and the methods used are varied, including any combination of clinical psychotherapy, group psychotherapy, family therapy, and concrete services and interventions on behalf of clients with social systems and the environment. (p. 255)

The definition applied primarily to social workers in health care and, although it included prevention, its major focus was clearly on psychotherapy. The primary knowledge base was described as being psychoanalysis and ego psychology. Only those theoretical approaches to practice that are based on that knowledge are considered to be included in the practice of clinical social work. Casework was clearly the "core process of clinical social work and the base on which work with groups and families must rest: the theoretical underpinnings of casework are crucial" (p. 260).

That definition set more narrow boundaries for clinical social work than did the California licensing law and subsequent developments. The authors noted that their views were controversial, aimed at stimulating a reexamination of social work practice and education.

NASW gradually became aware again of the needs of direct service workers, establishing a national register of clinical social workers in 1974 and a task force on clinical social work in 1979. The task force developed a definition of clinical social work and sponsored a national invitational forum for discussion of the definition and its ramifications.[17] According to the task force report,

> the purpose of clinical social work is the maintenance and enhancement of psychosocial functioning of individuals, families, and small groups by maximizing the availability of needed intrapersonal, interpersonal, and societal resources for the benefit of clients. The practice involves a wide range of psychosocial services to individuals, families, and small groups in relation to a variety of problems of social living.[18] Such practice is carried out under both private and public auspices. It involves intervention in the social situation as well as the person situation. The person-in-situation perspective is the base on which understanding of clinical practice is to be built.

That is a broader view of clinical social work than the earlier one of the clinical society.

The need for further work in defining clinical social work was stimulated by the fact that three interrelated organizations had the advancement of practice as their mission and were cooperating in setting standards for certification. In 1987, the Board of Directors of NASW, the Board of the National Registry of Health Care Providers, which had been established by the Federation of Societies of Clinical Social Work, and the American Board of Examiners in Clinical Social Work voted to accept the following definition of clinical social work:

> Clinical social work practice is the professional application of social work theory and methods to the treatment and prevention of psychosocial dysfunction, disability, or impairment, including emotional and mental disorders. It is based on knowledge and theory of psychosocial development, behavior, psychopathology, unconscious motivation, interpersonal relations, environmental stress, social systems, and cultural diversity with par-

ticular attention to person-in-environment. It shares with all social work practice the goal of enhancement and maintenance of psychosocial functioning of individuals, families and small groups.

Clinical social work encompasses interventions directed to interpersonal interactions, intrapsychic dynamics, and life-support and management issues. It includes but is not limited to individual, marital, family and group psychotherapy. Clinical social work services consist of assessment; diagnosis; treatment, including psychotherapy and counseling; client-centered advocacy; consultation; and evaluation.

The process of clinical social work is undertaken within the objectives of social work and the principles and values contained in codes of ethics of the professional social work organizations.[19]

That became the official definition.

The inclusion of the term "psychotherapy" in all of the definitions seems unfortunate to some social workers who fear it will dilute the strength and distinctiveness of the social aspects of practice. The term, however, is not a narrow one. Lieberman states that:

Social work psychotherapy has the objective of bringing about that change in behaviors that will improve individual functioning and the relationship between people and their social environment. In clinical social work, psychotherapy is always directed toward the interactions and transactions within the social orbit, in addition to addressing the internal life of the client. The maladaptive behavior of clients as well as malignant elements within the clients' environment become the focus of treatment as indicated.[20]

All of the definitions refer to prevention as an important function of clinical practice, but much less work has been done on defining that aspect of practice. Lurie argues for more attention to prevention, stating that clinical social work "must encompass a broader aspect of practice: prevention as well as treatment in all fields of practice."[21]

In their introduction to the *Handbook on Clinical Social Work*, Rosenblatt and Waldfogel contended that:

Whatever the actual definition of clinical social work, it is clear that the need for the term has been brought about by the following circumstances: (1) a blossoming of new theoretical bases used by social workers; (2) a change in the size of the "client unit" to include not only individuals but also families and groups, thus requiring a variety of modalities to fit new situations; (3) a renewed interest in the social environment; and (4) a renewed desire to establish an empirical research base to undergird practice.[22]

Any definition developed by a committee involves some compromises and, in a sense, is a political as well as a professional statement to be used for varied purposes, such as interpretation, public relations, examinations for licensing and certification, third party payments, and raising the status of the profession and its related organizations. A complex definition requires elaboration of its major characteristics to make clear the meaning of the terms used and their interrelationships, and it requires clarity about the skills and knowledge that are implied in the definition.

Characteristics of Clinical Social Work

Values

Clinical social work shares the values to which the profession is committed that derive from fundamental beliefs about people and society. An ultimate value is realization of the potential of people to live in ways that are personally satisfying and socially constructive. Implied in this value is simultaneous concern for personal and collective welfare and a conviction that each person has inherent worth and dignity, which means that he or she should be respected regardless of any likeness to or difference from others. Individuals should have the right to civil liberties, equal opportunities, and access to resources essential to meeting their basic needs. Since people are interdependent social beings, mutual aid and responsibility are desired. Each person, family, and group needs to be particularized. Personal and cultural differences should be respected. Social work embraces the great idea of democracy as a philosophy governing the relationships among people and their institutions. It is based on reciprocal rights and obligations and directed toward the welfare of diverse individuals, families, groups, and communities. These values are translated into the profession's Code of Ethics.

Purposes and Goals

Most important are the purposes and goals of practice, which are to achieve positive changes in the psychological and social functioning of individuals, changes in their families and groups, and changes in the conditions in their environments to lessen obstacles and provide opportunities for more satisfying social living. The key ideas are psychosocial functioning, empowerment, and person-environment interaction.

The term "psychosocial" is not a precise one. It has been used since 1930, according to Turner, to refer to feelings, attitudes, and behavior of persons in their relationships with others.[23] Coyle emphasized that the term also refers to the social conditions or situations which influence human well-being.[24] That is consistent with social work's long interest in people as social beings who are connected with various groups, social networks, and organizations and who live in social and natural environments.

Empowerment has become a major purpose inherent in clinical social work. The practitioner aims to empower clients. Pinderhughes and Heller define power "as the capacity to produce desired effects on others; it includes mastery over self as well as over the environment."[25] Solomon, writing of services to oppressed people, defines empowerment as "a process whereby persons who belong to a stigmatized social category throughout their lives can be assisted to develop and increase skills in the exercise of interpersonal influence and the performance of valued social roles."[26] It is a construct of person-group-environment interaction. The goal is to assist clients to achieve appropriate power.

Turner recently traced the evolution over a period of seventy years of a person-in-environment focus to direct the work of practitioners no matter what their particular orientations and specializations and regardless of whether practice was directed toward an individual, couple, family, or group.[27] There is strong, general support for the person-in-environment concept which deals with both internal and external influences on a client's condition and intervention in the environment as well as in the interaction between a worker and one client or between a worker and a couple, family, or other group.

Social Context

According to an NASW task force, the distinguishing feature of clinical social work, as compared with the practice of other professions, is the clinician's concern with the social context within which individual or family problems occur and are altered.[28] Included in the social context are society's institutions and organizations, programs, policies, and resources that affect health, education, and welfare services; environmental obstacles and supports; social networks, diverse population groups; and the effects of prejudice and discrimination on the lives of people. According to Papell, "A social worker practicing clinically joins with the profession in striving to alter societal forces that impact destructively on lives and in supporting and developing social resources that contribute to fulfillment in the quality of life for all humans."[29]

Breadth of Practice

A fourth characteristic of clinical social work is the breadth of its practice. Begun in medical and psychiatric settings, it is now practiced in all fields—child welfare, corrections, education, family service, health, mental health, and business and industrial settings. It is practiced with children, adolescents, adults, and older adults. It is practiced with a diversity of clients from varied racial, ethnic, sexual orientation, gender, and social class backgrounds. It is practiced in public and private organizations as well as in independent practice.

Knowledge Base

The definition of clinical social work specifies a broad base of knowledge derived from the biological, psychological, and social sciences for use in assessment and problem-solving. Although practitioners emphasize varied concepts and use different terminology, ego psychology combined with cognitive, cultural, and systems theories tends to predominate. Whatever particular concepts are selected, they are used within a frame of reference most often referred to as person-situation or person-environment interaction. The dual perspective, as formulated by Norton, is "the conscious and systematic process of perceiving, understanding and comparing simultaneously the values, attitudes, and behavior of the larger social system with those of the client's immediate family, and community systems."[30] This view has evolved into an ecosystem perspective for integrating understanding of the biopsychosocial functioning of individuals with knowledge of the functioning of families, groups, and larger social systems in a given habitat. Gordon believes that this frame of reference distinguishes social work practice from that of other professions.[31]

Integrated Practice

The rise of integrated practice is in harmony with knowledge about human behavior. The trend in the sciences is toward a holistic view of people as they interact in their social groups and networks and with the organizations and resources in their environments. The former artificial division of practice by the size of the system served is a contradiction of that knowledge. As Meyer has said, "the blurring of role categories is more consonant with the way people actually live their lives as individuals and as members of families, groups, and communities."[32]

With an adequate assessment of the individual or family in its situation, the social worker should have the ability to use individual, family, group, and community contexts singly or in combination in a purposeful and planned way. Baker has summarized well the major arguments for a generically oriented and skilled professional social worker. In order to begin where the clients are and meet their needs, the perspective is that:

> The individual or group that becomes the focus of social work intervention is caught up in a network of relationships, or psychological and social systems, that link the client to his physical and psychological past and present, his family, small groups, neighborhood, and community. When these systems are under excessive strain and in a state of extreme imbalance, social work intervention is likely to be needed. Thus, in his everyday practice, the social worker is faced with a wide range of psychological needs and unhelpful social systems which push him to act at individual, group, or community levels, either at the same time or in rapid succession. If method is to be his servant and not his master, then the social worker needs educating in a wide range of interventive strategies and to be given the opportunities to use them. . . . The human situation is always psychosocial.[33]

Assessment

A distinguishing characteristic of clinical social work is adequate appraisal of a person's biological, psychological, and social attributes, capacities, and resources as well as problems; the structure, and processes of families and other groups; and the inter-connectedness of people with their environments. Assessment goes beyond diagnosis of a problem or illness to a broader appraisal of the interrelationships between physiological, emotional, and sociocultural factors and the external environmental conditions that influence well-being.

Planning

Essential to effective practice is the process of planning a particular service to meet the needs of clients. The plan or contract for service includes agreement about the goals to be sought, essential resources, the modality and focus of practice, the anticipated length of treatment, the expectations of workers and clients, and such mundane factors as expectations concerning attendance, time, and payment of fees.

Treatment

The process of treatment is the essence of practice. The term is often used interchangeably with intervention. Treatment seems to be a broader term, however, that encompasses attitudes and processes as well as acts of a practitioner. It is the process of enabling people to make changes in their attitudes, relationships, and/or behavior and to make changes in some aspects of their environment, based on a sound assessment and sound plan. It involves the selection and use of a constellation of skills designed to meet the needs of the clients, and based on theoretical underpinnings and the ethics and standards of our profession. Skills are simply abilities to intervene well.

Treatment includes a cluster of roles: (1) psychosocial counselor or therapist; (2) resource consultant; (3) case advocate; (4) crisis intervener; (5) psychosocial educator; (6) facilitator of decision-making; and (7) placement counselor or provider of new living environments. This combination of roles to reduce or resolve problems in social relationships and in social resources and environments is central to clinical social work. In addition, social workers are collaborators with other members of a team or with practitioners in other organizations. Their special contribution to interdisciplinary teams is in-depth knowledge of the interaction among biological, psychological, and social processes combined with understanding of interacting social systems and social resources related to client needs.

Evaluation

Clinical social workers are expected to evaluate their own practice and to hold themselves accountable for their choice of models of treatment and specific interventive acts. They share responsibility with clients for the results related to the agreed-upon goals. The evaluation is dependent upon the plan of service and the contract established between the workers and the individual, couple, family, or group. They engage the participation of clients in the evaluation of both the process and the results. They follow ethical principles of confidentiality, informed consent, and the responsible use of information obtained.

Social work help is composed of complex skills. To put the skills into practice requires breadth and depth of knowledge mentioned in the definition. The definition is a generic one, that is it identifies what is common to clinical social work in all modalities or methods, fields of practice, and services to varied population groups. It is suggested that, if social workers can master the skills, based on knowledge and underlying theories, they can apply these to varied situations, but with further specificity and elaboration.

Trends in Clinical Social Work

Major trends in clinical social work have an impact on present and future practice.

1. Clinical social workers have come to recognize the inextricable interconnection between micro- and macropractice. For example, a great increase in managed care determines priority for services that can be provided, sets forth policies and procedures that may limit or enhance opportunities for effective practice, and increases pressures for cost containment and accountability. Social workers are increasingly eligible for third party payments from insurance companies and government. That is good, but it places certain controls over the nature of assessment, for example placing a label of mental disorder on a client or limiting the length of treatment, which pose serious ethical dilemmas. Clinical social workers are taking more responsibility to attempt to influence deleterious policies and practices.

2. There is an increase in the private practice of clinical social work. Once dependent on client fees, many services are now paid for, at least in part, by others. There is an increased use of contracts with schools, industry, probation and court settings, and other social agencies, so clinical workers can no longer work in complete independence from authority. They are accountable to licensing and certification bodies, courts, and funding sources. Changes in funding make it possible for them to serve clients from a much greater diversity of population groups.

In addition to the values, knowledge, and skills of clinical social work, private practitioners are managers of a business. Their income must provide not only personal income but also be sufficient to cover business expenses. Private practitioners are more subject to malpractice claims than are agency-employed workers. The NASW guidelines on private practice conclude that

> the private practice of clinical social work creates a range of challenges. A clinical social workers' success can be measured by his or her ability to blend the knowledge, skills, and values of the social work profession with sound business practices while earning a reasonable income. Social workers who follow these guidelines have a good foundation for an effective and rewarding practice.[34]

3. Clients of social workers often have serious and multiple problems these days, making it necessary for practitioners to have increased knowledge and skills in offering a continuum of services to meet the needs of clients. Offering a single service may not do the job: clients often need help through a combination of modalities, including access to a variety of social networks and resources in the community. They need a continuum of accessible services. Getzel, for example, reporting on services to poor

men with AIDS, pointed out that support groups were essential, but the group needed to cogwheel with requisite individual help, crisis intervention, advocacy, family services, and information and referral services.[35] Brown and Weil present a model of integrated services in child welfare from a family practice point of view that connects work with the child in need to work with families and with resources in the community, including placement as a last resort.[36] These are but two examples of clinical social work at its best.

4. Greater attention is now being given to the need for practice that is sensitive to human diversity. That is long overdue. Both the differences and the common bonds among people need to be understood and appreciated as they influence practice. Oppression, stereotyping, and discrimination exist. This problem requires the avid attention at both clinical and macro levels of practice. Models of practice have been or are being modified to give more attention to encompassing human diversity in all its forms.[37]

The thesis of this chapter is that clinical social work is an integral and essential part of our chosen profession. Competence in rendering services requires mastery of a system of values, knowledge, and skills that is generic or common to clinical social work in all modalities, fields of practice, and a variety of people of all ages, health conditions, social classes, sexual orientations, races, and ethnic backgrounds. The conclusion is that clinical social work help is composed of many interrelated skills. To put the skills into practice requires both breadth and depth of understanding. It is suggested that, if social workers can master the skills based on knowledge and underlying theories, they can apply these to varied situations and become truly competent. Thus, I am committed to the idea that social work is a necessary profession and take great pride in the progress being made, although much more work needs to be done.

Two | The Social Context

The social context for clinical social work is the set of interdependent circumstances and conditions that surround practice. In one sense, the context is international in scope with the growing interdependence of nations and the common, as well as different, needs and problems of people. Without denying that breadth, clinical practice is most directly influenced by the context in which it is practiced in a particular place. Context deals with the interrelatedness of people and environments in a particular supra-system. Even more directly, the social context for practice may be characterized by policies and programs, the profession of social work, the communities in which potential users of services reside, the population groups within the community, and societal problems that create the need for social work services.

Systems in Environment

Clinical social work is practiced within an ecosystem perspective. Ecology is the study of the relationship of plants and animals to one another and to the biological and physical environment. In the words of Cook, "The study of the interrelationship of living things with one another and with the basic natural resources of air, water, and food is called ecology, after the Greek *oikos* for house."[1] Ecologists use the term "ecosystem" to refer to a community of associated species of plants and animals together with the physical features of their habitat. The essence of ecology is that no organism can live alone: there is a web of interdependence among all living things and between these organisms and the physical environment in a given habitat. The environment provides the conditions and nutrients essential to survival and growth or it provides obstacles to survival and growth.[2] A neat fit between the organism and its environment is essential to survival and satisfying living. Ecology has become popularized by environmentalists, psychologists, sociologists, anthropologists, and social workers who are searching for ways to understand the interrelationships among people and between people and their environments. Each discipline makes its own modifications of the scientific base, selecting some major concepts from the whole.

According to Hazen and Trefil,

> The major principles of ecology are that natural systems are not static, but change constantly with the changing external conditions; species change or become extinct all the time; there is no real balance of nature but instead a dynamic web of living things interacting with their environment and each other, changing and being changed in return. Finally, we are learning that the entire biosphere is interconnected—that we can't change one thing without changing another. This in our view is the central great idea of ecology.[3]

An ecological perspective has been characteristic of social work since its early beginnings although the term was not used. In *Social Process in Organized Groups*, published in 1930, Coyle analyzed the literature on all kinds of groups and larger organizations. The first chapter is titled "The Organized Group in Its Social Setting." Groups are viewed as forms of reciprocal relations. Internal group influences interact interdependently with influences from other social systems. Characteristics of the community milieu such as ethnic stereotypes, social class differences, dislocations of families, and the pluralistic nature of society affect individuals and the groups to which they belong. A major theme is that a group must be viewed within the multiplicity and complexity of organized life. Coyle wrote: "the nature and quality of the community life . . . permeate the life of all the associations within it. The reciprocal action of individuals, groups, and the total milieu creates each organization and determines its functions and processes."[4] To help people, social workers strive to understand the complex environments in which they live.

Bronfenbrenner has proposed envisioning the environment as a nested arrangement of circumjacent contexts, including the microsystem or person, the mesosystem or interpersonal relations within family, school, and work contexts, the exosystem or social structures and institutions, and the macrosystem or overarching cultural patterns, values, and ideologies.[5] Each of these environmental contexts is recognized to have potential effects on health, illness, and social well-being.[6]

Germain has identified several of these environmental influences:

1. Modern technology affects health and disease. Examples are newly discovered chemicals that have great potential for both positive and negative outcomes; technological means for prolonging life which create stark moral dilemmas for the patient, family, and the medical profession; other advances that result in pollution and the rise of new environmental diseases; changing technology in employment which creates new opportunities for some, but unemployment and the need for retraining for others.

2. Informational storage systems, increasingly more sophisticated lead to violations of privacy that may prevent access to credit, employment, or health and life insurance. The explosion of knowledge and the development of new technologies make it difficult for practitioners to be up-to-date in their practice, which is one of their ethical responsibilities.

3. Statutory and regulative aspects of law influence the rights of some people, such as women and patients, and changing laws and regulations concerning such matters as divorce and school desegregation result in rapidly shifting expectations, demands, and opportunities. New statutes and court decisions influence practice in many ways.

4. The economic and political systems often produce inflation, inadequate housing, changes in Social Security, energy, and transportation problems which create hardships for many people.[7]

Developments within the exosystem have great influence on the way people live. Many years ago, Towle put it this way: "We know that unmodifiable adverse social circumstances are decisive and that the tender ministrations of an understanding relationship cannot compensate for basic environmental lacks, meager services, and restrictive agency policies."[8]

Policies and Programs

The policies, procedures, and programs of employing organizations are defined partially by numerous laws, governmental regulations, and mandated programs. Clinical social work is inextricably interrelated with legislative and administrative policies and programs of organizations in the agency's community and with local, state, and national levels of government. In chapter 1, it was clearly evident that clinical social work was legitimized through licensing laws and that additional certification is provided by professional organizations and other standard setting groups. Entitlements for financial assistance, health care, and Social Security have implications for social work practice.

Some social work services are mandated by government. For example, the Education of the Handicapped Act amendments of 1986 intends to ensure early service to children with handicapping conditions and authorizes the employment of social workers; another example is the Adoption Assistance and Child Welfare Services Act of 1980.[9] This program requires that a plan of family-centered services be prepared to (1) help families manage the tasks of daily living, adequately nurture children, and remedy problem situations and (2) safeguard children from being endangered by providing services to protect the right of every child to grow up with a sense of well being, belonging, life continuity, and, to the extent possible, permanence. That certainly is a mandate for high quality clinical social work services. But other public policies compromise, underfund, and fail to adequately implement such legislation.

The rapid increase in the costs of health and mental health care has stimulated the development of alternatives to the traditional fee for service payments for health delivery.[10] Managed health care is a growing trend in this country. It describes plans used to provide services in ways that contain costs while maintaining the quality of care. Managed care is implemented by health maintenance organizations (HMOs), preferred provider organizations (PPOs), managed care firms that provide utilization reviews, and traditional health insurance plans.

Managed care plans vary widely. They may include requirements for preauthorization to qualify a person for a particular service, precertification for a given amount of care, concurrent review of the treatment provided and the outcome, and predischarge planning to assure that the person received the care required and is ready for discharge. At its best, managed care is perceived as a program in which there is appropriate structure, control, and accountability to assure the most efficient use of health resources and positive outcomes.

Social work organizations depend upon many sources of funds for financing their services. They secure support from entitlements, insurance payments, government grants, and United Ways, which all have policies and procedures governing the use of the money provided. They often set priorities for the types of services to be funded.

The agency's functions and policies are defined partially by numerous laws, governmental regulations, or external financial arrangements. Confidentiality, for example, is compromised by legal requirements to report incidents of behavior such as child abuse. Statutes and court decisions govern commitment of patients to mental hospitals and patient rights. Many agencies are required to use the *Diagnostic and Statistical Manual (DSM IV)* of the American Psychiatric Association in order to secure reimbursement of funds for services to clients.[11] Too often, Yalom said, "The powerful invisible presence is the third-party payer—the financial denizen who has a shocking degree of influence over admission and discharge decisions and about every aspect of a plan for service."[12]

Since clinical social workers serve directly the changing needs of clients, channels need to be provided through which they can participate in review and modification of policies that influence the kind and quality of services given. Their status needs to be upgraded so that they have adequate power to carry out appropriate services of high quality. Reporting needs to reflect accurately the kind, as well as the quantity, of services given to people with particular kinds of needs and characteristics. Procedures of accountability and evaluation of outcome need to be in harmony with the goals of practice. Social workers need to use their influence to work toward clear policies that safeguard the clients' rights to privacy and informed consent and yet are flexible in such matters as intake, eligibility, fees, forms of service, assignment of workers, and workloads. Their commitment is to make it as easy as possible for prospective clients to have access to and continuity of services to meet needs and for practitioners to have access to needed resources.

The physical environment of organizations may or may not facilitate the effective use of services. The physical appearance of the agency gives messages concerning the extent to which people are welcomed and respected. One major question for workers is whether the physical space can be arranged so that it facilitates effective communication. It is important that spatial arrangements provide for adequate privacy and, at the same time, for desired social interaction. Physical settings influence behavior. Proshansky, Ittelson, and Rivlin demonstrate that: "Physical settings—simple or complex—evoke complex human responses in the form of feelings, attitudes, values, expectancies, and desires, and it is in this sense as well as in their known physical properties that their relationships to human experience and behavior must be understood."[13] Settings are characterized by continuous changes amidst regularity and stability. They include other people and their behavior, as well as walls, corridors, doors, arrangement of furniture, light, and decorations. The behavior of people and the physical characteristics are interdependent. A change in any component of the setting affects other components and thereby alters the characteristic behavior patterns of the people in that setting.

Fields of Practice

Settings are organized into fields of practice.[14] Emphasis on generic practice and specialization exist side by side in social work. The nature of specializations comprise an important aspect of the practitioner's social context. It was noted in chapter 1 that social casework, social group work, and social community organization were the major specializations, often combined with specialization in a field of practice. Now, the most frequently recognized form of concentration is field of practice, usually designated as health, mental health, education (school social work), family-child welfare, and occupational or industrial social work.

The need for some form of concentration in clinical social work seems to be indicated by:[15]

1. the varied and complex agencies, organizations, and auspices through which services are rendered and the policies and standards influencing practice in these settings.
2. the burgeoning knowledge about the large range and complexity of biopsychosocial problems for which clinical social workers have responsibility. Despite much overlapping, some problems are of primary concern to a given field and in-depth knowledge about them is essential.
3. the need for intraprofessional and interprofessional collaboration with members of numerous professions and disciplines.
4. the increasing knowledge about modalities or methods of practice (individual, family, group, community) and theoretical approaches or models of practice appropriate for particular purposes. Generic skills and knowledge are applicable to a particular configuration of services in each field.

The field of practice is an important context for the practice of clinical social work. Each field has its complex system of organizations, legislative and administrative policies, sources of funding, network of services, hierarchy of positions, and a place in the broader system of health, education, and welfare services.

Health

Social workers in the field of health work within a complex system of interrelated organizations.[16] They work in health maintenance organizations, private offices, acute hospitals, public health centers, rehabilitation facilities, home health care agencies, nursing homes, and outpatient clinics under either public or private auspices. Their work is regulated by a myriad of policies, regulations, and laws that are part of American health care. They need in-depth understanding of the multidisciplinary nature of health care and they need to find their appropriate roles to work collaboratively with physicians, nurses, physical therapists, and other personnel. They face legal and ethical issues posed by demands for cost effectiveness; by modern technology; by attitudes toward birth control, certain stigmatized illnesses and disabilities, and "death with dignity"; and by the many obstacles to access, quality, equity, and continuity of care for patients and their families.

More than other social workers, those in the field of health need to comprehend the nature of illness and disability and the usual forms of treatment for a given condition, the vocabulary used in medicine, and the psychosocial aspects of varied illnesses and disabilities. They most frequently apply the generic and specialized knowledge to relatively short term treatment of patients and their families, including individual counseling, discharge planning, psychosocial education, crisis intervention, and group work. There is an increasing use of a clinically oriented form of case management for helping chronically ill patients.

Mental Health

Mental health is an integral part of health care, but there are important differences.[17] Social workers are employed in a variety of settings, such as mental hospitals, day treatment centers, child guidance clinics, community mental health centers, and residential treatment facilities. Although social workers provide the bulk of mental health services, psychiatry still dominates the field, for example, in policies and procedures of diagnosis and assessment. The special knowledge concerns the organization and policies of the field and the types and causes of mental disorders and treatment options, with special emphasis on the psychosocial factors connected with a mental disorder. A wide variety of services are provided, varying with the site and the nature of the clients' problems. Psychosocial treatment usually needs to be coordinated with the use of psychotropic drugs, and for chronically ill patients, clinically oriented case management is essential.

Family and Child Welfare

Social workers in this field are located in public and private social agencies that deal with marriage and family counseling, protective services, parent- family life education, foster care, adoption, and residential care.[18]

It is the only field in which social work is the dominant profession. More than in other fields, the services focus on problems in family relationships and protection of children from abuse and neglect. These services need to be coordinated with a wide range of health, education, and welfare resources and practitioners need to collaborate with the judicial system on matters of abuse, neglect, and child custody. The special knowledge of behavior concerns the problems of children and their families that contribute to inadequate family functioning. When necessary for the welfare of the child, temporary separation and out-of-home care, combined with intensive counseling with both the child and family are required. The aim is family reunification and, when that is not possible, adoption or other permanent living arrangements for the child.

Occupational Social Work

Social workers in the field of occupational or industrial social work need more than average knowledge of the rapid changes going on in the world of work, including diversity of the work force, technological changes, and legal regulations. They need to adapt their clinical knowledge and skills to work in organizations that often have a profit motive.[19] The auspices vary, including business and industrial compounds, the military establishment, and trade unions. Learning to collaborate effectively with personnel directors, management, and representatives of unions—with their often conflicting interests—is crucial.

There is a great variation in the services offered by employers and trade unions. Services are designed to increase productivity, improve the stability of the work force, enhance the general well-being of workers, and strengthen the relationship of workers with their employers and/or unions. The services offered are usually time-limited, including crisis intervention, family counseling, psycho-education groups, and self-help and support systems. The interrelationship of work to family and community roles is recognized. Collaboration with business, industry, and labor organizations must be cultivated.[20] Occupational social workers must understand the personal, family, and community problems that interact with the problems that employees have in the workplace.

School Social Work

Social workers in schools are employed in complex organizations in which education is the primary function.[21] Clinical social workers need to understand the mission of education, the way that schools are financed and organized, the nature and structure of curriculums, and the legislation and other policies that mandate or limit the roles of social workers within the educational system. Schools are located in communities with their particular constellation of resources, environmental problems and opportunities, and varied population groups, necessitating close ties among pupils, families, school, and community.

School social work is usually one component of a division of pupil personnel services, requiring the clarification of roles of social workers in relation to those of guidance counselors, psychologists, nurses, teachers, and administrators. The special knowledge of social workers is the interrelated physical, psychological, sociocultural and environmental problems that create barriers to the child's academic achievement and social functioning in school. In addition to individual and family counseling, a major emphasis is on consultation with other school personnel and liaison between home and school.

Private Practice

The private practice of clinical social work is defined as the provision of clinical social work services by a clinical social worker who assumes sole responsibility for the client, regardless of the organizational structure within which the worker provides the service. Social workers establish their own conditions of exchange with the client and take full responsibility for the nature and quality of the practice within legal guidelines, professional standards and the *NASW Code of Ethics*.[22] They work not for a salary, but derive their income from fees for service from clients, third party payers, or contracts with social agencies or other organizations. They manage their own businesses and therefore need knowledge and skills in business administration to supplement their clinical knowledge and skills. They carry their own Social Security, and health and liability insurance. They do not have the range of employee benefits that usually accompany employment.

Many social workers have found satisfaction in private practice for the reason that, to some extent at least, they have control over the types of services offered and the types of clients served. They are able to earn higher incomes than if they were in agency-based practice. Studies tend to confirm their satisfaction. A comparative study of a random sample of NASW members indicated that practitioners in private practice fared better on scores of personal well-being than did those who worked in agencies.[23] Self-report instruments measured psychosocial strain, physical health, work performance, and life satisfaction. The private practitioners were not stress-free, however. They reported needs for a continuous flow of cases, were concerned about malpractice, desired adequate supervision and consultation and business supports.

In another study it was found that, compared with workers in agencies, they were significantly more likely to report greater opportunities to use their knowledge and skills, to do what they do best, and greater fulfillment of their expectations for professional practice.[24]

The benefits of private practice are many, but so are the risks and disadvantages. The costs of establishing a private practice are heavy, income is unpredictable, and there is a greater risk of malpractice litigation than for employees of social agencies. Private practitioners do not have the opportunities for learning in the form of supervision, consultation, peer groups, and training programs traditionally offered by agencies: these are safeguards for clients and provide support for workers. It may be a myth that they are fully independent and autonomous practitioners. They must meet requirements for licensing; obey numerous laws concerning reports of child abuse and threats to harm another; they are subject to all of the laws and regulations pertinent to owners of business; they must often gear their practice to the requirements of third party payers concerning, for example, the length of treatment and the diagnosis of psychosocial problems as mental disorders. They must adapt their recording to the specifications of each of the third party payers.

Work Satisfaction

Whether in private or agency-based practice, social workers, as do most people, desire job satisfaction. They need an opportunity to use their knowledge and skills with some degree of autonomy. In a survey of 275 randomly selected social workers in Maine in 1988, Arches found that perceived autonomy leads to job satisfaction.[25] She concluded that "workers are most satisfied when they have autonomy, are not limited by demands of funding sources, and are not stifled in bureaucracy." Isolation and fragmentation detract from satisfaction.

Clinical social workers ought to consult with administrators concerning elements of job satisfaction. Administrators desire practitioners who derive satisfaction from their work. They promote job satisfaction, according to Simmons, when they build an optimum environment in which excellent work can occur.[26] The need is for a philosophy of administration that emphasizes the qualities of optimism, persistence, and fairness. In such an environment, administrators and clinicians can collaborate in finding ways to bring about prized outcomes. Attitudes of hope and optimism contribute to the joy of working; persistence over a period of time in working to remove obstacles can pay off; and fairness involves respect for the needs and capabilities of staff, a shared view of the organization's mission, and shared trust. Given the power differential inherent in "boss-staff" relationships, special effort is needed to assume a fair, balanced, and accepting internal environment. Hartman offers similar thoughts on successful, satisfying practice within organizations.[27]

Although practice must be related to organizational policies and functions, as Glasser and Garvin state, "the profession of social work must not be coopted by organization needs and interests."[28] Pincus and Minahan take a similar stance in insisting that the "worker must be careful not to substitute agency conceptions, policies, and practices for independent professional judgment."[29] Social workers have both the right and responsibility to do everything in their legitimate power to influence the organizations that employ them in order to meet client needs as effectively as possible.[30]

Neighborhoods and Communities

People live in neighborhoods that are interconnected with larger community systems. The neighborhoods in which people live are characterized by their social history, diversity of population, distribution and succession of populations, variations in the presence and extent of social problems, availability and accessibility of resources, and the groups, networks, and organizations to which people belong. Each neighborhood has a distinctive environment in terms of geography, climate, flora and fauna, parks, hiking trails, beaches or other open spaces that influence the quality of living for its residents. The climate and scenery mean many things to different people. Shimer, a geologist, says that "Each part of this sculptured earth has its own characteristic flavor and its own special type of landscape, and each arouses unexpected and varied reactions in the observer."[31] Visiting a friend in a small, but culturally sophisticated city surrounded by ocean, forests, and mountains, a young woman said, "It's lovely, really beautiful, but I couldn't live here. I guess I'm an urbanite." The response was, "but I couldn't live in your concrete jungle. I'd go crazy there." Good friends, but worlds apart in their preference for a living environment. Some people feel depressed in rainy or clouded weather; others relish it. Some love the sun and dryness of the desert; others feel naked and exposed there.

People of similar ethnicity or religion tend to cluster in a particular geographical area, often reminiscent of the history of their families. Mormons, for example, tend to cluster in Utah; Scandinavians in Minnesota or the Pacific Northwest; Jewish people in such big cities as Los Angeles and New York; Mexican Americans in the Southwest; and Irish in the Northeast. By doing so, they are assured of living near people who share their traditions and customs, and provide mutual support and a sense of belonging. The sense of fit between people and their environments is enhanced.

People of fairly similar social class status also tend to cluster in particular geographical areas—the rich in the most desirable neighborhoods in terms of beauty and amenities and the poor in the most dilapidated and oppressed communities. For some people, regional identity is very strong. For example, when asked about their ethnic identity, a group of students in Alabama had trouble identifying with a given ethnic category. But, when one said, "I guess I'm a Southerner," there was general nodding of heads in agreement. Their families had been in this country for so long that they didn't think of themselves as English-Scots, Scots-Irish, or German-Scots, and even the black students said that most of their roots were in the Southern culture except, of course, that the color difference could not be denied.

Ecological theory in sociology is enlightening in terms of knowledge about the distribution of people and resources in a given community. Neighborhoods undergo changes in population over a period of time. A population often ages as children grow up, leave home, and establish residence elsewhere. A new wave of population takes over. Younger families may move in, requiring that schools again are needed as are more child-oriented resources. In one community that was largely populated by upper and upper middle-class whites of European origin, a few Chinese families, also of high economic status, moved in, so that now a large majority of the population is of Chinese descent. In another community, as many black families moved to outlying communities, a wave of poor Hispanic people moved in, requiring changes in the health and welfare systems to become sensitive to the special values and needs of the new population, including Spanish speaking personnel. The tendency of people to move out of inner city neighborhoods as they acquire higher incomes creates stark problems for those remaining behind and for those who take their places.

The city of Los Angeles is a clear example. It has become the most ethnically diverse city in the world. In 1980, a large majority of the population was white other than Hispanic. A decade later, it was 40 percent Hispanic, 37 percent other whites, 13 percent blacks, and 10 percent Asian, the latter being the fastest-growing population. It has one of the largest

Jewish populations in the world. Within each group, there is tremendous ethnic diversity as evidenced by the fact that almost one hundred different languages are spoken by families of children in the public schools. There is also tremendous diversity in socioeconomic status, but one half of the school children come from families below the poverty line. Unemployment has increased. Along with such changes come an increase in social problems and a need for more ethnically sensitive social work services.

Communities vary in the nature and quality of the environment that is built by humans, consisting of homes, buildings, roads, transportation systems and so forth. People's perceptions of the attractiveness of a neighborhood is influenced by the physical layout of buildings, houses, and streets as well as by its geography, climate, and space. The quality of housing, schools and other institutions reflect either a respect for the dignity of people or a devaluation of them. As one example of the influence of buildings on people, Cousins vividly describes how the hospital environment provides not only the essential medical care and treatment, but also creates severe stress for patients and families. He describes how the hospital environment imposes indignity and stress in terms of lack of privacy, separation, encouragement of dependency, disruption of sleep, painfulness of medical procedures, fear of bodily harm, adverse effects of drugs, loss of control, and uncertainty of recovery. These factors mobilize diverse emotions—anxiety, guilt, shame, depression, and a sense of helplessness and hopelessness.[32]

Horn reports that studies show that hospitals need not be dreary and anxiety provoking places.[33] Patients exposed to high noise levels and windowless rooms require more pain killers and have higher levels of delirium and depression. When patients can see trees, water, or gardens, blood pressure goes down, fewer drugs are needed, and less time is spent in the hospital. Both patients and staff feel greater satisfaction.

The setting in which practice occurs is as important as are hospitals to the welfare and satisfaction of clients and staff. The attendance of clients is influenced by the availability of transportation and the appearance of the agency. The appearance and location of the offices and meeting rooms provide an external structure and anchor for the clients. Hall points out that a person's "feeling about being properly oriented in space runs deep."[34] Such knowledge is linked to security and provides for a sense of continuity. The spatial arrangements within the room affect the experience of the participants. In Hall's studies of the reactions and perceptions of people to personal and social space, he found wide variations among ethnic groups concerning the social distance thought to be appropriate. Space perception is not only a matter of what can be seen, but also of what can be screened out as when Japanese people often use paper screens to filter out sight and sound. People differ in their sense of crowding. What one person receives as overcrowding, another may feel is adequate space. People from different cultures, when interpreting each other's behavior, may misinterpret the relationship or activity.

Social workers have traditionally advanced the belief that community and family support are major contributors to individual and family well-being.[35] Moreover, ensuring access to basic human services and resources within one's community has been a cornerstone of the profession's advocacy efforts. There is considerable evidence from clinical experience and research that the presence of appropriate resources and the ability to use them is critical in the family's ability to function, especially in the face of stress. Sources of support outside the family include friends and neighbors, church, organizational affiliations, and a community network of health and welfare resources. Of particular interest, is evidence that the family's ability to promote the health of its members is positively affected by its regular interaction with community organizations and resources.

Societal Problems

In the world in which we live, few people do not feel some stress and strain in daily living. Many people suffer from chronic or life threatening illnesses such as AIDS, cancer, and Alzheimer's, Parkinson's, diabetes, and heart diseases and do not have adequate health coverage or social support. Nuclear and toxic wastes threaten health and the quality of the environment. Economic changes lead to unemployment with its concomitant deleterious affect on personal and family functioning. Economic changes, combined with changes in the status of men and women, mean that more women are employed outside the home with advantages for some of them, but creating the need for child care and home help services that are scarce and costly. Notable increases in divorce, separation, remarriage, and birth to unwed mothers create problems.

Violence is endemic to our society as evidenced by gang warfare, murder, random shooting, spouse and child abuse, and the perceptions of even quite young children that they must carry guns to school for protection. Families with young children are becoming the fastest growing segment of the homeless, living on the streets. The raging drug epidemic, including drug abuse and trafficking, is a tragedy not only for individual users but for their families as well. The public education system is under attack, especially in urban areas, with large numbers of children who have academic and social problems and drop out of school. The judicial system is perceived by many, particularly members of minority groups, to be unjust and discriminatory. Racial tension is prevalent. Little progress has been made in eliminating the social problems of poverty, unemployment, sexism, homophobia, ageism, and urban blight. The marvel is that, despite these multi-faceted problems, many individuals and families do succeed in achieving a good life.

Human Diversity

Race

Race is a classification of people based on inherited physical characteristics, such as skin color, shape of eyes, hair texture, body build, and blood type.[36] Certain genetic traits occur more often in one race than in the others. There are no hard and fast boundaries between races; the categories are not mutually exclusive. There are many variations within a category, for example, the skin color of some whites is darker than the skin of some blacks. Within a given race there are many ethnic differences. Japanese, Koreans, Chinese and Vietnamese are all Asians, but their histories, values, place of residence, major interests, and customs differ widely; white people do not comprise a homogeneous category. The tendency to refer to all whites as Anglos hides the significance of many different sub- cultures and denies many groups a sense of identity. The Norwegians and Italians, for example, differ from each other in important ways and both differ from English persons. Among blacks, African Americans may be ethnically quite different from Haitians or Jamaicans. Hispanics in the Northeast tend to be Puerto Rican or Dominican; those in Florida, Cuban; and those on the West Coast Mexican American. Native Americans belong to hundreds of tribes and prefer to be identified by the name of their tribe rather than as Indian or Native American.

Attitudes toward race have a strong influence in determining the nature and quality of interpersonal relationships. Racism is a belief or doctrine that inherent differences among the human races determine achievement and behavior, usually involving the conviction that one's own race is superior, often leading to fear, hatred, or intolerance of another. The attitude of racism deters members of the races deemed inferior from the full exercise of their rights and opportunities. Within American communities, visible physical differences invite suspicion, fear, or distrust, creating interracial tension and conflict.

Ethnicity

Ethnic diversity is a fact of life in the United States and many other countries today, making it essential that clinical social workers practice with sensitivity and competence to meet the needs and build on the strengths of each group.[37]

In order to understand diversity, Solomon introduced the concept of ethnosystem. She points out that the United States is "an ethnosystem, that is, a composite of interdependent ethnic groups each in turn defined by some unique historical and/or cultural ties and bound together by a single political system."[38] The ethnic groups that comprise our society differ in terms of values, race, religion, and social class.

Ethnicity refers to a sense of peoplehood and belonging based on cultural commonality. Sotomayer's definition is: "Ethnicity refers to the underlying sentiments among individuals based on a sense of commonality of origins, beliefs, values, customs, or practices of a particular group of peoples."[39] The common factors include language or dialect, physical features, religion, kinship patterns, nationality, and contiguity. Everyone is a member of at least one ethnic group and increasing numbers of Americans belong to two or more because they have mixed ancestry. Ethnicity is an important component of both individual and group identity and serves as a reference group for its members. It may even be a critical lifeline for newcomers, providing for them at least some point of connection in an otherwise confusing and uncertain environment.

The ethnic groups that comprise the population of the United States, Canada, and increasing numbers of other countries are diverse in terms of their histories, needs, and resources. People in every sub-population may have great need and serious psychosocial problems, but members of some groups are in more dire circumstances than are those of the dominant white group. The neediest groups are generally recognized as being African Americans, Haitians, Mexican Americans, recent Asian refugees, Puerto Ricans, and Native Americans. As Toth reminds us, ethnic ties are important, but ethnic pride can be misdirected toward hatred and devaluation of others, as evidenced so clearly by the current ethnic cleansing movement in Eastern Europe.[40]

For groups that have been in this country for a long time, and are well established, ethnic identity may take on a new meaning. Such people have the freedom to choose whether or not they wish to be identified with an ethnic group and to be so construed by others. They may participate selectively in some of the traditional customs which tend to survive after a particular group has become well acculturated to the dominant society.

Religion and Spirituality

Religion is an important aspect of culture, yet social workers have tended to ignore their clients' beliefs, the meaning that religion has to them, and the possible conflict in religious values within the client or between the client and practitioner.[41] Religious beliefs provide conscious and unconscious norms by which people judge themselves and others. They provide a way of life for many people, influencing the food they eat, the friends they make, the holidays they celebrate, the norms of marriage, and ways of coping with death.

Religions may be positive aids in dealing with problems arising from a sense of uncertainty, powerlessness, and scarcity. Whether helpful or harmful to clients' psychosocial functioning, they define reality for them. Socialization of children has been influenced by religious assumptions and values, for example, Protestantism among African Americans, Buddhism among many Asian Americans, Catholicism among Latin Americans and Islam among Arab Americans. American Indians have a rich spiritual heritage specific to their tribes which gives meaning to their lives. An example from the Quinault tribe in the Pacific Northwest illustrates this.

> A rare reprieve, this night. There are no storms or rages or curled fists of seawater pounding Earth. Along the fringes of the village of Taholah, the shore sighs with each soft wave reaching to smooth rough stones. Usually quarrelsome, Ocean is peaceful this evening. In the ancient code of Quinault, Ocean is revered as father of life, and Earth as mother. Mountains and Forests are made from the bodies of those who lived in The Time Before Everything Changed—before the white man conquered them and took their land.[42]

According to Cornett, spirituality encompasses concern with the meaning of life, time, mortality, and beliefs about the existence of a higher power.[43] It involves individual responses to the events in life over which a person has no control. Religion interacts with ethnicity and social class in its influence on the life of a community.

Social Class

Societies develop a process of stratification through which people are assigned differential socioeconomic status. Research on social class in the United States identifies different numbers of social classes, ranging from six to three.[44] The criteria for assigning social class status also vary, but it is clear that some people have higher incomes, more education, more prestigious jobs, greater access to resources, and more power than do others. Rather than rigid boundaries, there is a continuum from highest to lowest status. People who come from Western European countries and who have been in the country for generations tend to cluster at the highest level, while African Americans, Hispanics and Native Americans tend to cluster at lower levels. Many of them are poor and beset by multiple problems that accompany poverty, lack of money, lack of social resources, discrimination and devaluation, lack of adequate educational opportunities, and unemployment. New immigrants and refugees also often fall within the lowest category. Devore and Schlesinger use Gordon's idea "that social class and ethnic group membership join to generate the class in action or the social reality."[45] The class exerts a profound influence on lifestyles and opportunities for finding satisfactions in living. Intertwining with ethnic and class differences, race, religion, age, gender, and sexual orientation distinguish one subgrouping from another.

Social class status is not rigid: many people are able to achieve upward mobility, but others, owing to a combination of circumstances, are downwardly mobile.

There are differences of opinion about the relative importance of social class and ethnicity. Since most immigrants and members of racial minorities have a common plight of economic immobility, Greer asserts that too much emphasis on ethnic differences tends to mask this important fact.[46] But prejudice and discrimination against racial minorities are important contributors to their disproportionate representation among the poor. There is a complex relationship between social class, race, and ethnicity. Understanding social classes and their major differences is necessary because social class status determines, to a large extent, the opportunities available for satisfying and effective social living. But, there is a danger that poor people will be stereotyped. Many of them have great capacity to pursue their desired goals in spite of obstacles.

From a review of the literature, Lieberman concluded that "though differences are believed to exist among different social strata in terms of attitudes and values and they have some relationship to treatability, the evidence is conflicting and controversial."[47] Accurate knowledge is necessary. Overgeneralization about differential characteristics of social classes may distort assessment and provide false criteria for planning. A systems orientation takes into account social class as one interdependent element in human behavior, not as a single causative factor.

Cultural Values

Within a changing society, it is becoming increasingly difficult to ascertain the dominant as well as variant values of the various segments of the population. There are many differences within ethnic and religious groups and between an ethnic group and the dominant white middle class. Using a value orientation framework developed by Kluckhohn and Strodtbeck,[48] Spiegel described the predominant American values in relation to orientations to time, activity, social relationships, relation to nature or the supernatural environment, and beliefs about the basic nature of people as good or evil.[49]

1. In regard to a time dimension, a preference is for a future orientation, as indicated by such matters as attention given to planning for the future, thinking about it, scheduling appointments, and valuing newness and youthfulness.
2. In regard to the activity dimension, the "doing" orientation predominates, focused on achievement. Success is recognized by others; competition is strong; there is striving for upward mobility; and social contacts are associated with the "doing."
3. Individualism predominates, reflecting the preference for horizontal rather than vertical relationships. Pinderhughes has said that "No other cultural group emphasizes autonomy and independence as much" as contrasted with responsibility to others. It places less emphasis on cooperation, friendship, and affiliation needs than on individual productivity and accomplishment.
4. In relation to nature, it is assumed that there are few problems occurring between humans and nature that cannot be solved by technology or money. These problems include the mastery of disease, space exploration, changing the natural environment, and pollution of air, water, forests, and the elimination of plant and animal species.
5. The final category concerns perceptions of the basic nature of humans. The predominant orientation is that persons are born neither good nor evil but more like a "tabula rasa" or blank slate on which the environment, the parents, the neighborhood and the school leave their imprint on the course of growth and development."

Spiegel summarizes the account of white middle-class American value orientations thusly:

It is evident that the first-order, or *dominant* American choices in each dimension fit together nicely—perhaps too well. If the personal achievement implied by "Doing" is to be facilitated, then it is good to be able to plan for the "Future," as an "Individual" not too constrained by family or group ties, with the optimism supplied by the "Mastery-over-Nature" orientation, and the pragmatic morality with which self-interest is justified afforded by the "Neutral" view of the Basic Nature of Man.[50]

Many ethnic groups vary, in small or large ways, from the pattern as do many individuals within a given group. Spiegel provides an example to illustrate the differences between the traditional American white value system and Italian and Irish populations. Anderson used the framework to compare subcultural groups in Singapore with the Western value system.51 The value orientations on which many ethnic groups, including some Asians and Hispanics, seem to vary from the dominant orientation most clearly is in regard to the strong priority on competitiveness and achievement of success in work and the extreme individualism and lateral relationships.

Determining the cultural values of any group varies greatly. McAdoo, for example, states that the diversity of black families, their value systems, and their lifestyles makes it impossible to be an expert on black families.52 Several diverse conceptualizations are offered: (1) black families differ from other families in having a greater level of poverty; (2) poverty, plus the experience of slavery and reconstruction, have left an indelible mark on families that has persisted; (3) black families are unique because remnants of African culture have been maintained and have adapted to discrimination. She supports the view that poverty and discrimination are the major factors.

The diversity of ethnic groups within each race and the varied experiences of their members make generalization difficult. It is in the process of assessment that clinical social workers need to review the latest information about the ethnic group to which their clients belong and then explore with them the meaning of their ethnicity and the difficulties they may have in adapting to what they perceive to be the differences between their culture and the surrounding culture. Knowledge of the dominant orientations is useful as a framework for understanding the values of any person or group.

Oppression, Prejudice, and Discrimination

Prejudice is an unfavorable attitude toward persons or groups which is based on preconceived judgments, rather than knowledge.53 Typically, such attitudes are directed toward people who differ from the prejudiced person's own reference group on some important dimension such as ethnicity, race, religion, sexual orientation, or political affiliation. The judgmental person has limited or inaccurate information about the group and usually has had little experience with that group. Prejudices are based on stereotypes, misperceptions that obscure the ability to view others as they really are in all their likenesses and differences from others.

Discrimination is, according to Newman: "any act of differential treatment toward a group or an individual who is perceived as a member of a group. . . the intent and/or effect of differential treatment is to create a disadvantage of some sort" (p. 149). Prejudice defines an attitude: discrimination defines behavior.

Discrimination against blacks and devalued ethnic groups is endemic in our society. The horrible history of slavery and legal segregation of blacks has passed, but devaluation and discrimination continue to be parts of their everyday lives. Solomon has described in detail how black people are devalued and discriminated against in all of society's institutions.[54] The institutional system has failed them, making it difficult for them to achieve upward mobility. Through both individual and institutional racism, they are trapped in bad environments and tend to feel powerless to achieve their life goals.

Other devalued ethnic groups, particularly Native Americans and Mexican Americans, have also found it hard to achieve "the American Dream." Many of them are poor, live in crowded or dilapidated housing and in neighborhoods that lack adequate health, education, and welfare resources. They have not had equal opportunities in education so they are relegated to the lowest paid jobs or are unemployed. Through both individual and institutional racism, they feel trapped in environments that do not foster satisfying growth and development which leads to feelings of powerlessness to achieve their cherished goals.

Gender

Men have traditionally had privileged roles and status in society.[55] In most cultures, women have been devalued, assigned to menial roles in the family and community, and deprived of opportunities to fulfill their potentials. It was a long hard struggle for women even to be allowed to vote, to participate in many community organizations, and to work outside the home except as domestic workers, teachers, or nurses. Higher education was virtually denied them until women's colleges were established, and they were discouraged, if not prohibited, from studying in such subjects as mathematics, science, engineering, and medicine.

Although these limitations on women's choices are now less frequent in the United States, women still suffer from prejudice and discrimination in many ways. They are just beginning to achieve political power in the form of election to Congress and appointments to important positions in government. They have witnessed the failure of passage of an equal rights amendment to the Constitution. Although they have achieved entry into many lines of employment, their wages have consistently been lower than those of men. A recent study by the U.S. Department of Labor concluded that women, as well as members of minority ethnic groups, never get past the promotional ladder by more than a rung or two. The report said, "The glass ceiling is much lower than we expected."[56] Recruitment policies that rely on networking, lack of access to training and development programs, and preferences of search firms for white males are discriminatory to many women.

Prejudice against girls and women begins at an early age. A report of a recent study by the American Association of University Women concluded that there are many inequities in education.[57] Girls received less attention from teachers than boys did, they were subject to sexual harassment by boys, and they had few opportunities to study mathematics and science. That organization is now engaged in activities to make education more appropriate and available to girls of all ages.

As changes are made in the status and roles of men and women, men experience stress in relating to the new expectations for equality.[58] Many men are modifying their lifestyles to give more attention to family interests, including child care. They learn that male dominance has had negative as well as positive consequences for their satisfaction in living. It is becoming more acceptable for them to express feelings, engage in family and recreational activities, and reduce the unreasonable pressure for achievement and success in employment.

Sexual Orientation

Strong prejudice exists against persons who are homosexual.[59] The irrational attitudes of fear, suspicion, mistrust, and hatred—homophobia—result in devaluation of gays and lesbians and discrimination against them. They may live in constant fear of rejection by family, friends, colleagues, and employers. They have faced discrimination in employment, housing, desire for child custody, recreation, the military, and social life. Extremely difficult for many of them is the decision concerning disclosure of their sexual orientation to particular people or in general. The fear of AIDS, which in the United States was first diagnosed in gay men, has exacerbated prejudice against them. Religions often consider homosexuality to be a sin, creating conflicts in values for members of those churches.

Power

Referring to prejudice and discrimination, Pinderhughes believes that, no matter the level of oppression and who is identified as minority or majority, the key issue appears to be that of dominance and subordination. Power thus becomes a primary factor in the cultural process. Stereotypes can be considered rationalizations to maintain the status quo and justify domination and immoral behavior on the part of persons in power.[60] People are oppressed when power or authority is exercised in a cruel or unjust manner. Discrimination is disempowering, denying social justice to those who are the objects of discrimination. Powerlessness stems from a complex and dynamic interrelationship between people and a relatively hostile environment.

The social context for practice has tremendous impact on the nature and quality of services provided to clients by social agencies and private practitioners. Knowledge about interacting systems in a given environment; laws, policies, and programs; the organization of the profession into fields of practice; criteria for job satisfaction; population distribution in neighborhoods and communities; major societal problems; human diversity; cultural values; and oppression constitutes a backdrop for practice. This knowledge of the social context needs to be integrated with knowledge about individuals, families, small groups, and social networks, which is the subject of the next chapter.

Three | Theoretical Perspectives

In order to practice effectively social workers need considerable knowledge about people and their proximate and distal environments. They need multiple perspectives in order to understand the range of human needs and problems, and the great variety of conditions that influence human development. They need a scheme for interpreting the needs of individuals and families who use social services. Treatment of any kind must be individualized, so that the means employed result in meeting specific needs and thus the achievement of goals. Individualization takes place only when a person's needs and capacities and the qualities of the environment are understood and taken into consideration.

The knowledge that is used as a foundation for a practitioner's activities should be such that it helps a worker to give service to all people in all phases of psychosocial development; to all socioeconomic, racial, religious, and ethnic populations; and to people with varied lifestyles and those who live under different environmental conditions. The theory should take into account behavior that explains how most people develop and cope with challenges in their lives, as well as taking into account difficulties and deviations in health and behavior. It needs to explain the continuum from very effective functioning to severe malfunctioning. The selected knowledge needs to demonstrate its relevance also for the conditions of life in our society. For many clients, poverty, illness, racism, crime, unemployment instability, natural disasters, and alienation erode the quality of life, making it difficult for people to develop their potentialities.

Contemporary practice theory is predominately eclectic in its knowledge base within a broad ecosystem perspective. Concepts from the biological, psychological, and social sciences are selected for their pertinence to the provision of direct services to people to help them achieve goals within the realm of psychosocial functioning. Psychosocial functioning involves a complex gestalt of emotion, cognition, and action as clients relate to and interact with other people and organizations in varied situations. The integrating idea is the dynamic interplay among person, family, group, and environment. What is needed is a multiple-angle lens.

Systems Theory

Formulations concerning complex adaptive systems in interaction with other systems in the natural and built environment are clearly useful in clinical social work. Such an ecosystem perspective provides a broad framework to guide practitioners in their observations and assessments of a person-family-group-situation configuration. It is to be noted that the idea of system has been put in a broad context of a network of interacting systems. The intersystems network, as it is referred to by Chin, is similar to what is called an ecological approach or perspective.[1] The perspective is concerned with "the relations among living entities and other aspects of their environment." It is "concerned with the growth, development, and potentialities of human beings and with the properties of their environments that support or fail to support the expression of human potential."[2]

Concepts about systems sensitize the social worker to the common properties and processes of human units of different sizes and complexities. Individuals, families, and formed groups may be viewed as biopsychosocial systems that are influenced by, and also influence other systems to which they are related. Hearn, a leader in the application of systems theory to social work, defines a system as "a set of objects together with relationships between the objects and between their attributes."[3] Bertalanfy says simply that it is "a complex of components in interaction."[4] He distinguishes a human system theory from a mechanistic theory. A system is composed of a complex set of interdependent parts related to each other in some fairly stable way. It is a holon, that is, an entity that is simultaneously a whole and a part. For example, persons are more than their skeletons, brains, muscles, organs, skin, and physiological processes: they are integrated wholes. The whole is more than the sum of the parts: the parts are organized and integrated. At the same time, all holons are components of a larger system. For example, a child is an integrated whole, but also a component of numerous other systems such as the family, extended family, school, play groups, and church or synagogue.

Changes in the system occur as consequences of changes within the system interacting with forces in the environment. Being adaptive, human systems have the capacity to react to their environments in ways that facilitate the continued operation and growth of the system.

It has been said that systems theory has been revolutionary in shifting ideas of causality from linear relationships to circular loops of influence.[5] It helps us to recognize the variability and complexity of the sociocultural world. It is, therefore, highly consistent with contemporary clinical social work.

Systems Concepts

Several major constructs from systems theory are particularly applicable to social work practice.[6] They are boundary, steady state, feedback, equifinality, social structure, and progressive differentiation.

Boundary

All systems have a semipermeable demarcation line that delimits and defines the components of the system. It distinguishes the system from its component subsystems and from the larger suprasystem of which it is a part—its environment. The environment consists of nature, institutions, human beings, and a network of social relationships, as these are influenced by the broader culture. The boundary between a system and its environment is partly conceptual and, to that extent, arbitrary. There is greater frequency and intensity of interaction and greater interdependence among the elements within than outside the system. The elements may be thought of as the substantive parts, such as individuals, or as the relational components, such as patterns of affection, roles, and communication.

Functionally, the boundary ties together the components into a meaningful whole and serves as a filtering device, admitting certain information into the system and blocking out other inputs.

Systems are more or less open to influences from the environment and more or less able to influence the environment. The more closed a system is, the less likely it is to have the wherewithal to meet its needs, because it cannot benefit from new stimulation that is essential to growth and change. A person, family, or other group can use new ideas, knowledge, or resources only when the boundary is open to such new information. On the other hand, some boundaries are so loose that the identity of a system becomes weak. In some groups, boundaries are closed to new members: in other groups, anyone can belong. When a boundary is too rigid or too loose, the system proceeds toward entropy, that is toward a loss of organization and function and eventual disintegration.

Steady State

Although human systems are constantly in a process of change, they also have a tendency to maintain a balance among their parts and between their own internal needs and external demands. This is known as the steady state, sometimes referred to as homeostasis or equilibrium. A steady state is a shifting dynamic balance rather than a static equilibrium. The term is used to indicate not only maintenance of or return to a prior level of functioning, but also movement toward change.

Stress and conflict are natural processes that disturb the steady state. Intrapersonal, interpersonal, and intergroup conflicts may occur. An individual may experience intrapsychic conflicts. An individual or family may experience unmanageable stress, resulting from a hazardous event, such as a natural disaster, loss, diagnosis of a life-threatening illness, rape, or physical abuse. The steady state is upset; the person or family is in a state of crisis. Parad, Selby, and Quinlan explain that "the crisis state results when new solutions to problems in living are called for, and habitual coping means do not suffice."[7]

Interpersonal and group conflicts arise out of differences among the participants' goals, values, norms, motivations, unconscious needs, and interests. They may also arise out of differences between the values and norms of the individual or group and those of larger systems in the community. Conflict disrupts the steady state; there is then an increase in stress. The need to reduce the stress leads to new adaptations so that a sense of stability and continuity is restored. Under stress, an individual or group operates either to maintain itself, to return to a prior state, or to move to some new state of being. Some stress is essential to motivate people to new and more desirable levels of functioning. People do not continually and only strive for tension reduction or even balance, but also strive for positive changes.

Feedback

Feedback is the response or reaction of one or more persons to a particular verbal or nonverbal behavior of another. It is a process that provides for self-regulation of subsequent behavior. Since it is an integral component of communication theory, it will be discussed more fully in chapter 5.

Equifinality

The principle of equifinality is that different initial conditions may lead to similar outcomes and that there may be different developmental routes to the same goal. The achievements of a system are not dependent upon the initial condition. Human systems are constantly in a process of change, as they seek to fulfill individual and group goals. The past is relevant, but it is not causally dominant. "Equifinality replaces the traditional cause-effect analysis by demonstrating its inadequacy to deal with phenomena such as emergence, purpose, goal-seeking, and self-regulation."[8] Equifinality is in harmony with the idea of people as creative and adaptable, not only being changed by, but also changing, circumstances.[9] There is also a complementary principle of multifinality, which states that similar conditions may lead to dissimilar end states.

An adaptive human system strives to achieve its goals through making internal or external changes, usually both. It can engage in problem-solving processes that consider alternative goals and means to its desired end state. A person or family can, to a large extent, go beyond its initial state. This is achieved through its ability to use new ideas, knowledge, and resources which again can happen only when the boundary is open to such new inputs. People have a certain degree of freedom to determine their own destinies. They act purposefully in relation to their desired objectives. They are influenced not only by their past experiences; they are also influenced by their anticipation of the future and by finding the appropriate means for making and implementing decisions.

Social Structure: Status and Roles

Structure makes it possible for social systems to create and distribute responsibilities and privileges, and to control individuals in relation to each other.

Status.   Status refers to a person's position relative to others in a hierarchy of statuses in a family, group, or society. Status may be ascribed to a person, based on such characteristics as color, ethnicity, social class, age, gender, physical condition, ancestry, or sexual orientation. Statuses are also assigned through achievement in such areas as education, occupation, or competence. The evaluation of these positions varies within a society and within its subpopulations.

Through a process of evaluation, people, individually or as a category, are ascribed to or achieve differential status of acceptance, respect, and power. High status enhances a sense of self-esteem and positive identity and low status has the opposite effect. In our society, one's status on a given dimension is either positively or negatively valued. White people of Western European backgrounds, heterosexual persons, and men have higher status in society than do members of minority ethnic groups, homosexual men, or women. In terms of achieved status, some occupations, levels of education, and types of competence have higher status than others do.

Role. Every social system has a structure of roles that accompany the status structure. Many definitions of role are similar to the one proposed by Hare: "a role is a set of expectations of a person who occupies a given position in the social system."[10] The essential idea is that a person in a particular position behaves with reference to expectations. Individuals are connected to social systems through the roles they occupy.

A role can be defined only in relation to its complementary role: for example, the role of husband in relation to wife, employer to employee, teacher to pupil, colleague to colleague, or friend to friend. Each system has its own pattern of roles. The nuclear family has culturally ascribed roles of husband-father, wife-mother, parent-child, and sibling. Other types of families have different sets of roles. In peer groups, the basic role is member or friend, but there may also be such roles as chair or committee member. Some roles are acquired through the interaction among the participants: members exhibit characteristic patterns of behavior, and they are expected to continue to behave in such ways. Examples are the scapegoat, clown, isolate, controller, or sick one. These roles tend to become stereotyped, limiting the range of behavior of the person in the role.

When people enact a role, they are responding to a set of expectations that they think others have for them. They also, however, adapt the rules that govern the role so that their performance becomes congruent with their own motives and expectations. People differ in the ways in which they interpret their roles, the positive and negative feelings they have about them, the extent to which they perform satisfactorily, and how they relate to their role partners. Roles are not static but undergo definition and redefinition as persons interact with each other. Although there are norms or standards of behavior that govern expectations, there is usually a range of acceptable behavior. Within each major role there is room for considerable diversity in ways of carrying it out.

Difficulties develop when there is lack of complementarity of roles, ambiguity or conflict about expectations, maldistribution of power and authority, poor performance, or when role behavior has become rigid.

There may be a need for shifts in roles with changes in status as, for example, when a wife-mother becomes employed and the unemployed husband assumes the duties formerly expected of the wife, or when patients are no longer able to perform their former roles. The idea of role emphasizes the importance of relationships between the role partners, whether they be in a one-to-one, family or group or institutional relationship.

Complementarity of roles—the harmonious fit of differences- -is a synthesis of components that make a whole. Mutuality of meeting a need results in creative adaptability of the members in a family or other group. It is the interaction among people that needs to be understood, as well as the internal motives and processes of the participants. A well-functioning set of roles in a family or other group is a means for integrating diversity into a functional whole.

Human Development

Progressive Differentiation

An important concept of systems theory is progressive differentiation. People develop in fairly orderly phases throughout the life course. In Freudian psychoanalytic theory, phases in psychosexual development were formulated, which ego psychologists have later integrated into broader psychosocial formulations. Models of human development assume that changes occur at different times, that the succession of these changes indicates that the system is moving in a particular direction; and that there are orderly processes to explain how progression occurs. These formulations emphasize the ego's adaptive capacities and its effort to achieve psychosocial competence.

Erikson (an ego psychologist) presents a formulation of psychosocial development that opens the personality system to interaction with inner and outer influences, without abandoning the significance of early experiences.[11] In each phase, individuals have new opportunities for psychosocial growth, but the manner in which these opportunities can be used is partially dependent on the individual's success or failure in dealing with the earlier maturational tasks. His formulation emphasizes capacity for continual growth throughout life and the influence of relationships and culture on personality development. In each stage, there are issues to be dealt with, needs to be met, tasks to be achieved, and hazards to, and opportunities for, growth. Sociocultural factors interact with physical and psychological ones in determining the adequacy of a person's functioning at a given time.

According to Erikson, development occurs in a series of eight epige-
netic stages, resulting in changes within the person and interconnections
between self and environment. The psychosocial outcome is a blend of
ego qualities from two polarities. The stages are:

Infancy: trust vs. mistrust
Early childhood: autonomy vs. shame and doubt
Play age: initiative vs. guilt
School age: industry vs. inferiority
Adolescence: identity vs. identity diffusion
Young adulthood: intimacy vs. isolation
Adulthood: generativity vs. stagnation
Old age: integrity vs. despair

Although the qualities of one pole will predominate, a person exhibits
a mixture of the qualities at a given time. Development is a process of person-environment interaction. When the environment does not support
and nurture effective development, the person's functioning is negatively
affected. Development occurs within an expanding sphere of relationships and mastery of developmental tasks.

The sequence of phases is thought to be universal, but the typical solutions vary from society to society and by subsystems within a given society. Human maturation cannot be viewed as separate from the social context in which it occurs. For every maturational stage, there always
appears "a radius of significant relations" who aid, abet, or hinder the
organism's coping with and resolving specific life tasks."[12]

Erikson urged that the relationship between "inner agency and social
life" be better understood, stating that "the rich ethological and ecological findings of modern biology need to be understood as to the major way
in which they shape the individual ego."[13]

Erikson's theory, according to Greene, has been misunderstood by
some critics.[14] It is not a deterministic theory: rather it is a process orientation in which there is renewed opportunity to integrate personality factors at each stage which covers a fairly large span of life. A person continues to cope with earlier issues throughout the life span. In spite of criticisms, his contributions are still widely acknowledged for shedding light
on psychosocial development and person-environment interaction. It is,
therefore, essential theory for clinical social workers.

Recent theorists have further emphasized the integral connection
between biopsychosocial factors and the environment. Maas has proposed
a scheme for understanding social development that incorporates knowledge concerning the mutual influence of individuals and their social contexts in each phase of development.[15] Under favorable environmental con-

ditions, development proceeds in the direction of increased complexity, greater differentiation, and better integration of social capacities. That is the systems construct of progressive differentiation. Somewhat similarly, Bronfenbrenner emphasizes that development is a function of the reciprocal role of person and environment across the life course.[16]

Numerous contributions have been made to special aspects of human development. One of the best known is Piaget's studies of phases in the development of cognition in children.[17] He has proposed four distinct stages, culminating in the acquisition and display of abstract and logical thought. A review of research by Vourlakis concluded that "in general, research suggests that children are competent in many cognitive tasks earlier, and have more conceptual ability than Piaget's stage theory predicts."[18]

In relation to human development, considerable criticism is made of inadequate attention to development in special populations by ethnicity, gender, age and sexual orientation. Gilligan, for example, points to the need to give more attention to the differential development of homosexuality and heterosexuality and for more complete descriptions of the processes of identity in varied ethnic groups in varied places.[19] Several writers have pointed out that developmental theories give inadequate attention to friendships, sibling, and other peer relationships and to work on subphases of development, such as research by Gilligan, Konopka, and Mishne on adolescence, work on midlife transitions by Golan and Schlosberg, and on gender differences in middle age by Neugarten.[20]

Longres has pointed out that developmental perspectives tend to focus on inevitable progress, but changes do not inevitably lead to progress.[21] The changes at any given time may or may not indicate improvement; the rate at which they take place may vary from time to time; while there are similar patterns of development among people, they may vary considerably among individuals. Thus, progressive growth in individuals is not automatic. The same is true for families, groups, and organizations.

Owing to the many variables that influence human development, Mailick and Vigilante have suggested substituting developmental need for developmental stage.[22] Such an approach would provide for simultaneous examination of psychosocial tasks at a given time in specific reference to personal, family, social, and environmental resources.

Family and Group Development

Families have developmental stages that mesh with the development of the individuals who comprise the group.[23] There are phase-specific and transitional tasks that need to be accomplished as the composition of the family, the developmental phases of its members, and the roles of members change. The wide variety of families in our society makes generalization difficult.

The most frequent delineation of stages deals with nuclear families in which the order of change is courtship, marriage, couple without children, couple with one child followed by the addition of other children, the leaving of the first child and then of other children, the couple alone, and then a lone person occasioned by the death of a spouse. The significance of such phases is in terms of the changes in the structure and size of the group; the division of responsibilities; the economic and psychosocial stresses typical of each phase; and the new demands each phase makes on all members of the family.

With a few exceptions, these formulations of developmental phases in families do not take into account single parent families in which the parent never married; those disrupted by separation, divorce, or early death of one spouse; extended family structures; foster families that include one or more nonrelated children; multigenerational families; and reconstituted or blended families composed of combinations of members from two prior families. These formulations do alert workers to changes that occur over time and their significance for family assessment and treatment. There are points of stress in transition to new phases which may tax the adaptive capacities of the members. There may be constructive resolution of the problems, regression, or maintenance of chronic difficulties. Each phase requires continual balance between stabilization and change in family structure, relationships, alliances, norms, and role transitions.

Other types of groups, except when the members first come together, have a past history.[24] They change in orderly ways as the members interact with each other and as the group develops patterns of structure and communication. There is an initial phase in which members become related to each other, oriented to the purposes and expectations of the group, engaged in the process, and achieve a working agreement. In one or more intermediate phases, the members explore and test the situation and work through conflicts concerning relationships, roles, norms, and power, leading to an appropriate degree of cohesiveness so that the members' major energies are directed toward working to achieve individual or collective goals, or both. The final stage is one of stabilization of changes made and termination, follow-up, and evaluation.

The principle of progressive differentiation from systems theory asserts that there are developmental sequences characteristic of systems. Development proceeds from a state of relative lack of differentiation to a state of increasing differentiation of the parts from the whole. But human systems are growth-adapting units that strive to maintain themselves through change, so that the differentiated parts are integrated into a functional whole.

Families and Groups as Systems

The most influential system to which most people belong is the family. Families are primary social systems consisting of two or more persons bound by ties of blood, marriage, adoption, foster status, or cohabitation, and characterized by continuity, mutual commitment, and emotional and economic interdependence. They exist within a broader extended family system and a network of other social systems, resources, and sociocultural environments that strongly influence the ways in which they carry out their emotional and instrumental functions. The family changes with the development of its members, the patterns of communication and affective relationships that exist, and the organization of roles. It changes with the members' capacities to solve problems, additions or losses of members, and the stresses, demands, and resources imposed from outside.

Families come from many ethnic, religious, and social class backgrounds with varied histories, traditions, norms of behavior, resources, and opportunities. These variations effect their relationship to other sub-populations and to the dominant society.

Knowledge of families and other groups as social systems comes primarily from sociology and social psychology, supplemented by psychoanalytic theory. Such knowledge is of special value to social workers in understanding the formation, development, processes, and relationships of the members who comprise the group and understanding the group's interaction with its environment.

Perhaps the best-known theoretical approach to the study of small groups is field theory, associated with the work of Lewin and his associates. Its basic thesis is that behavior is a function of the life space or field, which consists of the person and environment viewed as one constellation of interdependent factors operating at a given time. The personality includes the psychological and physical systems. The environment includes the immediate social group, the family, work group, and other groups to which the person belongs. It also includes the cultural system made up of the mores and norms of the person's nationality, racial, religious, and other reference groups. Lewin said that "to understand or to predict behavior, the person and his environment have to be considered as one constellation of interdependent factors."[25] Within a group, there is a continuous process of mutual adaptation of members to each other. Lewin's conceptualization is, indeed, in harmony with the intersystem, ecological, and biopsychosocial perspectives that are prevalent in today's direct service practice.

Complementing Lewin's field theory is sociometry, originated primarily by Moreno and Jennings.[26] It uses field theory, with emphasis on groups as networks of affective relationships and with individual differences and group conditions that account for a member's acceptance or rejection by others.

A third major contribution to group theory is Homans' formulation of the interacting concepts that define the group as an adaptive social system, surviving and evolving in an environment.[27] The whole is determined, not only by its constituents, but also by the relation of the parts to one another and to the environment which is everything that is outside of the group's boundary. Interdependence characterizes the relations of variables within the group and also the relations of the group to its physical and social environment. Members come together to form a group, motivated by their interpersonal needs and concern for a task. What emerges is a pattern of activity—whatever people do—that satisfies personal needs and gets tasks done. The verbal and nonverbal interaction patterns of activity established among the members move back and forth between socioemotional and task areas. An internal structure of interpersonal relations develops, interacting with the external system. The structure consists of norms; status and roles; and an affective structure. The group creates its own structure that consists of a set of norms, based on values, that differs in some ways from the culture of the external system influencing the group's norms and goals. A status hierarchy of roles develops through which power and influence are distributed. Sentiments are exhibited in the affective structure of liking and disliking among the members and result in greater or lesser degrees of cohesion.

Many factors influence the group's interactions, including the size and composition of the group, the structure of interpersonal relations, its capacity for adaptation, and the parallelism between what successful operations on the environment may require and what the group itself created. Homans' theory has made a major contribution to the person/group/environment perspective.

Psychoanalytic theory contributed to knowledge about families and other groups in terms of the influence of earlier social experiences on group behavior and the unconscious processes operative in group formation and interaction. Unconscious emotional factors partially explain the nature of the emotional ties of individuals with the group's leader or parents and among the members and such processes as scapegoating, contagion, conflict, and cohesion. This theory has contributed much to understanding family and group relations.

In addition to Freud's own work, some of the principal contributors to the application of psychoanalytic theory to groups are Ackerman, Bion, Durkin, Redl and Wineman, Scheidlinger, Slavson, and Yalom.[28]

Biophysical Factors

Biophysical knowledge comprises the structure and processes within the body that are necessary for the survival and functioning of the organism. Alterations in physical conditions may lead to alterations in cognitive, affective, or behavioral performance. Alterations in cognition, affect, and behavior influence the biophysical state. Research evidence supports the close interconnection of emotions, thoughts, actions, and physiological processes.

Genetic Endowment

Genetics is the study of inheritance that determines how physical characteristics are passed from one generation to another within a given species or among different species. The genes account for variations in sex, color, body build, and susceptibility to certain medical and psychiatric disorders. Although intelligence is thought to have some genetic base, the extent of that influence is not known because learning and environment play important roles. Genetic characteristics are sources of self-esteem and positive identity or the opposite. They also determine expectations of others for persons with a given characteristic. An extremely tall young man, for example, is viewed differently from an extremely short one by self and others, and there are different expectations concerning the types of activities in which each will be successful. Difference in skin color, even within a given racial group, elicit different feelings on the part of self and others. The dramatic maturational change that occurs at puberty is another example of natural physiological phenomena that influence the psychosocial functioning of the developing organism and make severe demands on adaptive capacities. Illnesses and physical defects that are hereditary or to which a person is predisposed not only threaten health and even life, but also tend to influence feelings of inferiority, stigma, anger at parents or other ancestors, guilt, and fear concerning transmission of a defect to others.

Organic and Mental Illness

Organic and mental aspects of illness are increasingly recognized to be indistinguishable. Classifications of mental disorders have in the past separated organic and nonorganic illnesses. There is growing evidence of the organic components of many mental illnesses. Based on a review of research on schizophrenia, Taylor concluded that "the biological concept of schizophrenia is fast becoming a scientific reality that social workers must understand and incorporate into their professional knowledge base."[29] But, he also said that psychosocial and environmental factors need to be taken into consideration in treatment. A task force on revision of the *Diagnostic and Statistical Manual (DSM III-R)* of the American Psychiatric Association reported:

> The accumulating knowledge about the numerous biological and physiological factors that contribute to a wide variety of traditionally "nonorganic" mental disorders has made the organic-nonorganic dichotomy obsolete. For example, few would now argue that schizophrenia cannot be related to some degree of dysfunction of the brain. In fact, the DSM III-R definition of organic mental disorders and syndromes might dictate that in DSM IV the majority of disorders should be placed in the Organic Mental Disorders section. Furthermore, the variety of factors (biological, psychological, and social) that contribute to the origin, onset, and presentation of virtually all of the disorders has made it essentially impossible to make clear distinctions between "organic" and "nonorganic."[30]

In situations in which physiological factors contribute to mental functioning, counseling or therapy alone cannot solve the problem. Medical treatment is essential, but is often insufficient. A combination of psychosocial and medical treatment seems most promising.

Psychotropic Drugs

Knowledge about psychotropic medication is essential for social workers in all fields of practice. Drugs are chemical substances that change the function of body organs or the process of a disease. In medicine, they serve such important purposes as the relief of pain or symptoms, the destructive action of bacteria, or stimulation of the body's immune system. The new antidepressants are revolutionizing the treatment of depression. The growing use and frequent abuse or misuse of psychotropic drugs clearly requires that social workers have knowledge about the major categories of drugs, their intended purposes, the real and potential side effects, the conditions that are amenable to drug treatment, and the psychosocial aspects of compliance or noncompliance to prescribed drugs. They need to develop the ability to integrate psychosocial and environmental interventions when working with clients who are using drugs, either prescribed or nonprescribed for them. They need to be clear about the patient's right to refuse medication.

The knowledge about psychotropic drugs is used in the processes of screening and assessing clients, interdisciplinary planning of treatment, educating individuals and families about the purpose and effects of specific medications, resource coordination, and monitoring of treatment.

Illness and Disability

The actual state of health, and persons' attitudes toward it, are important influences on the adequacy of their psychological functioning. When people feel good about the way their bodies are functioning, they generally feel good about themselves and are able to carry their roles with satisfaction and competency. On the other hand, illness or physical disability is almost always stressful for patients, their families, and significant others. Adaptive capacities are strained by severe pain and discomfort and by threats to body image and to the security and integrity of the person. Loss of satisfying roles or limitations on activities leads to the need for others to change in order to compensate for the changes in the patient.

Some diseases or handicaps holding little hope for cure or improvement require continual readjustment of the patient and others to a decreasing health status and capacity for assuming life tasks appropriate to the patient's developmental stage. Any surgery is not only life threatening; it is also threatening to the integrity of the body, the more so when there is serious disfigurement or impairment of functioning. Some illnesses and handicaps are accompanied by stigma and feelings of fear, guilt, or shame on the part of others as well as the patient: examples are AIDS, cancer, and epilepsy. Reactions to illness and disability vary according to the seriousness of the situation, the patient's and family's capacity to cope with stress, and the nature of the available care and resources.

The Use of Knowledge

Knowledge of the biological bases of human behavior is for use in practice. Saleebey describes the revolution that is occurring in knowledge of the biological foundations of human behavior and the need for practitioners to integrate such knowledge into their practice.[31] That social workers tend to neglect biological factors is indicated by research. He reports on a study of

2,090 patients screened at an out-patient psychiatric clinic, 43 percent of whom were suffering from a major physical illness. The social workers studied had no knowledge or even a suspicion of an existing major physical illness in 83 percent of the cases they referred to the clinic. 69 percent of these major medical illnesses contributed significantly to the psychiatric state of the patients. Saleebey argues that social work education and practice should use knowledge of the biological foundations of human problems.

> We cannot claim to be guardians of the person-in-context perspective, the ecological framework, without this knowledge. In addition, failing to provide clients with full understanding of the physical dimensions of their troubles is to render them less able and less powerful and, most important, to deny them access to the forces for wholeness and health that rest within every individual.[32]

Ego Psychology

Freudian psychoanalytic theory has alerted clinical social workers to a number of concepts that aid in understanding person-environment interaction. Most social workers do not accept Freud's view about determinism in behavior, that is, that earlier experiences determine later events, but they do accept the idea that there are connections between past and present experiences, preconscious and unconscious forces as well as conscious ones, that motivate feeling, thought, and action. Behavior is shaped by the interplay among a set of interacting subsystems of the personality which are labeled id, ego, and superego. Rationality and irrationality are regular parts of people's thought processes.

Ego psychology builds on, but also diverges from, early psychoanalytic theory in important ways. It is essential knowledge for social work because as described in Erikson's work, it emphasizes the personality's differentiation and development in relation to the environment. It offers a theory of adaptive behavior that involves understanding of the interaction between internal and external influences on human development and behavior. The underlying philosophy is that people are connected to other people and to the environment. Connectedness is reciprocal.

Goldstein, a social work scholar of ego psychology, has offered seven propositions from ego psychology that are useful to social workers.

> 1. Ego psychology views people as born with an innate capacity to function adaptively. Individuals engage in a lifelong biopsychosocial development process in which the ego is an active, dynamic force for coping with, adapting to, and shaping the external environment.

2. The ego is the part of the personality that contains the basic functions essential to the individual's successful adaptation to the environment. Ego functions are innate and develop through maturation and the interaction among biopsychosocial factors.

3. Ego development occurs sequentially as a result of the meeting of basic needs, identification with others, learning, mastery of developmental tasks, effective problem solving, and successful coping with internal needs and environmental conditions, expectations, stresses, and crises.

4. While the ego has the capacity for functioning autonomously, it is only one part of the personality and must be understood in relation to internal needs and drives and to the internalized characteristics, expectations, mores, and values of others.

5. The ego not only mediates between the individual and the environment but also mediates internal conflict among various aspects of the personality. It can elicit defenses that protect the individual from anxiety and conflict and that serve adaptive or maladaptive purposes.

6. The social environment shapes the personality and provides the conditions that foster or obstruct successful coping. The nature of cultural, racial, and ethnic diversity as well as differences related to sex, age, and life style must be understood in the assessment of ego functioning.

7. Problems in social functioning must be viewed in relation both to possible deficits in coping capacity and to fit among needs, capacities, and environmental conditions and resources.[33]

Adaptation

The ego has a degree of autonomy to function independently of instinctual impulses and drives. It is adaptive, able to adjust harmoniously to the environment. According to Hartmann, "adaptation is primarily a reciprocal relationship between the organism and its environment."[34] Adaptation may be achieved by changes in the psychosocial system of the person, by restructuring and modifying the environment, or both; or by the choice of a new environment. In systems terms, these processes maintain the steady state or enable the system to move toward a changed state. Adaptation is a circular process in that the environment is adapted to the system's needs; the system then adapts to the changed or new environment, and so forth.

Adaptation is clearly linked to the concepts of stress and coping.

Stress

Stress refers to any interference that disturbs a person's physical or mental well-being. People may experience stress in response to a wide range of situations, including illness, internal or interpersonal conflict, and significant life events. When faced with a stressful situation, the body responds by increasing production of certain hormones, leading to changes in heart rate, blood pressure, metabolism, and physical activity. At a certain level, they disrupt a person's ability to cope. Continued exposure to stress may lead to mental or physical symptoms.

Many of the stresses are biological or social intrusions. Major changes in life are stressful. Holmes and Rahe have developed a scale for ranking life events that provoke stress.[35] Losses in relationships are by far the most stressful experiences. But any change can disrupt the steady state and contribute to stress.

Coping

Coping is a process of facing and dealing with problems that create stress, protecting people against anxiety and guilt. Adaptive coping devices vary with a person's age, past experiences, and culture. They may include seeking and using relevant information, requesting support from other people, changing environments as in getting a new job or moving to a new neighborhood, searching for the meaning of an event, praying and meditating, using a problem solving process in making decisions, or using defense mechanisms.

The use of mechanisms of defense to ward off anxiety may or may not be adaptive. Among the common defenses are:

Projection: the attribution of unacknowledged feelings and thoughts to other people
Displacement: the transfer of feelings and thoughts that refer to one person to another person
Regression: reversion to an earlier phase of development in thoughts and behavior
Repression: unconscious forgetting of an anxiety- producing thought, emotion, or memory
Projective identification: projections onto others aspects of a person's own unacceptable impulses or self image
Sublimation: alteration of drives and impulses directing them toward creative or socially productive activities
Denial: refusal to recognize the existence of an anxiety-producing thought, emotion, or conflict.

Other defenses are rationalization, intellectualization, identification with an aggressor, reaction formation, suppression, altruism, avoidance, empathy, and splitting. Woods and Hollis present a more thorough discussion of these mechanisms.[36]

Mailick notes that it is likely that clients will often use a mix of adaptive coping mechanisms and maladaptive defenses.[37]

Social Relationships

An article by Goodman begins:

> Not all that long ago, people pictured the newborn as a helpless blob, a tabula rasa waiting to be molded into a human being. Experts presumed infants spent their first weeks not only unable to speak, but also unable to see, hear. or think. In the 1940s, even as progressive a scientist as Arnold Gesell, M.D., of the Yale Clinic of Child Development, didn't begin studying a baby's development until he or she reached one month of age. He noted in the book *The First Five Years of Life*: "In a sense, he (the human infant) is not fully born until he is about four weeks of age. It takes him that long to attain a working physiological adjustment to his postnatal environment."
>
> Then, about 25 years ago, scientists started taking a more careful look at the newborn—and realized the babies were looking right back![38]

People are, by inherent nature, social organisms. People need people to survive and grow.

Based on a review of research, Carlton concluded that: "research has made it possible to state, without equivocation, that people are social beings by nature and not as the result of socialization after birth."[39] Even conception is a social process, requiring two people to create a third one. Even the fetus responds to others: it hears the mother's heartbeat and startles at the sound of a cymbal. Babies come out of the womb with senses sufficiently developed to take in information and adapt to the environment. They turn toward human faces, can distinguish patterns, movement, light, color, and taste. They can communicate their needs and respond to the behavior of people around them. They influence and are influenced by others. Bowlby's work on attachment theory concluded that the infant's propensity for attachment to other persons is a genetically endowed capacity.[40] But, that does not mean that the environment does not impede or promote the development of that capacity.

Gilligan provides references that document the social nature and capacities of young children and their responsiveness to others. She says: "Previously described as 'locked up' in egocentrism or fused with others, as capable only of parallel play, the young child now is observed to initiate and sustain communication with others, to engage in patterns of social interaction with others, and thus to create relationships with others."[41] It is now evident, according to Sanville,

> that there is both a sense of self and a sense of relatedness from the moment of birth and that the lines of development are intertwined. Development does seem to proceed, as some of us have long imagined, in the form of a dialectical spiral, each rewarding experience with others resulting in an enhanced sense of self and each fresh sense of an ever changing self permitting richer exchange with others. And all the while the infant is organizing these experiences into a world view.[42]

Human relatedness is the key to healthy psychosocial development. According to Imre, "Because humans are essentially social beings, lives and meanings are intertwined. No person can know who he is without reference to others. For most people, purposefulness and usefulness are vital parts of the meaning of their lives and these are found in the community of other persons. Relationships are complex and many faceted."[43]

Object Relations

People have the capacity to develop and sustain mature object relationships. The word "object" seems an odd one for designating social relationships among humans. It involves the capacity for developing relationships and internalizing them. It involves the internalized sense of self as a distinct person, interdependent with significant others. Early patterns of object relationships have a crucial influence on subsequent ones.

The internalization of object relations forms the bridge from external reality to internal reality. The meanings of internalized relationships, especially those absorbed in the early stages of life, appear to be of crucial importance to the nature and quality of further psychological development.[44]

Internalization is lifelong. Thus, new object-relations are internalized and old ones are both reinforced and modified. Object relations address not only the images a given person might have of the others, but also the cognitive and the affective aspects of such relationships. The cognitive aspect deals with the facts of relationship, such as persons involved, time, place, words, and circumstances. The affective deals with feelings that are involved in them. Feelings range the entire spectrum of human emotion from love and hate, to anger and joy, to disgust and stimulation.

A typical example is the man who, at age fifty, remembers little more about a childhood teacher than that the teacher loved him. He has forgotten the subject the teacher taught, but in his mind's eye he can see him. His present feelings about him are warm and affectionate. He refers to him as his favorite teacher. Another example is the sixty-three-year-old client who feels that if his now-deceased mother had known that her granddaughter had an active sex life at age sixteen, she might have been ashamed—not only of the granddaughter, but of her son who thought no better of his own mother than to permit his daughter such leeway.

Object relations theory emphasizes that psychosocial development occurs through relationships with other people. Its focus is on internalization of interpersonal relations, their contribution to normal and pathological ego and superego development, and the mutual influence of internalized and actual relationships. The fundamental idea is that people develop in relation to those persons in their environment and in relation to the internalized representations of their relationships with others. Dealing with both actual and symbolic relationships, object relations theory can aid social workers in understanding their clients' capacities and problems in relating to other people.

Interpersonal and Group Relationships

The family is the primary and most intimate group to which most people belong, and a high quality of family relationships is crucial to their happy and healthy development. Children need above all the care, protection, and love of a family, but they need, too, extra-familial relationships that enhance their self-esteem and sense of efficacy. Very early in life, they begin to reach out to peers and other adults in the community. They participate in informal play and often attend day care centers, nursery schools, and inter-family get-togethers. Their affiliations change as they grow older and assume new roles with their peers and in organizations.

Grunebaum and Solomon report on research findings that peer relationships, both with friends and siblings, are probably as important to social development as relationships with parents and other adults are.[45]

The smallest group is the pair or dyad, which is the most intimate and personal of all patterns of relationships. Dyadic relationships include mutual pairs in which the give and take between the members is about equal; courtship pairs in which a person is seeking and the other being sought after; dominant-submissive pairs in which one tends to control and the other to defer; sadist-masochist pairs in which one is attacked by the other but seems relieved by it; and complementary pairs in which the qualities and needs of one supplement those of the other.[46] In the pair, harmony brings greater advantages than in any other relationship, and discord brings greater disadvantages.

The triad, or group of three persons, is another system to be understood. It is famous in fiction as the love triangle for the reason that a third person has an effect on the pair; in a group of three, there is usually rivalry of two for the affection or attention of the other. There may be a two-person coalition against one, or one may serve as a mediator between the two others who are in a state of conflict. When a close relationship between two people becomes tense, the couple may involve a third person on whom their anxieties are displaced. Family therapists call this process by the term "triangulating." The triangulated person often becomes a scapegoat.[47] A third person may increase the solidarity of the pair or may bring discord into the relationship. Larger systems comprise various combinations of singles, pairs, and triads. As a family or other group increases in size, sub groups tend to become more prominent.

In order to meet their needs, people develop complex patterns of social relationships that are significant to their psychosocial functioning.

Acts of communication in a relationship convey positive and negative expressions of emotion, as well as of opinions and facts. Both in verbal and nonverbal ways, the members communicate their feelings toward each other. Phillips notes that in every human relationship, there are "emotional reactions to one's self, to the other person, and to the specific content of the material expressed."[48] The varied responses of persons toward others are means through which they attempt to satisfy their own needs for relationships with others and to avoid threats to self.

Schutz has postulated three basic interpersonal needs: inclusion, control, and affection.[49] Persons differ in the extent to which they seek out and desire meaningful relations with others as contrasted with their desire for and use of privacy. To a certain degree, they indicate a desire to have others initiate interaction toward them or to leave them alone. They express behavior toward others in terms of inclusion or exclusion as well. They differ, too, in their need to control others and in preferences for being controlled by others. The balance of power may be stable or shift in different situations. Power, according to Pinderhughes, often is an unacknowledged dynamic in human relationships.[50] In a power hierarchy, some people control others who are in subordinate positions. Too often, people in minority racial and ethnic groups, the poor, and other oppressed populations lack sufficient power to control their own lives. Although everybody needs to love and be loved, people vary between preference for intimate, personal relationships or for more impersonal and formal relationships with others. Again, persons behave toward others and prefer that others behave toward them in certain ways with respect to affection. The responses of persons toward others and of others toward them may or may not be reciprocated.

Bronfenbrenner has a similar formulation but places greater emphasis on reciprocity. He identifies the basic needs as reciprocity, balance of power, and affective ties.[51]

The way in which persons relate to each other is the heart of the interpersonal process. The attitudes that people have toward each other are naturally somewhat ambivalent. Human relationships are characterized by various positive ties—love, affection, empathy, cordiality, and positive identifications. These are associative and tend to unite people. Relationships are also characterized by various negative ties—hatred, hostility, repulsions, fears, prejudice, and indifference. These are dissociative, separating in their effect. When persons come together, they may accept each other, reject each other, or be indifferent to each other. They may seek to establish intimate, personal relationships or behave in an impersonal manner. They may prefer that others respond to them with a particular degree of closeness or distance. A positive orientation to others is often reciprocated by the other, but not necessarily. There may or may not be compatibility between the needs of persons for relative intimacy or distance. The extent to which persons find acceptance in any situation depends upon the complex interaction between their own needs and attributes, those of other individuals, and the social context.

The combination of affectionate and hostile feelings between people is very subtle at times. It is difficult to know the reasons for liking or not liking others. Positive or negative feelings may be based on distortions in interpersonal perception. A person may have false perceptions of another owing to ineptness in communicating intent. A child, for example, tries to express friendly interest in another child through a push, but the gesture is misinterpreted as one of hostility. Ignorance of the nuances of language of various subcultural populations often leads to the use of words that hurt, when no hurt is intended. People tend to stereotype others, that is, to perceive them according to preconceived notions about what they will be like or how they will behave, representing failure to individualize them and to recognize them as they really are. There is a tendency to stereotype persons who differ from oneself in such characteristics as race, religion, gender, social class, appearance, sexual orientation, or age.

A person may have a false perception of another based on transference reactions.[52] Many relationships have within them feelings, attitudes, and patterns of response transferred from other, earlier relationships, particularly those with parents. Some persons misunderstand the present relationship in terms of the past. They tend to relive earlier attitudes with the persons in the present situation and react in ways that are not logical or appropriate to the current relationship. Transference will be discussed more fully in chapter 6.

Be it a couple, family, or peer group, the specific feelings that members have toward each other and the ways these are exposed differ from one group to another and will vacillate from time to time in any group. Ambivalence is characteristic of all relationships. Feelings shift and change: love may turn into hate or love may deepen, and so forth. There are differences in patterns of feelings, typical of different types of groups. In the family, for example, relationships are continuous, feelings run deeply yet may vacillate extremely from time to time; or they may become stabilized and resistant to change. Within a peer group, on the other hand, there are opportunities to develop new relationships of a more or less intimate nature according to need, choice, and the availability of appropriate persons. Although members of peer groups tend to bring to the group already learned patterns of relating to others and may transfer to others feelings that had their roots in the family, the intimacy of relationships is usually diluted, as contrasted with the intensity of relationships in the family.

Cultural Factors

In the preceding chapter, culture was presented as a major social context in which practice takes place. Here, the focus is in terms of its influence on the feelings, attitudes, behavior, and problems of clients.

The family and other groups to which persons belong comprise the context and means for acquiring and changing attitudes, interests, and values. Ego psychology postulates that cultural factors are important determinants of personality formation. A person knows himself not as an idiosyncratic individual, but by his cultural affiliations and heritage. Cultures prescribe the content and methods whereby people are socialized and resocialized. In order to understand people, it is necessary to know their cultural orientations. These are often difficult to determine; for cultures are not static but changing, and people increasingly vary in their own attitudes and behavior from the typical or ideal model. As discussed in Chapter 2, within the American culture, there are multiple cultures and subcultures, "carried by relatively autonomous groups or strata within the larger society . . . each with its own comparatively distinct value system, its special problems, its distinctive social perspectives."[53] These may be based on combinations of gender, ethnicity, race, and religion, interacting with social class.

The values, norms, language, customs, and traditions of a culture or subculture influence a person's opportunities for effective functioning or they become obstacles to achieving desired goals. An individual's and family's reference groups, based on religion, ethnicity, race, social class, or common interests, serve as a point of reference for self-evaluation and evaluation of others.[54] Some of these reference groups may be mutually sustaining or there may be conflict in purposes, values, and demands made by them on individuals and families. They play an important part in one's sense of identity and self esteem. The problem of achieving a positive sense of identity may be more serious for persons who are members of ethnic minority groups.

Adaptation to new situations is complicated for persons who have been socialized into one culture whose values conflict with those of one or more other cultures. Chau refers to this problem as cultural dissonance.[55] Many people must learn to integrate some aspects of two or more cultures, often made more difficult because their own culture is devalued by the dominant society.[56]

Culture conflict often is the outcome when a person is caught between the expectations of various reference groups: for example, family and school, ethnic norms versus predominant group norms, culture transmitted by parents versus that transmitted by peers or teachers, and intergenerational conflict between parents and children.

Many factors promote or retard social and economic upward mobility: the size of the ethnic group; the length of time in this country; urban or rural background; facility with English; extent to which discrimination has been encountered; the availability of social and political leadership within the population; the nature and influence of religion; and the extent of deviations from the majority group in fundamental values concerning human relationships, authority, orientation to time, and family structure. Unfortunately, upward mobility tends to be associated with the giving up of certain cultural values and often former friends, groups, and even relatives.

There has been a tendency to view minority cultures as negative in their effects on their members, when indeed each culture has many positive characteristics. Many factors promote effective individual and family functioning. As one example, Sotomayor has described elements within the Mexican American family that have promoted individual integration and group cohesion, including the extended family pattern, respect for the aged, family role patterns, and language.[57] As another example, Locklear has described the attitudes and practices of American Indians that are still valued by them, such as generosity, priority of family and interpersonal relationships, an extended family system, and preference for work that provides inner satisfaction as well as income.[58] Problems are created when these values are not appreciated by other people and when they conflict with those of the predominant culture.

Members of racial and minority ethnic groups have developed varied patterns of coping with negative stereotyping and discrimination in which their dignity and worth are demeaned and their rights are violated. Myths have been perpetuated about minority groups, which are rationalizations of members of the predominant group. Even in social work, it has been noted that "to rationalize their failure to serve, they (social workers) have projected such negative stereotypes as unmotivated client, the lack of communication skills, the inability to deal with abstractions, the notion that illegitimacy carries no stigma in minority group communities, and the myth that black people do not adopt."[59] Other myths can be added, such as the idea that members of minority groups are better served by untrained workers than by professionally qualified practitioners. The fact is that clients from these groups can and do make good use of professional service when the service is appropriate to their needs and if the workers have desire, knowledge, and skills to serve them.

Religious beliefs are an important part of culture, yet social workers have tended to ignore their clients' beliefs and the possible conflict in religious values between the worker and the client.[60] Religious beliefs provide conscious and unconscious norms by which people judge themselves and others. They may be positive aids in dealing with problems arising from a sense of uncertainty, powerlessness, and scarcity. They may be used in harmful as well as helpful ways. Whether helpful or harmful to a client's psychosocial functioning, they define reality for the person. Socialization has been influenced by religious assumptions and values: for example, Protestantism among African Americans, Buddhism among many Asian Americans, and Catholicism among Latin Americans. Religion interacts with race, ethnicity, and social class in its influence on psychosocial functioning.

An ecosystems perspective that incorporates biological, psychological, social, and cultural knowledge provides a framework for understanding the range of influences on the psychosocial functioning of individuals, families, and other groups. Clinical practice is consonant with a set of professional values and ethics. The violation of them constitutes malpractice. That is the subject of the next chapter

Four | Values, Ethics, and Malpractice

Values are an important determinant of the social worker's selection of knowledge for purposes of assessment and treatment. They are ideas about what is worthwhile or useless, desirable or undesirable, right or wrong, beautiful or ugly. They include beliefs and ideologies, appreciative or aesthetic preferences, and moral or ethical principles. Translated into ethical principles of conduct, values guide the practice of a profession. They derive from a few fundamental beliefs and attitudes about people and society.

Values are preferences: they are propositions about what is considered to be desirable. They indicate a "desirable mode of behavior or an end state that has a transcendental quality to it, guiding actions, attitudes, judgments and comparisons across specific objects and situations and beyond immediate goals to some ultimate goals."[1] Values, translated into ethical principles, guide the practice of any profession. They derive from a few fundamental beliefs and attitudes about individuals and society.

Professional Values

As noted in chapter 1, the ultimate value of social work is that human beings should have opportunities to realize their potentials for living in ways that are both personally satisfying and socially desirable. Montagu has said that "The deepest personal defeat suffered by human beings is constituted by the difference between what one was capable of becoming and what one has in fact become."[2] Most social workers would agree with this statement. Underlying the value of realization of potential are many more specific ones that elaborate its meaning. Implied in the basic value is simultaneous concern for personal and collective welfare for the mutual benefit of all concerned. As Silberman has said "Successful social work service should benefit the child and the family, the patient and the hospital, the employer and employee, the member and the group; not one at the expense of the other, but for the benefit of both."[3] Implied also is social work's concern with the quality of social relationships and with positive development and prevention, as well as therapy. Two primary values elaborate the meaning of realization of potential.

A primary value is belief in the inherent worth and dignity of the individual. People have worth and dignity simply because they are human beings. About the importance of the value of the worth and dignity of the individual, Younghusband has said, "it is ultimately in this, in the dignity and worth of man, that the philosophy of social works rests."[4] If this belief is accepted, then certain other ideas follow about individuals in relation to society. Persons should be accepted as they are and treated as whole persons in a process of development. They should be treated with respect, in spite of their likenesses or differences in relation to other individuals and population groups. They should have freedom to express themselves without fear of negative sanctions. They should have the right to privacy; information given by or about them should be treated with confidence or given to others only with their informed consent.

Since all people are worthy, social justice is due each one. Everyone should have the right to civil liberties and equality of opportunity without discrimination because of race, ethnicity, social class, religion, age, sexual orientation, or gender. Persons should have access to resources that are essential to meet their basic needs, not only for survival, but also for the development of their potential. They have a right to make their own decisions and to participate in making group decisions, within the limits imposed by the particular culture and status and with regard to the rights of others. The right to self-determination is not absolute. As Hans Falck believes, it should be re-labeled social self-determination.[5] It needs to be reinterpreted to encompass certain rights of families and other social networks which, in many cultures, take precedence over rights of individuals to make certain decisions. Belief in the worth and dignity of the individual does not obviate belief also in the worth and integrity of the family and extended networks of relationships. There is a delicate balance between individual and group welfare.

The delicate balance between individual and group makes interdependence among people essential to fulfillment of potential.[6] Thus, a second primary value is mutual responsibility. People are not in complete control of their lives; neither are they simply the victims of external circumstances. They are neither dependent nor independent beings. Rather, they are interdependent one upon another for survival and for fulfillment of their needs. They interact with other people and with the social and political institutions of the society in which they live; they both influence and are influenced by others. Mutual responsibility supplants the concept of rugged individualism. Persons are and should be interacting members of society, both giving to, and receiving benefits from, others to the extent of their capacities and the opportunities that are available to them.

People are interdependent. Konopka eloquently reminds us that "All lives are connected to other lives. . . . It is the vital interrelationship of human beings that is the heart of social work. The focus is on *freeing* individuals while helping them to support each other."[7] Interdependence implies mutuality in relationships among persons and among groups and organizations. It acknowledges the diversity of groups and cultures that comprise society. Each individual, family, and group needs to be particularized so that there can be opportunities for each social unit to maintain many aspects of its own culture and to make a contribution to the whole. Interdependence is essential to democracy. A democratic philosophy, according to Pray, rests upon a deep appreciation of the validity and the value to society as a whole of these individual difference in human beings. It conceives of social unity and progress as the outcome of the integration, not the suppression or conquest of these differences. Accordingly, it tests all social arrangements and institutions by their impact upon human lives, by their capacity to use for the common good the unique potentialities of individual human beings, through relationships that enlist their active and productive participation.[8] Group, as well as individual difference should be accepted and used for the welfare of all.

The ideology of social work from a broad psychosocial perspective views individuals as whole persons, interacting with others in the systems and the subsystems in which they find themselves. It is humanistic, scientific, and democratic. It is humanistic in its commitment to the welfare and rights of clients and the social systems of which they are a part. It is scientific in that it prefers objectivity and factual evidences over personal biases. It emphasizes that the practitioner's judgments and actions are derived from a reasoning process, based on scientific knowledge to the extent that it is available. It embodies the great idea of democracy, not as a political structure, but as a philosophy governing relationships among people, based on reciprocal rights and obligations, and directed toward the welfare of the individual, family, group, and society.

Ethics

"Ethics, in effect, is values in operation."[9] Ethical principles derive from values. Professional ethics are a set of moral principles regarding practitioner's conduct in their relationships with individuals, groups, and organizations. An ethical principle sets forth what practitioners are obliged to do under certain circumstances. When accepted by a profession, a code of ethics becomes a means of social control of the behavior of practitioners. It specifies certain norms or rules that govern behavior. Thus, no code of ethics can give absolutely clear guidance to a practitioner. There are ambiguities and dilemmas around any ethical issue. A code of ethics alerts practitioners to principles that need to be taken into account in making a choice of plan or action. The major ethical principles are concerned with competence, integrity, propriety, commitment to client welfare, and protection of rights.[10]

1. A moderate amount of professional competence must be assumed before a practitioner can contend with ethical issues. The absence of competence is itself an ethical issue. It is unethical to attempt to render a service when one is not competent to do it well. According to Levy, the principle of competence asserts that workers are ethically accountable for what they do and the way they do it. Workers are expected to be equipped to undertake social work service and to perform the specific function which they undertake.[11] The NASW Code of Ethics states: "The social worker should strive to become and remain proficient in professional practice and the performance of professional functions."[12] Social workers should retain ultimate responsibility for the nature and quality of the services which they provide.

2. A second major ethical principle is integrity. According to the NASW Code of Ethics, social workers should act in accordance with the highest standards of professional integrity and partiality. They deal with all people with whom they have a professional relationship in a manner that will validate the trust and confidence in them and the profession. They are expected to serve all types of clients on a nondiscriminatory basis. Services are to be given according to the needs of clients, not the social workers' personal preferences and prejudices. Workers do not exploit relationships with clients, colleagues, or significant other persons for personal profit or advantage.

3. A third major principle is propriety. Social workers should maintain high standards of personal conduct in their identity as social workers. Their private conduct is a personal matter to the same degree as is any

other person's, except when their conduct compromises the fulfillment of professional responsibilities. They do not condone or participate in behavior that is fraudulent, deceitful, or otherwise damaging to people. It hardly seems necessary to say that they do not engage in such behavior as drunkenness, sexual intercourse with clients, filthy language, or uncontrolled anger.

4. Still another principle is that social workers' primary responsibility is the welfare of their clients. They protect them from physical or mental harm and unwarranted stress. They assure that services and resources to which clients have a right are accessible to them. They are expected to provide the best service of which they are capable and to treat clients with respect, acceptance, and objectivity. They must often weigh the balance between the welfare of clients and the welfare of others, when these are in conflict. Indeed when clients are a danger to someone else, workers have a responsibility to exercise their responsibility to society and take steps to protect a potential victim.

5. Another interrelated principle is that social workers protect and safeguard the rights and prerogatives of clients.[13] A number of specific principles that elaborate this one are self- determination, confidentiality, social and human relatedness.

Self-determination.   Self-determination is defined by Barker as "an ethical principle in social work which recognizes the rights and needs of clients to be free to make their own choices and decisions."[14] The value occupies a central place in the profession. Yet, it has increasingly become recognized as one of the most complex principles to apply to practice.

Rothman, in an analysis of the principle, found that it is used as an absolute value by some social workers and as a relative term by others.[15] He reviewed literature on the factors that limit self-determination. His review of the literature indicated several factors that limit self-determination, including differences in the capacity of clients to make choices, restraints in the social context that affect choices, other values that may have priority, and other professional considerations that influence practice. Research bears out Rothman's conclusion that self-determination is a confusing and complex value. Kassel and Kane, based on interviews with a homogeneous sample of social workers, found a high level of variability in interpreting and applying the principle.[16] Weil and Sanchez also found diversity of beliefs regarding the principle and a desire for greater clarity about its meaning.[17]

Clinical social work entails a joint relationship in which clients play important parts. Self-determination then is interpreted as optimal client participation in all aspects of assessment and treatment. The word "client" often is used to mean one person, but it must be extended to include couples, families, and groups. As discussed earlier, the values of many ethnic groups place higher value on family and cooperative decision-making than do mainstream white Americans. Abramson says, "Following an approach of self-determination requires social workers to be responsible, in principle and in practice, to both clients and community."[18] A belief in the most essential capacity of humans is the power to reason, the ability to determine their own actions. The idea of humans as rational social beings who must adjust within a community suggests a social context to the concept of self-determination, a sense of belonging places relative limits on self-determination. Clients have an inalienable right to participate actively in making decisions that affect them. The client-worker relationship is an alliance, not one of control. In clinical social work, the practitioner is concerned with aiding clients to make choices based not only on their immediate desires but also on consideration of the alternatives and consequences for selves and others.

Confidentiality.   One of the most important values is the obligation of social workers to respect the clients' right to privacy.[19] The confidential information provided by clients to their workers must be protected and not given to anyone else without the clients' informed consent. Confidentiality is essential to the development of trust between the worker and clients, leading to the free communication of facts, feelings, and thoughts relative to the practice situation. Assurance of confidentiality enables clients to seek and use resources without fear of stigma, disapproval, or damage to other relationships.

There are several exceptions to the general principle of maintaining confidentiality. Social workers are not obligated to protect confidentiality when the client reveals an intent to commit a crime or other harmful act such as child neglect or abuse or one that is detrimental to public health. In such instances, it is desirable that the social worker inform the client of the legal requirements that the intent or act be reported to the designated authority and encourage the client to take responsibility for reporting it.

A feature of social work in many settings is that information is used for numerous purposes, such as recording, case consultation, supervision, or collaboration with other staff. The social worker is obligated to inform the clients of such uses and secure their informed consent.

In work with families and other groups, there is an additional concern with the ethics of each member in the use of information one member receives about others. As members disclose their feelings, ideas, and experiences to each other, the workers cannot make promises about the members' use of knowledge about each other. But this fact does not absolve them of ethical responsibility. They make clear to all that they hope that members will be able to express what they feel and think without fear that this information will be disclosed outside the group without the members' informed consent. In this respect the worker serves as a model for the members; in addition, the worker expresses expectations that they will hold in confidence information they derive about each other.

In matters of confidentiality, ethics and law generally reinforce each other. According to a NASW commission, "law ensures that the client's rights are guaranteed against those who do not act from ethical motives; ethics guarantees that the institutional conscience will transcend law and attend to obligations, whether guaranteed by law or not."[20]

Levy sums up the issue by saying, "in one sense, this principle may be summarized as the social worker's obligation to use the client's confidences for him, not against him, and to permit himself to receive confidences from the client only when he may be able to do something constructive with them."[21] When clients are served within their families or other groups, there are special complications in the assurance of confidentiality. The worker, of course, behaves in accordance with the ethical rules, but has a further responsibility to work with the client system toward the acceptance of a norm of confidentiality among the members.

Social justice.   Justice, in its simplest meaning, is to act fairly toward people. Sample, president of the University of Southern California, made an impassioned plea for social justice in a message to the university community. He began it this way:

> In his famous letter from the Birmingham jail, Dr. Martin Luther King, Jr. wrote that "injustice anywhere is a threat to justice everywhere." Today, over twenty-five years later, we have made some significant progress toward securing the civil rights and personal freedoms of every American, yet we must continue to be vigilant in protecting the human dignity of each member of our society. And we must struggle against injustice and intolerance at all levels, from the national to the local.[22]

Kurzman wrote that social justice is a matter for society's institutions to take steps to assure that justice is done.[23] Action at the macro level is important. Sample continues, however

> But institutions and officials can do relatively little about the small everyday acts of harassment and intimidation which we as individuals may allow

to go unchallenged. As long as we let those small moments pass without calling attention to the injustice they represent, the threat to justice everywhere will continue.

Thus, I call upon all of us to remember our responsibilities to ourselves and each other by speaking out against bigotry and intolerance whenever and wherever they occur. Only by this vigilance in our daily lives can we help make justice everywhere possible.[24]

That statement captures the profession of social work's commitment to social justice. Lewis wrote: "A helping profession not based in some morality that inspires a just order runs the risk of encouraging a practice that promotes an unjust one."[25]

Caring and social connectedness.   In chapter 3, individualism was presented as a major value in middle-class white American culture, as contrasted with the emphasis on mutuality and affiliation in many other cultures that comprise our country's landscape. The Code of Ethics still supports emphasis on individual welfare. In the not too distant past, a person tended to be regarded as a separate entity rather than as an integral component of social systems ranging from mother-child to large group relationships. A growing number of social workers, however, give priority to caring, relatedness, and interdependence and this value is supported by research on the social nature of humans.

It is a fact that, as John Donne wrote a long time ago, "No man is an island, entire of itself." Many social workers identify with Ryan's concern for "a world that would de-emphasize the exaltation of the individual as some kind of disconnected, omnipotent being and that would accept the reality that human accomplishments are the results of the actions of many persons working together." As Griffith Humphreys said, "There is something stronger than each of us individually, and that is all of us together."[26]

Caring is a mutual emotional process. Mutual caring and responsibility supplant the concept of rugged individualism. People are and should be interacting members of families and groups, both receiving from and giving to others to the extent of their capacities and the opportunities that are available to them.

Ethical Dilemmas

Most social workers probably accept these values and ethical principles as stated in their broad and abstract forms. But the principles do not give adequate guidance to a practitioner, posing dilemmas and requiring that practitioners use their professional judgment in resolving ethical problems. An ethical dilemma, according to Linzer, "represents the need for a choice between two actions affecting others; it has its source in conflicting values. The conflict in values is not between a positive and a negative one or between right and wrong, but between two positive values and two right choices. That is what makes the decision difficult."[27] The practitioner is in doubt about how to act in relation to personal and/or professional values, norms, or attitudes.

Ethical matters cannot be separated from clinical decisions in goal setting, assessing, contracting, and selecting modalities and techniques of practice. They are an aspect of almost every decision made by a social worker because decisions made are thought to be better than other ones.

Differences occur in all phases of the social work process. Ann Conrad conducted research, using questionnaires with a sample of fifty-eight field instructors in the Northeastern region of the United States.[28] The purpose was to learn what salient issues were of concern to these social workers. The most intense source of ethical conflict related to conflicts between professional values and the organizational setting and policies that interfere with social work functions. Other ethical dilemmas centered around limits to confidentiality, the duty to report potentially dangerous clients, competing rights of members of families, needs of clients for and inadequacy of resources, discharge of clients from hospitals regardless of their needs. Despite the ethical issues that troubled them, the social workers who participated in the study reported relatively high levels of satisfaction with their membership in the profession.

The duty to aid.   Reamer sets forth "the duty to aid" as a fundamental ethical principle concerning which many dilemmas require the social worker's attention.[29] The NASW Code of Ethics says that social workers "should act to ensure that all persons have access to the resources, services, and opportunities which they require." For some social workers, their personal attitudes and pressures from others may lead to a desire to refuse to work with persons of whose behavior they disapprove. A dilemma for example, is the conflict between a social worker who opposes abortion and a client's desire to have one, or a worker whose religion still considers homosexuality to be a sin and the needs of gays and lesbians for service. Other social workers may, even in the fact of contrary evidence, fear contagion from persons with AIDS.

Professional power and self-determination.   Ethical issues which concern clinical social workers reflect the special status of the profession as one whose practitioners have power to intervene in the lives of individuals, families, and groups. The principle of self-determination provides a guideline for limiting that power. But there often are conflicts between clients and practitioners, social agencies and practitioners, or policies, laws, and court decisions that seem to detract from the power of clients to determine the choices they desire to make.

Social workers often face dilemmas concerning their rights to abrogate the self-determination of clients. An example relates to AIDS and other contagious diseases concerning mandatory testing and the need to inform significant others that one has the disease. Mandatory testing is viewed by many as a necessary measure to protect other people's health, and provide prospective foster and adoptive families with information about the health of the children being considered. Others view mandatory testing as discriminatory, contributing to emotional trauma, and preventing people from seeking treatment. The social worker then has to decide how to help clients make decisions concerning testing and disclosure.

Another frequent dilemma concerns the authority of the practitioner and the rights of clients when the behavior of clients is harmful to others. Examples provided by Kurland and Salmon include the case of a mother who reported that she disciplines her son by making him kneel down with his knees on a potato grater for an hour, saying "You've got to be firm."[30] Another example is of a group of care givers of patients with Alzheimer's disease who were discussing the supports they could use to make their lives easier. "I needed to get an aide," Mrs. P. said, "but I stopped because all they ever sent me were blacks and you can't trust them." Clients certainly have the right to express their points of view and determine their own behavior if it is legal. The worker may aim to help the clients to explore the issue and their feelings and thinking about it.

The authority of the social worker is a key variable. It may be based on legal power as in protective services or in professional competence. In some instances, the principle of social self determination may be compromised to the extent that social work service is involuntary. Even within such circumstances, there is ample opportunity for clients to make many decisions within the limits that are set.

There are times when social workers, particularly in mental health settings, may have to make decisions about certifying a client for involuntary hospitalization. In a study by Dworkin, it was found that the major reason for certification was the dangerousness of the patients, especially dangerousness to others, and the major reason for a decision not to certify was the use of available resources as alternatives to hospitalization.[31] Patients with schizophrenic disorders were most frequently certified, while depression and neurotic conditions predominated in the non-certified cases. A similar issue concerns the involuntary placement of adolescents in residential treatment facilities.

Truth telling.   Clients have a right to know.[32] That rule poses dilemmas for some practitioners. The questions include: when is it acceptable to withhold information? What harmful consequences can there be in telling the truth? Are there times when the truth should be withheld in order to avoid a more serious threat to a client's well-being, such as a loss of life or serious emotional trauma? An example concerns patients who are terminally ill and whose adult children urge that the patient not be told the truth and predict horrible consequences if the patient is told, ostensibly for the benefit of the patient but more often, self-protective. Parry points out that "the right to know when you are sick what is happening to you, how it is happening, by whom, and under what conditions of risk, is a basic human need."[33] "A corollary to the client's right is the issue of how and when a person is informed. Adler makes a similar point, saying "The problem is often not with the truth but with insensitive and inflexible communication. . . . A social worker's primary responsibility is to defend the dignity and autonomy of the dying patient."[34]

Another ethical dilemma concerns the use of records with clients. In general, clients have the right to know what is in their records. Hafferty explains that technically, the information about the client in agency or private practitioner's files belongs to the client, but the file itself is the property of the provider of service.[35] He reports on research indicating that clients who are routinely given their records and are involved in their treatment have better outcomes than others do. Access to information is often denied because health care providers are afraid the data may be interpreted incorrectly, patients may try to treat themselves or draw the wrong conclusions. The practitioner, however, has the responsibility to explore the meaning of the information to the client and provide clear and accurate information that the client can understand.

Divided loyalties.   Social workers often feel torn between satisfying the interests of varied parties when there is conflict around an ethical issue. A frequent example is an agency's eligibility requirements which a prospective client cannot meet - yet the client desperately needs the help. What can the social worker who processes the initial request do about this? Similarly, a client may become unable to pay the fees that were initially agreed upon and the private practitioner or agency takes the position that it cannot afford to serve the client unless the fees are paid. The duty to aid should take preference over rules and regulations that deny services to people who need them, but the social worker often does not have the power to change the rules, creating stress for the practitioner. In private practice, social workers face the dilemma when a client's needs for service cannot be met owing to the policies of third party payers or managed care organizations. In some instances, the only alternative is for the practitioner to seek out and find a suitable alternative resource for the client while simultaneously working with others to change the policies and procedures that mitigate against the welfare of clients.

A common dilemma is divided loyalties between members of a family when the rights of one party take precedence over those of the other members. An elderly father wishes to remain in his own home; the adult children urge the social worker to arrange for a nursing home placement to protect his safety and their own peace of mind. In child welfare, the conflict may be between the rights of children and those of parents. The child has a right to a safe environment and freedom from harm and parents have a right to privacy and freedom from interference in family life. Legislation may deal with this issue, but won't resolve the ethical dilemmas for social workers. In the State of Washington, for example,

> The Legislature declares that the family unit is a fundamental resource of American life that should be nurtured. . . . When the rights of basic nurture, physical and mental health, and safety of the child and the legal rights of parents are in conflict, the rights and safety of the child should prevail.[36]

A child's right to be nurtured, to be mentally and physically healthy, and to be safe from harm overrides the legal rights of parents to have the child at home. Social workers face many dilemmas in making decisions concerning when a child is abused or neglected and when parents are unable to maintain or reestablish a family in which each member can have their needs satisfied.

Another dilemma for social workers in child welfare concerns their positions on what foster parents perceive to be their rights to intervene in court proceedings about the children in their care and to be able to apply for adoption of a foster child.

In occupational social work, questions are raised as to whether social workers are on the clients' side or management's side; yet the social worker needs to attempt to serve the interests of both clients and management. The organization's goals of productivity and profit may not be congruent with clients needs for a satisfying work environment, including attention to the impact of employment on family life and the stress of family life as it affects clients' competence in the world of work.

Bioethical dilemmas. Today, society is faced with bioethical dilemmas that concerned fewer people until recently. These include the most basic of all questions concerning when human life begins and how it should end. They include the issues concerning the rights of women to have abortions and use particular methods of birth control. They include issues concerning the growing number of alternative forms of treatment such as chiropractics, herbal medicine, acupuncture, and folk medicine. In the absence of clear norms, families are called on to make wrenching decisions about their own care and the care of members who are sick or disabled. Examples of the plight of families are numerous. A young couple viewing the fetus during ultra-sound imaging may experience severe stress and conflict in reaching a decision about abortion or intrauterine treatment. It is no longer unusual to be faced with a decision about continuation of life support systems. And adult children are often distressed by numerous decisions related to the medical and long-term care of their elderly parents. Under some circumstances, families are faced with a decision about the donation of organs while others question whether and/or in what way and at what time to tell the patient and other family members that the patient is dying. Conflicts tend to be severe when the desires and needs of the patient differ from those of other family members. These problems become ethical dilemmas for social workers who try to help their clients to make appropriate decisions, particularly when their own values conflict with those of their clients.

Resolving Ethical Dilemmas

Moral philosophers have developed theories and principles of ethical problem-solving. They have directed their efforts to theories intended to guide decisions in ethically complex situations. Two major schools of thought have developed as means of resolving ethical dilemmas.[37]

The *deontological* theory claims that certain actions are inherently wrong or right. An example would be that it is inherently wrong to lie to a client, therefore the principle is absolute. No exceptions can be made. Critics argue that rules and principles may need to be broken in extreme cases to protect a client or third party from harm. The competing *utilitarian* theory claims that actions are not inherently right or wrong, but that the rightness of an action is determined by its consequences. Its emphasis is on the outcomes of actions and it supports those actions that result in the greatest good for the greatest number of people. Thus, a breach of confidentiality might be justified if the benefits for many would outweigh the harm done to one or a few. Critics argue that utilitarianism is impractical owing to the difficulty in weighing harmful and desirable consequences, and that it can be used to violate the rights of a minority.

Many social workers are familiar with Dewey's and Lindeman's views that ends and means must be compatible, that "good" ends do not justify "bad" means.[38] Reamer reflects this point of view. "Our professional history," he says, "is too full of too many instances when appealing outcomes have been brought about through unconscionable means . . . we have learned that our concern about the consequences of our decisions and actions must be tempered with a concern about the means used to pursue their effect upon individual freedom and well-being."[39] There is a need to add that clinical social workers are concerned with the freedom and well-being of couples, families, and groups as well as of individuals.

Linzer concludes a discussion of the issue in this way: "By being open to both ethical theories—the deontological and the utilitarian—the social worker creates wider options for decision making and confronts greater conflict in situations that present ethical dilemmas."[40]

Holland and Kilpatrick conducted an exploratory study using interviews on the nature and types of ethical dilemmas.[41] A sample of twenty seven social workers in Georgia were interviewed. The research identified the ethical dilemmas by dimensions of competing values: (1) the focus of ethical decisions which ranged from an emphasis on the ends sought to an emphasis on the means by which decisions are made; (2) an interpersonal orientation ranging from priority on the autonomy and freedom of individuals to pursue their own self-actualization to priority on mutual responsibility, relationships with others, and group support even at the cost of some individual liberty; and (3) the locus or source of decision-making authority, ranging from reliance on internal or individual choices and judgment to compliance with external rules, norms or laws. They found that intermediate positions were more prevalent than the extremes. "Respondents tended to describe how they understood and responded to problematic case situations in patterned ways that emphasized typical responses along these three dimensions." These three dimensions influence professional judgment in making decisions about resolving ethical problems.

Malpractice

Violation of ethical principles and inability to meet standards of practice are considered to be forms of malpractice. Recent literature and research suggest that social workers are aware of the risk of malpractice but are not well informed about legal and relevant practice issues.[42] Many social work authors emphasize that the best defense against malpractice litigation is competent practice. Overall, the literature tends to address only a few select legal issues such as privileged communication, child welfare and school liability, informed consent, supervisory and field practicum risks, misdiagnosis, use of contracts, duty to protect and warn, the fiduciary relationship, and legal issues with AIDS clients. Generally, the literature does not delineate a practice oriented conceptual framework for helping practitioners to resolve legal ethical dilemmas and mitigate against malpractice hazards. Practitioners need a framework to guide their practice behavior in accordance with sound principles, legal duties, and ethical responsibilities.

Defining malpractice.   Professional malpractice is a form of negligence on the part of a practitioner who is required to perform in a manner that is consistent with the way an ordinary, reasonable, and prudent professional would act under the same or similar circumstances in their profession as defined by Bernstein and by Cohen and Mariano.[43] A social worker can be held liable when a client is harmed because the worker's performance did not meet the profession's standard of competence and conduct. Intentionally or unintentionally doing nothing or doing wrong can cause potential liability.[44] As stated in *Black's Law Dictionary*, malpractice is "any professional misconduct, unreasonable lack of skill or fidelity in professional or fiduciary duties, evil practices, or illegal or immoral conduct."[45]

The NASW Code of Ethics and statements of professional standards set forth minimum standards of professional conduct by which the practitioner's practice is judged.[46] Liability can be established based on the grounds of failure to follow a rule, law, administrative procedure, or professional standard. Also, if a social worker's negligent or wrongful actions contributed to another's erroneous decision, the worker can be found liable. An outstanding career history, lack of knowledge of a rule, or inadequate supervision or training are not sufficient defenses. In general, criminal and civil liability vary from state to state. What is considered good practice may vary by geographic region.

Malpractice in Social Work Process

As social workers engage their clients in treatment, they face numerous risks of malpractice. The most frequent ones are related to informed consent, differential diagnosis and assessment, the nature of the social work relationship, inappropriate treatment, termination of services, and evaluation of outcome.

Informed consent. A typical malpractice risk is related to failure to secure informed consent during the initial phase of practice. Social workers may not clarify with clients the nature of the proposed treatment and secure their informed consent to the plan.[47] Included are failure to determine the client's competency to give informed consent; using undue influence and coercion leading to involuntary treatment; failure to inform the clients of the potential benefits, risks, and alternatives to the planned service; and failure to secure parental consent for treatment of children with the child's knowledge that the parent is being informed. In other instances, the worker may insist on getting parents' consent when the child has a right to secure help without it, as when adolescents in many states have the legal right to have abortions or use school health clinics without parental consent or when adolescents have the right to refuse treatment.

Social workers may fail to give adequate attention to the principle of confidentiality.[48] Included are failure to discuss the limits to confidentiality, including the duty to warn specific others to protect them from harm; failure to secure a written agreement to have information released to other sources; and breach of agreed-upon confidentiality by giving information to other staff, team members, or other agencies without the client's knowledge and informed consent.

During the first sessions, the worker's aim is to identify the client's need or request, begin a psychosocial assessment and formulate a diagnosis when that is needed, orient and engage the client, set clear expectations, and plan a course of action. The purpose is to move the applicant who requests services to a client who employs services. Jones and Alcabes propose that applicants do not become clients until they have been socialized to the expectations for clienthood and are considered novitiates until socialization is completed.[49] They found that nearly one-half of the malpractice claims were made by novitiates. Research by Besharov and by Jones and Alcabes substantiate the need to facilitate the novitiates' understanding of treatment and to secure their informed consent to the plan of treatment.[50] That includes attention to the purpose and goals, roles of practitioner and client, the risks and benefits of services, alternative approaches, limits of confidentiality and privilege, fee setting and collection procedures, the anticipated duration of services, and the basic rights and responsibilities of becoming a client and using services.

Differential assessment and diagnosis.   Accurate, differential, multidimensional, and individualized assessment provides the foundation of sound social work practice. Assessment is an ongoing process that is guided by agency purpose, functions, and policies, and above all, by client needs. In accordance with the value of the right to privacy, it should be limited to what is essential to achieving agreed-upon goals. There are, however, areas of assessment that social workers are legally and ethically responsible to identify, report, and act upon that may appear to intrude upon the client's rights to privacy, self-determination, and confidentiality.

Within the realm of professional liability, a variety of assessment and prediction risks occur with clients who are potentially dangerous to self or others, victims or perpetrators of child, spouse, or elder abuse, incompetent, or gravely disabled. Malpractice claims have been made against social workers for not identifying or documenting factors that predict a risk for danger to self or others; not reading or gathering information from collateral sources that documented potential risk; defamation of character by the use of derogatory words or wrongful reporting; and liability for the actions made by others based upon the worker's negligent or inaccurate assessment.

Claims may be made for the practitioner's failure to make an accurate diagnosis of mental disorders when that is a possibility, and failure to assess accurately the environmental situation, such as the suitability of a family or residential setting for the placement of a child or handicapped adult; failure to consider biological factors that influence psychosocial functioning; and failure to refer a client to a physician for a medical diagnosis when indicated.

Findings from a study of the use of mental health benefits by Sharfstein, Towery, and Milow, indicate that diagnostic information submitted on insurance claims forms is often inaccurate.[51] The authors conclude that legitimate concerns about confidentiality influence practitioners' decisions to submit inaccurate information, but that does not make it right or legal. In an analysis of malpractice claims from American Home Assurance, Alexander found that half of the claims related to misdiagnosis of disorders with underlying physical conditions that required medical treatment.[52] If an inappropriate or inadequate diagnosis harms a client, the social worker can be held professionally liable and found to be practicing medicine without a license.

An example of a dilemma regarding a diagnosis concerns a social worker who is employed in a private for-profit hospital and completes an intake interview on a patient. The diagnosis is clearly polydrug abuse, requiring hospitalization. The patient's insurance does not cover treatment for substance abuse. The patient is very motivated for treatment and payment is the only obstacle. If the social worker decides to secure treatment for the client by listing a different diagnostic label, such as depression, that is clearly fraudulent and the worker has engaged in malpractice.

Fiduciary relationships. Social workers have fiduciary relationships with their clients. "A fiduciary relationship is one based on trust and in which power is entrusted for the benefit of another."[53] It involves duties and liabilities. Clients trust their social workers to act in their best interest. Practitioners are prohibited from using their power to exploit or harm clients. Definitions of fiduciary relationships emphasize these points: "(1) special duties arise because of the trust or confidence reposed in the fiduciary; (2) the fiduciary has special powers to dominate and influence the client because of the nature of the relationship; (3) as a consequence, the fiduciary must act in the best interest of the client and cannot take advantage of the client to promote the fiduciary's own interests" (p. 107). To prevent the abuse of power by fiduciaries, there is increasing reliance on judicial action. The practice principles include the duty to tell the truth, to secure informed consent, to maintain confidentiality, and to be loyal to the client. Practitioners have been held liable for intentional injuries and for negligent performance of their duties. The relationship between the clinical social worker and the individual, family, or group is a crucial component of practice from the initial contact to the ending of the relationship.

As the client and worker engage in treatment, interdependence, acceptance, and mutual trust are reinforced. A stronger attachment between the practitioner and client emerges, and the client is freer to risk disclosure of problems and both negative and positive feelings. The worker's aim is to create a relationship and system in which the client can make and maintain changes in some aspect of psychosocial functioning. The result may be that a worker becomes more reticent to follow laws concerning a breach of confidentiality or change the course of treatment that may endanger the therapeutic relationship. Malpractice risks are exacerbated by the client's transference and the worker's countertransference reactions. The major malpractice behaviors are sexual misconduct, assault and battery, defamation of character, failure to be available when needed, abandonment, and inappropriate or abrupt termination.

An example of a dilemma concerning confidentiality concerns a clinical social worker who recently began a group for male batterers who are separated from their wives. The worker is encouraged by the rapport between the group members. During the second session, a member indicates that he is very angry with his wife. The practitioner is aware that he has seriously abused his wife in the past. The worker is concerned that breach of confidentiality will break the group members' trust and impede their willingness to disclose their true feelings. The social worker has to make a decision about whether or not to report the danger.

Landers reports that there has been an increase in malpractice claims and ethical violations related to the boundaries of the client-worker relationship.[54] Based upon our code of ethics and standards, the worker must set appropriate limits with clients. Any type of interaction outside of the therapeutic relationship, such as friendship, can lead to confusion and confidentiality issues can be jeopardized. Clearly, sexual relationships are prohibited. Yet, as reported by Kurzman of the NASW Insurance Trust, there has been a significant increase in sexual malfeasance suits.[55] In 1985, the NASW Trust's malpractice insurance terminated coverage of claims for sexual impropriety.[56] Practitioners need to be mindful of the use of touch, which can be perceived as a sexual advance and may, in some cases, precipitate undue emotional suffering leading to psychiatric hospitalization.

As the relationship develops, social workers may respond inappropriately by becoming too intimate with the client, by abandoning the client in times of crises, or by becoming judgmental, punitive, and unable to relate to the client with empathy, acceptance, and authenticity.

Inappropriate treatment.   Social workers have a professional, ethical, and legal duty to provide a reasonable standard of care to their clients. Mental health and other laws specify that the proposed treatment should first consider the least restrictive environment based on the client's competency, danger to self and others, and grave disablement. Social work treatment can pose many risks, particularly if the practitioner deviates from the use of treatment approaches that are accepted and endorsed by the profession. The profession does not endorse or recognize treatment models or techniques that deceive the client or that inflict excessive emotional suffering or physical harm. The use of confrontational approaches, fight techniques, or physical encounter can lead to assault and battery charges. The use of approaches that emphasize regression, "early childhood work," group confrontation, and experiential "in vivo" activities must be based upon an adequate assessment of the nature of the client's problems and current situation. The client must have the capacities and strengths to benefit from these forms of treatment without precipitating further crises or regressive states that can lead to emotional or physical harm. An example follows:

Recently, a clinical social worker attended a half-day experiential workshop on techniques to discover the "inner child." The worker has been treating a 29-year-old client who is diagnosed as having a borderline personality disorder. On several occasions, the client has had vague recollections of sexual abuse as a child. The practitioner thinks that the client would benefit from "inner child work" and would like to use some of the new techniques that were presented at the workshop. What should the clinical social worker do before using this new treatment approach?

Termination.   Termination or transfer of a client to another service can be difficult for both clients and clinical social workers. Malpractice risks emerge around lack of preparation for expected and unexpected events such as a worker's change of job, insufficient or conflicting evaluation of outcomes, and worker's and client's feelings about and responses to termination. When terminating or transferring a client, professional liability suits include failure to refer, consult, transfer, or terminate when appropriate, abandonment or abrupt termination, improper withdrawal of services, continuation of treatment when it is ineffective or no longer needed, inappropriate bill collection, false promises about outcome, and failure to achieve expected results.

An example of a risk of malpractice is one in which the practitioner has been working with a depressed client for the past year. The worker likes the client and feels that progress has been made. However, the client's depression continues, and agreed-upon goals have not been achieved. The questions are: What should the worker do? What are the malpractice risks if treatment is continued?

It is the clinician's responsibility to evaluate the outcomes of the services provided. The means of evaluation should have been discussed earlier during the planning stage. If there is difficulty in making the necessary changes and achieving the specified goals, the practitioner should seek consultation or supervision. The worker should document in the record the dialogue with the consultant and the consultant's recommendations about how to improve the course of treatment. If, after consultation, there is disagreement among professionals, a mutually acceptable compromise should be reached and implemented involving maximum participation of the client. If there is substantial disagreement, the client should be given the option to continue with the original clinician, obtain another consultation, or transfer to another professional. If the client fails to improve or gets worse after a reasonable trial of treatment based on recommendations made by the consultant/supervisor, the practitioner should consider referral, transfer, or termination. It is the ethical responsibility of the practitioner to transfer or terminate services when treatment is not effective or no longer needed. Clients have sued because treatment was extended beyond the point it was needed, continued when it was unsuccessful, or required expertise beyond the worker's knowledge and skills.[57]

If the clinician decides to refer or transfer the case, an explanation should be given to the client about what information will be shared with the referral or transfer contact. Again care should be taken not to abandon the client. If the practitioner anticipates an interruption or termination of services to a client, the client should be notified promptly and plans made for transfer, referral, or continuation of services in relation to the client's needs and preferences. It is important to facilitate a smooth transition and explain the decision to transfer, refer, or terminate treatment. Workers should deal with their clients' feelings about termination, including their dissatisfactions, possible sense of rejection, and anger toward the clinician.

Before clients are terminated from service, it is the social worker's responsibility to follow certain guidelines.

GUIDELINES FOR TERMINATION

The social worker should:

1. Examine each objective agreed upon during the initial phase and evaluate the outcome with the client.
2. Document the fact that evaluation has taken place and termination is agreed on. If there is disagreement, a compromise should be reached.
3. Insure that abandonment has not taken place.
4. Insure that termination is timely, not prolonging treatment unnecessarily.
5. Deal with clients' feelings about termination, including their dissatisfactions, possible sense of rejection, and anger toward the clinician.

Problem-Solving

Social workers are often confronted with situations in which a code of ethics and professional standards conflict with laws, statutes, and agency policies, or where there are few or no standards or guidelines set forth. In order to prevent malpractice, the social worker not only needs to be well informed, skilled in "good practice," and prepared to resolve ethical legal dilemmas, but also equipped to make sound decisions.

Examples of the dilemmas faced by social workers include: (1) the problem of the rights of HIV clients and those with other contagious diseases to privacy and confidentiality versus the responsibility to warn others; (2) ethnic minority groups, refugees, and new immigrants who are particularly vulnerable when workers have inadequate understanding of their cultures, leading to inaccurate assessment and treatment or when our laws differ from theirs; (3) differences in laws regarding whether suicide is a viable option or is illegal; (4) the rights of children to live in a safe home and environment versus the rights of parents to raise their children; and (5) agency policy requiring that treatment must be short-term versus client's needs for more prolonged help.

A set of guidelines for problem-solving was proposed by Houston and Northen to assist the social worker in making sound and competent decisions and maintaining good practice.[58] These procedures are to be applied when confronted with ethical-legal dilemmas or conflicting practice decisions.

GUIDELINES FOR PROBLEM-SOLVING

The social worker should:

1. Identify the problem and potential areas of risk.
2. Identify the parameters set by professional ethics and standards, laws, statutes, and agency policies that pertain to the area of risk.
3. Determine a course of action for each parameter based on principles of practice.
4. Identify conflicting courses of action or alternative solutions.
5. Describe the risks of each course of action. Specifically identify risks of physical or emotional harm to the client or others, the likelihood of the risk in the current situation, and the consequences of violating the code of professional ethics and standards, laws, and agency policies.
6. Weigh the risks and evaluate each course of action, consider which courses of action are within the norms of reasonable and good practice, and whether or not there is risk of negligence, error, omission, or intent of harm.
7. Choose or formulate a new course of action that best reconciles the conflicts and risks.
8. Before implementing the course of action, identify strategies and precautions to mitigate against harm to others; violation of professional ethics and standards, laws, and agency policies; and to protect against possible malpractice claims and suits.

9. Seek professional supervision and consultation if appropriate. Remedy gaps in knowledge and skills specific to the identified problem and take action to remedy deficits.
10. Implement the action and evaluate the results.

Social workers who follow these guidelines will likely be competent practitioners in implementing professional values and ethics.

The prevention of malpractice and professional liability litigation poses many complex and contradictory issues. Social work professionals need to be informed about changes in tort actions, professional standards, laws, statutes, and agency policies. Furthermore, legal vulnerability needs to be placed in proper perspective. A social worker who follows principles of practice, abides by the Code of Ethics and professional standards, and resolves ethical-legal dilemmas and practice decisions based on a problem-solving process has little need to fear malpractice claims and, in the unlikely event that happens, will be able to defend against such claims.

Five | Communication

Clinical social workers are engaged in face-to-face interaction with individuals, couples, families, and groups: their interest is primarily in interpersonal communication as distinguished from communication through the use of mass media. The process by which a steady state is maintained or a new level is reached is communication among people.[1] As systems theory has evolved to take into account the greater complexity of human beings in their organized relationships, it has incorporated knowledge that was developed originally by scholars interested in human communication.

Social interaction is a term for the dynamic interplay of forces in which contact between persons results in a modification of the attitudes and behavior of the participants. Communication, both verbal and nonverbal, is basic to interaction.[2] There is a structure to communication in that each social unit carries on its communication through certain agreed-upon channels, but it is a process, too, of exchanging meanings and making common meanings.

Interpersonal communication is a complex social process through which information, feelings, attitudes, and other messages are transmitted, received, and interpreted: it is the very essence of a social system.

Essentially, communication is a process of formulating and exchanging meanings. As people communicate with one another, they learn about each other's feelings, hopes, ideas, and values. They exchange feelings, thoughts, and actions. Through verbal and nonverbal communication, there is a reciprocal and cyclical influence of the participants on each other. These transactions may or may not promote positive growth of individuals; they may or may not be constructive for the environment. No system moves toward its goals unless communication is adequate enough to prevent entropy. Without adequate exchanges in quantity and quality, growth and development are limited or distorted; a system needs new inputs in order to move toward a new state.

Communication theory does not explain the facts that bring about a given pattern of behavior in communicating with others. It does give clues concerning what patterns of verbal and nonverbal communication may be perpetuating particular behavior, which can be interrupted through new inputs into the system.[3] Other knowledge, such as ego psychology and sociocultural theories, contributes explanations for the patterns of communication that have evolved.

The Communication Model

The basic model of communication is that of a system in which a sender encodes a message that is intended to convey a particular meaning. It is sent along a channel, such as speech or gestures, to a receiver who decodes it, interprets its meaning, and sends a message back to the sender or to another destination.

Sending Messages

The sender of a message formulates a fact, thought, idea, or feeling that one or more other persons will hear and use in some way. Every message sent has a purpose. Shaw points out that the intent of messages may be to: understand other persons; initiate or maintain a relationship; impress others in some way; discover how one's position on an issue stands in relation to others; persuade others to change their thinking; provoke reactions from others; defend oneself; seek a favor or resource.[4]

The sender needs to consider how the message will be received, which influences the form of the message; for example, a firm statement, an anecdote, a tentative suggestion, an exploratory open-ended question, or a closed question. Once the message is encoded and sent the receiver has control over what happens to it.

The message sent may not be the one that is received. "Noise" may interfere with and distort the message at any point in the process. Noise, as used by communication theorists, refers to such interferences as actual noise, distractions of various kinds, faulty perceptions, difficulties in hearing or seeing, or the language used.

Receiving Messages

A distinctive characteristic of a human being is the ego's capacity for integrating and using input, any information or resource that has been made available to the person. Receivers of a message listen and observe selectively according to their knowledge, psychological state, past experiences, the social context of the interchange, and the nature of their relationships with the particular persons in the communicative network. They respond selectively to messages, according to their judgment of the intent and meaning of the message sent. Each message contains both a content and a relationship component. The former conveys information about facts, opinions, feelings, or experiences and the latter defines the nature of the relationships between the communicants.

There is "an elaborate set of implicit conventions and rules which govern the origin, flow, and effects of a message."[5] Understanding a message is influenced by the clarity of the message and by its appropriateness to the social context. It is influenced also by certain characteristics of the participants—their past and present experiences with each other and the subject matter, their cognitive capacities, and their language skills. In communication theory, the attribution of meaning to a message is called decoding or processing.

Feedback

The result of processing a message is some output. The responses to the message sent are fed back to the sender as new input. Some action is taken. The receiver of the message becomes a sender back to the original sender or to another person who decodes the message, interprets it, and responds to it. Feedback is a process that allows a system to check out its effects on its environment through a channel looping back from the output to the input. By this process, a system can maintain its steady state or become motivated to change. It has been defined as "the property of being able to adjust future conduct by past performance."[6] Feedback to the sender may take the form of a verbal message or a nonverbal one, such as the nod of a head, a smile, a puzzled expression, or a negative shaking of the head. Ideas are exchanged primarily by verbal means; emotional content by nonverbal means, such as gestures, posture, silence, and action. "Words mean nothing in themselves. They are tools to convey meaning," according to Day.[7] In clinical social work, the client's responses to the practitioner's message are varied, depending upon the message itself and the client's decoding of it. Clients may respond by continuing to explore the content being discussed; to provide further information to the worker; or indicate that they understood or did not understand the message sent. Phrases like "no, that's not what I meant," "I just don't get it," "yes, that's it," "yeah, I understand," "so what!" "are you telling me that. . ," convey whether or not the worker's message was understood but also, particularly when combined with tone of voice, the quality of the relationships. The practitioner often seeks feedback from the clients in such common phrases as "I noticed you smiled when I said that," "does that make sense to you?" "what questions do you have about what I've said," "would you like me to say more about that?" or, "you looked puzzled."

Feedback is not necessarily self-correcting: it can further disrupt the steady state. It can multiply the errors or deviations. One example concerns a student who expresses great anxiety over an examination; the other participants pick up the anxiety and exaggerate further the difficulty and importance of the examination; contagion of anxiety occurs. Energy is directed toward perpetuating the anxiety rather than to preparing for the examination. On the other hand, a different response from a second person might have lessened the anxiety of the first student had the anxiety not only been recognized and accepted, but also if a corrective idea about the realistic expectations and consequences of the examination had been added. In such ways, feedback can serve to maintain the steady state or initiate changes in the system toward a new state.

The Process in Practice

An example illustrates the need for alertness to the inconsistency between verbal and nonverbal messages.[8] A social worker recorded:

> Mrs. Gandy's child, Jim, was referred to the clinic because of his serious acting-out behavior in school. While we were exploring the feelings about the referral, she said that she understood Jim, but the teacher certainly did not. She gave many abstract explanations about his problems. She wanted me to help the teacher to understand Jim because that was all that Jim needed. She said several times that she loved Jim and he loved her and that she never got mad at him because she understood him so well.
>
> As she talked about her relationship with Jim, her physical appearance and tone of voice suggested to me that she really was feeling depressed. When she interrupted her monologue, I said that I heard her saying that everything was fine between her and Jim, but

I felt she looked as though she might be feeling sad or upset. I tried to convey the empathy I felt by posture and tone of voice.

After a brief startled silence, Mrs. Gandy lowered her head and started to cry. I offered her a tissue and remained silent. She then slowly told me that she was very upset. She knew down in her heart that she really was a failure as a mother. She felt completely hopeless about it all. Having acknowledged her feelings to herself and to me, she could move toward exploration of the facts that were contributing to the situation, including her part of it. She requested help for herself in relation to Jim, as well as help for Jim.

In analyzing this incident, the worker reported that she commented on the difference between Mrs. Gandy's verbal and nonverbal messages, after deciding that it would be appropriate to disclose her observations to the client. Before doing this she considered how the client, as a recipient of a message, might respond to it. She recognized her own initial hesitancy to share her observation directly with the client. She felt somewhat anxious about upsetting the client's steady state by puncturing a necessary defense. She felt uncertain about her ability to deal with the response should the client become angry with her or reject the message. She examined her own feelings toward Mrs. Gandy, recognizing that she felt empathy toward her, and knowing that her own feelings could convey as much as the words.

The message was encoded and transmitted to Mrs. Gandy through words, gestures, and tone of voice. The message was received first with a startled response, but with a minimum of distortion, which is not always so. To have a message sent through appropriate words and gestures depends upon adapting one's vocabulary to that of the recipient. For a message to be received, there must be shared definitions of meaning.

Mrs. Gandy received the message that was sent and responded to it by crying and then disclosing previously unacknowledged feelings. The worker remained silent in order to give the client time to ventilate her feelings, to think about the message, and to convey her acceptance of the crying. The client was ready to hear the message and was able to decode it accurately, in spite of her strong emotional response to it. If the worker's message had been ignored or seriously distorted, the client's response would serve as feedback to the worker, who would try again to formulate and send a more helpful message.

Language itself is basically social, learned through experience in the context of human relationships. Imre explains how "throughout life the self becomes known, insofar as it is known, primarily through verbal and artistic activities and images."[9] People have the ability to reason and to use language for cognitive and expressive purposes. It is the mixture of thought and feeling which makes up much of human experience. "Attempts at precision in language are necessary, in fact vital, to the consensually validated messages required for effective communication."

Variations in Ability

Ability to communicate with other people is basic to effective psychosocial functioning. Unless persons understand the intent of messages sent to them they cannot respond in a way that meets the expectations of the other. Likewise, unless persons can convey their intents to others in such a way that they can be perceived with accuracy, they cannot make their desires known. When people cannot understand others, they tend to become anxious. The result is often confusion, misunderstanding, and distrust. Many difficulties in interpersonal relations and role performance derive from inability to make clear one's desires, knowledge, feelings, and ideas. If members of groups do not participate actively in the communicative network, they miss an opportunity to give to others and to receive validation of their feelings and thoughts from others. It is not implied that each member must "tell all," but rather that each is entitled to what privacy is needed at a given time. The development of a sense of identity is dependent to some extent upon validations from others. Without feedback from others, there is a lack of knowledge about the extent of congruence between one's own perceptions of self and the world and the perceptions of other people.

To enter into verbal communication with other people requires many interrelated skills, which vary by developmental phase, abilities, and culture. It requires ability to listen to others and to make sense out of what is heard; to present information in such a way that others can understand the message; to relate what one is saying to the ongoing discussion; to subject one's feelings and ideas to the scrutiny of others; to consider the rights of others to express themselves; to physically face those with whom one is interacting; and enter into the mood of the interaction. These skills are required of both worker and clients. These demands are present in the client-worker interaction and in family and group interaction.

Not all clients are ready and able to verbalize their feelings and attitudes. Polansky and his associates have studied what they refer to as verbal accessibility, which is the degree of clients readiness to use words to describe their feelings and basic attitudes. Verbal accessibility is determined by a complex of elements: the client's capacity for self observation, motivation, freedom to communicate verbally, and the worker-client relationship.[10] Relatively nonverbal clients can be helped, however, if the worker uses nonverbal activities through which clients may express themselves and through which their capacities for verbally expressing their feelings and attitudes may be increased.

People vary in their abilities to send clear messages. They screen messages so that they are congruent with their belief systems. The way messages are decoded is influenced by values, stereotypes, earlier experiences, and the status of the communicator.

People vary in the problems they have to send messages to others, perceive those sent by others, and respond appropriately. Messages may have hidden meanings for the receiver. They may become distorted through language barriers, stereotypes, hearing losses, noise or other disturbances, or dysfunctional mental processes. The messages sent may be contradictory; they may be ambiguous in that the message has little meaning or several possible meanings; and there may be confusion because words may generate different messages for different people related to culture, education, and social class.

A halo phenomenon may be operating, whereby people tend to have a unified impression of others—for example, an overall like or dislike of a person—instead of differentiating the person into aspects that are of unlike value. Selective attention and selective interpretation distort communication. An overload of new information into the system makes it impossible to process all of it, often leading to confusion or anxiety. Nonverbal messages may sustain the flow of conversation or be incompatible with the verbal messages.

Cultural Variations

Some cultures place much more value on verbalization than do others, so that members from different cultural backgrounds may have different perceptions about the relative importance of verbal and nonverbal forms of communication. Middle-class families tend to have the resources that facilitate the development of formal language, which gives their children an advantage in the use of verbal skills.

There is, on the other hand, evidence that persons identified with lower and working classes share some characteristics that impede their ability to participate in the verbal world of the dominant middle class.[11] One such characteristic is the first-person perspective, in which reality is described through the person's own perspectives and in relation to one's self only. Modes of conceptualization tend to be oriented to the concrete.

Both depth and breadth of verbal communication are therefore somewhat curtailed.

Furthermore, such persons are further impaired by the inadequate grammatical structure of their communication. Clients often use the colloquial language indigenous to their cultures and communities rather than formal speech or writing. There are many variations in spoken and written languages, which should be viewed as contributing nuances and richness of expression rather than only as problems.

Some clients may have a tendency to communicate ideas and feelings by analogy rather than analysis. Feelings of depression may be described as, "I feel like I do not have a real friend in the world," rather than, "I am depressed." Clients' tendencies to give examples of their experience of a problem rather than to isolate and analyze specific factors is often considered reflective of a lack of insight or cognitive ability, rather than a style of communication which needs to be accepted by the worker. Furthermore, the kind of response the social worker makes to the client may cause additional problems. Lee, for example, has noted that in describing poor people, social workers use language that disempowers and dehumanizes them.[12]

Culturally derived attitudes toward authority influence the nature of interpersonal communication. For example, in many Japanese families, ultimate authority is vested in males. The nonacceptance of the authority of women, combined with conventional courtesy toward them, might be reflected in an overly polite manner and avoidance of expression of feelings. In some cultures, as in some segments of the Mexican and American Indian cultures, persons are taught not to share personal problems with outsiders. Some ethnic groups, such as Haitians, consider eye contact to be disrespectful. Social distance, due to such cultural differences, can be reduced through discussion of feelings about various forms of self-expression.

At the other extreme, some middle-class clients of European origin have a pseudosophistication with verbalization that masks misunderstanding of reality and that makes the expression of feelings extremely difficult. Words are used as a defense against understanding, or as an avoidance of taking responsibility for behavior. Overintellectualization can be a common defense against involvement.

Nonverbal Communication

Nonverbal communication accompanies the use of words: such messages are essential to understanding the meaning of what is being communicated.[13] But nonverbal means of communication are often primary, with verbalization supplementary to the medium of action. People send messages through their behavior, which often speaks "louder" than words. Pounding on a table, slamming a door, walking away, crying, hugging, or holding hands convey particular meanings to the persons who are present much more clearly than words can.

Paralinguistics are the vocal, but not verbal, sounds, that convey meaning. The meaning of spoken words can be modified by the articulations accompanying them. The same words have different meanings, depending upon these other clues. Emotions are often expressed through paralinguistics: sadness, for example, by slowness of speech, many pauses, low pitch, and sighs; anger by relatively rapid speech, loudness, and brief pauses.

Body language. Body language, or kinesis, is concerned with movements, gestures, and posture. Facial expressions include yawning, forehead wrinkling, blushing, closed or wide-open eyes, nodding or shaking the head, frowning, smiling, laughing, making or avoiding eye contact. They are important components of behavior that communicate feelings.

Movements of hands, arms, feet, and legs also give off messages. Hands and fists can be open or tightly locked; fingers can be used to point, scratch, rub, fidget; hands can be used to cover the mouth, pull, slap, clap, support a chin or face; shoulders can be shrugged or relaxed; feet can be stamped, moved in rhythm with slow or rapid movements; legs can be crossed in a variety of ways, and kicked back and forth. All of these movements provide clues for the social worker's assessment of the emotional state of the client.

Vision. The nonverbal messages received by the eye confirm or disconfirm the validity of the spoken words. People in interaction tend to synchronize their nonverbal behavior, mirroring each others' posture, speaking in similar tone and tempo. Gestures, posture, and other actions of the recipient of a message provide clues to the sender of how the message is being received, for example, with intense interest, hostility, or boredom. They provide information about feelings and attitudes. Much nonverbal communication is enacted below the level of conscious awareness through blushes, grimaces, twitching, or sweating, that erupt before the person gets control of the feelings. Nonverbal messages confirm, amplify, contradict or emphasize the verbal message.

In inferring the meaning of a message, it is the pattern of the total configuration, rather than a single component, that is important and that includes the social context in which the interaction takes place.

Touch.   In the predominant American culture, touching is the most intimate form of nonverbal communication. Acceptance of different forms of touching varies widely among ethnic groups. Middle-class white North Europeans tend to be inhibited in their use of and response to touch, as Borenzweig found in a study of clinical social workers.[14] The taboo against touching was strong. Although the respondents had positive attitudes toward the selective use of touching based on the needs of clients, they were hesitant to use that means of expression.

The typical handshake contrasts sharply with the use of three kisses on the cheek in Iraq. Some forms of touching on the shoulder or holding a hand may express support, warmth, or caring. Particularly with children, touch may serve as an expression of love and comfort. But separating the clinical use of touching from the sensual, affectional aspects is open to interpretation. Sexual harassment and seductiveness are clearly unacceptable. Because touching clearly indicates the difference in power between practitioners and clients, there is a danger that the invasion of privacy will be resented. The social worker, however, can explore with clients the meaning of touch to them.

Appearance.   Material objects observed through sight or touch are powerful sources of communication, making different impressions on different people. Clothing, grooming, hair styles, make-up, jewelry, and color express personal tastes, lifestyles, and culture. Mode of transportation, type and location of home, and interior decoration provide indications of social class status, personal values, and interests.

There is a tendency to stereotype people on the basis of their possessions and appearance. Both practitioners and clients observe and judge each other. An example is of a parent of a child in a residential treatment setting who requested the Director of the Social Work Department to assign a new social worker to her child because "that scruffy, long-haired young man with one earring can't possibly help Jeanie or me." Whether formally or informally defined, there is a loosely structured dress code that persons in particular positions are expected to follow.

Use of time.   The use of time is a frequent indicator of feelings and attitudes. An old story told by a psychiatrist is that "if you come early, you're anxious; if you're right on time, you're compulsive; and if you're late, you're hostile. So you can't win."

Those patterns in the use of time are sometimes quite reflective of a person's motives: there is some validity to the story. The person who comes early may indeed be anxious or there may be practical reasons such as the schedule of a bus or lighter traffic than usual. Some people are compulsive about coming right on time or just being thoughtful by not arriving before others are ready for them, or not keeping others waiting. Some people do arrive late to keep others waiting, signifying hostility or resistance or a different value concerning the importance of time. Persons of high status often come late, giving the message that their time is more important than the time of the one who is waiting. Some cultures have more relaxed attitudes toward time than does the dominant one; punctuality is not always perceived as the virtue it seems to be in middle-class white American culture.[15] As described earlier, different ethnic groups have different orientations to time.

Space. Space has great significance for interpersonal, family, and group relationships and for the practitioner-client relationship. Physical closeness or distance influences a person's sense of comfort and varies with many personal, social, and cultural factors. The need for more or less space between people depends at least partially on whether the relationship is viewed as public or private, personal or impersonal, intimate or distant. It depends also upon the social context in which communication occurs, including the expected content of the conversation.

Hall notes the sense of crowding that some people develop, depending on whether they have been acculturated to a sense of propriety about contact with others. Some people set "an invisible bubble around themselves" to keep others outside; they feel crowded when their space is invaded.[16] Such behavior may be interpreted as rejection by others. Other people require close physical contact with others: they consider persons who remain at a distance as aloof and unfriendly. Hall reports there is evidence from research to show that people brought up in different cultures "live in different perceptual worlds" as found in their manner of orienting themselves to space.[17] According to Germain, Latinos tend to prefer closer positions than do North Americans.[18] Jews, according to Nelsen, are more comfortable standing very close to a friend than is a Caucasian non-Jew.[19]

Furnishings. The arrangement and nature of furnishings of rooms send clear messages about the intended interactions among the people who use them, conveying a sense of comfort and respect, or the opposite. The room arrangements influence the ways that people are expected to behave toward each other. A waiting room in a public welfare office too often forces people to sit side by side in bleak rooms, with the expectation that they sit quietly until their names are called, often for long periods of time. The opposite is a waiting room in a children's clinic furnished with comfortable chairs and coffee tables, bright pictures on the walls, coffee, puzzles and modeling clay on a table, and current magazines for both children and adults. That space is supportive and reassuring and presents an atmosphere of respect and caring for the clients.

The way people arrange themselves in a room reflects the purpose of their being together, how well they know and are comfortable with each other, and their cultural backgrounds. In families and groups, members who choose to participate less actively tend to sit further away from the center of action. A fear of criticism tends to increase distance but seeking approval from others tends to increase closeness to those from whom approval is sought. People also tend to seat themselves farther from a person with a stigmatizing illness, undesirable characteristic, or one who is in a wheel chair. Thus, interpersonal communication is greatly influenced by the context in which it occurs.

Action-Oriented Experiences

Action is a crucial means through which people communicate with each other.[20] Action-oriented content is useful to facilitate communication with clients of all ages, but it is essential for young children and people, whatever their age, who have low tolerance for or lack of ability to communicate verbally in effective ways. Some activities tend to lower defensive barriers to verbalization so they are often used to facilitate discussion. Sharing of food, working with clay, or the use of audio-visual aids are common experiences for achieving this purpose. Engaging in some activity permits a person to enter into conversation when ready to do so, without the sense of pressure that is often present when discussion is the only activity.

This is not meant to imply that some anxiety, discomfort, or pressures toward verbal participation are not useful motivations. Rather, it is meant to emphasize the value of aiding discussion under circumstances in which the clients could not participate otherwise or in which the quality and content of communication is enhanced through such devices. Frequently, the discussion stimulated by an experience is of at least as much value as the activity itself.

Speech is but one means of communication, but it is a basic tool for all human beings. Nonverbal communication usually must be understood in verbal terms before it can be integrated and used by a person. Verbal skills are essential to success in education, and to the successful fulfillment of almost any role.

There is a close interrelationship between facility in verbalization and exposure to and use of experiences in the physical and social environment. Stimulation from dealing with a variety of nonhuman objects, within supportive social relationships, seems essential to the development of adequate verbal skills. In the course of normal development, the basic speech skills are acquired during the preschool years. The progression is from experiencing many objects to learning the verbal symbols for these things and experiences. Dearth of language skills may often be reflected in poor performance at school or work.

In working with clients who have suffered early deprivation in this respect, development of skills in verbal communication may be dependent upon the provision of experiences with objects and people to make up for these lacks. Some action-oriented experiences provide a means for the free communication of feelings, desires, and ideas; some involve nonverbal communication, a primary means of communication as contrasted with the more abstract medium of language.

In working with children, play tends to predominate. In play, for example, the children express feelings and perceptions about their world which they cannot verbalize. Through exploration with many materials, they begin to learn cognitive skills in understanding colors, shapes, textures, sounds, and spatial relations, and to identify many common actions. Later they learn to label what they have experienced. They draw upon prior experiences and repeat those that have made an impression upon them. As they relive experiences in play, they express anger, hate, love, joy, and other emotions. Not only does the unpleasant character of the experience not prevent children from using it as a game, they often choose to play out the unpleasant experience. By so doing, they attempt to master the problematic situation. The content of the play indicates with what basic problems the child is coming to terms and it gives clues as to what is disturbing.

But at least as important are the patterns that occur in play. Some of these, for example, are rigidity or functional adaptation, evidence of body image and identity, stereotyping or creativity, accommodation to cultural norms, balance of emotional attachment to things or to people, activity or passivity, and realistic use of objects as contrasted with objects used in a highly affectively charged way.

Social workers need to learn to understand the meaning of play, gestures, and other actions just as they need to understand the verbal language of the persons they serve. Words and actions are seldom separated. Many activities make use of words, but within a framework of playing, rehearsing, or learning something new, one step removed from the demands and consequences of performance in the world outside. It must be remembered that the development of facility with language remains an important area of ego adequacy. Clarity of understanding by the worker is equally important, whether the medium of communication is verbal, nonverbal, or a combination of both. The two tools of conversation and action-oriented experiences are closely interrelated. The essential question for the worker is when and under what conditions can an action-oriented experience contribute to the clients' abilities to communicate more effectively.

Communication in Groups

In families and other groups, communication becomes quite complicated. The larger the number of participants, the greater are the potential misunderstandings and confusion. A message may be sent to a particular person, who does not respond; instead, an unintended recipient decodes the message so that the intended message is not completed, from the viewpoint of the sender. A message may be intended for the group as a whole, but only some members hear, see, and understand it. With those who receive it, each often decodes the message differently; and the one who sends a message back may not represent the feelings or thinking of the group. More than one member may want to send a message at the same time, which results in confusion and inadequate communication. Each member, with particular values and styles of communication, needs to be understood and to be responded to in appropriate ways. Within the interacting processes of the group, correction of distortions in perception of intent and content of communication may be delayed. Some messages may get lost in the welter of competing messages so that responses are missing. Lack of commonage of experience may make communication difficult.

An open system of communication, based on the right of each individual to be recognized and heard, increases the chances that members will face and solve their own problems and the problems of the group. Within the system, the worker's role is to behave in ways that will facilitate the group's effort. Positive change is facilitated by interaction which is honest, sincere, and meaningful to the participants. It is more likely to occur when an individual is involved in the group and has responsibility for some part of the group's effort to realize its purpose. Thus, each member shares some information and attitudes with others. A member does not feel the need to withhold participation due to fear of reprisal, or lack of confidentiality concerning what is shared. The desired pattern of channels of communication is one that is group-centered as contrasted with a leader-centered group in which all communicative acts are channeled through the worker or a particular member of the group. Instead, members communicate with each other and with the worker. With genuine involvement in the process, new ideas, experiences, points of view, and emotional responses may become incorporated into the personality of an individual.

Although the particular pattern of communication will shift as the family or other group deals with varied situations, the social worker's efforts are directed toward the achievement of a pattern that is predominantly one of integrated interaction. This fact points to the necessity for concern with affective forces of attractions and repulsions among members of a group which comprise the emotional bond among the members.[21] Acts of communication convey positive and negative expressions of affect as well as of opinions and information. Both in verbal and nonverbal ways, members communicate their feelings of love and affection, hate and dislike, and indifference toward each other. The content of conversation is significant as members tentatively approach each other to learn to what extent they share common orientations toward relationships and interests. But nonverbal communication through actions and gestures is the principal means of expressing and exchanging emotions.[22]

Problems in Communication

There are guidelines to aid social workers in their assessment of the adequacy of the communication. Adequate communication is direct and open, and conveys the intended meaning with clarity. If communication is adequate, there is consistency between the intents and the words or actions used, and consistency between affect and cognition; there is a balance between listening to or observing others and contributing to others; and there is acknowledgment of personal responsibility for the intent and content of the communication. Such communication assumes a high degree of emotional maturity, and expectations therefore need to be in line with the developmental phase of clients and their particular vulnerabilities.

Many problems occur within a therapeutic session that makes communication between a worker and one client or a worker with a family or group difficult, requiring great knowledge and skills on the part of the practitioner. Among the most important problems are the following:

1. *Failure in receiving messages.* Listening is an active, not a passive, response to a message being sent. It requires following the verbal content,

the underlying meaning, and the nonverbal accompaniments. It requires that the intended recipient pay close attention. Intended recipients may be preoccupied with their own thoughts, uninterested in the subject matter, or just waiting to talk and therefore are unable to respond to the sender of the message in a way that encourages the continuation of purposeful communication.

2. *Lack of clarity.* Difficulties in expressing thoughts, feelings, or opinions are typical of practitioners as well as clients. The messages sent are often vague, confusing, or incongruent. Two contradictory messages may be given which puts the receiver in a "double bind." The words used may be ambiguous, the accompanying nonverbal behavior may be inconsistent with the words, the message may contain more than one central idea. These faulty messages make it difficult for the listeners to respond in meaningful ways.

3. *Language.* Ability to speak a common language is essential to effective verbal communication. Difficulties occur through the ambiguities and deficiencies of the language. The English language has numerous meanings for the same word and many idioms, creating particular difficulties for clients for whom English is a second language. A student from an Eastern European country, for example, sought out her adviser, saying she did not understand what an instructor meant when she asked him if her proposed topic for a term paper was acceptable. He said, "you bet" on his way out the door. She thought she knew what a bet was, but looked it up in the dictionary. She asked, "Does `you bet' mean that I'd be taking a chance if I wrote that paper?"

Problems occur when there are differences in language due to ethnicity, social class, regionalism, education, or literacy. Technical language and professional jargon are hard for many clients to understand. The most obvious difference occur when clients do not speak English and practitioners are not available who speak the client's language. Or clients and practitioners may speak in different dialects which stem from differences in social class, region, ethnic group, and age. Clinical social workers need a vocabulary broad enough to adapt to that of their clients. In assimilating a language, a person inherits the symbols, definitions, and way of life expressed by the culture. Language communicates the values, norms, and folkways of the culture. Social workers need to respect the complexity of adaptations a client must make in becoming bilingual.

4. *Divergent purposes.* When people do not agree about the purpose of their work or play together, communication is difficult.

Failure on the part of the worker to make explicit the purpose of an interview may lead to a condition in which the worker and client hold differing, perhaps contradictory, purposes. Given such confusion of purpose, both client and worker will then interpret their own and each other's communications in light of their particular understanding of the objective of the session. As these subtle distortions continue, the client and the worker will be going in two entirely different directions.

In families, there may be differences in goals among the members that inhibit discussion of a problem. An example concerning a severe illness of a child is one in which the practitioner may want to help the child to express concerns about what is happening and to further the expression of feelings and reactions between parents and with siblings. Parents, on the other hand, may desire to protect each other and the children from the reality of the medical situation.[23]

5. *Emotional factors.* Emotional factors often serve as inhibitors of effective communication. Transference reactions, to be discussed in chapter 6, distort the reality of the nature of the relationship between the social worker and a client or among members of a family or other group, resulting in distorted messages. Sending of desired messages is often blocked by anxiety, fear of rejection, or a judgmental response.

6. *Cultural norms.* The workers' lack of knowledge about cultural norms may limit the client's initial participation in the helping process. Clients may expect, as is probable in the Japanese culture, that they should give only polite answers to questions, suppress strong feelings, be indirect in their patterns of speech, and be apologetic for the slightest lapse.[24] If social workers do not understand the values on which such behavior is based, they are apt to interpret these behaviors as resistance rather than as efforts to behave appropriately in an ambiguous situation. If workers are able to understand the meaning of the behavior, they can respect it, listen attentively to the client, and gradually reduce the ambiguity in the situation for the client.

Clients may be less open to share private feelings with an outsider to the family and, in particular, one from a different background.[25] Or, as in the Mexican American culture, an extended period of informal social conversation may be expected to take place prior to initiating the official reason for the visit or session.

7. *Use of stereotypes.* Stereotyping of other persons is a clear barrier to good communication. It exists when individuals are viewed and treated as members of groups, rather than as persons who are both alike and different from other members of the group in many ways. Clients may have stereotypes of practitioners and practitioners of their clients, interfering with realistic perceptions of each other and concomitant distortions in the communication process. Stereotypes are used when adequate knowledge

of people is lacking. When comparing one population group with another, it is necessary to understand that only some members of both groups will exhibit the dominant characteristics or behavior of their group: the principle of individualization is essential.

8. *Attitudes toward authority.* Another obstacle to achieving mutual understanding of effective communication, often unrecognized by workers, is conflict concerning authority. The client needs to come to understand the nature and extent of the worker's legitimate authority, and the worker needs to come to understand the client's need to control or to submit to the worker's power. Typical of many clients is an adolescent's statement. "I don't know whether what I say is what you want," looking directly at the worker, who said that whatever she wanted to say would be just fine. "Well, it's so lonely here—I haven't run into any of my old friends from James School. I just don't know anybody." Many clients need to be assured of their rights to participate in the process.

Clients may attempt to control the process and content in many ways, for example, by using either silence or long monologues that are difficult to interrupt, or by coming late or leaving early. In families there may be the struggle of one member to control the messages sent or the behavior of others or to expect the worker to control the process of communication or the behavior of members. In formed groups, there is often a struggle for power among the members or between the worker and the group. Whether it pertains to individual, family, or peer group, the usual initial pattern is for the clients to accede to the worker's authority; then challenge some aspects of it; and gradually develop an appropriate balance of control in the worker-client interaction. When clients discover that they have both rights and responsibilities to participate freely within certain agreed-upon parameters, both the relationship and the motivation for change are enhanced.

9. *Taboos.* Certain subjects are taboo in a given society.[26] These taboos reflect a general consensus to block or prohibit discussion in areas of sensitivity and deep concern. Having internalized these taboos, consciously or not, people are hindered from talking directly about them. Sex, use of condoms, incest, death, race, power, and money are examples. Yet, to get help with the accompanying problems, it is necessary to open the boundary of the human system to accept information and discussion of it. Social workers often fear or hesitate to initiate discussion of subjects that tend to elicit deep emotions or interpersonal conflict. By avoiding discussion of the taboo subject, the practitioner often engages in a "conspiracy of silence," thereby depriving clients of an

opportunity to understand the issue and when deemed desirable, to work toward change.[27]

The Social Worker's Role

Social workers need to be particularly sensitive to the client's ability to understand what they are trying to communicate and, at the same time, to test out their understanding of the messages being sent by the client. Self-evaluation by workers as well as evaluation of the adequacy of the client's communication is necessary. Among the characteristics of communication to be taken into account are: clarity of speech; change of topic; the transactions that do not get completed; who is in control and under what conditions; the appropriateness of affect; the message about relationship that is embedded in the words; and congruence between the manifest or literal and latent or more hidden content.[28] There is an underlying meaning behind the words of which the speaker may not be aware. In work with more than one client at a time, the task is more complicated in that workers need to understand the meaning of the messages sent by them or by one member to each individual and to the group as a whole. They need to assess the speaking order: who speaks to whom; who is left out; who speaks for whom. For example, if mother talks to father, does the child usually interrupt? If the oldest child talks, does the father lecture? The nature and extent of each person's participation influences the individual's use of the service and also the progress of the treatment.

Clients often need help to learn how to communicate more effectively in a particular situation so that they are understood by others and, in turn, become able to understand others. This process lays the groundwork for other forms of change. Modeling and teaching communication skills are important parts of the worker's activity. Change in dysfunctional communication patterns may lead to change in interpersonal behavior, and enhanced capacity for effective communication may result in more positive responses from other people.

An illustration of practice in helping clients to communicate more effectively concerns a group of young adult patients with diagnoses of schizophrenia. The setting is a ward in a state mental hospital.

I had begun the second meeting by asking the members what they thought we might do to make our group a useful one for them. After several minutes of discussion, it seemed that learning to communicate better was a dominant theme. I said, "Well, it seems that we would like to try to understand better what each of us is trying to say—it can be very difficult sometimes to get across a simple message." The members picked up on this comment and talked about how hard it is for them to say what they want to say.

One member, who thus far had given the impression of taking the group as a joke, became very serious and said, "I been in lots of groups. Who knows which way the wind blows? There's too much hate in this room. It might kill us like it did the beautiful people. I feel the edge of pain and the what of sane." There was absolute silence.

After waiting for some response, I said "Mark, I'm confused about what you want to tell us. I gather you have fears about being in this group." Mark did not reply, but Bob said, "That's the way Mark always talks—he says a lot of poetic bullshit that always turns me off." Shirley said, "That's what he's trying to do—get you to leave him alone."

I asked, "Mark, do you want us to leave you alone or were you trying to tell us something else?" He replied, "I just dig weird language." Minnie said, "He's always talking that way when he wants to fox us." Mark then responded to my earlier statement, ignoring Minnie's remark. "I try to say what I mean—what I feel inside—but most of the time I can't do that so I talk in images."

I would have supported Mark at this point, but several members started grumbling, telling me all at the some time about Mark's refusal to talk to people directly. I wondered, "Can you talk to Mark directly instead of talking about him to me?"

There was surprised silence. Minnie said, "Mark, I think you're playing games with us." Bob said, "I don't know about that—are you scared to say what you mean?" Mark responded, "I guess it's true. Talking to people scares me so I guess I try to throw them off balance by making myself hard to understand."

The members responded to this statement with considerable approval, culminating in the statement by one withdrawn girl, Cindy, who said, "I know how it feels to be scared, but it feels even worse to be lonely." I said that I understood it could be very painful to feel scared or lonely or both scared and lonely. Mark said, "Yeah, I'm both."

I said that other members might have some fears, too. There was strong nodding of heads as Bob said, "You've said it directly to us all." I said the group could help them with these feelings as we learn how to talk more clearly to each other about things that matter to us. [29]

This vignette of practice illustrates the principle that practitioners need to follow the manifest content of the conversation at the same time that they seek to understand the latent content. The manifest content consists of the literal and obvious meanings of the verbal messages; the latent content is what is below the threshold of superficial observation. It may be just below the level of awareness, subject to ready recall, or it may be at the unconscious level. The latent content may extend and add meaning to the manifest content or may contradict it. If the former, the process of communication is enhanced; if the latter, mutual understanding is hampered.

Social workers help clients to identify the roadblocks to effective communication. These were noted earlier, as when one person dominates the conversation or withdraws from active participation. One illustration is the treatment of a family consisting of Mrs. Kopper, who is in the final stages of getting a divorce; Mr. Prince, who has been living with her for several months and whom she plans to marry when the divorce becomes final; her two children—Cathie, age four, and Tommy, age eight. Tommy was brought to a mental health center because of severe temper tantrums and refusal to talk. One part of the treatment plan was to work with the two adults in relation to Tommy's needs. The worker recorded:

> For several weeks Mr. Prince participated very little in the discussion, despite my efforts to draw him out. Mrs. Kopper speaks for both of them. His silence has appeared friendly. He often smiles or nods, which behavior was interpreted by me as agreement with Mrs. Kopper's statements.
>
> Yet, feeling uneasy about Mr. Prince's continued silence and noting a sudden and fleeting look of distress on his face, I said I wondered if his silence might mean that he did not really agree with Mrs. Kopper's opinion that the status quo was just fine for both of them. This comment led to a flood of feelings about how awkward the present arrangement is for him, how uncertain he feels about the ambiguity of his place in the family, and how uncertain he feels about his responsibility to the children once the marriage takes place. Thus, an area of conflict was opened up at a new level of communication. I recognized that I should have been active much earlier in bringing him into the conversation.

The focus of work with the couple then shifted, with their agreement, to recognizing the differences between each person in feelings and perceptions of the situation, helping them to listen actively to each other and check out with each other the accuracy of perceptions about the message; expressing both loving and caring feelings and hostile ones in a nondestructive manner, and then moving into decision-making concerning their futures.

Some forms of family treatment are based almost entirely on changing the communication process.[30] For many individuals, families, and small groups, however, improved communication is not the primary goal for its own sake. Rather it is sought as a tool on the way to achieving the major purpose of improved social functioning.

As the practitioner assesses and influences the way the client/worker system is developing, these efforts result also in positive changes in the clients' patterns of behavior, for "the relationship between task and socioemotional activities is complex."[31] If clients are able to develop meaningful relationships with the worker and often also with other participants, it is expected that they will carry these attitudes and abilities over to other vital relationships. If they can sustain motivation to work toward their individual or collective goals, the sense of hope and successful effort will be carried with them after they leave the social work situation. Similarly, if they have been able to modify their role behaviors and communicate more effectively within the helping system, these gains may be transferred to other social situations. Thus, as practitioners are paying attention to the maintenance and development of the system, they are simultaneously intervening to help clients meet their needs and solve their problems in psychosocial functioning.

Knowledge about people's differences in comfort and facility with verbalization has several implications for social workers, particularly in work with families and other groups. The workers consider verbal accessibility and styles of verbalization in setting realistic expectations for the participation in the group's discussions or action-oriented experiences. The expectations take into account the members' own expectations for each other. When a member feels incapable of meeting the worker's or the group's expectations concerning verbal communication, feelings of inadequacy are bound to be accentuated. The outcome may be reticence to participate, withdrawal from the group, or assumption of a role of dominator or monopolizer. Practitioners are concerned with whatever hinders a client from learning to communicate effectively.

In most situations, social workers direct some effort toward helping the members to communicate more effectively with other people. The ways they do this depend upon the particular problems that the members are having in communication, the values and norms of the members related to communication, and the motivation and capacities of the members to work on this particular aspect of functioning.

Young children need to learn to communicate with the social worker, often in new ways. Many children are expected to listen to and obey adults and to respond only to specific questions asked them. Often they are not expected to enter into discussions with adults present—to give as well as take in reciprocal verbal communication. Workers need to develop interest in the children's viewpoints and to be able to enter into the world of childhood so that they and the children can talk with each other. To talk with children in language suitable to the children's level of understanding without talking down to them is a precious attribute in a worker. Children are not as nonverbal as is often assumed. The clue, to a large extent, is in the adult who is able to listen, to enter into the child's world, to talk simply and concretely, with the appropriate amount of seriousness or playfulness that is indicated by the child's moods. Adults, too, have their troubles in listening and talking. Observations of the capacities for communication of the members are used by the worker in making a professional judgment about when to enter the conversation, or intervene in an activity for a particular reason, and when to support silently the client's style of communication.

With small children, workers may teach them the elements of verbal communication: how to label the sights, sounds, colors, and objects they encounter. They may teach them how to ask questions or make a request of an adult or another child. Often children need to talk about those things with which they have direct experience, so that social experiences and conversations go hand in hand. With older children and adults who have difficulty in the use of verbal communication, workers may need to provide indirect modes for practicing communication through such experiences as role playing, sociodrama, use of microphones, puppets, word games, or charades. Clients may move into direct verbalization as soon as they are ready to benefit from it.

There often is a need to help persons to check out the intent of a message with the message as perceived by others, through such means as questioning them as to what they understand, and requesting restatement of the message that was sent.[32] The workers may seek feedback from the clients as to whether or not their own intent was perceived accurately by the others, and correct themselves when necessary. They may mirror back to the clients what was felt, seen, or heard. When clients have expressed an emotion or an idea, a reaction is expected which contributes to the extension, clarification, or alteration of the original message. When they are aware of the results produced by their own actions, their subsequent actions are influenced by this knowledge. Some members of groups need to be asked to listen to others, to indicate when a message is not clear, and to offer correction of messages, when requested.

Workers may need to point out to members when their messages are not clear, when they are confused, incoherent, or incongruent, or when others have misinterpreted an intended message. There is a need to call attention to double-bind messages and ask that they be clarified. A double-bind message is one in which the latent message contradicts the manifest or cognitive message, or in which one set of words contradicts another. Words may convey one attitude or request, and tone of voice a different one. In double-binds, there often is no right response, so that the person is caught in a dilemma and may become anxious, inactive, or withdrawn.

Communication in the Torres family provides an illustration of a double bind. Mr. and Mrs. Torres have an eight-year-old daughter, Juanita, and a son, Ramon. In a meeting with the family, the worker recorded that Mrs. T. complained that Ramon refuses to talk with them about his school and friends. When asked to respond, Ramon said that he does want to tell his parents about his friends, but when he starts to talk, his mother tells him to shut up and stop bothering them. The only thing he can do is go upstairs to his room. Then his mother calls out that he doesn't love her. If he loved her, he wouldn't ignore her. He tries to please her, but he just can't seem to win. Mr. T. said, "You know, Ramon is right—that's the way it happens over and over again."

The specific acts of social workers in opening up and clarifying verbal communication are varied and many. In families and groups, they may make comments and ask questions that invite certain members to speak. They may need to limit a member who attempts to monopolize the conversation. They may request further amplification of a feeling or thought or may connect up what one member says with what has gone before it in order to help the members follow the sequence of communication. They may ask for reactions from others to the comments of one member. They may notice points of difference or stress, and help bring these into the open where they may be examined and explored, through sharing their observations of these tensions with the members and eliciting broad and varied reactions to this observation. They may restate an idea to verify their and the group's understanding, which tends to make it the possession of the group, as well as to make its understanding clear. Whenever this happens, the commonage of experience of the group is broadened which, in turn, facilitates communication among the members. Above all, perhaps, the practitioner's own skills in communication are important. If they are direct, clear, and honest, there will be consistency between their verbal and nonverbal acts of communication. In these respects, they need to be a model for the clients to emulate. The concern is with communication both as a tool in working toward other goals, and with ineffective communication as a problem in itself. The level of communication sought is, therefore, of a practical applied nature, as contrasted with abstract thinking.

Members of groups, including families, often continue to need help to communicate effectively about more difficult subjects within the group itself. When members of a group find it difficult to talk about their feelings and problems, comments from the worker that mention the universality of certain feelings and concerns, if appropriate to the situations of the members, often release inhibitions. Examples would be the recognition by the worker that it is perfectly normal for teenagers to feel rebellious against their parents at times, or to have frightening feelings about sex. Those things that people are often ashamed of, or are embarrassed about, are also of deep concern to them, for example, sexual attitudes and experiences, racial differences, and failures.

It is through a process of communication that clinical social workers and their clients initiate, sustain, and terminate relationships with each other in order to achieve mutually agreed-upon purposes. Relationship is the subject of the next chapter.

Six | The Professional Relationship

Professional relationships—the emotional connections between social workers and their clients—are developed and sustained with the intention of supporting and enabling clients to work toward the achievement of their desired goals. The nature and quality of social workers' relationships with their clients and significant others have an important influence on the success of treatment.

In work with individuals, emphasis is on the nature and quality of the relationships between the social worker and the client. In work with families and other groups, there is an equally important emphasis on the relationships among the members. In all models of practice, relationship is accorded great importance as a dynamic for positive change. Basic to all aspects of practice is the planned development of a relationship, defined in terms of the client's needs and capacities. The relationship itself has potent and dynamic power for influencing feelings and behavior. It is not only a context for treatment, it is also a dynamic element of treatment.

According to Perlman, "relationship is a catalyst, an enabling dynamism in the support, nurture, and freeing of people's energies and motivations toward problem-solving and the use of help. . . . It is 'a human being's feeling or sense of emotional bonding with another."[1]

Although there are varied definitions of relationship, its essence is a sense of being connected psychologically with one or more persons. The dynamics of relationship in treatment are related to the basic needs for love and social connectedness. Social connectedness refers to the feeling that one is recognized and included in a social system—a sense of being meaningfully connected with another or others.

A helpful relationship requires a set of values, attitudes, and interpersonal skills that reflect the concern for others and knowledge about social relationships. In order to develop and sustain a relationship that has the qualities that help clients to feel loved and connected socially with another or others, social workers indicate their concern for the well-being of clients, that they respect them, accept them, and desire for them to be happier in some way. In the relationship, the worker becomes a reliable environment—reliable in the consistency of attitudes and reliable in time and place.[2] The values of social work are thus implemented.

Social workers have long referred to the ideal worker-client system relationship as being characterized by the qualities of acceptance or nonpossessive warmth, empathy, and genuineness or authenticity. Other helping professions with different theoretical orientations also agree on the importance of these three ingredients. There is a substantial body of research in counseling and psychotherapy with both individuals and groups that supports the view that these are necessary qualities to successful outcome.

Acceptance

"Nonpossessive warmth" is a term used to indicate the practitioner's acceptance of, or love for, a client. In Rogers' view, nonpossessive warmth means caring for a client, but not in a possessive way or to satisfy the practitioner's own needs. It means caring for clients as unique persons with a right to have their own feelings and thoughts.[3] This quality is akin to what social workers have referred to as "acceptance."[4]

Feeling accepted by another human being tends to help clients feel that they are of some worth and that they are understood by another. In such an atmosphere, clients become free to explore their capacities, goals, and problems, discover their own identity, and set forth realistic aspirations for themselves. The value underlying the concept of acceptance is the innate worth and dignity of human beings.

Evidences of an attitude of acceptance are showing genuine interest in one's clients, giving them recognition, listening sensitively to what persons say, paying attention to what they do, conveying a desire to be helpful, and really caring about them.

Acceptance does not require the approval of behavior; it does, however, convey the hope that clients will be able to move away from self-defeating behavior toward the realization of their potentialities. As representatives of a profession and of society, social workers are the bearers of values, feeling accepted makes it possible for the clients to feel secure and worthy of respect and consideration, even when workers cannot approve of their behavior. Thus, acceptance does not mean that the workers do not make judgments about the clients but rather that, although they evaluate, they do not condemn.

Comments by the social worker that convey acceptance of the person, but not the behavior, are those that imply the message, "I accept you, but not what you did." To a sixteen-year-old adolescent who had stolen a car, a worker said, "I know you did what you felt you needed to do at the time, but because I care about you, I'd like to help you to stay out of trouble with the police from now on. How do you feel about what I said?" A nonblaming attitude and words that indicate understanding of what was said may open up communication about the problem and ways of solving it. For example:

> Mrs. Nelsen, a mother of two preschool-aged children and a secretary, is married to an engineer who travels a great deal. The children need to be taken to a day care center every morning. She has been reprimanded by her supervisor for frequent tardiness and is in danger of losing her job. The practitioner followed the mother's telling of her story, nodding occasionally to indicate that she was listening. When Mrs. Nelsen paused and was silent, she asked if Mrs. Nelsen had anything else to say. With an agitated voice, she replied, "I just can't get to work on time. I cannot do it." The worker responded, "that is really bothering you?" "Yes" sighed Mrs. Nelsen.

The worker's response was an accepting one, different from such blaming responses as "well, you can if you try," or "why don't you organize your time better?" or "if you'd just get up a little earlier, everything would be all right."

In research by Shulman, the skill of acknowledging the client's feelings appeared to contribute substantially to the development of a good working relationship as well as to the worker's ability to be helpful.[5] Acceptance of clients is indicated by many small actions of courtesy: greeting clients in ways appropriate to their cultural traditions, making them comfortable, orienting them to the available resources, and calling them by their preferred form of address. Acceptance of clients requires self-awareness concerning differences in values, tendencies to stereotype clients, abhorrence of certain behaviors such as violence or dishonesty or prejudice toward men with long hair or beards, older people, women who are obese, or clients who have difficulty in abstract reasoning. It is difficult to face a ward of severely retarded clients for the first time, children who have lost their hair through leukemia, dying patients, fathers who have sexually abused their daughters, or children who wear torn and dirty clothes and live in shacks. It is easy to personalize questions asked by clients, such as "Do you have a license?," "Are you married?," "How can a person as young as you are help me?" Becoming defensive when such questions are asked does not convey acceptance. As social workers develop greater understanding of people and their environments, as well as of their own values and attitudes, they become increasingly able to really care for their clients.

Empathy

The Minnesota Native Americans, according to Konopka, have a proverb that says, "Never judge a man until you have walked a moon in his moccasins."[6] That picture indicates the need for empathy, which is closely related to acceptance. It is the ability to project oneself into the thinking and feeling of another in order to understand what that person experiences. An anonymous English writer is credited with the statement that empathy means "to see with the eyes of another, to hear with the ears of another, and to feel with the heart of another."[7] Being closely linked to intuition, it is not primarily intellectual. The most distinguishing feature of empathy, compared with other kinds of fellow feelings, lies in the fact that the person's ego boundaries and coherence of self are maintained. It is a process of what Kohut calls "vicarious introspection."[8] It is to be distinguished from the related concepts of sympathy and insight. It "allows ourselves to sympathize with enough of the clients' situation to experience their emotional state without allowing ourselves to be undone by the weight of the burden. At the same time we use insight to apply this experience to what we know of the client's experience" (p. 59).

Objectivity, essential to empathy, is the capacity to see things and people as they are, without bias or prejudice. Workers focus on the needs of the clients, being aware of their own values and feelings, they are more able to refrain from imposing them on others. They are able to evaluate realistically the feelings expressed toward them. In perceiving other persons, there is a tendency toward a halo effect, that is, to see only positive qualities in persons who are liked and only negative qualities in persons who are disliked. That is a form of stereotyping. Self-awareness lessens the likelihood of making faulty judgments about others.

Objectivity involves understanding the motive of clients in their reactions toward the worker, so that the workers are realistic in evaluating the feelings and behavior expressed toward them. It involves as well understanding one's own reactions to the covert or overt feelings expressed by clients. Self-awareness is pursued, not for the satisfaction it brings workers in their introspective activities, but for use in practice wherein some of their own feelings and reactions may hamper their ability to understand others or to use themselves appropriately as they interact with individuals, families, or groups, and systems in the social environment. Workers need sufficient self-acceptance and security to permit disengagement from their own feelings in order to be able to focus on the feelings of others. Dealing with such feelings necessitates some emotional maturity. Self-centeredness is incompatible with effective practice. Indeed, if workers are preoccupied with their own feelings and reactions during a session, rather than focused on the feelings and reactions of the clients, they may not be able to empathize with particular clients or act appropriately in response to the interaction.

An example of empathy concerns Mrs. Payne, age 50, whose husband died in an accident a month ago, and who last week lost her job as a computer programmer because the firm was moving to another state. She could move with the firm if she wished to do so. That would remove her from her two sons and their families, many friends, and community associations.

In preparing for her second session with Mrs. Payne, the worker reviewed what she knew about Mrs. P. and her social situation and reflected on what it might be like to be in Mrs. P.'s position. During the session, the worker summarized briefly what she understood to be Mrs. P.'s concerns. The response was tears in Mrs. P.'s eyes and head facing down, followed by crying. The worker observed Mrs. P.'s behavior, handed her a tissue, touched her hand, and then waited until Mrs. P.'s tears stopped flowing. Then, in a soft voice, she said, "You lost your husband and your job and are now faced with a tough decision about moving." "That's exactly what I'm up against," replied Mrs. P. The worker's response was to ask Mrs. P. if she would like to talk about it some more. Mrs. P. sighed and then told the worker a fuller story about her life, to which the worker listened, interrupting only occasionally to indicate that she was paying attention or to request elaboration of some information. When Mrs. P. stopped, she looked directly at the worker and said with sobs, "and all of a sudden, my life is really messed up." The worker responded, "Yes, and you feel strongly the loss of James (her husband) and the job which you liked." Mrs. P. nodded, and the worker then continued, "Do I understand that you don't want to move, but you desperately want to work?" "You've summed it up in one sentence," replied Mrs. Payne.

Accurate empathy requires the presence of several sets of behavior on the part of practitioners.

1. It involves a process of sensitive anticipation of the feelings and concerns that clients might bring to the session. From whatever information practitioners have, they reflect on the possible feelings that clients might have when coming for help in similar situations so that they are attuned to the client's emotional state and concerns.

2. It requires the verbal facility to communicate one's understanding in language that is clearly understood by the other person. Feelings of empathy are communicated through the consistency of the verbal and nonverbal acts which convey a sincere desire to understand, avoiding such statements as "I know" or "I understand" when indeed one does not and cannot. It is much more useful to say, "No, I really don't understand now, but I want to. Can you help me to really understand?"

3. It involves the ability to facilitate expression of both positive and negative feelings and exploration of them through sensitive listening and observation. Exploration involves the use of comments and questions that draw out bit by bit the clients' feelings and perceptions. No judgment is made about what the client should feel; rather efforts are made to discover what the client does feel.

4. It involves the use of feedback to clients, checking out what the practitioner understands with what the client meant, for example, "You seemed to be feeling angry about that." The feedback is based on noticing "the subtle and not so subtle ways that people manifest emotion without words—their nonverbal acts of communication." Helpful feedback is dependent upon having a large vocabulary of emotional terms so that one type of feeling may be distinguished from others. Hepworth and Larsen present a list of words that describe human emotions.[9] They are: competence and strength; happiness and satisfaction; caring and love; depression and discouragement; inadequacy and helplessness; anxiety and tension; confusion and puzzlement; rejection and abandonment; anger and resentment; loneliness and isolation; and guilt, shame, and embarrassment.

Accurate empathy involves the crucial capacity to imaginatively consider the lives of clients in their environments, that is, to reflect on what it would be like to "walk in their shoes." Polombo has pointed out that "only through introspective merging with another person's feeling states, while simultaneously maintaining cognitive awareness of the merger, one can begin to know what another feels."[10] Practitioners draw on their own relevant life experiences to aid them to understand the client. A professional detachment follows which makes possible an objective analysis of what the worker has perceived.

Authenticity

Authenticity, also referred to as genuineness, is the third ingredient of a helping relationship. The terms refer to such qualities as honest, reliable, free from pretense, trustworthy, and sincere. To be genuine does not mean that practitioners disclose their own feelings and experiences to clients except for a carefully thought through purpose. It does mean that they do not deceive their clients about themselves or their situations. Authenticity requires considerable self-awareness on the part of practitioners so that their verbal and nonverbal messages are congruent and they are able to control negative or defensive responses so that they will not harm clients. What is effective is the absence of phoniness and defensiveness. Honesty and freedom from defensiveness provide a model for clients to emulate.

Authentic social workers admit their mistakes, fulfill the conditions of their contracts, provide rather than withhold knowledge, and answer clients' questions according to their assessment of the meaning of the question and the clients' needs. Telling the truth is the essence of authenticity; yet the quality of the relationship in which truth is told is crucial. Cousins, in writing about medicine, says that "certainly the physician had the obligation to tell the truth but he also had the obligation to tell it in a way that did not leave the patient in a state of emotional devastation - the kind of emotional devastation that could compromise effective treatment."[11] The same is true for social work.

A common concern of inexperienced workers is how to respond to clients' personal questions about their age, ethnicity, religion, marital status, or life experiences. Workers tend to evade answering the questions or do so in a defensive manner. An example of a non defensive response concerned a mother who asked a young female worker, "You don't have any children, do you?" The answer was an honest, "No, I don't have children," and a wait to see what the response would be. When the client didn't respond, the worker said, "I wonder if you're concerned about that." "Not really," said the client. "Oh," replied the worker, "I thought maybe you'd feel that, since I don't have children, I might not be able to help you with yours." That opened up the topic for further discussion.

Practitioners' capacity for authenticity may be severely tested, especially in work with troubled and aggressive children. Kolodny reported an incident which happened one day when he took a group to a zoo and wildlife refuge that was frequented by many children's groups in the area.

The time we had spent there was apparently enjoyed by all. An unfortunate corollary of the enjoyment was, of course, that nobody wanted to leave. I attempted to cajole the members into the van as, all about us, cars and buses filled with children and their adult leaders came and went in the parking lot. Next to the lot was a huge field and next to this a number of cages filled with birds and fowl of various types. . . . Just as I thought I had all of the youngsters in the van, three of them ran pell-mell for the cages and, with wild yelps, opened them. Pigeons, pheasants, their exotic cousins and distant relatives flew madly out of the cages. . . . The reactions of all the people present can be imagined. I stood crestfallen, with upturned palms, while my young charges ran back to the van for protection. After about three minutes of silence, during which I attempted to maintain my composure, the members began to whisper to each other, "He's mad now," as if I could not hear them. They continued this for some time until one of them, plucking up his courage, asked me directly, "You're mad, ain't ya?" "No, I'm not mad," I said, meanwhile seething with rage. "I'm just sorry that you guys spoiled a good time for yourselves."

The lie deceived no one. It simply confused the members and left them silent for another few minutes. I finally decided that none of this was helpful, but that perhaps, strangely enough, my obvious dissembling could be made use of clinically. "What I just said was not true," I said, loudly. "You made me feel like a fool out there and I was mad at you for it, but I did not want to show it." Silence again followed, and shortly afterward, agitated whispers. A number of these youngsters came from backgrounds in which adults in their lives were constantly angry at each other, separating, and sometimes leaving forever. This suggested to me the tack I should take. I repeated that I had been mad and still was, but that, at the same time, I was wondering what they thought was going to happen now that I had gotten mad. The answer came back, almost in chorus, "You're gonna stop the club," "You ain't coming back after today," I assured them that I would continue to work with them as I had been doing.[12]

Authentic behavior is essential to the development of trust. Trust develops as clients have experiences that successfully test their practitioners' honesty and integrity. Achievement of trust is relatively easy if the social worker merits it and if clients have previously achieved a basic sense of trust in other people. Many emotionally disturbed clients, however, have not had opportunities to work through the basic issue of trust versus mistrust. They may feel unloved or rejected, suspicious of other people, and lack confidence in themselves and the intentions of other people. Each new relationship offers some occasion for mistrust until the unknown becomes known. The less the capacity to trust, the more difficult it will be for clients to move into a therapeutic alliance with their social workers, and in families and groups, with other members. As clients develop trust, they gradually become ready to take more risks in participating in the helping process. The worker's responsibility is to act in ways that are authentic and trustworthy.

Clients often recognize the practitioner's authenticity by expressing such phrases as "you kept your word"; "you didn't bitch on me"; "as I look back, I'm glad you really leveled with me"; "she said she could not promise I'd get my children back from foster care, but she'd help me to try to do what was necessary to get them back." The skills that contribute to the development of authenticity, based on the values of the profession, include truth telling accompanied by empathy; provision of realistic, rather than false, reassurance and support; examination of one's own feelings and biases in order to prevent them from harmful expression; and creation of a social environment that reduces social distance between the worker and clients and the social distance between the members in work with families and groups.

Assessments and Ratings

Scales have been developed and used for measuring each of the components of the worker's relationship with individuals and groups.[13] There is considerable evidence from research in counseling and psychotherapy to support the view that the quality of the relationship is a necessary, but not sufficient, condition for successful outcome. Numerous studies of both worker-individual and worker-group relationships confirm "the potency of relationship in bringing about positive outcomes."[14] The outcomes seem to hold for a variety of counselors and therapists regardless of their theoretical orientations for a variety of clients, and for both work with individuals and work with groups. Although workers must have acceptance, empathy, and authenticity for clients, the clients play a part in eliciting these qualities. It would seem, then, that the presence of these qualities is a product of the interaction between clients and the practitioners.

Within social work, too, there is evidence that these qualities are primary factors in both continuance of treatment and positive outcome. Ripple and associates found that a relationship in which the social worker has warmly positive feelings toward the client increased motivation and was an important factor in whether or not a client continued in treatment and outcomes.[15] Sainsbury, in a report on a study of families with multiple problems, found that clients preferred workers who were informal, patient, and caring, and who displayed warmth, empathy, and ethical integrity toward all members of the family.[16] From a nationwide study, Beck and Jones concluded:

> This factor (relationship) was found to be twice as powerful as a predictor of outcomes than any other client or service characteristic covered by the study and more powerful than all client characteristics combined. An unsatisfactory relationship was found to be highly associated with client-initiated disengagement and with negative explanations by the client of his reason for terminating.[17]

Mullen found that social workers' sensitivity to and ability to communicate understanding of feelings in a language that is attuned to the client's current feelings are positively associated with depth of self-exploration and are frequently associated with attitudinal, cognitive, and behavioral improvements.[18] Other studies by psychologists provide support for these findings.[19]

In a recent review of research on clinical social work, Russell reported that "The conclusion reached by a majority of the studies has been that a positive relationship exists between these clinician attributes and client therapeutic gain."[20] She points out that the qualities can be viewed as independent attributes of the practitioner or a product of the client-worker relationship with both clients and workers contributing to the process, referred to as "the therapeutic alliance." A positive alliance contributes to positive outcomes. From a systems perspective, it is clear that the attitudes of clients and practitioners are interdependent. But it is the social worker who is primarily responsible for influencing the process.

In a review of seventeen studies on relationship variables in groups that incorporated the qualities of warmth, empathy, and genuineness, Dies concluded that the results "generally demonstrate that the quality of the therapist-client relationship is important for group process and therapeutic outcome."[21] Although these qualities are essential for successful group treatment in many settings and types of groups, they comprise only a part of the successful attributes of a group leader. That holds true also for practice with individuals and families. In groups, the group itself is the primary agent of change; therefore, research suggests that the relationship established among the members also relates significantly to outcomes. The practitioner has an important role in cultivating helpful relationships among the members. Elliott's research indicated that empathy may play a more crucial role at certain moments in the helping process, for example, following a new and highly intimate disclosure.[22]

Research provides evidence that, in spite of the importance of the qualities of acceptance, empathy, and authenticity in determining outcome, many practitioners do not have high levels of these qualities.[23] When they lack these qualities, they are possibly ineffective or harmful to clients. But there is also evidence that these qualities can be learned or enhanced.[24] The qualities are not inherited and their lack is not an unchanging aspect of personality, even though some people seem to have more of them than others do. There is some evidence from research that these ingredients of effective relationships can be learned through training and education. That is the good news.

Several theoretical explanations seem to account for the value of these qualities in practice. One explanation is that they are potent positive reinforcers that elicit a high degree of positive feelings from clients.[25] Positive feelings increase the client's self-esteem, decrease anxiety, and increase the level of acceptance communicated to others, thereby reciprocally increasing the positive appeal and reinforcement received from others. Feeling accepted, understood, and cared about tends to enhance self-esteem and feelings of being valued by other people. In an atmosphere in which people feel valued, they are free to explore their feelings and ideas, set forth realistic aspirations for themselves, and develop motivation toward achievement of their goals.

Another explanation is that the relationship itself is a source of gain because the client has a sustained relationship with others without getting hurt, i.e., the relationship provides a safe environment.[26] A person's intimate feelings and concerns can be discovered and evaluated only if there is mutual trust between worker and client. When the worker is genuine, accepting, and empathetic, then clients tend to feel free to communicate their feelings, concerns, and ideas.[27] When clients perceive that the workers are attempting to understand, rather than to judge, it is not necessary for them to cling to dysfunctional defensive maneuvers.

With some clients the relationship is in itself a corrective emotional experience. It does not repeat the condemnations, rejections, or authoritarian controls that have characterized one or more significant relationships in the past. Clients often expect that practitioners will respond to them as they feel others have done. Through consistent attitudes on the part of the worker, clients are able to change their feelings and behavior that have a destructive influence on them.

Power

A professional relationship conveys acceptance, empathy, and genuineness. It also carries *power* in that the social worker assumes some degree of authority to influence the initiation and development of the relationship. Pigors explains that this authority is vastly different from the exercise of authoritarian power over others for personal gratification or for the achievement of one's own ends.[28] The authority is derived from knowledge, professional skill, and power invested in the worker by licensing, certification, and the agency or other institution.

It is also derived from the power the clients give the practitioner to influence them. The nature and degree of the worker's direct influence on individuals, or the group process, vary with the capacities of the clients to make their own decisions. When clients are unable to cope with a situation, workers actively use their authority. On the other hand when they are able to participate responsibly, the worker supports autonomy. When on rare occasions, the worker must use coercive authority because clients are hurting each other, destroying property, or engaging in such behavior as child abuse, which must by law be reported, the coercive authority is vested in the professional role and its legal sanctions.

Being in a position of power is often an issue for social workers.[29] They may deny that they do have authority and its concomitant responsibility for the welfare of the client. The worker's feelings about power and sharing it with their clients can be tested by clients. Workers may have had negative experiences with figures of authority and thus be uncomfortable with the role. They want to be liked by the cllients, to be thought of as a friend, and to be democratic. They confuse democracy with laissez-faire leadership. They may deal with their feelings by abdicating the role or becoming authoritarian. Such behaviors tend to provoke severe testing by the clients, who expect the worker to give professional opinions and take appropriate action, while always respecting the clients' right to question these opinions and actions and to make their own decisions.

Clearly tied to the conflict over the workers' power and the way they exert it are the clients' continual concerns about their status and power in their families, groups, and institutions, combined with ongoing concerns about trust and acceptance.

If social workers can come to care about, accept, empathize with, and demonstrate authenticity, they will not need to worry about using the power that is inherent in the professional relationship for purposes inimical to the well-being of clients.

Cultural Influences on Worker-Client Relationships

Ethnicity, race, social class, and gender of clients and workers influence the development of effective working relationships. Characteristics of the worker interact with those of the other participants in the process. First impressions are important. Each person, worker and client alike, often unconsciously tends to evaluate the other in terms of certain stereotypes based on ignorance or preconceptions about differences between them and on prior experiences with apparently similar people.

Depending upon prior experiences with people of other races or ethnic groups, a quality of mutual strangeness may pervade the initial meeting. All parties to the relationship feel uncertain about the other's feelings and expectations, with accompanying suspicion or fear. White workers usually feel guilty of being part of a racist society and may have feelings of discomfort when they are with a client who differs from them in color. When working in a cross-cultural situation, the practitioner is faced with challenges in establishing personal and professional credibility.[30] Stereotyping is a major deterrent to developing and sustaining effective relationships. Some practitioners are not able to respond to a client of a different race as a separate person, instead of as a symbol of a particular category of people.[31] It is imperative that differences be recognized and respected and that racial and ethnic identity be fostered. Attention to culture must not, however, be at the expense of individualization. Both Cooper and Kadushin point out that practitioners may emphasize ethnic factors to such an extent that individual problems and solutions become obscured.[32] Cultural factors need to be viewed as they interact with psychological and environmental ones in a particular situation.

Race is a problem in establishing relationships; it is a problem to be worked on, particularly when the race of the client and worker differs.[33] Clients from minority groups of color have valid reasons for initial distrust of white practitioners because many white people are prejudiced and discriminate against these people in many subtle and overt ways. The barriers between white workers and clients of different races need to be recognized and dealt with early in a relationship. Traditionally, practitioners have tended to avoid color differences. If workers are able to communicate their awareness of the difference in a sensitive manner, the potential for developing a helping relationship is enhanced and the client is more apt to continue with the worker than if these differences are denied or ignored. The worker begins to bring differences into the open by introducing the subject at an appropriate time and then responding sensitively to the client's feedback.[34]

Clients who have experienced discrimination are often particularly sensitive to the social worker's attitudes in the initial contact. They value being treated with respect but they have often not been so treated. Effective work with clients requires that the worker observe those formalities that are overt indications of respect, such as proper introductions, use of titles and surnames, and shaking hands. Such formalities are important to black clients who have been denied these symbols of courtesy. They are important to people of ethnic groups also.

An example is given by Velasquez and associates, who point out that the Spanish language includes two terms for use in addressing another person, depending upon the person's status as to both age and social role.[35] Addressing an older person or one of higher authority by his or her first name is not perceived as just a friendly gesture, but rather as a lack of respect: a social worker is in a position of authority and therefore should be addressed by surname and title. It is a sign of disrespect for a Latino client to disagree with a person in a position of authority. If unaware of this cultural norm, a worker may misinterpret the client's behavior, which militates against the development of a relationship characterized by mutual trust.

Another example is provided by Aguilar.[36] In the Mexican American culture it is the custom to have an informal and personalized conversation before entering into a business transaction. In making initial contacts with Mexican Americans, it is essential to begin the interview with an informal and leisurely conversation. Hammond also emphasizes the importance of informality and personalized contacts in establishing relationships with Native Americans.[37]

Within some Asian cultures there is a similar expectation that time will be taken for social amenities and for getting to know a person before "getting down to business."[38] The offering and acceptance of a cup of tea is frequently an important part of setting a climate which will be comfortable for the discussion of problems. In the Japanese culture, for example, respect for authority is a basic part of behavioral expectations. For persons reared in very traditional families, it may be exceedingly difficult to disagree with someone in a position of authority.

The social worker in such a situation must be very careful not to press family members for agreement or a conclusion before there is sufficient comfort to express difference. In a cultural situation where the expectation is to agree with the expert, it becomes important for the worker to pose options and to foster discussion rather than assume that the first "yes" signifies agreement or support of an idea. Etiquette may dictate agreement when an "expert" makes a suggestion. The worker needs to develop a climate that is sufficiently supporting to allow for discussion and sufficiently safe to allow for expression of feelings rather than the enactment of expected role behavior.

Cultural differences may intensify feelings of suspiciousness and distrust toward the worker. Problems in relationships often derive from differences in perceptions of social institutions. Social workers may view police, schools, recreation centers, public welfare departments, and health facilities as supportive and protective agencies. Some clients, however, associate such institutions with unsavory past experiences of failure, rejection, devaluation, or prejudice against them. There is ample reason for them, therefore, to distrust the social worker and the social agency until the worker can demonstrate interest, acceptance, empathy, and ability to help. Social institutions are potential resources for clients, but their effective utilization is dependent upon the clients' perceptions of, and prior experiences with, them. If the worker understands the basis for clients' attitudes, ways can then be found to help them make use of available opportunities.

Anger of an oppressed person toward institutions may be displaced onto the worker. Even when a worker displays acceptance, empathy, and authenticity, clients may not feel that the worker cares for them. The client may distort the worker's intent and behavior. A worker is often hesitant to discuss such problems with the client. But in order to develop the understanding of self and others that is essential to social competence, clients need to have workers who can explore the feelings that the client has toward them and then, when indicated, confront the client with the facts of distortion. When the worker is too threatened to open up the issue, clients are denied an opportunity to learn something about themselves and how they relate to others.[39] The worker's countertransference interferes with the development of a helping relationship.

White workers attempt to defend themselves in many ways against the anger and distrust of some clients of other races and against their own feelings of guilt toward them. They may deny the differences, overidentify with clients, or set lower expectations for them than they would for a white client. On the other hand, they may feel a need to set such high standards that the client is doomed to failure. They may have fantasies that they can make up for all of the clients' past deprivations. The basic solution is introspective efforts to recognize their feelings and then to focus on the clients in their situations with efforts to accept them as individuals and to empathize with them.

Workers of minority racial or ethnic backgrounds may have similar difficulties in relating to clients of a different group. As is true when white workers connect with clients, minority workers need to be able to accept their own and the clients' ethnicity.[40] All workers need to respond appropriately to the prejudicial comments made by clients.

Social workers, regardless of ethnicity, tend to belong to the middle class by virtue of their advanced education. Munoz notes that those who have emerged from circumstances of poverty may have a sense of guilt and conflict in the process of leaving behind their loved ones.[41] These factors may lead to either denial of identification or overidentification with clients of their own ethnicity. Maki says that essentially these clients are not helped to differentiate themselves from the worker and are maintained in a dependent position consistent with some of the authoritarian aspects of some ethnic minority cultures, for example, Latinos and some Asian groups.[42]

When workers and clients come from a similar racial background, it is often easier for the worker to accept and empathize with the client. Matching worker and client in regard to race has the advantage of fostering a sense of comfort in sharing certain identifiable physical and social characteristics and of understanding the culture into which both were socialized.[43] It is, however, easy to overemphasize the similarities within a category and to fail to take into account the many individual, family, and environmental differences.[44] It has been noted, for example, that in black client-black practitioner relationships, problems often develop because of the practitioners' tendencies either to deny the common tie with the clients or to overidentify with them. In spite of sharing a common racial experience, unless workers can recognize their own countertransference reactions and learn to control them, it is unlikely that an effective working relationship will develop.

There are both positive and negative implications for work across racial and ethnic lines. It is possible to capitalize on the values that come from learning about and facing differences as well as from learning about and facing similarities. The social distance between people can be reduced. In Kadushin's words:

> If the worker's professional training enhances the ability to empathize with and understand different groups and provides the knowledge base for such understanding, the social and psychological distance between worker and client can be reduced. If the gap is sufficiently reduced, clients perceive

workers as being capable of understanding them, even though they are the products of a different life experience.[45]

Similarly, Solomon emphasizes that one of the characteristics of non-racist practitioners is the ability to feel warmth, genuine concern, and empathy for people regardless of their race. A further skill is the ability to confront members when they distort or misinterpret the positive feelings that the worker has for them. When workers are too threatened to open up the issue, "the client is denied an opportunity to learn something about himself and how he relates to others."[46] The worker's failure to explore the issue with the client interferes with the development of relationships.

Other Influences on the Worker-Client Relationship

Ageism. The stereotyping of older adults as physically or mentally impaired, rigidly set in their ways, isolated, and dependent on others, is all too prevalent in society.[47] Too often social workers consider anyone over age sixty-two or sixty-five to be too old to benefit from counseling or therapy concerning psychosocial problems. They tend to limit their services to management of resources. When a social worker labels clients as elderly, that label often mitigates against the provision of individualized services to them and their families.

On the other hand, many older adults often have their own intergenerational stereotypes about younger people. The perceived social distance between older adults and younger social workers is illustrated by a group in a senior center.

CLIENT: There's no way a younger person like you could really understand and help us. Not that there's anything wrong with that—but I mean, how could you?

SOCIAL WORKER: I've often thought about this matter. How do you think I'm unable to help you, Ralph?

CLIENT: I'm eighty-six years old, have physical problems I never dreamed of when I was your age, and I've had many more experiences and lived much longer.

SOCIAL WORKER: All that is true, but might it not be possible for me to help you, even so? Do the rest of you feel as Ralph does about an older person being helped by a younger one?

The social worker has anticipated the problem and is able to control defensiveness about it and open up the subject for group discussion.

Sexual Orientation. The development of an effective social work relationship is influenced by the sexual orientation of the participants.[48] In a heterosexually oriented society, homophobia is prevalent; bias against homosexuals is rampant; heterosexual relationships are viewed as more natural and healthy, with some lingering attitudes that gays and lesbians are abnormal, despite the fact that, based on evidence, homosexuality is no longer classified as a mental illness.

Heterosexual practitioners may exhibit homophobia, making it difficult to relate to gays and lesbians with acceptance, empathy, and genuineness. Gay and lesbian clients may distrust heterosexual practitioners owing to the discrimination and negative attitudes to which they have been subjected. Their sexual orientation is not visible: they are identified as such when they decide "to come out of the closet" and find acceptance within their own reference groups.

Gender

Gender differences influence the nature of the worker-client relationship. Many women are concerned that counselors and therapists tend to perpetuate traditional sex-role stereotypes that may harm clients by expecting them to conform to narrowly defined roles and limit their life choices. Gilligan's studies suggest that there are differences in basic values between men and women, characterized by women being more apt to value caring and men more apt to value justice.[49]

Transference

Relationships develop through verbal and nonverbal communication in which both realistic and unrealistic forces operate. An emotional bond between two or more persons operates at both conscious and unconscious levels. According to psychoanalytic theory, people may displace feelings or attitudes that they experienced earlier toward a member of their family or other very significant persons in their lives.[50] Clients interpret the current relationship in terms of earlier ones. They expect that the worker will respond to them as they perceive that their parents or other significant persons would have done. The worker, however, does not respond in the anticipated ways, but expresses empathy, acceptance, and authenticity and responds to the client as a social worker, not as a person from the client's past. Through experiencing this different relationship, and sometimes also through developing understanding of the transference reactions, clients enhance their ability to relate to others on a realistic basis.

In numerous ways, hostility may be expressed against the worker who represents a parent or other significant person in the client's past. Clients often complain about persons in authority—father, boss, teacher—when it is the worker toward whom they have the feelings of hostility. Even though such hostility stems from feelings that were realistic in the past, the irrational elements are not appropriate to the present situation. Likewise, some clients with a need to be the "one and only" cannot bear to tolerate the fact that the worker has a close relationship with other clients. They develop fantasies about the worker's relationship with other clients and become jealous or feel rejected by the worker. They may feel criticized by a worker when the worker's comments were intended to be constructive. Some clients are extremely sensitive to subtle nuances that indicate less than total acceptance by the worker. They may anticipate criticism and interpret noncritical comments or questions as criticisms.

Clients often develop strong positive feelings that are expressed in a desire to have the worker to oneself, difficulty in sharing, strong overidentification, or prolonged dependency. In some instances, clients want to be nurtured by the worker, unconsciously expecting what they wanted but did not get from their parents. They may endow the worker with even more power than the worker has. They may withdraw from the relationship if they become overwhelmed by the intensity of their feelings. They may fear becoming totally dependent or helpless. Some clients present themselves as being very independent: with trust and reassurance, they can dare to express needs for help from others. Some clients present themselves as being helpless, and perhaps, also hopeless, incapable of doing anything on their own. Here the worker must give a great deal of support, but also work toward self-direction.

These unrealistic feelings toward practitioners are often referred to as "transference reactions," that is, the unconscious and inappropriate repetition of reactions and feelings from the past in a present situation. They involve a reliving of past experiences by transferring reactions from earlier to present relationships. The workers' task is to develop and sustain the relationship on a realistic basis. They do not actively encourage these feelings and actions, but evaluate their impact on the progress of the work. They cannot ignore them. Their feelings need to be recognized and understood and dealt with as they occur.[51] At times when clients are ready, workers may comment on the underlying feelings. They may comment that, although a client sees the worker this way, the worker is not parent or teacher. and cannot behave as such a person would.

In group situations, social workers need to understand that there may be multiple transference reactions not only to themselves, but also among the members.[52] When an atmosphere of trust, acceptance, and mutual aid has developed in the group, feelings which have been taboo may be expressed. Group interaction often facilitates the expression of hostile feelings toward the worker as a symbol of authority. When one member dares to express hostility, other members may react with shock. When they realize that the worker does not retaliate but continues to accept the person, they become more able to express their own conflicts toward the worker. A process of contagion has occurred. Irrational attitudes are easier to see in someone else, yet gradually the implications of one's own behavior become clear. Particular members may be stimulated by the special characteristics of other group members who remind them consciously or unconsciously of earlier relationships with parents, siblings, or significant others. Sibling rivalry is often reenacted in group situations, with certain members reminding one of being the less-favored child in the family.

As clients develop relationships with the worker, they often request personal favors. These may vary from a small boy's request that the worker give him the toy he has been playing with, to a man's request that the worker go to lunch with him, lend him money, or do other such favors. The worker's understanding of the meaning of the request determines the response. Early in the relationship, clients may be testing the worker to clarify their respective roles; they may be wanting reassurance that the worker really cares enough for them to give or do something special; they may be seeking means to have more time with the worker and turn the relationship into a personal one. Practitioners can ask clients about the reasons for requesting the favor. Such requests for time, attention, or gifts are handled within the agreed-upon norms and rules, and according to the worker's judgment about the effect that granting or refusing the request will have on the progress of treatment. In a family or other group situation, of course, the worker's relationship with other members must be taken into account.

Children particularly may have strong positive feelings toward a worker who represents a mother figure to them. This type of transference is illustrated by a social worker's visit to a ten-year-old girl in a hospital who was to have surgery the next day.

When I entered the room, Catherine saw me and burst into tears. I approached her with a smile but with concern, too. I put my hand gently on her shoulder. She looked up and said tearfully, "I'm going to surgery tomorrow." I said that I knew and that she is worried about it. She started to shake her head negatively but then slowly changed and said, "Yes, I am." I asked if she wanted to tell me about it. She said, "There's a sticker up my spine and it hurts a whole lot." I said I knew it hurt and asked if she was afraid of what would happen tomorrow. She nodded her head.

There was silence, during which time she stared intently at my earrings. She asked, "May I see your earrings?" I took one off and gave it to her. She patted it very lovingly and said, "My mother has a lot of earrings." This was the first time she had ever mentioned her mother. I said it must be hard for her not to be able to have her mother here when she goes into surgery. She agreed but said she understood. Then she asked if she could touch the pretty buttons on my blouse. She touched them slowly, each one. I knew she was grasping on to every bit of security she could find and that I was in a mother role with her.

In groups, members develop positive and negative feelings and reactions to each other, similar to those they develop with the worker.[53] For example,

In a group of women, Mrs. Jerrold glowered at Mrs. Pascoe when the worker asked Mrs. J. to wait until Mrs. P. had a chance to speak. Mrs. P. asked Mrs. J. why she was angry with her. Mrs. J. looked startled and then said, "Well, I've a right to be angry—you cut me off." Mrs. Balcof said, "But the rest of us have a right to talk, too." Mrs. P. said she could not understand why Mrs. J. acted so strongly against her. Mrs. J. did not reply. There was a silence, which I did not interrupt. Mrs. J. broke the silence, saying that she did react too strongly; Mrs. P. had done nothing to her. I commented that I was the one who had requested that Mrs. P. be given a chance to speak. Mrs. B. asked Mrs. J. if she might be jealous of Mrs. P. because the worker had turned her attention away from Mrs. J. and toward Mrs. P. Mrs. Williams said she agreed with that idea, commenting that it was natural to be jealous of the attention another member receives "just like children who want the mother's attention all to themselves." The members all laughed at this, including Mrs. J.. Mrs. W., in a light manner said that the group sometimes acted like a family of kids who get jealous of each other. Mrs. J. thought it was natural for kids to feel this way but not for adults. The members continued to talk about the incident and reassured Mrs. J. that other adults often reacted as she had done.

This example is but one of the many ways in which member-to-member rivalries may be expressed in the group and of how the group process can be used to help members understand themselves better. Note that the predominant social climate was one of mutual acceptance and support, allowing for the expression of negative and positive feelings, and that the worker was comfortable in setting a limit, using silence to stimulate reflective discussion, clarifying her part in the process, and trusting the group process. Note, too, that the members of the group explore the problem, offer interpretations of behavior while simultaneously providing support, and then universalize the situation.

Gradually, as clients begin to trust the worker, and as they develop more confidence in their own abilities, they tend to identify with the worker. Such identification is manifested in various ways. They may begin to dress like or imitate some aspect of the worker's appearance or mannerisms. They may comment that they try to think about how the worker would handle a particular situation, or that they did something to please the worker. Often such behavior is an unconscious incorporation of some part of the worker into themselves. Gradually, they move from identification with the worker to an enhanced sense of their own identity.[54] Such identifications occur also among members of groups. They enhance the sense of relatedness and, in addition, lead to changes in attitudes and behavior. The worker tends to foster identifications, but also to help clients move to an enhanced sense of their own identities and mature object relationships.

Another special challenge to workers and their use of relationships and possibly a form of transference involves the response to and management of seductive behavior. These sexual advances are not limited to the worker-client dyad, but may also take place within families and formed groups. In one study, it was found that encounters with seductive behavior were common.[55] These experiences were mildly to markedly discomforting to the workers. Some workers felt angry that their professional interest, concern, and caring had been misinterpreted. It is possible, of course, that workers themselves might unwittingly behave toward clients in seductive ways, based on their own interpersonal needs. To be able to recognize one's feelings and refocus the relationship on a professional basis is the challenge to the worker. Unfortunately, there are instances of practitioners' rape of clients, a highly unethical and criminal act.

Countertransference

When it is the worker who transfers feelings and reactions from earlier relationships onto one or more clients, the term "countertransference" is used. Imhof defines countertransference "as the total range of possible emotional reactions, attitudes, values and beliefs that the helper may have toward clients."[56] The helper has disrupted the relationship through some error in perceiving the client realistically. Countertransference components of the relationship need to be recognized and, if they are harmful to the progress of an individual or the development of a group, they need to be understood and controlled.

Countertransference reactions are evident in many ways; for example in the use of time by being late, absent, forgetting appointments, keeping clients waiting, ending sessions early or prolonging them beyond a reasonable time, dreading going to sessions, being unable to accept and empathize with a client, engaging in arguments, defending a position, or engaging in erotic fantasies about a client. These reactions tend to interfere with the worker's ability to relate to the client, to perceive the client realistically, and to be helpful to the client.

Imhof gives two examples of a worker's recognition of countertransference. The first example is a worker's comments that "I really feel sorry for the woman. I know I should have taken a tougher stand about her drinking, but—I don't know—I just had this overwhelming sympathy for the problems she has." And in the second example, the worker said, "It sounded like my own story when I was drinking just a few short years ago. I know how much going to Alcoholics Anonymous helped me and naturally I felt it would be the only treatment approach I would suggest."

A social worker's values can lead to countertransference reactions. Awareness of one's own values is crucial to understanding and helping others, for people's values determine many of their choices and actions. In writing on psychotherapy, Buehler has said:

> One cannot live without encountering the problem of values. . . . Nor can one be a therapist without bringing certain convictions about values into one's work. These convictions may or may not be specifically communicated to the patient, but they help determine the goal he sets for himself and his patient; and they are consciously or unconsciously reflected in his questions, statements, or other reactions.[57]

Herein lies the need for self-awareness so that social workers can honestly and openly recognize their own values, distinguish them from those of the clients, and act on the basis of knowledge about the distance between their values and those of the clients, rather than deny that values do enter into practice.

Understanding and coming to terms with the values of one's own important reference groups is necessary for anyone who hopes to understand the values of other people. Konopka points out that the worker needs "to realize that he sees others through the screen of his own personality and his own life experiences . . . This is why a social worker must develop enough awareness of at least the make-up of his own particular screen."[58] Fortunately, workers may correct this screen through careful analysis of their own behavior in relation to others and through the use of supervision or consultation. Such efforts help them to take into account their own bias, even though they cannot completely eliminate it and thus make it possible to understand better the persons with whom they work.

An important step in becoming able to develop effective relationships with clients is to recognize one's own distortions but then to move from self-awareness to self-control; that is, as Solomon said, "the ability to control heretofore unconscious aspects of one's personality which have served as an obstacle to establishing warm, genuine, and empathic relationships with certain kinds of people."[59]

Practitioners may not recognize how certain unresolved personal conflicts may lead to errors in assessment and treatment. The conflicts may vary with the nature of the clients' problems and situations. Wellisch, for example, described the intense personal emotions engendered in therapists working with chronically ill children and their families.[60] These countertransference errors include

1. overidentifying with the family, which may be due to unresolved object losses from the therapist's past.
2. being rigid with the family (e.g., refusing to see the family anywhere but in the office), which may be a defense against overinvolvement with the family.
3. pushing for more change than is possible, which again may reflect the therapist's own unfinished business with family matters.
4. overdoing (e.g., overinvolvement in medical issues), which may be a defense against the inevitability of the disease process.
5. buying into the family projective process (e.g., not raising certain issues because the child "may be unable to bear it").

6. taking the side of the family against the primary physicians, which is usually an indication of the therapist's need for omnipotent control.
7. being utilized by the physician as a crisis interventionist (e.g., allowing physicians to wait too long to refer families).

Sprung describes issues of countertransference with older clients related to ageism and Wallerstein with clients in a crisis of divorce.[61]

Another potential problem is related to a tendency by workers to empathize more readily with one member of a family or group than with another. In a relationship with one client, the worker's empathy may make it difficult to see that client's significant others realistically. Often, for example, a worker finds a small child very appealing and tends to blame the parents for the child's difficulty. Unconscious parental urges may be stimulated by the neediness of clients, and these attitudes may reinforce the client's needs to look for gratification that was not given in earlier phases of development, rather than to work toward more satisfying and effective relationships in the present. In sessions with a mother and child, a worker's positive feelings for the child and the child's responses to them might arouse jealousy or fear in the mother. When workers get cues that such a situation is developing, they reflect on their own attitudes toward child and mother. They may then be ready to talk with both parties, for example, to explain that the child seems to want all of the attention and that the mother has feelings about this; that the worker is there for both of them.

The social work relationship provides a therapeutic milieu within which practitioners and clients together pursue agreed-upon goals related to enhanced psychosocial functioning of individuals, improvement of the functioning of families and groups, and desirable changes in the environment. Developing and sustaining a relationship characterized by acceptance, empathy, and authenticity is one crucial force in assuring positive outcomes. But the competent use of a repertoire of skills or techniques is also essential. In chapter 7, these skills are described and illustrated.

Seven | Intervention

Intervention consists of using a series of skills or techniques to help clients achieve their goals related to the enhancement of their psychosocial functioning.

Numerous attempts have been made to develop categories of specific forms of help, often referred to as procedures, tasks, techniques, interventive acts, or skills. The term "skill" now seems to be preferred: it denotes the ability to do something with competence. In spite of somewhat different perspectives, there is considerable agreement about a number of clusters of interventive skills.[1] These are support; acceptance of feelings; structuring; exploration; education; advice; confrontation; clarification; interpretation; and facilitation of family and group processes. They are based on theoretical propositions about the dynamic processes through which changes are brought about. They are generic clusters, that is, they are applicable to work with individuals, families, or groups and to both direct and indirect service activities.

An ecosystem perspective emphasizes that there are mutual and reciprocal influences among the parts: change in one part of the system affects other parts; any change upsets the steady state.[2] A system needs inputs of new information in order to change; it corrects its operations through the process of feedback; the system and its environment influence each other; and similar goals can be achieved from different initial conditions. In helping clients to change, social workers have available to them a repertoire of clusters of techniques or skills for selective use with clients at a given time.

Support

Support is an essential ingredient of clinical social work practice. To support a person means to sustain or keep steady, to give courage, to express faith and confidence, and to give realistic approval to an individual or group.

Supportive techniques sustain the motivation and capacity of people while they are using a social service. Clients have varied degrees of positive and negative motivation to enter into and use treatment. Particularly at the beginning, there is some natural anxiety, doubt, and uncertainty, but later on there are also times when some aspects of the situation become threatening. At these times, motivation is sustained by reducing the threats. Support from the practitioner—and in a group, from other members as well—tends to keep anxiety at manageable levels. As anxiety lessens, clients feel comfortable enough to remain in the situation and develop confidence that they will not be hurt in it. In accepting help, they recognize that some changes will be expected of them. These anticipated changes may be threatening.

In individual treatment, the client may fear the loss of self-control, invasion of privacy, inability to meet expectations, loss of self esteem, or the demands of the intimate relationship. In families and other groups the client may also fear a loss of status, possible recriminations by other members, loss of individuality, rejection by others, and fear of exposure of one's self to others. In order to minimize these threats, the ego needs to be supported in its efforts to cope with new and difficult situations, What is supported are the client's capacities, constructive defenses, and efforts to work toward goal achievement.[3]

In system terms, the steady state needs to be maintained in reasonable balance so that the upset is not beyond the person's coping capacities. A moderate level of tension may motivate a person to attain a goal, but when tension becomes extreme, it is disruptive and even incapacitating. Support is an important motivator, not only because it reduces anxiety and enhances self-esteem, but also because it is a prerequisite to change through other means.

The social work relationship is itself a means of support through which clients are sustained in their efforts to use the clinical experience for their benefit. Feeling accepted, receiving empathic responses, and being helped by someone who is genuine is a rare experience for many clients. People often bloom when they are the beneficiaries of such a relationship. In groups, there is the additional potential of mutual support among the members. The worker sets the tone for mutual support through expressing the expectation that members will become able to do this themselves. To a large extent, however, the members become supportive of each other as they become aware of their common purposes, interests, and needs and as they work out their positive and negative feelings toward each other. They become supportive of each other as they feel trust and security in the worker, as they come to identify with, and to integrate some of those patterns of support into their own personalities.

Support is demonstrated through a variety of specific skills, implemented according to the worker's understanding of the individual's or group's feelings and readiness at a given time. The major skills in the use of support are attending and realistic reassurance and encouragement.

Attending

Attending is the ability to pay attention to what is being said and done. Its purpose is to convey a message of respect and a feeling that what is being said or done is important. While essentially silent, practitioners are actively observing, listening sensitively, and following the flow of verbal and nonverbal communication. They note not only the manifest content but the underlying feelings as well. They send back cues that they are interested in and understand the information through what Hepworth and Larsen refer to as furthering responses.[4]

Attending is conveyed by such messages as head nods, leaning toward the speaker, murmurs and eye contact when appropriate. It is conveyed through such verbal messages as "uh, huh," "mm," "yes," "I see," "and then?," "that's important," "would you tell me more?"

Purposeful silence and sensitive listening are powerful aids to self-revelation and examination of self and situation. Purposeful silence often indicates that a worker is listening and following what is being said. Such a stance tends to induce the talker to continue in the same vein. In other instances, purposeful silence indicates that clients are expected to mobilize their thoughts and then express them. A worker's personal need to fill in a short period of silence with words often interferes with clients' efforts to get ready to share pertinent information.

Reassurance and Encouragement

Provision of realistic reassurance is an important supportive skill. Reassurance tends to reduce feelings of insecurity and anxiety and to let clients know that, with help, they can cope. Persons often come into a new situation, especially if they have been referred to it for help with a problem perceived by a relative or person in a position of authority, with feelings of stigma, abnormality, or guilt. A moderate level of stress may motivate a person to attain a goal, but when it is extreme, it is disruptive and incapacitating. Realistic reassurance instills hope that things can be better, thereby enhancing motivation for trying to change oneself and one's situation. In order to be reassured by comments made by the worker or by another member, clients must feel some trust and confidence in that person. The worker may reassure clients about the normality and acceptability of their feelings, behavior, or situation. Universalization tends to reduce anxiety by lessening the fear of being different from "normal" people. Such reassurance is based on realistic knowledge about, and appraisal of, clients in their situations; otherwise, the worker is being deceitful or not genuine. Such attitudes are sensed by clients.

When realistic reassurance cannot be given, it is apt to be more supportive to acknowledge the difficulties and to suggest what can be done within a difficult situation. Denial of reality is not supportive. In using reassurance, "relief comes not from self-understanding but because the worker in whom the client has placed confidence has said in effect that it is not necessary to be so worried. The dynamic is not one of reasoning but of faith dependent upon the client's confidence in the worker's knowledge and good will."[5] Expressing confidence in clients' capacities and recognizing their achievements, or at least their efforts, is often preliminary to the development of self-confidence. It is a powerful incentive to continue to try new solutions or to continue on a successful path.

Encouragement and reassurance may be conveyed by such messages as: "I can see you're really trying"; "Its not easy to be a parent and also have to earn a living, but I think we can find ways to reduce the stress you're feeling"; "I see you've given a lot of thought to that matter since our last meeting"; "Other clients have been in a similar boat and made it." To a child, the worker may say: "lots of children come here to get over their troubles"; "It often feels scary to come to a new place, but you'll soon want to come"; "It's OK to cry here."

Acceptance of Feelings

There is a close interconnection between support and motivation and capacity to express feelings. Support is an essential condition for the expression of genuine feelings and concerns. When clients feel supported, they find courage to express feelings and thoughts that would be suppressed in usual situations, to expose some of their vulnerabilities, and to dare to risk trying new things.

As feelings of love, satisfaction, and happiness are expressed, these feelings are reinforced if the responses to them show acceptance. Feelings of anger, sadness, hopelessness, hostility, and fear are also often expressed, usually leading to a reduction in anxiety. If they are accepted, clients can recognize the universality of their feelings, as well as the unique meaning to them, and their anxiety tends to lessen. Some anxiety is, however, helpful and used for productive work in problem-solving. Feelings often lose some of their intensity and hold on a person once they are expressed to and accepted by others. Yalom, in writing about therapeutic factors in groups, has said: "the open expression of affect is without question vital to the group therapeutic process; in its absence a group would degenerate into a sterile academic exercise. Yet it is only a part process and must be complemented by other factors." He suggests that it is the "affective sharing of one's inner world and then the acceptance by others" that seems of paramount importance.[6]

Acceptance of one's feelings by others tends to be supportive. Although disclosure of facts is of value, expression may often need to be contained. Clients may get gratification from talking about themselves without being able to make progress toward any change. They may get caught up in their own sense of hopelessness or helplessness in a repetitive recital of content. If they are in a group, other members may react negatively to the monopolization of time by only a few. Such group responses to the nature and amount of self-disclosure by these few need to be assessed. The worker may have to stop the outpouring of feelings. At such times, limiting expression is supportive.

Several specific skills are used to encourage the expression of feelings and have clients feel that they are accepted. Encouraging expression of feelings may be aided by making comments or asking questions about feelings, for example, "What were you feeling when that happened?" or "People often feel shocked when they get that kind of diagnosis." Encouragement of expression is often followed by identifying the feeling if the client has not done so. Examples are: "That was devastating, wasn't it?," "Did you feel embarrassed about that?," "You are really very angry, aren't you?"

Reflecting back the feeling enhances the client's awareness of the particular feeling. "You seemed to be saying that you have been depressed all week." "Yes." "And can you tell me more about the feeling of depression?" The client may not be able to identify the feeling by name, but give vague indications instead, implied by tone of voice, a nonverbal gesture such as a tight fist, coming into the room with a light tread and bright smile. "You look like you're feeling downcast today," or "you really are looking happy today." The worker assures clients that all feelings are acceptable.

Structure

People are influenced to move toward the achievement of their goals through participation in a treatment experience whose structure meets their needs and provides direction for their participation in treatment.

The intent of the social worker is to create a special environment conducive to the achievement of goals that have been mutually determined by worker and client. The techniques in this category comprise activities by the worker concerning "the structure and direction of the interactions with the client."[7] For work with families and small groups, it is necessary to add "and interactions among the members." The objective of structuring is to create an optimal milieu for work. It primarily lays the groundwork for skills more directly concerned with influencing attitudes and behavior. Structuring includes skills to assure the flexible use of policies and procedures, the definition of limits, and the focusing of interaction on key issues.

Policies and Procedures

The policies and ways of work of an agency provide a framework within which the worker and the clients operate. To work together effectively, workers and clients need to be clear about the policies and procedures concerning purposes of service, use of time, duration and frequency of sessions, fees, principles of confidentiality, and the major focus of the sessions. Such agreements provide a boundary within which the worker and clients are free to operate.

These policies and procedures should be used flexibly and changed in accordance with the clients' needs and capacities. Achieving clarity about the structure of the service reduces ambiguity and confusion and thereby provides support so that energies can be released for working toward the agreed-upon goals. The skill is in the timely presentation of information by the social worker, responding to clients' reactions and, when necessary taking steps to change dysfunctional policies and procedures.

Limits

Limits and rules are important forms of structuring. They define the boundaries of acceptable behavior. In defining limits, the worker intends to help clients to adapt to the realistic demands of the situation. A person needs to learn to meet these demands and to be protected from the destructive tendencies of self and others. Limits provide a sense of safety, diminishing fears of going too far and losing control of oneself. Such limits are more acceptable than the use of power by the worker in the form of punishment or negative criticisms.

Some people need to learn to overcome too rigid conformity to policies and rules in order to develop spontaneity in relationships and to use their capacities in more creatively adaptive ways. They need permission to try out different modes of behavior. The social worker needs to balance the use of permissiveness and limits based on differential assessment of the individuals and the group as a whole.

Structural controls are not an end in themselves but serve as a means to the goal of self-control and self-direction. The worker presents the limits clearly and concisely and seeks feedback from the clients as to their acceptability to them. The practitioner might say: "You're not allowed to smoke here, but you can smoke at the rear of the waiting room before you come to our meeting and on your way out. Can you live with that?" "It's our policy that, if you miss a session, you'll be charged for it unless you call us in advance. Does that seem fair to you?" Clients generally understand the need for limits and appreciate having them made clear early in the helping process.

Exploration

Exploration is one of the dominant sets of techniques used in social work practice, and its use has been well documented in the clinical research literature.[8] It is a means for examining a situation by bringing facts, opinions, and feelings into the open so that sufficient understanding of the person-group-situation configuration is obtained to work toward goal achievement. It is used to elicit necessary information, to bring out details about experiences and relationships as clients perceive them, and to identify the feelings connected to the relationships and experiences. Through exploratory skills, the worker draws out descriptive materials, perceptions, and emotions connected with the facts and explanations. It is an important step in the problem-solving process. Along with support and structuring, exploration lays the groundwork for skills more directly intended to influence the individual's or group's functioning.

The skills or acts of the social worker engaged in the process of exploration with an individual, family, or group consist primarily of comments and questions, in addition to the provision of requested information. The skills are used within the purpose of the practice, the content of the communication, and the social context.

Comments

Comments are usually more effective than questions in encouraging clients to give information on pertinent matters, allowing for freedom to decide what to present and how to do it. The specific skills include reflecting back, as when a worker comments, "You said it was scary to come here at night all alone." They include requests for elaboration, such as "I'd like to hear more about how you were able to work out that problem with your employer." They include suggestions of topics, such as "I wonder how you happened to come here for help at this time." Another skill is sharing an observation as when a worker said, "I noticed you were listening intently when I mentioned _____." Or, a worker may restate an idea to clarify the meaning of a client's message as in the following: "Another way of saying that might be _____." Still another skill is summarizing the content of a session or a segment of one: "I recall that today we talked about your difficulty in making a decision about a divorce and your sense of responsibility as a parent. Perhaps you could add other things to what I've said."

Questions

Questions asked by social workers for purposes of exploration tend to fall on a continuum, from open-ended to closed.[9] Open-ended questions are similar to comments but in a different form. They are used to seek description or elaboration of events, experiences, situations, and problems. They permit clients to tell their own stories in their own ways. They may elicit information that might not come out in a more structured interview. Clients have the opportunity to reveal their own subjective frames of reference and select those elements of their situations that are of greatest concern to them.

Open-ended questions optimize self-determination. They give clients the power to find their own style of communication and the content to be covered. "Could you tell me about your problems and what you've tried to do about them before you came here?" is a typical question asked in first sessions. Semiopen questions request elaboration of the client's story to elicit more specific information about some facet of the story, for example, "Could you tell me more about the trouble you're having with Jane?"

Closed questions are asked when specific information is sought, such as identifying information about the client and situation. They are as simple as: "How old are your children?" "Did you see your doctor last week?" "Then you've decided to join the group?" They require specific answers. Open-ended questions, followed by probes, allow clients to tell their stories in their own ways and then help them to amplify the story with relevant details.

Some practitioners tend to shortcut exploration out of a desire to reach a resolution to a problem quickly. They accept a client's or a group's first proposal: the focus is on action—"what are you or we going to do?," rather than on the means to achieve the best possible action—"how can we make a good decision?," "what is really going on here?," "what seems to be contributing to the difficulty?" as perceived by the clients. Some practitioners may also be uncomfortable with the ambivalence, differences, and uncertainties that exploration often accelerates. So, in a rush to bring certainty to an issue or get busy with a task, workers may avoid or shortcut exploration. The process of exploration furnishes a necessary foundation for moving beyond eliciting and elaborating information to using the information for other helpful purposes.

Psychosocial Education

The purpose of education is to provide new knowledge and skills required for coping with a particular problematic situation. People often change if they know what is desirable and effective with respect to rational self-interest. Lack of knowledge and skills in role performance contributes to ineffective functioning. Assimilation of information from the social environment is central to the process of problem-solving. Positive change may be influenced by an educational process that offers tools and resources useful to clients. Education is woven into the ongoing helping process when the client is an individual, but educational goals are more frequently achieved in work with families and formed groups.

Knowledge is one road to ego mastery; it is a source of power.[10] Providing information, rather than withholding it, is the best safeguard against dependency upon the worker. Knowledge is provided or new skills taught when the material is clearly relevant to the clients' situations and when they do not have ready access to the information. The information that is given needs to be accurate: the worker needs to know the facts and how they relate specifically to a particular person's or the group's needs.

People often need new information or reinforcement of knowledge in order to make sound decisions about themselves and other persons who are significant to them. They often need specific details about community resources and their use. They often need to understand general principles of human growth and development or the implications of an illness or physical handicap for themselves or their families. They may need to learn some basic skills that can help them to enter into new relationships more effectively, as for example, appropriate approaches to a teacher, stepparent, or prospective employer. They need information about laws that affect them concerning such events as abortion, marriage, adoption, divorce, discrimination in housing or jobs, and consumer protection.

The appropriate use of education is a crucial skill. It is based on exploration, involving searching for information, exploring alternative solutions to problems, and encouraging clients to share their knowledge and skills with each other. The worker may provide relevant data, teach the steps in the problem-solving process, seek responses to the information given, and ask members to apply the information or skills to their own situations. The teaching methods may include verbal presentations of information or the use of environmental resources and such media as audiovisual aids, role playing, and demonstration. They also involve the selection and use of persons not in the group to provide information or teach relevant skills.

Information is given in ways that relate clearly to the goals of clients. In providing information, practitioners do not usually follow a fixed agenda or outline. They pay attention to the cognitive and social needs of the clients at a given time. One skill is to offer information briefly in language that can be understood and in a tentative manner, making it clear that it is open to examination by the clients who may question and refute it. The worker then seeks feedback to discover whether the message sent was the message received through such comments and questions as: "What questions do you have about that?" "Do you understand what I said?" "Were you able to follow me?" Clarification of the message may be required.

A third skill is to encourage the expression of feelings concerning the content or the way it was presented. When workers observe nonverbal cues that indicate doubt, skepticism, disagreement, or anxiety about the information, they may call attention to these observations. "You look puzzled," "That information is sometimes upsetting to clients—was it upsetting to you?" "How do you see it?" Such comments and questions stimulate the clients to come to grips with the issue being addressed.

There may be a need to assist clients to recognize and cope with their emotional reactions to the information through the use of exploration and clarification. Kane has reminded us that education and therapy are closely akin.[11] Emotions and relationships can obscure educational messages and people need help to bridge the cognitive and affective aspects of learning.

Learning to perform tasks and participate in activities is essential to the acquisition of effective role performance. It is necessary that clients be provided with knowledge and skills essential to functioning in various roles or in negotiating external systems. In imparting information and teaching skills, the social worker uses a variety of media and resources: for example, demonstration or modeling of skills, role playing, using audiovisual resources, constructing genograms, family sculpting, anticipatory planning, and practice of new behaviors. These are but a few of the activity-oriented experiences that facilitate interpersonal learning and the improvement of role performance.

Education is used not only with clients but also with significant people in their behalf. Workers may, for example, give information to a teacher about a child's family situation or to a prospective employer about the kind of jobs that can be performed by a client with a particular handicap. They may give advice in the form of a recommendation, for example, that a child in residential treatment be moved to a cottage more appropriate to the child's current needs. It is to be remembered that it is ethical to intervene with others about clients only if it is done with their informed consent, except under the most unusual circumstances.

Advice

Advice is a form of direct influence that suggests or recommends a particular course of action. Social workers offer advice to serve two functions: to give specific recommendations that, if carried out, may further the attainment of the clients' goals; and to provide an important source of emotional and cognitive stimulation.[12] They share their opinions, based on knowledge, and explain the reason for the recommendation, a form of information-giving. They offer advice cautiously, so as not to hamper the clients' efforts to arrive at their own decisions. They offer such advice as tentative ideas for consideration by the clients, rather than as commands. Although workers are often hesitant to give advice for fear of encouraging dependency, or violating the clients' self-determination, they probably do so more often than they acknowledge. Clients resent advice at times and do not use it, but this is most often true when advice was not sought or when it was inappropriate to their needs.

Clients often want and need suggestions and advice from workers. In one study, it was found that clients were more likely to be satisfied with a service if the worker gave appropriate advice. The clients perceived lack of advice as lack of interest in resolving their problems.[13]

In another study of clients' reactions to casework, it was reported that lack of advice-giving was the most frequent complaint about the service. If the worker was marked relatively high in the use of advice, clients were less likely to be dissatisfied than if the worker made little use of this technique.[14]

In another study by Sainsbury, it was indicated that clients tended to reject advice when it was perceived as an order to do something, but accepted advice when it was perceived as a suggestion for their consideration. This finding suggests that it is the way advice is given that makes a difference in its usefulness to clients.[15]

In still another study, on the use of advice by eight social workers in a parent-counseling program, Davis concluded that working-class parents received more advice than those of middle-class status did. All of the social workers gave some advice, and parents' reactions to advice tended to be more negative than positive. Parents also said, however, that they liked the workers to give advice and none wanted less advice than they received. This paradox may be resolved, according to Davis, by realizing that advice may serve an important therapeutic function other than guiding actions. It may stimulate a person to think of alternative ways for dealing with problems.[16]

In a study of groups by Lieberman, Yalom, and Miles it was found that the members valued direct advice or suggestions given by the practitioner or other members of the group about how to deal with some life problem or important relationship. Those who made large gains in treatment marked this item as important significantly more often than those who made few gains did.[17] In a recent survey of research in outpatient mental health settings, Videka-Sherman found that advice is one of the interventions that is associated with positive outcomes.[18]

Advice is generally accepted by, and useful to, clients if it is what they really need, if it is presented in a way that connects it to the current life situation, if it is ego-syntonic, if it is presented in a manner that conveys genuine interest in the person's welfare, and if the person's own decision-making processes are engaged in responding to the advice.

Skills in Giving Advice

Most advise is given in the form of tentative suggestions, either in the form of comments or questions. Examples of suggestion would include such phrases as: "Some clients have found it helpful to _____. Would that be helpful for you?" "There are many home health care resources in the community that you could use." "Have you tried to tell your teacher about that?" "Could we go over your budget to see if ways can be found to get out of the debt that you say is driving you crazy?"

There are times when advice is given in the form of definite recommendations, such as "You really should tell your partner that you are HIV positive" "You need to keep your appointments with your probation officer" "You need to get some respite from your caretaking duties. Here are ways that can be done."

A powerful, but somewhat risky, skill is the use of paradox, a form of advice that is being used primarily in family treatment. For example:

In work with the family of a patient, Mrs. Varick, her therapist hypothesized that the family was locked in a tight pattern of communication in which Mrs. V.'s talk of worries generated responses from family members that she should not worry. That behavior perpetuated the problem. The family was advised that when Mrs. V. starts to worry, the members will say, "You're right, it worries me, too," "You are right, it is worrisome."

The paradoxical prescription was aimed at disrupting the interactive pattern and initiating a new one, with the hope that the symptom would disappear. An ethical issue concerns how one gets informed consent to use such a procedure.

Several principles of practice guide social workers in their decisions to give advice to clients. These principles are similar to those suggested by Kadushin.[19]

1. Provision of advice usually comes after a request for it by clients or is based on assessment of need for it.
2. The advice offered is grounded in knowledge and based on a sound rationale.
3. The social context in which the advice may be implemented needs to be considered, including cultural values, realistic conditions, and support from others.
4. With some exceptions, advice should be offered tentatively with an ample consideration of alternatives and recognition of clients' rights to ignore or reject it.
5. Advice should be offered after the clients have tried to find solutions to their own needs or problems, building on their capacities and maximizing self-determination.

6. Giving advice needs to be accompanied with support and hope, and within a good worker-client system relationship.

Confrontation

Confrontation is a form of statement that faces a person or a group with the reality of a feeling, behavior, or situation. Its dictionary meaning is to face boldly, to bring a person face to face with something. Its purpose is to interrupt or reverse a course of action. It is a form of limiting behavior that faces a person with the fact there is some inconsistency between his or her own behaviors or between his or her own statements and those of other sources, that such behavior is irrational, or that it is destructive to self or others. It is concerned, not with the meaning of the behavior, but with stopping it and redirecting the course of the discussion or activity. Although usually viewed as dealing with negative behavior, it may be in the form of challenging positive attitudes or performance as well.

Confrontations stimulate self-examination. They usually challenge a client's defenses, such as denial, rationalization, projection, or displacement, or they challenge unacceptable behavior. They upset the person's emotional balance, creating temporary discomfort or anxiety, and thus unfreeze the system and make possible a readiness to change in order to reduce the discomfort.

A confrontation disconfirms the acceptability of what is happening. It provides information that contradicts distortions of blindness to facts, directly and openly. It provides a force that challenges obstacles to the achievement of goals. Overton and Tinker say that confrontations are direct statements, but they need not be harsh: the firm challenge should be "with an arm around the shoulder."[20] There is a vast difference between confrontation that is accusatory, such as, "Stop lying to me," and one that deals with denial by such a statement as "I know it's hard for you to tell me, but I already know that you are in serious trouble with the police," accompanied by a gentle tone of voice.

Hallowitz and associates report that there is some empirical evidence for the view that, when confrontation is accompanied by a high degree of empathy, it is an effective therapeutic technique; when employed by practitioners with little empathy, it is not.[21] Citing various studies, Nadel concluded that a challenging comment by a worker may be effective with certain clients who need more than a reduction of restraints to express their unconscious negativism.[22] A challenge is a form of confrontation: it calls into question and takes exception to what is being said or done. Confrontation may be of a person's verbal or nonverbal behavior or of the interactional patterns among people.

Confrontation needs to be based on sound assessment of individuals, families, and groups. It is not the worker alone who uses confrontation. The members confront each other, often quite bluntly, requiring that the worker evaluate the impact of such statements on particular individuals and on the group, following up in whatever way seems necessary. The worker may ask the group itself to evaluate the consequences of such confrontations on the progress of individuals and the movement of the group. In order to find patterns of behavior, the worker may comment on omissions and contradictions in the descriptions of the members. A comment that seeks to understand what happened tends to be more effective than questioning why it happened. It tends to focus on the chain of events, and this makes clear the nature of the behavioral patterns to the members.

Confrontation can be a somewhat risky technique because some clients may interpret it as criticism, verbal assault, or rejection. To avoid those responses, it needs to be accompanied by empathy and the message needs to relate to specific behaviors, not the total personality. Effective confrontation, according to Hepworth and Larsen, involves an expression of concern; a description of the behavior of the individual, family, or group; reference to the particular discrepancies or inconsistencies; and the possible consequences of the behavior.[23]

The skill is in making challenging statements in words the clients can understand. Such statements might be: "I've been trying to figure out what you were thinking when you told me you were going to school regularly, but the vice-principal informed me that you've been truant a lot—that's getting you in real trouble at school." Another example is: "I'm concerned because you insisted that you did not beat your son, but the doctor found severe bruises on him and reported your child abuse to the protective service agency." Another example is: "Whenever you begin to talk about your sexual problem, you talk very briefly and then change the subject." And, "We've talked a lot about some of the discrimination you've faced and I've agreed with much of it, but when you insist that there's no chance for you to get admitted to the community college, I must disagree. There are many students of Mexican background there."

Confrontation is an essential skill that is used to help clients to face behaviors that are obstacles to the development of power to control their own lives and achieve their desired goals. Solomon writes forcefully of its importance in serving oppressed populations. A major criterion of nonracist practice, she writes, is "the ability to confront the client when true feelings of worker empathy and genuineness have been expressed but have been misinterpreted or distorted by the client." That skill is combined with the "ability to feel warmth, empathy, and genuine concern for people regardless of race, ethnicity, or color."[24]

Clarification

Clarification is widely used in social work practice. To clarify simply means to make understandable.

Clarification involves reflection, an introspective thought process that promotes understanding of oneself in relation to other people and situations. Both clients and practitioners engage in reflection. According to Schon, reflection in action is "reflective conversation with the situation."[25] It is central to the art through which practitioners sometimes cope with troublesome divergent practice situations. It begins with an effort to solve a problem, remaining open to the discovery of phenomena incongruent with the initial problem-solving. That leads to reframing of the problem, and reflection on the consequences of these efforts.

Practitioners recognize that the action may have different meaning for clients than is intended. The task, then, is to discover what these meanings are. They also need to make their meanings accessible to the client. This view is similar to Saari's proposal that clients and worker, within a therapeutic concordance, practice and refine reality-processing skills which clients can use later in situations external to the treatment relationship.[26]

Other writers have referred to the use of introspection and to the worker's formulation of hypotheses concerning the interrelation between behavior and environment.[27]

Effective psychosocial functioning requires some scheme for organizing and interpreting events. If this scheme is distorted, a person has difficulties in relating to other people and in performing valued social roles. Through reflecting on problems, recognizing difficulties in perception, and then acquiring more accurate perceptions of self, other persons, and the environment, changes are likely to occur. By reducing discrepancies between internal perception and external reality, a person is able to function more effectively. Current experience can be used as a corrective in modifying attitudes and behavior if a person is helped to reflect on and reevaluate significant experiences, situations, and relationships. Growth in ego capacity is achieved by facing and coping with the reality of one's thoughts, feelings, and behavior.

Skills in Clarification

The primary skills used in clarification are encouragement of reflection on feelings; reflecting or paraphrasing; making connections; identifying patterns of behavior; and reframing.

Reflection on feelings. Going beyond the acceptance of expressed feelings to provide support, feelings are examined. There is often a need to understand their impact on cognition and behavior. Ability to associate emotion with words and actions supports the ego's capacity to cope with them. Feelings may be denied or their expression may be out of proportion to the reality of the situation. By being able to identify and describe a feeling, for example, a child may learn to substitute verbal symbols for harmful actions.

Practitioners encourage reflection on feelings by making comments and asking questions to elaborate on and understand the feelings. Examples are: "Are you afraid that I'll criticize you if you tell me more about your fear of 'coming out of the closet?'" "Have you felt this depressed for long?" "What do you do when you feel depressed?" "You're troubled about Jennifer and infuriated with her, aren't you, and she knows this is how you feel," "You seem embarrassed to tell your parents that you have AIDS—how do you think they are going to feel when they know?" "You're afraid your father will kill you when he learns you are pregnant—can we look more closely at the basis of your fear?"

In a study of clients' reports on their experiences with therapists of different theoretical orientations, there was considerable consensus that the most helpful procedure, in addition to the relationship, was the recognition and clarification of feelings which clients had been approaching hazily and hesitantly.[28]

Paraphrasing. Paraphrasing is a way of mirroring behavior as it is observed by another. The workers or other members of a family or group may rephrase a statement so that the problem and situation are seen in a new way. Sometimes clients are not sure what they have said, because so many confused thoughts and feelings are connected with the words. When workers or members of groups can express what they heard, the sender of the message can decide whether what was heard was what was intended. The receiver of the message may respond with a request for clarification, It may then be possible to pursue the subject in more depth. Such an act may also enlist the participation of other members, since the worker's reflection of client activity is like an invitation to react further to what is being said.

Some examples are "Was the main point you were making that you don't know how to tell your fiance that his way of starting sex displeases you?" "Would another way of saying that be _____?" "Do I understand that you have definitely decided to get a divorce?" "You indicated that your anger with your son's behavior has become uncontrollable."

Making connections.   Perceptions of self in relation to others may be changed through bringing to consciousness and then understanding material that was previously suppressed. Through recognizing the connection between past experiences and current responses, a person may come to recognize that the present is not the past, but that some past experiences are messing up the present. Although many adaptive patterns can be modified with little or no clarification of the relation of past to present, some destructive patterns of behavior may be modified only if a person examines and reevaluates significant past experiences and their consequences for current functioning and future living. Reviewing past situations is a tool for helping people to learn from experience. Hutten has said that "allowing clients to talk with feeling about past traumas when they are re-evoked by present experiences is one of the opportunities we do have to intervene 'preventively' in relation to the future."[29] She notes that the discovery of continuities of experience can reopen a person's potential for further development. Coping capacities can be released when past experiences can be integrated into the personality "instead of having to be cut off or kept at bay by heavy psychic expenditure."

Reframing.   To reframe is to change the conceptual and emotional meaning of a situation or a set of facts. It is used to enable clients to put a new perspective on their problems. Segal gives an example:

> We treated a salesman who stuttered and wanted to rid himself of his speech impediment so he would make a better impression on people. The therapist was able to reframe his stuttering as an asset, distinguishing him from the usual high-pressured salesmen who people immediately turned off. Once he accepted this reframing, he viewed his impediment in a radical new way—as an advantage. In doing so, he no longer tried to stop himself from stuttering, and the problem all but disappeared.[30]

Middleman and Wood present the following example:

> After talking and playing with the anatomically correct dolls for a while, five-year-old Jennie told me that when her daddy bathes her, he gets into

the tub with her, puts her on his lap and pokes her peeper with his hot dog. She picked up the little girl doll and banged its head on the floor. I said, "Jennie, you didn't do anything bad." I picked up the daddy doll and compared it to the little girl doll. "Look," I said, "Daddy is a lot bigger than you. You were too little to make him stop." Then I cuddled the little girl doll and said, "The little girl wasn't bad. The big daddy was bad." She looked up at me with big eyes. "You're a good little girl," I said. She reached for my hand.[31]

Interpretation

Interpretation is a process of creating meanings. A major form of feedback consists of interpretations about the meaning of behavior. An interpretation is a statement that explains the possible meaning of an experience or an underlying motivation for behavior, or it is a seeking out of reasons for a particular difficulty in psychosocial functioning. It offers a new frame of reference for the client's consideration. It is a reconceptualization of the reasons for behavior, based on the practitioner's theories of human behavior and social environments. Interpretative statements are generally not offered until other forms of clarification have been used. They are directed toward the conscious or preconscious level of the personality. They are not offered by the worker until the clients have tried to find their own meanings. When workers add their contributions to the clients own efforts, they participate according to their judgment that the clients are ready for this, that they are almost ready to acknowledge the meanings themselves, and that there is a strong relationship to support and sustain the members in their work.

Interpretative statements are usually made in tentative forms of suggesting that something may account for something else, commenting that there are explanations for an event and requesting that the clients think of alternative ones, or putting an explanation in the form of a question that asks for consideration of its applicability to the particular situation. In a sense, any interpretation is a tentative hypothesis or a hypothetical question based on the worker's knowledge of people in their environments.

Within a therapeutic relationship, clients acquire enhanced understanding of themselves and other people when they discover explanations for their behavior. When the clients are not able to find their own explanations and the social worker has arrived at one or more tentative hypotheses, this understanding is offered to the clients. To a parent, the practitioner might say "You've said you don't want to be like your father was in disciplining you, but aren't you doing the same thing with Bobby?" Or, "I've noticed that whenever the group is talking about their mothers, you remain silent and look sad. Is that because you haven't yet been able to accept the fact that your mother is dead?" Or, "There seems to be some connection between your extreme anger and your father's illness that we need to try to understand."

Even young children can understand an appropriately worded interpretation. With a four-year-old boy, for example, a social worker said, "When you yell those curses, you are showing how very mad you are"; and to a little girl, "Your crying tells me that you feel very hurt about having been called names by the boys."

In a study of practice with families by Brown, it was found that practitioners often have difficulty in communicating the intent of their messages effectively.[32] The comments which were most effective were those that were clearly stated and contained only one basic idea: accurate, specific, and to the point; focused on the central problem under consideration; offered in a mood of sharing a perception with a client and in words that were consonant with actions; and offered in a tone of voice that was supportive and non-threatening. The comments tended to be effective when the worker was sensitive to the feelings and differential readiness of clients, thereby conveying acceptance and empathy. They were effective when the worker avoided taking sides in arguments and did not attack defenses; focused on relationships and interactions among people; encouraged clients to respond to the statement and allowed adequate time for the response; and offered opportunities for members to respond to each other. The comments tended to be effective when they related primarily to process as distinguished from manifest content; when there was emphasis on positive feelings and behavior as well as negatives; and when the message got at a theme that drew the members' ideas together.

Interpretations were judged as not helping clients when the worker's statement included numerous ideas so that clients did not get a cue as to which idea they were to respond to, or when too much information was given in a single message; such messages were vague, ambiguous, long, complex, and difficult to understand. They were not helpful when the worker inappropriately interrupted a client, allowed one member to respond for another, did not return to the first member's concern when others had interrupted, or inappropriately changed the subject. They were not helpful when workers enhanced defensiveness and withdrawal from participation. One of the judges summarized one worker's use of interpretation with the comment, "How we can deluge the client with words." Such volubility is something to be watched. Although the research on the use of interpretation was limited to meetings with families, it can be assumed that many of these findings would apply as well to work with individuals and formed groups.

A number of principles govern the use of techniques aimed at interpretation:

1. Interpretations should be based on sound assessment. They are helpful only if they are accurate, based on observation of the client and knowledge of human development and behavior in a network of interacting systems.

2. Assessment must be made of the families, groups, and the social context as well as the individuals. The worker needs to consider the phase of family or group development and the readiness of particular individuals to understand the what or why of their behavior, the emotional ties among them and the cohesiveness of the group.

3. In interpreting the meaning of feelings, behavior, or events, workers should usually offer their comments as impressions, suggestions, and opinions, not as facts. They encourage the individual, families or group to test out the meaning of their comments and to respond to them.

4. Workers should avoid generalizations that deal with the total person. Rather, they partialize the comments or questions to a particular feeling, behavioral pattern, or situation.

5. Comments and questions are most helpful when they are expressed clearly, simply, and directly. Usually the briefer and more concise the comments are, the better. It is important to present only one fact or thought at a time.

6. Workers need to follow through with considerable exploration of the reactions of an individual or members of a group to interpretations. Furthermore, whatever understanding has developed needs to be repeated in different forms over a period of time if it is to result in more adaptive behavior.

7. Interpretation is done at the conscious or preconscious levels of the personality. Usually, the focus is on the present. Recall of the past is facilitated and past events interpreted when such recall helps the person and other participants to understand the present.

8. Offering interpretations that explain the underlying meaning of behavior may threaten the ego's defenses; children and adults with weak egos need considerable support rather than attack. Anxiety that does not overwhelm the ego is useful so long as it is within a range that can be dealt with constructively.

9. As with any other activity, the worker's aim is to help individuals or groups to do as much as possible for themselves. Hence, questions that help people to identify and explain feelings, behavior, and situations are usually more effective than interpretations given by the worker in that the persons are helped to find the meanings themselves, But when meaning eludes people and is considered by the worker to be important to progress, interpretations are useful and sometimes essential.

10. A special characteristic of the use of interpretation in a group is that, to be useful, it need not be directed specifically to a person. During a period when a problematic situation develops, various members may present experiences, feelings, and make relevant comments. To the extent that the underlying theme of the content is relevant to a particular client's concerns, they may derive understanding of themselves and their experiences. Often when feelings or explanations are universalized, they touch closely on some member's particular concerns. This dynamic is what Konopka refers to as anonymity of insight.[33]

11. When working with more than one person, the worker needs to pay attention to the group process—the continuity of content, communicative abilities and patterns, emotional ties, and roles of workers and members. Individual reflection and introspection are pursued when they can be connected to the needs of others. The worker finds the thread of connections between one individual's need and the needs of others. There is a tendency for social workers to direct interpretation to individuals rather than to the group system. If more interpretations were directed to the group, it is likely that a greater sense of relatedness and cohesiveness would develop.

In a review of several studies on the use of interpretation in short-term groups, Dies concluded that: "The accumulated evidence, then, strongly supports the value of interpretation as a vehicle for therapeutic change."[34] Another study also found that the qualities of relationship were necessary ingredients in successful outcome, but only when combined with work toward improved cognitive understanding.[35]

Facilitation of the Group Process

Work with families and other groups utilizes all of the skills or sets of techniques that are used in work with individuals. There are also, however, techniques that are specific to the group system, whether family or peer group. There are generic skills, but there are additional ones that are used when the client system consists of two or more persons. The common element underlying these techniques is that of using the group interaction in order to maximize the value of the group for its members. The worker's focus is less concentrated on each individual and more on connecting members to each other so they can be of greater help to each other. The group is a mutual support and mutual aid system.[36]

The social worker guides the group process so as to maximize its value as the primary instrument of treatment. In order to achieve this intent, the worker needs to understand process as a series of psychosocial interactions between and among all the participants, including the worker. Group discussion is not a series of conversations between the social worker and each member serially; rather, it engages as fully as possible each member in a group-centered interaction process, usually reflective in nature. The worker does communicate with specific individuals, but also observes the effect of their actions on the group. Focus on the group does not negate the importance of the individual. When the focus is upon interpersonal interaction, neither the individual nor the group is submerged: both are viewed as equally important. Neither can be fully understood without the other.

The social worker follows several lines of communication simultaneously: the needs and contributions of individuals related to the group; the interplay between emotion and cognition; the interplay between manifest and latent content; and the patterns of communication among the members. These thought processes get translated into the differential use of the other skills and a decision as to whether to address an individual or the group as a whole.

The special skills are attending to the family or group system, encouraging participation, and exploring for common and diverse interests,

Attending to the Group System

Attending involves scanning and using nonverbal messages to indicate that each member is valued and addressing the group as a whole. Comments might include "I notice that we're all here today," "I see that the couples are sitting together but are talking across couples also." Practitioners avoid engaging one member in a dialogue for an extended period of time, with others as an audience. When that happens, other members tend to become passive and bored, and the group becomes ineffective as a means of help. They do not respond verbally to every contribution made by each member for that would detract from the give and take among the members. Rather, they request that others respond to the messages that have been sent and tend to address their own comments and questions to the group as a whole, rather than to a particular member. The worker, however, does pay attention to the needs and contributions of individuals, but, in doing so, observes the effect this has on other members and on the group.

Encouraging Participation

Social workers make efforts to involve each member of the group as fully as possible. They do this through such means as inviting participation in general or of particular individuals. Examples of comments might be: "Jane, you look like you may want to say something," "What do the rest of you think about what Mr. James has said?" "Let's play a get-acquainted game," "It's all right to remain silent now, but you'll get more out of the group when you're ready to participate more actively," "I notice the boys have done most of the talking: could we give the girls a chance now?" Most importantly, such comments demonstrate that an individual's needs and interests can be met, at least partially, by participation in the group. Exploratory questions and comments that ask members to talk about their goals and interests and indicating that these are appropriate to this group, tends to enhance participation.

Exploring for Common and Diverse Interests and Needs

Through exploration, practitioners bring out the common and diverse attitudes, feelings, and ideas about the members and their situations. In family treatment, for example, the practitioner said: "Mr. Matson thinks it would be good if the family went camping for your vacation. Mrs. Matson seems to think it would be better to go to a nice resort. What about you children: you might have even different ideas." To a group of foster adolescents, "some of you like your foster parents very much, but Joan and Kathryn don't have such good feelings about theirs. But, you all have said you would rather be back in your own homes." Or, "Donna has said that she feels she has been discriminated against on her job. Have any of the rest of you had such an experience?" The practitioner recognizes the differences, but simultaneously searches for the common ground.

The practitioner recognizes the underlying agreements and explores disagreements among members in order to help the members to clarify their own positions, to understand that their position is not the only one and, when appropriate, to move toward resolution of conflicts that are created by differences. Some differences are due to lack of accurate facts or misrepresentation of facts; some are due to differences in values that concern what is desirable or worthwhile. What needs to be dealt with is the meaning of these differences in relation to a particular situation, not at an abstract level of generalization. In order to find the sources of conflict, the worker listens and watches the facial and body expressions of the members to understand the approvals and disapprovals, questions, or concerns. The worker may respond to help the group accept the right of members to hold unpopular opinions, and to accept and appreciate differences.

The worker is concerned with group process because the primary means of help when using a group are the support and stimulation that members give each other, supplemented by the worker's direct contributions to the work of the client system. Changes in attitudes and behavior occur when members are actively involved in the group; when they are able both to give and to take from others. They benefit from perceiving both their likenesses to, and differences from, others. Thus, the focus is on the development of meaningful group interaction without losing sight of individuals. Sharing of individual thought is necessary so that each member can become aware of what others are feeling and thinking and use this knowledge for appraisal of that individual's own feelings, thoughts, and actions. Individual satisfactions are essential to the development of cohesive groups which have great influence on their members. The worker therefore needs to make sure that the group becomes a mutual aid and mutual need-meeting system.

All of these skills involve give and take among the members with the worker in providing mutual support and mutual help for the benefit of all. The selection of skills is always specific to a situation. No one skill results in positive changes; rather a constellation of skills is used to meet the particular needs of members of particular groups. There are clear indications from the study by Lieberman, Yalom, and Miles that practitioners who convey acceptance, empathy, and genuineness: provide support for the members' efforts; use a cognitive framework that enables members to understand themselves, other people, and their situations; and facilitate the group processes so as to ensure the working of positive forces, generally have the best results.[37] In the use of any of the skills, the mutual aid potential of the group is furthered when the object of the worker's intervention is the group as a whole or the interrelations among the parts, as contrasted with work with one member at a time. The particular combination of skills used are based on the assessment of the clients as members of families or groups. Assessment is the subject of chapter 8.

Eight | Assessment

Throughout most of the history of social work practice, efforts have been made to understand persons in their situations and thus to provide services that can meet their needs. Helping individuals or families to meet their needs more adequately is based on particularizing them in their environment, that is, in the network of interlocking social systems of which a person is a part. It is a basic principle of practice that workers individualize their work with people. Individualization occurs when people's needs and capacities and the special qualities of their environment are taken into consideration.

Regardless of whether the early pioneers were most concerned with individuals, groups, or communities, they gradually learned that problems are caused by multiple transactions within a system and between the system and the environment. Jane Addams, that great pioneer in the settlement house movement, wrote dramatically about a lesson learned the hard way. Scientific knowledge of social and political situations had always guided Addams' approach to neighborhood improvement and broader social reform. She insisted that social action should be preceded by carefully ascertained facts. She learned, through trial and error, that this is true for help to individuals as well.

In one example, she notified a man that employment was available on a drainage canal and advised him to take the job so that he could receive assistance for his family. He went to work, as she recommended, but he died of pneumonia shortly thereafter. In focusing only on employment, she had failed to acquire other knowledge about the man and his family. From such experiences she learned that "life cannot be administered by

definite rules and regulations . . . the wisdom to deal with a man's difficulties comes only through knowledge of his life and habits as a whole:
and to treat isolated episodes is almost sure to invite blundering."[1] She
concluded that it is necessary to know people through varying conditions
of life. She accepted the need to understand individuals, their families,
and their other social relationships as these interconnect with the conditions that affect their lives.

Mary E. Richmond, in 1917, espoused the idea that social workers
need to understand clients in their social situations. In what she called
social diagnosis, the social worker makes as exact a definition as possible
of the person and the situation, "that is, in relation to other human beings
upon whom he in any way depends or who depend upon him, and in relation to the social institutions of the community."[2]

That theme of person-situation has persisted over time. To achieve
such understanding, scientific knowledge about individuals, families,
small groups, and environments is necessary. The emphasis is on the connections between the individuals, families, and networks of social relationships and community conditions and resources. The need, as
expressed by Lee, is "direct simultaneous concern with people and environments."[3]

Defining Assessment

All definitions of clinical social work regard assessment as a necessary
process. Assessment is the process whereby a clinical social worker, with
maximum participation of clients, acquires differential and accurate
understanding of the person-family-situation gestalt. Consistent with a
generic biopsychosocial systems perspective, Vigilante and Mailick state
that "the assessment process is based upon a triumvirate of assumptions.
It assumes that all human phenomena are best understood in a multi-
causal interacting framework; that the concept of needs and resources
reflects the intentions, purposes and values of the social work profession;
and that person-in-situation can effectively become the vehicle for selection of the unit of attention."[4] Meyer writes "assessment is a cognitive
process, a form of logical analysis, where a practitioner comes to know
his or her case through acknowledgment of the client's own story, interpreted through the screen of an available knowledge base that is relevant
to the case situation."[5]

The term "diagnosis" continues to be used by some social workers
interchangeably with "assessment." The term "assessment" has become
prevalent in order to distinguish the process of biopsychosocial *assess-*

ment from clinical or medical *diagnoses*. Assessment takes into account not only the definition of the problem or disorder, but the motivation, capacities, and competence of persons interacting in their networks of social relationships in a given community with its environmental obstacles and opportunities.

A social worker uses knowledge of social systems, first to understand individuals, families, and groups in situations and then to plan and guide treatment. Skill in analysis of the situation requires the ability to use a conceptual framework for organizing observations and for planning services. The behavioral science base, as previously described, is used as a guide to determine what the practitioner takes into account in formulating an assessment. Even when it is predetermined that individual help will be given, it is important for the worker to understand the structure and processes of the client's family—the mutual impact of members on each other and problems and strengths in the family's functioning. It is important to assess the influence of the individual's and family's reference groups on their values, goals, and behavior. Likewise, it is important to assess wider environmental influences, regardless of the nature and size of the client system that is to use the service.

A basic assumption underlying the framework for assessment is that human behavior is the product of the transactions between individuals and their environments. Individuals have an interdependent relationship with others; they are part of a number of interlocking social systems, and certain dimensions of their behavior can be understood only in terms of the purposes, structures, functions, and development of these networks of interaction and a given individual's status and role in them. The worker's assessment is, therefore, related both to individual and social dimensions. At both individual and group levels, the practitioner is concerned with the nature of stresses derived from internal and external forces that disrupt the steady state; and the capacity and motivation of the persons involved to withstand stress, cope with change, and find new or modified ways of feeling, thinking, and behaving.

Needs and Problems

The needs and problems of clients are greatly varied. Although each individual and family is different from all others in some respects, their problems typically fall within a limited number of categories.

Reid has developed a classification of problems for task-centered social work practice and tested its reliability. The categories were built upon earlier formulations by Reid and Shyne and Reid and Epstein,[6] and include interpersonal conflict, dissatisfaction in social relations, problems with formal organizations, difficulties in role performance, decision problems, reactive emotional distress, inadequate resources, and psychological or behavioral problems not elsewhere classified.

Building on the work of Reid and his associates and knowledge of types of problems occurring frequently in the biopsychosocial system approach to practice, the following categories are suggested.

Lack of Economic and Social Resources

Many clients of social and health agencies face a frustrating array of social problems occasioned by the lack of adequate income, housing, employment, day care facilities, legal aid, medical resources, and discrimination.[7] Many neighborhoods lack adequate health, recreational, and educational opportunities, aesthetic qualities, and public transportation.

In many such situations the problem is created primarily by external factors over which an individual has little control and is responding in normal ways. Deficiencies in tangible means and resources restrict and thwart the ambitions of people and limit their abilities to relate to others. Lack of essential material resources may lead to stress in personal and family functioning and also may deprive people of opportunities to associate with others in mutually enriching ways. In our society, money is highly valued and necessary for fulfilling personal, social, and emotional needs as well as for physical survival. Unemployment or dependency on public welfare often brings stigma and disrespect to persons and their families, leading in turn to loss of self-esteem and self-confidence. "All poor people do not have psychological, social, and relationship problems, but being poor greatly increases one's vulnerability," Orcutt observed.[8]

Unsatisfactory Role Functioning

Problems in role functioning often are in the nature of lack of preparedness for the role, lack of clarity about expectations as in step-parent families, failure to meet expectations of other people, loss of a valued role such as that of employee, conflict in carrying two or more roles, too many responsibilities in a given role, such as single parent, or unavailability of suitable roles to match the interests and abilities of a person.[9] Lack of knowledge, skills, opportunities, and resources often contribute to the problem. In many instances, socialization into roles has been inadequate.

Loss of Relationships

Separation from some significant relationship or set of relationships with particular others is a source of many difficulties. Separation of children from one or both parents creates serious psychosocial problems for both the child and the parents. Filial deprivation experienced by parents when children enter foster care is a complement to the more widely studied concept of maternal deprivation.[10] Loss of meaningful relationships with relatives and friends usually accompanies placement of elderly persons in nursing homes, particularly when relocation is not voluntary or when refugees leave relatives and friends behind in the old country. Loneliness, a sense of loss, and grief accompany separation from others.

Death of a loved one, of course, is the most devastating form of separation, at whatever phase in the life cycle it occurs. The survivors must cope with intense feelings of sorrow, loneliness, isolation, guilt, grief, and depression. They must cope with changes in economic and social circumstances. In addition to the emotional reactions to the loss of the deceased person, the survivors experience strains in relationships with other people and difficulties in developing new relationships or deepening existing ones.

Dissatisfactions in Social Relationships

Relationships with other people are influenced by intrapsychic and interactional problems.[11] People often feel severe dissatisfaction with their relationships. They perceive deficiencies or excesses in their relationships with others. They may fear intimate relationships or be unable to develop intimacy when such a relationship is desired; they may feel concern about the inadequacy of their sexual adjustment. They may suffer from extreme shyness or timidity, leading to deep feelings of loneliness. They may feel that they are unable to be assertive in appropriate ways; that they are too abrasive or overly aggressive; or that they are excessively vulnerable to the criticism of others. Low self-esteem or a distorted sense of identity may prevent them from entering into and maintaining relationships with desired others. Research by Gilligan concludes that "the central theme of girls' own stories is an intense concern and a persisting quest for authentic relationships and genuine connection." Konopha's research on the problems of adolescent girls confirms this finding. Inability to develop and maintain affectional bonds with others is one major difficulty in mental disorders. Whittaker, for example, found that the most severe disturbance in autistic children is the failure to develop satisfactory social relationships.[12]

Interpersonal Conflict

Conflict in central life relationships is frequent, predominantly between marital partners, partners living together outside marriage, parents and one or more children, siblings, or other relatives.[13] There may be conflict in other relationships also, such as those between close friends, pupil and teacher, worker and supervisor, or colleagues.

Conflict may be overt as evidenced in uncontrolled arguments or physical violence. Spouse and child abuse, incest, rape, and assault have become major problems with which social workers increasingly are dealing.

Conflict may be covert and expressed through such means as withdrawal from open communication or displacement of hostility onto other people, as when one member of a family or group becomes a scapegoat or rejected isolate. All interpersonal conflict manifests as difficulties in relationships among people. Essentially, interpersonal conflict involves interlocking patterns of interaction between and among people.

Psychosocial Components of Illness and Disability

Problems in psychosocial functioning are associated with particular illnesses and disabilities.[14] Various social, emotional, economic, and environmental stresses accompany mental or physical illness or physical handicaps. Illness is a stressor that renders a person vulnerable to other problems and other problems aggravate the illness. Ell and Northen reviewed research on the effect of illness on the patient's family and the effect of the family's response on the patient: patient and family well-being are inextricably interrelated.[15] In addition to the illness itself, both patients and their families often face the stigma associated with such life threatening diseases as AIDS and cancer or illnesses and handicaps that are visible, such as epilepsy and loss of limbs.

Culture Conflict

In our society, there is often conflict among persons and between groups, based on cultural differences, prejudice, or discrimination.[16] Interpersonal dissatisfactions and conflicts are often based, at least in part, on cultural differences. Certain ethnic groups have values that may not be understood by others, creating problems for their members in making choices and adapting effectively to their environments. Differences in values may be expressed in attitudes toward time, material possessions, work, family structure, role expectations, individual versus family decision-making authority, and competition versus cooperation. Members of minority cultures particularly are faced with such decisions as holding to or violating norms regarding food preferences, customs and traditions, family planning, divorce, premarital and extramarital sex, and other personal morals. Adaptation is complicated for persons who have been socialized into one culture whose value system conflicts with the value system of one or more other cultures of which the person is a part. Many people must learn to integrate some aspects of two or more cultures, often made the more difficult because their own culture is devalued by the dominant society. Chau refers to this problem as cultural dissonance.[17]

Members of one culture may become hostile toward the dominant culture when they know that their rights are violated through legal and social inequities and discrimination in housing, employment, education, and health care. Feelings of distrust, suspicion, resentment, and hostility often characterize relationships between members of groups who differ in regard to race, ethnicity, or religion. The result may be negative stereotyping, interpersonal or intergroup tensions, even violence. People may hold attitudes that restrict their own choices or they may be the victims of the attitudes of others toward them. Insecurity in a parental role may be aggravated if the family's own values and norms are too different from those of the groups which influence the child. Parent-child conflicts develop when children reject their parents' values and expectations, wanting to adapt to the majority culture when the parents are trying to maintain the culture into which they were socialized. Conflict between cultures, then, can result in a variety of intrapersonal, interpersonal, and group conflicts, particularly for new arrivals.

Conflicts with Formal Organizations

Problems of this type occur between an individual and another person, but the difficulty is not with the person per se, but with a position or role in an organization.[18] The person in the role represents the organization which is perceived to be withholding desired services or otherwise acting against the best interests of the client. Adolescents, for example, do not experience authority in school and law enforcement agencies as particular persons, but as strangers or impersonal enemies who make demands on them. Another example is common distrust of the welfare system. The conflict occurs with a representative of the system, but the major dissatisfaction is with the policies, procedures, values, or functions of the system itself. Clients often feel powerless to secure the information or resources to which they feel entitled.

Making Decision

Clients often need help to make decisions,[19] the outcome of which are important to their well-being and future satisfactions. Important life choices include marriage, divorce, birth control, disclosure of a serious illness or sexual orientation, a move to a new environment, changes in work or education, and awesome decisions concerning medical care and treatment. Clients need to resolve their ambivalence and clarify the probable consequences of alternative choices. The decisions that are made will affect not only the client, but family members and significant other persons as well.

Maladaptive Group Functioning

Difficulties often occur at a family or group level of functioning.[20] The condition or situation that is thought to be undesirable is dysfunction in the properties of the group. Interpersonal relationships may be unsatisfying to the members or dysfunctional to the welfare of particular individuals and the group as a whole. There may be lack of mutual affection and acceptance among members: the members may be unable to enjoy each other. The group may need to isolate, scapegoat, demean, or glorify one or more members. There may be discrepancies among individuals' orientations to love, authority, and group identity or conflicting loyalties between members of the group and between the family and other significant persons in the environment.

The composition of a group may be faulty, for example, when a foster child is placed in a family inappropriate to the child and the family's needs or when a group is so large that individual needs are unknown or ignored. The "fit" between the person and environment is faulty.

The roles in the group may contribute to inadequate group functioning. There may be a missing role, as when one parent separates from the family or an elder child leaves home, requiring a redistribution of the tasks performed by the missing member. Some members may perform their roles inadequately, resulting in disequilibrium and conflict. Members may disagree about what to expect of a person in a particular role, or they may not be clear about roles and responsibilities. There may be lack of sufficient differentiation, constancy, and flexibility in the social organization of the group.

Patterns of verbal and nonverbal communication among the members are often faulty, so that individuals lose touch with each other. There may be lack of opportunities for some or most members to express their concerns, opinions, and desires and to learn how these tie in with concerns, opinions, and desires of others. There may be inappropriate balance between the demands for self-disclosure and privacy. There may be inadequate mechanisms for making decisions and solving problems that affect all members of the group. Patterns and means of communication are closely tied to the achievement of individual and group goals. There may be little mutual understanding of goals. If goals are known, there may be lack of support of individual goals or lack of means to achieve group goals.

All these factors are interrelated and interdependent, since a group is a system of interdependent components. As a result of the interaction among many facets of the group, there may be lack of cohesiveness. The members are not attracted to each other and to the welfare of the group, resulting in apathy and lack of group identity and loyalty. Such groups do not share common goals, values, and norms and are unable to meet the needs of the members.

Medical and Psychiatric Diagnoses

In medicine, diagnosis is defined as the art and science of identifying a disorder or disability. In contrast, social work deals with psychosocial problems. The use of medical and psychiatric diagnoses is an issue for the profession. It is generally agreed that if a physical disease is suspected, a physician makes the diagnosis and is responsible for the medical treatment. Even so, social workers need to be alert to symptoms that suggest an illness, to the symptoms of drug use and the effects drugs have on people, and to the psychosocial aspects of illness and disability. Physical, social, and psychological well-being are intimately interrelated: when medical problems are suspected, it is necessary to rule out the presence of organic conditions through referral to, or consultation with, physicians. Social workers practicing in health settings need considerable knowledge about diseases to make appropriate psychosocial assessments.

The use of diagnoses of mental disorders in social work practice is another matter of controversy in the profession. Regardless of their attitudes toward attaching diagnostic labels to clients, many social workers are now required by government, insurance companies, or funding agencies to classify their clients' difficulties according to the categories in the *Diagnostic and Statistical Manual* of the American Psychiatric Association.[21] First published in 1980, *DSM III* was intended to clarify many of the commonly used diagnoses. *DSM III-R*, a revised edition, was published in 1987 and has recently been revised for publication.[22] This manual is generally consistent with the International Classification of Disease (ICD) developed by the World Health Organization, which covers both medical and mental diseases. *DSM* conceptualizes each disorder as a clinically significant behavioral or psychological syndrome, which is typically associated with painful symptoms or impairment of functioning.

Surveys have indicated that DSM is widely used in social work education and practice, but there is controversy concerning its suitability to assessment, planning, and treatment in the profession.[23] Many social workers strongly favor the use of classifications of mental disorders. Perhaps, the strongest favorable statement is that of Fishman, who said, "It is argued that DSM is a fount of helpful information and a source of reassurance: to name the demon is to take a step toward taming it."[24] She recognizes that it, however, is only a point of departure for a psychosocial assessment. Turner agrees that labels are important aids to conscious and deliberate planning and treatment. Williams asserts that the use of DSM III categories is important for social work because it contributes to effective communication among mental health professionals; to effective evaluation and treatment planning; it is useful in teaching psychopathology; and has potential for furthering research. Woods and Hollis have made similar points in their support of the use of DSM.[25]

Classification and Labels

The objections to the use of the classification of mental disorders concern the unreliability of some of the diagnoses, the impact of a diagnosis of mental illness on clients, and the danger of overlooking physical conditions that often accompany mental problems.

The primary objection refers to labeling persons as "deviant." The use of labels is thought to play a crucial role in the development and maintenance of deviant behavior: people tend to behave according to the expectations conveyed by the label.[26] The label also tends to create stereotyped reactions from others. When categories are not adapted to new information, they become perpetuated in their initial form. The label may then become an instrument of social control, as when children with handicaps in the use of English are labeled mentally retarded and progressively denied equal educational opportunities. When people are inappropriately labeled, they are devalued and stigmatized. The diagnosis can become a self-fulfilling prophecy: the way a problem is defined determines its solution.

Labels tend to be unidimensional, whereas people are multidimensional. As Reid notes, most mental disorders are a product of complex interactions among the client, other persons, and collectivities; diagnoses, particularly of mental disorders, do not account adequately for the sociocultural and environmental aspects of problems. Labels often give practitioners a false sense of confidence in their understanding of clients. Furthermore, they emphasize problems rather than positive motivations, capacities, and achievements. Reid noted that "categories of deviance, particularly psychiatric labels, are given more weight than they merit."[27]

In spite of reservations, most scientists argue that some form of categorization is necessary. Lewis strongly asserts the need for typologies to serve diagnostic ends: " A sound assessment scheme should free the worker to consider more carefully the unique aspects of individual requests and to tailor the process of intervention to fit the peculiarities of each instance of a class of cases."[28] Lewis was not referring to any particular kind of classification scheme, but emphasizing the point that categories are essential to orderly thinking.

Kutchins and Kirk offer a set of principles for assuring the proper use of classifications of mental disorders:

1. All diagnoses should be made with scrupulous regard for correct procedures.
2. Careful attention should be paid to organic conditions.
3. A physician should be routinely consulted about the medical aspects of a diagnosis.
4. Every diagnosis should be accurately reported to the client and to the insurer.
5. Clients should be advised, preferably in writing, that no diagnosis is meant to indicate a definitive judgment about any physical condition.
6. Clients should be referred to physicians for the evaluation of any medical condition.[29]

Identifying Psychosocial Problems

Assessment in clinical social work may include diagnosis of physical or mental disorders, but goes beyond that to a focus on the interrelation of physical, psychological, and sociocultural factors related to a particular difficulty. Certain principles serve as guides to clarifying the nature of the clients' problems.

1. The problem should be based on facts, not inferences, and it should be defined in operational terms.

2. Classifications are merely tools that alert a practitioner to major combinations of relevant factors. They are thus useful in communicating the central tendency of the condition to colleagues.

3. The classification influences what is perceived and how the perceptions are organized for action. Formulating a useful psychosocial assessment requires knowledge beyond that in the classification. The evaluation is of patterns of behavior or sets of environmental obstacles, not of a person or family.

4. Classification is a means of ascertaining what characteristics a person or family has in common with other individuals or groups in a population. It emphasizes also what is unique in the person or family, that is, how an individual or group differs from others of its type. This is the well-known principle of individualization.

5. Problems are viewed not as existing in the person only, but as a characteristic of the person-situation interaction. Interpersonal, environmental, and intrapersonal processes are all taken into account in defining the problem.

6. In undertaking service with a client identified as having a particular type of problem, the social worker does not permit the label to obscure the client's strengths or the value of intervening in a variety of systems to meet the client's needs.

7. The search for understanding is reciprocal between a practitioner and a client. In line with social work values, workers have a right and a responsibility to participate actively in the process, but so, too, do the clients, for they are full participants in all aspects of the process. The assessment is tentative, to be modified in the crucible of client system-worker interaction.

Sources of Information

The psychosocial study of the individual-group-situation configuration is accomplished through a variety of means. *Epidemiology*, according to Meyer, is as essential for a social worker as for a doctor.[30] Knowledge about the characteristics of caseloads and the common needs of people living in an agency's catchment area is important in setting priorities for service. Preventive, developmental, and community action services are based on knowledge of the extent of the problem or condition and the demographic characteristics of persons affected by the condition.

Even in treating one individual, neglect of epidemiological data can distort the reality of the lives of people. If, for example, a social worker assumes that a seven-year-old girl who is failing in school, both academically and socially, is an isolated instance of deviance, she is treated individually and labeled as a deviant. If, however, a survey is taken of the school population of seven-year-olds, the social worker may discover that the condition is widespread, especially among children from minority groups or those living in poor neighborhoods. Such a survey was made in one large city, resulting in the implementation of social work services under the joint auspices of the public schools and a voluntary agency.[31]

Although the worker still has a responsibility to help the initial client, the incidence of the difficulty also suggests broader programs of reaching out to offer services to all those who share a common condition or of participating in community action toward solutions to the problem. Awareness of the common need of families for information about diabetes and its consequences, for example, resulted in the provision of informational meetings for patients and their relatives.

Direct service workers have a responsibility beyond that to their clients. Agencies should be concerned with translating private troubles into public issues.[32] When workers have encountered a number of similar needs or difficulties among those whom they serve, it becomes a public issue. They have a responsibility to address themselves to the policy issue, at least by reporting the situation to relevant persons and groups in the community who can work on it. Through this process, social problems of significance to many people are identified and a start is made in the assessment of their nature, extent, and severity.

Individual Sessions

The most frequent source of data for use in assessment is the personal interview with prospective clients in which facts about them and their situations are elicited and in which there is exploration of their view of their needs and situation. Individual interviews are thought to be especially useful in understanding and clarifying the particular goals that clients hope to achieve and their reactions to the available services and the conditions under which they are given. They offer an opportunity to explore feelings and information which, at this time, might not be shared within the family or other groups until there is enough trust and support by a worker for doing so. They are useful in screening, referring, and preparing individuals for experiences in groups. It must be remembered also that many persons are not living in a family, so they need to be interviewed individually at the outset.

Within the interview, Goldstein emphasizes that "the approach to the client should be self evident; combine what we now know about the boundless ways by which people create their respective realities with basic practice principles and values" in order to give persons as Richmond put it, "a fair and patient hearing."[33] With sensitive listening to the clients' own stories, a practitioner can discover the meaning of the problems and the situation to the clients and begin to develop a relationship based on trust, acceptance, empathy, and genuineness.

Worker-Client Relationship

The relationship between a worker and the individual or group is a crucial source of information for use in assessment. Practitioners can learn much about an individual or a group through examining their own spontaneous reactions.

The idea is that emotional reactions are provoked by clients. A worker may identify strongly with a person, desire to become intimate with that person, or have feelings of pity, hopelessness, anger, or rejection. Workers consider not only what it is within them that stirs up these reactions, but also what there is in the relationship between worker and client that results in such behavior. It is often true that a person or group elicits similar reactions from other people also; a pattern of interpersonal behavior that is destructive to the client may be involved.

The other side of the reactions of the worker, of course, is the client's reaction to the worker. Some of the reactions are realistic perceptions of the other people, but some of them are in the nature of transference or countertransference reactions. It is a two-way process: both worker and client behave in ways that affect the other: a process of mutual influence is occurring.

Couples and Family Sessions

Increasingly, joint and family sessions are used as the major procedure or as supplementary to interviews with individuals. Joint sessions usually consist of two clients, such as husband and wife or parent and child. There are special values in the use of joint and family interviews for purposes of assessment. In a nationwide survey of agencies affiliated with the Family Service Association of America, there was more use of joint than of family interviews, but the values for both types were similar.[34] With the exception of one local association that was opposed to all multiple-client approaches, all respondents were enthusiastic about the many values of joint interviews with couples who were seeking help for marital problems. Although fewer social workers used interviews with family units, those who did concurred that there were unique values in both modalities. The values stemmed from the opportunity provided for simultaneous observation and evaluation of both partners or the entire family. The most frequently mentioned value was improved understanding of each individual and of the interactional patterns among them. Family sessions revealed interaction in ways similar to joint interviews, but there was a sense of increased subtlety of understanding and greater illumination of marital relationships and family functioning.

Five major contributions of joint and family interviews to the assessment of marital problems were found:

1. They reveal often hidden strengths and positive mutual bonds within the marriage and the family that may become essential therapeutic aids.
2. They illuminate the way in which family members interact with pathological destructiveness, restrictiveness, and mutual pain.
3. They provide greater clarity about the life situation of the couple or family, especially when home visits are used.
4. They make possible greater speed and accuracy in assessment.
5. They provide improved opportunities for the worker to observe the impact of treatment on the couple and the members of the family. (p. 53)

From a review of the literature and this empirical study, Couch concluded that there is emerging a fairly consistent approach to assessment. There is a decided trend toward emphasis on the current situation, although historical data are not being neglected. Another trend is to assign to intake the same worker who will have ongoing responsibility for the case, so that assessment and treatment are interwoven.

> Finally, the diagnostic microscope has been fitted with a wide-angle lens, with the result that the picture under scrutiny looks different. No longer does the individual loom largest, with marriage, family, workaday world, and the wider society seen as background for him. Instead, he is now viewed at one and the same time as a unit and as a functional part of various groups, each of which is in turn part of a larger cluster—the marital combination, the family group, the work group, and similar face-to-face associations. Beyond these, the wider society and the great universe itself form, as it were, concentric circles infinitely expanding outward, with no hard and impenetrable lines dividing the individual unit from the marital or family constellation or from other family groupings and the encompassing wider circles. (p. 54)

Group Services

Similar values accrue from meetings of clients in small groups for purposes of assessment: for example, with adoptive parents, children referred to child guidance centers, and patients or their relatives.[35] Such group procedures have been found to have values similar to those of family sessions, but with additional values in providing insight into the nature and quality of relationships with peers. In children's groups, the relationship with an adult practitioner gives clues concerning strengths and difficulties in relationships with other adults, both parents and others with whom the child has an association. Such groups augment the limited information provided by parents, teachers, nurses, and doctors. In one family service center, it was found that groups provided an accurate and vivid vision of the child's level of functioning.[36]

Measuring Instruments and Graphics

Measuring instruments are increasingly used by social workers to obtain and analyze data relative to the assessment of problems and person-situation configurations.[37] Many social workers make little use of scales and other instruments, preferring to use unobtrusive methods in which observation and data collection are part of an ongoing process of interaction between the worker and clients. They often distrust devices that might intrude on the developing professional relationship and the exploratory dialogue between the worker and clients. Some practitioners have learned, however, that selective use of such tools can improve assessment, further the treatment process, and document the outcome of the helping endeavor.

Manuals of mental and physical disorders are forms of instruments. A wide variety of other instruments are available, including self rating inventories, questionnaires, formal scales, and simulations that measure some aspects of psychological or social functioning. Some of the instruments and descriptions of others can be found in Ell and Northen, Hudson, Levitt and Reid, and Toseland and Rivas.[38] The tools used need to be clearly related to the goals of service and to the particular needs of the individual, family, or group that is being served.

Graphics present data in pictorial form to help the reader to quickly grasp the essence of the phenomenon being considered. Statistical graphs and tables have long been used for presenting complex data in forms that can be easily understood. Sociograms have long been used in group work to depict the relationships among members of a group in terms of leadership-followership and positive and negative ties.[39] Similarly, the eco-map pictures a person's relationships in the family or household and also in the extended family and groups and organizations in the community.[40] The genogram or family tree has gained popularity, particularly among family therapists. It records information graphically about family members and their relationships and ancestry over a period of at least three generations.[41]

Eco-maps that trace an individual's or family's social network are useful in assessment and decision-making processes. In a recent book, Meyer devotes an entire chapter to a presentation of the use of graphics for assessment.[42] She emphasizes that pictures do not substitute for words: rather they are intended to simplify complex data. Words are necessary to describe, elaborate, and explain events, behavior, emotions, attitudes, and relationships.

Content of Assessment

The amount and nature of the data sought vary with the many facets of the service, particularly its purpose and structure. The understanding of the client-group-situation gestalt that is sought cannot include all aspects of the individual's or group's functioning. In accord with the value of the right to privacy, it should be limited to what is essential to achieving agreed-upon goals. If a service is one of primary prevention or enhancement of development, the data obtained are often limited initially to the descriptive characteristics common to the clients, such as phase of development, common experience or status, and certain potential risks to healthy development. Later, during the process of service, the worker may elicit additional information as it seems particularly relevant, or as individuals who exhibit special problems are identified. If the service is a therapeutic or rehabilitative one, helpful treatment cannot be given unless the worker has adequate understanding of the nature, causative factors, and course of the problematic situation. Such understanding must be combined with understanding of the psychosocial aspects of the problem and the adequacy of the client's current functioning in particular situations.

The structure of the service provides boundaries for exploration concerning people in their situations. For example, when an individual is in a state of crisis, the information sought centers around the precipitating events and the emotional reactions to it. In short-term formed groups, the goals are usually specific to a problem or status shared by members, and the content of the assessment is thus limited to that which is most pertinent to the focus of the group. In work with a family or other natural group, a major focus will be on the adequacy of the structure, composition, relationships, communication, and decision-making processes. In work with formed groups, the worker will be alert to cues to understanding the patterns of relationships, communication, and problem-solving as these develop; be aware of sources of conflict among members or between the group and other systems related to differences in values, goals, role expectations, status, and power; and evaluate the influence of the composition of the group on its functioning. The need is to base the content of the assessment on what will aid the practitioner in understanding a particular client system in a particular situation.

Gordon Hamilton, an early social work leader, said that "diagnosis is not a secret labeling of the client, it is not an uncontrolled adventure into the mysteries of life: it is a realistic, thoughtful, frank, and scientific attempt to understand the client's present need, which is always a person-in-situation."[43] Although she used the term "diagnosis," her statement clearly applies to psychosocial assessment. Content to be considered in formulating assessments of individuals and groups may be outlined as follows:[44]

INDIVIDUALS

1. Description of the agency or other setting in which service is given.
2. Identifying information about the primary client and family.
3. Presenting problems and precipitating factors.
4. Relevant historical data.
5. Assessment of personality factors: adaptation, stress, coping, and ego functions.
6. Status, roles, and relationships.
7. Relevant functioning of the family system.
8. Individual and cultural values and experiences of oppression related to race, ethnicity, religion.
9. Biological factors: health, illness, medications, drugs.
10. Diagnosis of mental disorder, when appropriate.
11. Relationship to the community including social supports, use of resources, and environmental obstacles.

GROUPS, INCLUDING FAMILIES

1. Goals that are common among members and those that are specific to individuals.
2. Strengths and difficulties in the quality, depth, and patterns of relationships.
3. Structure and composition of the group and recent changes in membership.
4. Effectiveness of patterns of communication among the members.
5. Flexibility and adaptability to maintain a dynamic steady state.

6. Influence of the history of the group on current functioning.
7. Major subsystems and alliances and their impact on the group.
8. Decision-making processes: who makes what kinds of decisions?
9. Major conflicts around what issues and the means used to cope with them.
10. The degree of cohesiveness of the group. In families, consider individual differentiation and group identity.
11. Relationship to the community.

Case Illustration

Description of the agency or setting. The setting is a Catholic parish in a Haitian community in a large city in the southeast. Through word of mouth and participation in activities and church services, members of the Haitian community know that social workers are available to help them with problems or refer them to appropriate resources.

Identifying information. The primary client is Mr. Lyon, a Haitian male, age fifty, a practicing Catholic, married, speaks Creole, has a fourth grade education, is employed as a gardener, has been in this country for eleven years. The family members are Mrs. Lyon, age forty-two, with a second grade education, employment as a maid, recently separated from Mr. Lyon, living in a nearby city with a brother and two-year-old daughter. Four children presently live with Mr. Lyon—a male godchild, age seventeen, two daughters ages seventeen and eight, and one son, age nine. Three other sons live in Haiti, ages 21, 20, and 18, who are in school and supported by their parents.

Presenting problems and precipitating factors. Several problems were presented by Mr. L. in the initial interview. His seventeen-year-old daughter is in the United States illegally: she came as a visitor and stayed; he needs to find ways to legalize her presence here. He and his wife are saving money in order to pay the exorbitant costs of bringing the sons to this country. The most important problem is his wife's infidelity. When he confronted her with the facts, she denied the charge, which made him furious and he beat her, emphasizing that this was the only time he had done so, and he regrets it very much. The result was a joint decision that she go to another city to live with her brother, where she could find a job as a housekeeper and be away from the man with whom she was having an affair. For the past year, this has preoccupied Mr. L.'s thoughts: he can't eat or sleep and has lost weight.

Relevant historical data. In Haiti, education is available only to those who can afford it. Mr. L. came from a poor peasant family that needed him to work in the fields in order to sustain the family. Because he had only four years of education, he reads and writes with difficulty. Economic conditions in Haiti influence many couples to postpone marriage and live together until the partners can afford the elaborate wedding ceremony necessary to comply with society's requirements. The Lyons were married only after their fourth child was born. Mr. L., unable to find work in Haiti, came to the United States as a refugee twelve years ago, being one of the "boat people." When the boat was sinking off the coast of Florida, the U.S. Coast Guard picked up the people and placed them in jail. He was released when a friend paid a bond for him. He wanted his wife to wait until she could enter the country legally, but she became impatient and boarded a boat just as he had done. She spent only a short time in prison because he was able to pay for her release. Two years later, they sent for their daughter. Mr. and Mrs. L. became legal residents under the General Amnesty Act.

Assessment of personality factors. Mr. L. appears to be motivated to work on the problems. He came to the office on his own initiative; listened intently and asked appropriate questions, was able to verbalize his problem and situation, responded to questions, and seemed to reflect on what he was saying. He feels guilt and remorse over beating his wife, but blames her for being unfaithful. He is under great stress, with which he copes by means of prayer, using altruism as a defense by helping others, using some denial of the seriousness of the marital conflict, and reaching out to communicate with his wife. He has a great deal of hope that things will work out, combined with discomfort and anxiety about the way things are now.

Status, roles, and relationships. Mr. L.'s role as head of the household with his wife at his side has been threatened. He has been able to succeed in his work role over a period of many years, and feels secure in that role. His role in the church is a sense of pride and status. Part of his sense of identity comes from his membership and participation in the church. He is not a member of any other organization but participates with male friends in following Haitian politics, and playing dominoes and card games.

Relevant functioning of the family system. Little is known about the actual way the family system functions, but its boundaries have been loosened with three separate subgroups: Mr. L. and the four children; Mrs. L. and the two-year-old girl; and the three sons who are in Haiti. The absence of the mother from the main family must pose problems for the children as well as for Mr. L. The marital conflict upsets the system's steady state and creates stress for all members of the family, threatening the very survival of the group.

Individual and cultural values.   Mr. L. places high value on education, asserting that all of the children will go as far as they are able and making sacrifices to provide for their education. He values strong ties to the family and extended family, in harmony with Haitian values of the male as head of the household. He has strong faith in religion, valuing strong relationships with other members of the church. He values hard work and maintains an attitude of optimism that there will be improvement in his situation and that of the children.

Biological factors.   There are no indications of illness or disability in any of the family members, except for Mr. L.'s complaints about occasional low back pains.

Diagnosis of mental disorder.   There have been no diagnoses of mental disorders in the family.

Relationship to the community.   The L. family has had numerous problems with immigration officials in relation to their status as undocumented residents until the General Amnesty Act was passed, and they are still struggling to find the resources to legalize their daughter's status and to arrange for the sons to come to this country legally. Mr. L. and Mrs. L. have had no difficulty fulfilling their work roles in a satisfactory way, but the family income is meager.

Mr. L. does not verbalize his awareness of the extent of prejudice and discrimination against Haitians that exists in the community. He has insulated the family, to some degree, by living in a Haitian neighborhood, going to a Haitian church, and participating in groups of Haitians. There is yet no information about the children's relationships in the community, except that they are all in school. Mr. L.'s attitudes toward white-dominated institutions seems to be one of passive acceptance. Being from a poor Haitian family and speaking only Creole, he has limited access to the resources of the broader community and distrust of bureaucracies.

Analysis of Data

Several interrelated problems are evident in the information available from the initial interview. The primary problem may be one of long-standing, namely transition from Haiti to the United States: first Mr. L.; then Mrs. L.; then the oldest daughter, who is still an illegal resident; and then the godson. Three sons are still in Haiti, hoping to immigrate to this country, and three children have been born in the United States. The need to support such a large family, including members of the extended family in Haiti, creates situational stress, as do the problems in negotiating with immigration authorities. Lack of knowledge of English and illiteracy compound the problems. These stresses have been exacerbated by the separation of Mrs. L. and the youngest daughter from the household, owing to marital conflict precipitated by the wife's infidelity. The meaning of the marital problem to Mr. L. seems to be the loss of status and role as head of a two-parent household in a culture in which the male role is dominant, with the accompanying loss of self-esteem. As the children grow older and the sons immigrate here, additional stress may occur as members have increased contact with the dominant culture.

Mr. L. has a great deal of anger, grief, and embarrassment over the wife's infidelity and separation. Although he acknowledges his part in the problem by beating his wife, he perceives the solution to the problem as being a change in Mrs. L.'s behavior. But since marital and family problems are interpersonal, Mrs. L. needs to become involved in working with him. It is, however, not known what her views are and whether or not she wishes to preserve the marriage.

Mr. L.'s goals are to work to reestablish the family; be able to communicate more effectively with his wife; secure legal status for the daughter; and bring the sons to this country. The first task for the worker then would be to clarify Mr. L.'s role in the family, his relationship with his wife, and the impact of the wife's separation on the children. He will be helped to learn to communicate with his wife about the marriage and bring her into marital or family counseling to determine whether his goal of family reunification is a shared one and, if so, to find ways to enhance the family's functioning. An additional goal will be finding ways to legitimize the daughter's status and bring the sons to this country.

Mr. L. has many positive attitudes and ego strengths to bring to the tasks. He has demonstrated capacity to survive in harsh and hostile environments; he has high motivation to find a solution to the problems; he has the ability to express his feelings and concerns; and he is able to take responsibility for his part in the separation, the beating of his wife, for which he shows guilt and remorse. Mr. L. has found adaptive ways to cope with the stress through religion, helping others, and making efforts to communicate with his wife. His unselfishness and concern for the needs of others can be used in the problem-solving process. His competence in group participation can be built on, and his strong religious faith can be channeled to help him resolve his grief and anger, which has been sublimated for the time being. He has accepted the social worker's suggestion that he and his wife meet together to try to find solutions to their problems.

Formulation of the Assessment

The information elicited in the initial phase of practice needs to be integrated into a formulation that attempts to describe and explain problems, capacities, motivation, and goals of clients as was attempted by the student who worked with Mr. Lyon. The analysis takes into account the client's functioning in relation to norms, knowledge about problems, ego capacities, cultural values and traditions, and varied explanations. The purpose is to identify the most critical factors that are operating in it, and to define their interrelationships. It is the worker's professional opinion about the facts and their meaning; understanding of the configuration of the facts in order to determine how the person, family, or group can be helped. Perlman and Somers have referred to this process as one of problem-solving by the worker, done through a process of reflective thinking.[45] It is a logical process, although it incorporates intuitive insights.[46]

Realistic appraisal provides the basis for action that should be guided by facts, not myths. What is to be understood is the nature of the need or trouble, the factors that contribute to it, the participants' motivations and capacities, and an assessment of what can be changed, supported, or strengthened in the person-group-situation configuration. To be properly understood, an individual or group is assessed in relation to the particular category of clients who have similar characteristics. It is to be reemphasized that classification pertains to certain aspects of the functioning of an individual or group, not to the person or group as a whole.

Assessment is not completed when a problem or condition has been classified. There remains the need to construct some explanation of how it has come to be the way it is. A worker draws inferences from what is learned about the person-situation configuration and relates these judgments to the service that can be given. The behavioral science theory that is used determines largely the inferences that are made.

Use of Norms

Within any given culture, there are norms or expectations that are used to judge the extent to which a person or group is functioning adequately. Assessment of a person's position on a continuum, ranging from very effective to very ineffective functioning, cues the worker into both problems and capacities. Although norms are necessary, rapid changes in the conditions of life and lifestyle pose problems for both workers and clients in assessing the adequacy of functioning. Such assessment is made, not against absolute norms, but in relation to adaptation that is primarily "a reciprocal relationship between the organism and its environments."[47] Changes in either the person or the environment can bring about a state of adaptation in which there is a fit between the person and his or her environment that is favorable to the person's survival. There are certain average expectable situations or average atypical situations with which a person deals. The term "average expectable" signifies that which is within the range of expectations for the fit between person and environment.[49] According to this idea, expectations are differentiated according to such important influences on psychosocial functioning as gender, community, school grade or occupation, status of health, race, ethnicity, religion, and social class. The social worker seeks to learn the client's perceptions of, and attitudes toward, the norm of the different subsystems of his environment. It is to be noted that there is always some range of acceptable behaviors that are functional in the client's social context.

Assessment of behavior needs to take into account such judgments as whether it is a reaction to change in circumstances such as death of a loved one, immigration, illness, or arrival of a new baby; whether it is socially acceptable behavior in the client's sociocultural group; the extent of disturbance in terms of whether the behavior interferes with any one or several areas of functioning; the type, severity, and frequency of symptoms; and whether there are changes in behavior of a kind that are not expected in terms of normal maturation and development. Although practitioners do not focus on symptoms per se, they do need to know their significance. Rutter gives the example that nail biting tends to be an indication of stress, but is not associated with psychiatric disorders. In contrast, "disturbed peer relationships are more commonly associated with psychiatric disorders and, as such, warrant more serious attention."[49] It is important to be clear about the amount of suffering that symptoms cause the clients, the extent to which the symptoms prevent them from achieving their goals, the ways in which symptoms interfere with clients' normal progression in development, and the effect of the resultant behavior on others.

The social worker takes into account the fact that all phases of human development overlap; persons have their own rates of maturation and development within what are average expectations; there are many variations within a normal pattern of functioning; and the norms themselves are in a process of change. The standards that persons set for themselves in relation to those that others set for them influence their success or failure in the major tasks in each phase of the life cycle. People's feelings about their assigned roles, the way they interpret them, and their responses to the expectations of others give clues to the fit between the person and the environment. A person may adapt well to one situation and poorly to another. The worker, therefore, is concerned with variations of effectiveness of functioning in different social systems—whether ineffective functioning in one system is affecting ability to adapt elsewhere, and if successful functioning in one system can be used as a bridge to more effective functioning elsewhere.

Stereotypes

Making judgments about the adequacy of a person in relation to norms cannot be avoided, but it poses problems. One challenge is in ascertaining the influence of socioeconomic status, race, and ethnicity on psychosocial functioning. Although there are certain characteristics, for example, that differentiate one group from another, efforts to define these characteristics, often combined with personal and institutional prejudice, may lead to negative stereotyping. Persons in positions of power, including social workers, come to expect stereotyped behavior and plan and act accordingly.[50] Pinderhughes and Solomon point out that it is easy to label some behavior as pathology when the clients' responses are to a sense of powerlessness.[51] This difficulty points to the need for sound and current knowledge about social class, race, and ethnicity.

Another challenge to judgments about adequacy of functioning stems from a tendency to hold absolute criteria. Writing about the family, Goldberg notes that, consciously or not, practitioners carry some ideal about what "normal" family life is or should be—there is an unrealistic model concerning what is good, adequate, or ideal family living.[52] In reality, there are few objective and universal criteria. Terms such as authoritarian husband, overprotective mother, and rejecting parent are used in varied ways, without precision, and without regard to the expectations for parental behavior in particular cultures. Extended families do exist and are functional in many cultures, including Asian, Mexican, and American Indian cultures. Goldberg provides evidence that the modern family is not isolated, as is so often stated. Three-generation families exist. The nuclear family is often embedded in a close network of family and neighborly relations.[53]

Such research dispels certain myths about the family. It is to be remembered, however, that many families are indeed isolated from sources of support. Anther myth is the one that the more separate and distinct are the roles for men and women, the better it is for them and their children. In opposition to this traditional myth is acceptance of more joint and interchangeable roles for men and women. Pollak indicates that there are great variations in patterns of family structure that are within a normal range. He refers, for example, to the fact that concentration of authority in one member of the family is probably not an expression of pathology. More often it is an expression of the history, religion and ethology of a population group. It may be pathological, however, if it occurs when it should not be expected to happen, according to the culture of the group to which the person belongs.[54] Yet, individuals and families may need to deviate from the norms of their cultures if they are to exemplify the values of human dignity and justice for both sexes.

Goldberg suggests that, in spite of difficulties, there is a way of determining the effectiveness of family functioning. In the family which is adapting fairly successfully there is "a tolerable fit between what members of a family seek from each other and receive in return, and also perhaps a fit between their values and ways of living and those of the social group or network to which they belong."[55] It is to such interactional patterns among members of groups and with their reference groups then that assessment should be addressed.

Self-Awareness

In eliciting data from the client system, the values of practitioners influence greatly the information they seek and the inferences they draw from the data. They are guided by the values and ethical principles of the profession, as elaborated in chapter 4. Their own personal values may, however, make it difficult to implement professional values. Often, workers may not even be consciously aware of their own values' effect on their practice.

Awareness of one's own values is essential, for they determine choices and actions, including goals, perceptions of capacities and problems, and the means to be used in the helping process. The practitioner needs "to realize that he sees others through the screen of his own personality and his own life experiences."[56] Some individual and family values are changing rapidly, offering many more options for choice. These relate, for example, to sexual behavior, forms of family structure and composition, marital separation, joint custody of children of divorce, self-gratification, and individuation. With a variety of fairly acceptable lifestyles, practitioners may unwittingly impose their own preferences on clients' views of themselves and their situations.[57]

Alternative Explanations

Explanations, according to Lewis, are most useful when they account for all of the known facts and suggest others not previously identified.[58] The explanations that are arrived at through logical thinking are not for all occasions, but applicable to a particular case only. Lewis illustrates the point by noting that not everyone who has been subjected to social injustice has developed the same responses. The assessment must explain how a particular individual or family was actually victimized and what its responses to this event did or did not bring about. Not everyone who has experienced the death of a parent or spouse responds to this event in the same way. The assessment should explain the connection between a particular death and the functioning of a particular person or family.

Strengths as well as difficulties are located as the worker seeks for alternative explanations. Such an approach tends to deemphasize stereotyping of clients through establishing the unique as well as the common responses to factors that contribute to a particular condition. In searching for explanations, it is usually necessary to give some attention to the nature of past experiences that have precipitated or contributed to the current condition. There may have been a gradual building up of inner and outer stresses; or there may be truly traumatic experiences from the past that contribute to the current difficulty.

Accurate assessment requires the ability to consider alternative explanations of behavior. Solomon gives the example of a black child who is assessed as being discriminated against in a new school or, alternatively, as a child who is having difficulty adapting to a new school in which she feels isolated and lonely. Assessment requires determining which alternative is most probable by means of careful exploration of one's own feelings and exploration with the client.[59] The practitioner might further hypothesize that both may be intervening factors, along with the need to adapt to a new neighborhood and find new friends and resources to make up for their loss in the old neighborhood.

Social workers intend to understand the present, but they intend also to influence the future. They are interested in preventing a harmful event or further damage from occurring as well as in promoting desired events. The worker has tremendous authority in assessment but so, too, do the clients, for they are full participants in all aspects of the process. The assessment is tentative and on-going, to be modified in the crucible of interaction between worker and clients.

The initial assessment leads to a plan of service for an individual, family, or group. Planning is a complex process and that is the subject of chapter 9.

Nine | Issues in Planning Services

Planning for a specific service to clients is one of the most important processes in social work. It is largely a cognitive activity, with an emphasis on mapping the components of intervention. The need is for explicit reasons for selecting each component from among alternatives.[1] It may be viewed as a bridge between assessment and the problem-solving work that follows.[2] Social workers, in collaboration with clients and often with other practitioners, make certain choices concerning the nature of the services and the resources to be made available to particular clients. Although planning, like assessment, is an ongoing process, certain decisions need to be made prior to and during the initial meetings with an individual or family. The result of the planning process is a contract or working agreement.

Planning is necessary because social workers seek to provide individualized services to meet needs. Meyer has suggested that the primary focus of social work is a process of differentiating particular people from the mass.[3] Within common human needs and situations there are particularized needs to be taken into account. Thus, a plan must be made for each individual, family, or group to be serviced. The plan is based on knowledge of legislation, agency policies and procedures, and assessment of clients in their networks of interacting social systems.

Kurland has noted that planning has been a neglected process in social work and that "the price for lack of thoughtful and thorough planning is high,"[4] Frequently, it is paid in clients who drop out, sporadic and irregular attendance, and lack of successful outcomes. It is paid also in workers' lack of confidence to take on new types of clients and new responsibilities. Main's research on social work with groups has implications for all of social work practice. One of her major conclusions was that the degree of development of assessments, treatment goals, and plans for individuals are positively associated with the degree of appropriateness of the worker's use of self with individuals and with the group.[5] Treatment planning is a basis for purposeful service, and is associated with the nature of the worker's engagement with the members. So the price of thoughtful and thorough planning is high in aiding the use of oneself effectively with clients. The ultimate value of planning is "the likelihood of reaching the desired outcomes is better than chance."[6]

Preliminary planning includes decisions concerning:

1. The needs and problems of clients that will serve as the initial focus of service.
2. The goals, mutually arrived at between the practitioner and clients, that specify successful outcome, and
3. The means to be undertaken to achieve the goals, including the modality or unit of attention; the structure of the service, including decisions as to the make-up of the client system; the number and type of personnel to be involved; the duration of service; and the means for entering into the service system.

In relation to each of these components, there are alternatives to be selected, based on the professional judgment of the practitioner, the potential clients' preferences and capacities, and on the organization's policies, procedures, and resources. In order to make sound decisions about the means to be chosen, practitioners must have a body of knowledge about them.

Flexibility in Choosing

Within the approach to practice described herein, a flexible and individualized consideration of multiple alternatives for meeting the needs of clients is valued. This approach is not congruent with organizational policies and practices that limit service to casework as a one-worker-to-one-client endeavor or to a worker-family or worker-small group or community endeavor only. Nor is it congruent with policies and practices that require that services be given through only one type of activity, for example, verbal communication, play therapy, behavior modification, or transactional analysis. A growing body of literature calls for complementarity, cooperation, and integration of treatment modalities and illustrates how the use of individual, family, group, and community services can potentiate each other.[7] Multisystems models of practice are essential for some clients whose problems are at different levels, ranging from intrapersonal to community.[8]

Not all prospective clients need service through multiple modalities. The challenge to the practitioner is to aid clients to decide which one, or which combination, shows promise of being most productive in relation to the goals of service. To meet this challenge, social workers need knowledge of the common and specific characteristics of types of systems. They need to be able to select a target system, that is, any persons the worker attempts to influence in order to accomplish the desired goals.[9] For example, work with people who are not themselves clients in behalf of clients is very important. Thus, other systems may need to become the target of intervention; for example, in addition to helping a schoolchild with social difficulties that hinder learning, a parent or teacher may need to be involved as well as representatives of environmental resources.

Selecting a Modality: Individual, Couple, Family Group

Clear criteria for the use of individual, couple, family, group, or community services do not exist. Professional judgment is required. Any decision needs to be based on an assessment of the persons who are involved in the situation, the goals of the service, and the values and risks involved in varied modalities of practice. Understanding the special characteristics of different forms of treatment and their uses is essential to planning a service for an individual or a family.

The Individual

In the one-to-one relationship, privacy is the major characteristic. The client also has the undivided attention of the practitioner. In the one-to-one relationship, there is only one interactional bond between the worker and client. Both have the power to break the relationship. By virtue of their positions in an organization or the sanction derived through licensing and professional knowledge and skills, the practitioners are the primary influence over what is done and the means to be used. It is true that they have the power, even though they seek the client's active participation.

The exclusiveness of the relationship, unless it is brief and task-oriented, tends to foster intimacy in disclosing feelings, thoughts, and experiences to a relatively benign and trusting worker. The client expects that all of the messages sent will be evaluated and responded to by the worker. Clients invest themselves in the relationship in various ways and with different degrees of intimacy. The relationship usually develops around fairly realistic expectations and perceptions of each partner. In some situations, clients may become deeply invested in their relationship with the worker and quite dependent upon the worker for emotional gratification. Strong identifications and positive transference reactions may develop, usually combined with some elements of negative transference.

The focus of the work tends to be on the unique and specific characteristics and behavior of clients in their situations. Although clients may be helped to work on problems in social relationship, the other persons are not directly present. Practitioners perceive these relationships only through the clients' verbalizations and actions.

The individual client-social worker dyad, with its unique characteristics of privacy, one-to-one communication, potential for intimacy, and exclusiveness seems to be the modality of choice under certain circumstances.

Intrapsychic and interpersonal problems may at times require individual help. A private relationship may be desirable when clients have trouble coping with highly sensitive matters and painful emotions which are very personal in nature.[10] It may be indicated when there is severe pathology, with low tolerance for anxiety and frustration and inability to empathize with others: individual treatment may be necessary because in groups there are pressures for realistic relationships, responsive interactions, and competition for time and attention that may be too stressful.[11] It may be indicated when there is a need for clients to develop self-understanding of the dynamics of unresolved conflicts with parents or other significant persons in the past. When clients have intense emotional needs, such as fear of abandonment, narcissistic injuries, or strong feelings of deprivation, individual treatment may be used in collaboration with group counseling to help the client to tolerate the stresses arising in the group experience.

Individual help is chosen when clients need to have some psychological distance from a living group, such as a family or dormitory, in order to be able to perceive it more realistically and to evaluate their place in the system. It may often be the preferred approach for exploring and resolving problems not suitable for discussion in the presence of family members or peers, whose needs might redirect the focus and divert the content from the task at hand. It is usually preferred when a person has a salient need for rapid restoration in a crisis situation and either does not live in a family or the family cannot be engaged in the helping endeavor. It is probably preferred when the situation requires people to make a crucial, specific, personal decision that has long-term consequences for them and others, and they need to do the problem-solving work free from undue influence exerted by peers or family. Examples are decisions about whether or not to have an abortion, relinquish custody of a child, drop out of school, file for divorce, reveal one's sexual orientation or diagnosis of a fatal illness. In such situations, individuals need to clarify their feelings and thoughts as to what they really want to do, make a decision, and consider and face the consequences of the decision for themselves and significant others.

When a marital couple has separated, individual treatment is best, according to findings from a large study based on the counselors' ratings. Once separation has occurred, partners need the one-to-one relationship to sort out, cope with, and integrate the trauma and anxieties stemming from separation.[12]

Some people refuse to participate in family or group treatment; the only alternative then is individual help. This is true also if a person is imbued with the idea that the problem is so unique and difficult that only an expert can help and that the presence of other clients would dilute the change effort.[13] Some persons are too fearful of groups or they are governed by a value that forbids discussion of personal feelings and problems with others. It may be that these are the people who most need a corrective group experience. Nevertheless, individual help is required, at least until the initial resistance to family and group forms of help can be modified.

An individual relationship is essential to develop and coordinate environmental resources or reduce environmental stress through resource consultation with the client, case advocacy, or to identify a network of positive supports for a particular client.

The Couple

There seems to be considerable agreement that working with couples together, either in joint interviews or in groups of couples, is most appropriate when marital conflict is a major problem. In a large study by the Family Service Association of America, for example, couples treated together showed significantly greater change than did those treated through individual interviews, as rated by both counselors and clients. Treatment of couples in groups was also found to be more effective than individual interviews.[14] Gurman came to similar conclusions. He surveyed seventy-three journals and concluded that conjoint treatment of couples generally produces the best results, although in certain circumstances each of the other forms may have particular advantages.

The rationale for this choice is that marital maladjustment is an entity having its own dynamics apart from individual maladjustments; therefore, one treats the marital pair. Groups of couples with marital problems were almost as beneficial as conjoint treatment and were superior to that form among people who divorced.[15] The group modality also seems to produce the highest social as well as marital adjustments. In another study, by Macon, couple treatment and group treatment of marital problems were found to be equally effective.[16]

The Family

In the family, each member has a history of relationships with each other member. The members live with the assumption that destruction of the group is a threat to their emotional survival.[17] The nature and quality of these relationships is based partly on realistic experiences with each other, but also partly on distortions of perceptions of each other's intents, behaviors, and status in the family. When the family system is the unit of service, the members enter into a new arena in which the expectations are that they will share with each other and with a practitioner in different ways than have been characteristic of them. The worker is an outsider who enters into an established system of relationships, evaluates the system's functioning, and attempts to support or change certain elements of the system. The worker's primary tie is to the process between and among the members, but each subsystem must be considered as well as each individual in their relationships with other individuals and subgroups. The relationships between husband and wife, parent and children, and siblings are of utmost complexity.

Family relationships are almost always intense, for each member is dependent upon others and the group for meeting basic needs. For this reason, members may feel there is a great risk in entering into family treatment. There are apt to be fears of rejection or retaliation from the very persons upon whom one is dependent for emotional and sometimes also for physical survival. The social worker's influence is greatly modified by the patterns of authority that have been established in the family. Some of this authority is legally defined and some of it is culturally defined concerning the power of parents in relation to children. In families, the practitioner individualizes each member from within the interacting processes of the group. Although the goals of each member are considered, so are the goals of every other member. But the primary goals concern the family itself—changes in the family's structure and communication systems.[18] The family will continue as a unit when the worker's particular relationship with it has terminated.

Research indicates that, despite some differences among practitioners, a systems perspective is prevalent.[19] There is agreement, too, that

> the main purpose of therapeutic work with a family is to improve members' functioning as a working, interdependent group . . . each member should derive personal benefit . . . the goals are to facilitate communication of thoughts and feelings between family members; to shift disturbed, inflexible roles and coalitions; to serve as role models, educators, and demythologizers, showing by example how best to deal with family quarreling and conflict.[20]

In harmony with these goals, family treatment is particularly useful when the difficulty is in the functioning of the system itself. Examples are ineffective patterns of communication and lack of satisfying relationships among the members, lack of clarity about role expectations, conflict among the members concerning goals and decisions, and inadequate ways of coping with problems in daily living. Family treatment is usually the modality of choice in parent-child relationship conflicts. Perlman notes that joint and family interviews may be uniquely suited to the clarification of role requirements, role allocations, and role performance within the family, since the participants can simultaneously become aware of their own perceptions related to those of others and may mutually experiment with revised role definitions.[21] Work with families is essential when one of its members has a serious illness or disability. The illness or disability disrupts the family's functioning, which has an impact on the patient's well-being. A substantial body of research supports the interacting influence of patients and family units.[22]

The Group

In formed groups, practitioners have responsibility to initiate and develop a system of relationships among people who often have had no prior acquaintance with each other. They need to develop a relationship with each member and with the group as a whole, which consists of the intricate network of changing relationships among the members. As in work with individuals, the worker and the members come together for a limited period of time. The worker influences relationships in order that the group can become the principal means of help, yet also eventually become no longer necessary as a source of psychological and social support for the members.

The intensity and intimacy of relationships vary with the purpose of the group and the needs of the members. Relationships may become very intense; nevertheless, they are diluted by the larger number of interactional bonds and the limited time that members spend together. Strong identifications may develop between one or more members and the worker, or between two or more members. As cohesiveness develops, there is often strong identification with the group as a whole.

Transference reactions often develop between certain members and the worker, often predominantly positive, but tinged with negative aspects. There is the added complexity of transference reactions among the members themselves. The pattern of reactions, based on a combination of realistic and distorted perceptions of others, creates a very complex network of positive and negative ties.

The practitioners' influence is reduced by their presence in a group in which members influence each other. This shared authority requires that the workers understand and then either support or challenge the processes among members rather than assume direct control, except when members are unable to control themselves. The group, with its competing demands, shifting alliances, and complex emotional network, does not allow for the protection of an individual to the extent this may occur in the one-to-one relationship. But the group does afford more psychological space for individuals permitting them to move into relationships of greater and lesser intensity, according to their own readiness and interpersonal needs. The needs of each individual are important, but they fall within concern for the needs of each and all. In some groups, there may be a collective goal as well as shared individual goals.

Groups are powerful means for influencing change. The dynamic processes operating therein have the potential for making groups the principal means for helping people to meet certain needs or to cope with certain problems in social living.

Yalom has done considerable research on what he calls the therapeutic factors in groups and research by social workers and psychologists confirm his findings.[23] Although their influence varies with different persons and with different types of groups, in general, the five most potent factors are:

1. *Interpersonal learning.* This is a primary dynamic because working with two or more people simultaneously is a unique experience. Interpersonal learning is based on our knowledge about the critical nature of people's social needs; about how human development thrives under conditions of constructive relationships. One sees the influence of acceptance

and empathy on learning; the fact that groups can provide a corrective emotional experience for past destructive social experiences; and that people reveal their interpersonal styles—their positive capacities for relationships and their maladaptive behaviors in groups. Group members can learn from each other. In the group, people can work through distortions and develop understanding of their relationships, and it is through a combination of support and challenge among the members that this occurs.

2. *Self-understanding.* Through the observations of others, reflective thinking, and feedback from other members, persons develop understanding of their own patterns of feeling, thinking, and behaving and the impact of these patterns on their relationships with others and on their competence in role performance. Such understanding is a step toward changes in self-defeating attitudes and behaviors.

3. *Catharsis.* This goes beyond mere ventilation of feelings and thoughts—it does not mean "let it all hang out." It refers to the relief that comes from learning how to express one's own feelings and one's feelings toward others in constructive ways, and to have these feelings accepted by others.

4. *Cohesiveness.* Cohesiveness is the group bond—the "we" feeling, the attractiveness of the group to its members. It is a necessary condition for effective group achievement. In a cohesive group, there is a high degree of mutual acceptance, support, and aid. There is the feeling of belonging, or being accepted for what one is which is prevalent when groups have an appropriate degree of cohesiveness. In cohesive groups, members can live through the inevitable conflicts that occur from time to time—the group is strong enough that conflict does not destroy it.

5. *Acquisition of knowledge and skills.* The actual learning of new information and skills is essential to effective social functioning. Many people encounter difficulties in social living because they lack information and skills in relating to other people and in satisfactorily performing their social roles. Groups are the most natural environment for such learning.

These five forces have repeatedly been found to be those that potentially make the group a powerful positive force for the members.

Other somewhat less significant factors or those that are more important in the beginning stage than throughout the life of the group are:

6. *Universality.* This dynamic is crucial during the beginning phase of treatment. Typical comments are: "I'm not alone with this condition," "We're in the same boat, brother, after all," "I'm so relieved to know it isn't only me." Such awareness tends to release debilitating anxiety as

members learn knowledge that certain feelings and situations are not abnormal and unique.

7. *Instillation of hope.* Hope is essential if a member is to continue in the group beyond the first meeting or two. A sense of hopefulness provides motivation for working toward something better.

8. *Altruism.* The ability to give as well as to receive enhances self-esteem and social competence. Recognizing that one has helped others is a powerful motivation. Solomon, in her book on social work practice in oppressed communities, notes how very important this factor is in working with poor black people and it applies as well to other population groups.[24]

9. *Other factors.* Also identified as influential in many groups are imitative learning or, more importantly, identification, first with the practitioner and then with the group; corrective recapitulation of the family group; and what Yalom calls existential factors, primarily that motivation that comes from recognizing that only individuals can take responsibility for the way they live.

What is the purpose? From a review of the literature, it becomes clear that *first* the group is usually the preferred modality when the purpose is some form of enhancement of social relationships.[25] As stated by Goldstein, "groups often aim to correct maladaptive patterns of relationships."[26] The particular dynamics of groups as described previously make them ideal environments for coping with deficits or difficulties in social relationships. Many people with problems in relating to others need considerable acceptance and support from others who are in a peer role with them. They need to learn how others perceive them and to practice new behaviors in a social situation that is removed from their daily relationships, one in which feedback comes from other members as well as from a professional person. The perspective provided by multiple views of problems, people, and situations provides a context for reality testing and makes the group particularly desirable when clients have unrealistic perceptions of themselves or others or when they suffer from a low sense of self-esteem or personal inadequacy. A small group that is meaningful to its members affords an ideal environment in which individuals can be helped to work on dependence-independence conflicts, sibling rivalries, or problems with authority and to cope with problems of loneliness and loss.

Even when the major problems are in the functioning of the family system, usually indicating service to the family, a member may benefit from a group service. Clients may not be able to bear the anxiety of family sessions or may not be able to overcome a fear that other members will retaliate for their expressions of feelings and ideas. When the boundary of the family is closed to new inputs, multiple family groups may stimulate the members to new ways of feeling, communicating, and decision-making. In groups, the relationship with the worker and other members can begin at whatever level of participation each person is ready for until, through observation of what happens to others, the members learn that the worker is interested in them as well as in each other member.

A *second* purpose of social work service, which usually calls for the use of the group, is that of enhancement of social competence. For purposes of preventing problems in social functioning, the group is clearly the predominant modality.[27] The goals are to help the members to function more adequately in their vital social roles and to cope with changes in role expectations and social situations.

The need for service stems from lack of adequate knowledge, social experiences, and skills for coping with an anticipated event or situation, usually a new phase of psychosocial development or a transition to a new or changed role. Based on intensive study of socialization theory, McBroom concluded that the group is the most effective and natural modality for intervention in such situations because social competence can be developed only through relationships with other people.[28] Similarly, Germain and Gitterman have said that when members share a common set of life tasks, the group provides multiple opportunities for human relatedness, mutual aid, and learning task-related coping skills.[29]

A *third*, interrelated purpose of social work for which the group is often the preferred treatment is the development of capacities to cope with devastating events, such as a life-threatening illness, rape, natural or physical violence.[30] After the initial crisis, support and stimulation from peers aid in the disclosure and management of emotions, the release of tension, the enhancement of self esteem, and the discovery of new ways of coping with stress and with the reality of the situation. There is some research that indicates that people who have had traumatic experiences often feel isolated, lonely, and depressed. Such people are more apt to have serious difficulties in coping realistically with the consequences of the event than are those with supportive social networks.[31] Such people are particularly suitable for a carefully planned therapeutic group experience. Groups are also obviously the modality of choice for services not aimed primarily toward helping clients within direct services, but for purposes of staff training and development, collaboration, planning, and social change. Such groups, however, are beyond the scope of this book.

From a review of surveys of the use of groups in the United States and Canada, Russell concluded that "the consistent finding among these surveys, therefore, has been that groups are utilized by social workers primarily for therapeutic goals."[32]

In addition to the primary criterion of group purpose, the characteristics and conditions of prospective clients may influence whether or not they will benefit from a group experience. Some indications for groups relate to the personality or behavioral characteristics of prospective clients. Understanding of the dynamic processes that occur in groups suggests guidelines for selecting persons for whom the group might well be the modality of choice. Sherman has proposed that: (1) groups are particularly suited for isolated individuals because the group can be a controlled and relatively nonthreatening social experience and a vestibule to expanded human relations outside the group; (2) the group provides a more diluted multiplicity of relationships for clients threatened by the closeness and dependency aspects of a one-to-one professional relationship; (3) clients with limited verbal abilities usually make better use of groups than of individual help; (4) group experience is usually appropriate for persons whose affective responses need to be stimulated, for they can gradually become involved vicariously with the intimate feelings of others, matching them mentally or verbally to their own; (5) clients for whom projection is a major ego defense may learn to see themselves and others more realistically as they learn about multiple views of problems and behaviors.[33]

Other social work writers have proposed criteria for selecting the group for persons who have been diagnosed as suffering from physical, social, and mental disorders. These suggestions include the following:

1. Persons with serious chronic illnesses. Participation in a peer group releases tension, enhances self-esteem, and facilitates effective coping with changing body images and issues concerning losses, life changes, and the need to confront the reality of the disability, through shared experiences and group support and feedback.[34]

2. Patients suffering from schizophrenia or from personality disorders. Many often find therapeutic group work is the modality of choice.[35] Study of the symptoms of patients who have been diagnosed as mentally ill indicates that most of them feel isolated, suffer from low self-esteem, and behave in ways that disturb other people.[36] A properly designed group can give clients the support, acceptance, and mutual understanding that exceeds anything an individual worker could supply, and provides opportunities for feedback, reality testing, and learning essential social skills.

3. Persons who are addicted to alcohol. Turner suggests that group treatment may be the preferred modality.[37] The advantages attributed to group work are the nurturance of interpersonal relationships in a population characterized by social isolation, group support for identifying with the role of a recovering alcoholic, direct observation of interpersonal behaviors, and peer modeling by successful members.

Note how these proposed guidelines are harmonious with knowledge about the dynamic change forces in groups and with the purpose of improving relationships, developing social competence, and coping successfully with traumatic life events.

Client Choice

Practical matters need to be recognized and taken into account in making decisions about the type of service to be offered or provided. Obviously, one of these considerations is client choice. People have different attitudes toward, and different experiences in, individual, family, or group modalities, which influence their motivation to use a particular type of service. The important point, however, is that the choice should be an informed one, so that the client can understand some of the benefits, risks, and consequences of a particular decision. Another consideration is the obvious one that, if a person is not currently a part of a family constellation, the choice is limited to an individual or formed group modality. The size of an agency and its caseload, or the caseload of a private practitioner, influences the extent to which formed groups can be utilized. There must, of course, be a sufficient number of applicants or clients with a common need to make possible the formation of a group.

Multiple Modality Practice

Understanding the particular characteristics of individual, couple, family, and group and the primary purposes for which they are used is essential to the development of treatment plans for clients. Increasingly, it is recognized that the need is for a combination of modalities combined with the use of environmental resources.[38]

The need for using modalities of practice simultaneously or successively is clearly indicated, for example, for patients with AIDS and their families. In addition to the illness itself, families must deal with isolation, fear of contagion, stigmatization, and confronting the precipitant of the illness, such as unsafe sex practices, tainted blood transfusions, or the use of needles in taking drugs. Individual counseling to the patient or family members, supportive and therapeutic groups, are combined with a range of health and welfare services, and social networks, all coordinated through clinical case management, Getzel provides illustrations of such multiple services in his articles on serving AIDS patients.[39]

Similarly, in work with abused or neglected children, the trend is clearly toward the provision of integrated services to the child, the child's family, and the foster family or personnel in residential settings, combined with the range of environmental resources and opportunities that are necessary.[40] A recent handbook on social work practice with clients with a variety of problems in psychosocial functioning delineates how the need for multiple services is clearly evident.[41]

Selection of a Practitioner

The particular constellation of persons who interact with each other is an important determinant of whether the clients will be satisfied with the experience and the hoped-for outcomes achieved. In a worker-individual client situation, administrative decisions usually govern the assignment of a particular client to a practitioner. Often this occurs in as simple a way as assigning a client to whatever worker has the time to undertake the service. But if there is more than one alternative available, attention should be given to the compatibility between workers and clients.

The issues are primarily concerned with ethnicity, race, social class, sexual orientation, gender, and age. Differences in ethnicity between the worker and clients are usually accompanied by differences in socioeconomic status as well. When an ethnic group is also of a minority race, color differences have an influence on interpersonal relationships. Members of minority ethnic groups have ample reasons to distrust "Anglo" social workers because of the negative valuations that have been attributed to them in most of our society's institutions. White clients may carry over society's negative valuations of practitioners who belong to minority ethnic groups. Differences in religions with the accompanying values and attitudes toward such issues as birth control, homosexuality, use of alcohol, behavioral expectations, and preferences in food, manners, holidays, and traditions create discomfort among some people.

The variables of gender and age interact with other factors of difference between the practitioner and clients. Kadushin reports research findings indicating that clients tend to prefer male to female practitioners and older to younger ones.[42] These preferences are probably changing, however, with the rise of women's movements and changing attitudes toward well-qualified younger professional persons.

In considering the desirability of matching workers and clients according to factors of similarity and difference, Kadushin concluded that with too great a similarity between the worker and clients, there is a risk of overidentification and lack of objectivity; with too great a difference, it is harder to achieve empathy and understanding. Similarities tend to promote an early sense of trust and comfort while differences provide for stimulation toward changed ways of thinking and behaving. The weight of the evidence from research is that competence is a more important consideration than the descriptive characteristics of the worker are as these match or are different from those of the clients.

Differences can be overcome by competency. Solomon sets forth the knowledge and skills required of nonracist practitioners, whatever their own race and ethnicity.[43] The nonracist practitioner is able to perceive alternative explanations for behavior; collect those verbal and nonverbal cues that are helpful in choosing the most probable alternative in a given situation; feel warmth, genuine concern, and empathy for clients regardless of their race, color, or ethnicity; and confront clients when they distort or misinterpret the real feelings of warmth, empathy, and concern that have been expressed. The same characteristics would apply also to practitioners working with clients who differ from them in other important ways.

Make-Up of the Client System

Families.   Decisions concerning which members of a family should be included in family treatment for a particular purpose needs to consider the varieties of family life. Variations in family structure influence the ways in which families perform a broad range of functions and tasks and distribute their roles.[44] Although increasingly less frequent, the predominant structure continues to be a family consisting of two parents and one or more children. Roles of spouses in these families, however, change as both parents are increasingly employed outside the home. Blended or step-families are numerous, varying in their structural complexity; many include children from both prior marriages. As homosexual men and women are accepting their identity, they are living in domestic partnerships, sometimes with children in the home. The extent to which these couples and unmarried heterosexual couples who are living together assume the obligations and commitments to family life varies. Single-parent families, most often headed by a woman, are increasingly prevalent, owing to no marriage, divorce, or separation. They tend to have less income than two-parent families, even though a large proportion of the women are employed. Although a large majority of these families are white, a disproportionate number are African American or Hispanic.

Knowing who belongs to the family is a necessary prelude to determining who should be included in family sessions. In much of the literature on social work with families, it is interesting that only a small proportion of work is done with the total family.[45] More often than not, treatment is targeted to individuals; for example, the parents of a child or a spouse of an adult patient or to a married couple, excluding children or members of the extended family. When the family system is viewed as the modality of choice, practitioners strive to interest all members of the defined family in the endeavor, except perhaps for very young children. When all of the members attend the first session, they sense that each one of them is important to the task of working together to deal with the difficulties of one member that affects them all or to deal with a problem in the family's functioning.

The interdependence of members of a family, mutually influencing each other, suggests the desirability of service being given to the family rather than to one or two members. Family sessions have therapeutic values that benefit all of the members. Practitioners enter into the family as caring and yet temporary helpers who respect the family's culture, structure, and autonomy.[46] All of the members are simultaneously exposed to the worker, which tends to develop mutual understanding of their roles. All members can directly experience the practitioner's empathy, acceptance, and genuineness for each one and for the family as a unit. The members develop common knowledge of the problems of concern and the similar and different views that each one has about the situation. That open communication enhances the cohesiveness of the family and the members' sense of family identity. As members participate together in finding solutions to problems or making decisions, they gain self esteem and an increased capacity for recognizing and solving problems. They learn that differences can be expressed, weathered, and dealt with. When people participate in making decisions, the decision is often more acceptable than when others make it for them.

In reality, it is not always possible to get all of the members to attend all sessions, so practitioners begin with whichever members of the family are able or are willing to attend the session.

Because of the practical problems in insisting upon the presence of all family members, it is helpful to use the definition articulated by Wells and

Dezen. "A therapist engages in family therapy when he sees natural units as parents and children, spouses, or members of the extended family, together as a group over most of the duration of treatment with the goal of improving their functioning as a unit."[47]

Groups. It is in relation to formed groups in which the social worker makes the decision concerning whether to suggest membership to an applicant or client that there is most concern about group composition.[48] "The very fact of group mixture in itself," according to Redl, "may sometimes play a great part in what happens in a group, even when the best conditions and the most skillful professional leadership are taken for granted."[49] If persons are placed in unsuitable groups, they may become a serious disturbance to the group, be harmed by the experience, or drop out of the group. If the composition of a group is faulty, it is less able to become a viable and cohesive social system. The principle is to pay attention to the person-environment fit.

Knowledge of the factors that influence the participation of people is used by workers to determine which ones seem most crucial to the purpose and the anticipated focus of the group. There is no such thing as a perfectly composed group, but it is important that workers know with what they are dealing in this respect. Two basic questions to be raised are: Will particular individuals benefit from the group? Will they be able to participate in such a way that their presence will not interfere seriously with the realization of the purpose of the group for others? This is true for families as well as for formed groups.

Although there are many opinions about criteria for group composition, there has been little systematic study of who fits together in groups. Perhaps the most generally accepted principle is what Redl calls "the law of optimum distance": groups should be homogeneous in enough ways to insure their stability and heterogeneous in enough ways to insure their vitality (p. 82). This principle is based on the premise that the major dynamics in a group are mutual support and mutual stimulation among the members. Some balance is necessary so that no single member represents an extreme difference from other members, for this usually makes integration into the group unlikely. Clients who represent extremes of any one factor of significance in human relationships are usually not placed together.

The most important consideration in group composition is its purpose. The specific goals and needs of prospective members should be those that can be met through the purpose of the group. Whatever the purpose, it is essential that there be some common need or problematic situation to provide some focus for the content of group life. Goals of individuals need to be complementary and in harmony with the general purpose of the group.

Similarity in descriptive attributes can enhance the functioning of a group. People hesitate to join groups in which they feel very different from the other members. Similarity makes for compatibility and facilitates communication. Members of groups who share the experience of being in a similar stage of psychosocial development tend to face common life tasks to master and certain common interests to pursue.

Within the several stages in the life cycle, differences in age influence group participation. Levine, in a study of twenty-four outpatient therapy groups, found that similarity of age was the one factor significantly related to interpersonal attraction and freedom of expression.[50] Unless there is some strong sense of common fate that can overcome age differences, groups are most productive when members' ages are fairly similar. Age is a more important factor in relatively short-term groups than in long-term ones. It is also more important in childhood than in adulthood.

Gender-linked values and norms of behavior in our culture are important to the development of identity and successful role performance, even though these are changing rapidly. There are also values and norms for heterosexual relationships. Grouping by age and gender is often useful in that these similarities provide support for learning social roles. In spite of changes in expectations, women and men in groups are apt to use power and handle opportunities for intimacy differently. A study of groups by Garvin and Reed suggests that such groups have different effects on men and women and that some of these effects tend to restrict women's options and relegate them to less powerful positions within the group.[51] Daley and Koppenaal studied transition groups for women related to role changes and their effect on age-specific tasks. They found that, compared with cogender groups, the women's groups facilitated more self-disclosure of feelings and relationships, decreased the likelihood of acceptance of stereotyped roles, and provided greater opportunity for empathy and role modeling for sex-specific conflicts.[52]

In a review of research, Carlick and Morton found that, in groups which were segregated by gender, women concentrate on socioemotional expressive content; in integrated groups they tend to focus on task-oriented behavior.[53] Mixed groups may be preferred for certain other purposes, as in groups whose members need help to understand and improve heterosexual relations.

There is a tendency for small groups in our society to be based on similarity in cultural values and practices associated with social class, race, religion, and nationality. Difference in such characteristics tend to separate people from one another in work, play, education, place of residence, and lifestyle. These factors may be relevant to the purpose of the group; for example, when groups are formed to work toward improved interracial relationships, or to help members of a minority group to accept their own cultural background as a basis for integrating this facet into their basic sense of identity. These factors may not seem relevant to the purpose of the group but, since cultural differences influence attitudes, patterns of behavior, and interests, they cannot be ignored. They must be recognized. Plans must be made for utilizing differences as positive dynamics toward growth and change rather than as impediments to such movement.

The social worker is concerned not only with the nature of the capacities and problems of people, but with modes of coping with problems. How individuals express themselves, deal with tension and conflict, and defend themselves from threat and hurt, influence the nature and content of group interaction. Diversity of ways of coping with problems facilitates the exchange of feelings and ideas among members, providing there is a potential for a strong bond in relation to the purpose and focus of the group.

An individual's tendency to withdraw from relationships or to reach out aggressively to other people is especially important. Usually, extremely shy persons are not placed with extremely aggressive ones because of what is referred to as "shock effect." Members who are too far from the behavioral level of others in the group may find themselves in intolerable inner conflict, stirred up by the faulty placement.

An individual's ability to communicate through the use of verbal symbols is another important factor. If a group is to use predominantly verbal means of communication, the ability to express oneself verbally is essential. A nonverbal person often finds the problem intensified in a group of very active, talkative members. In groups of relatively nonverbal members, however, there is need, for some who can stimulate conversation at a level others can achieve.

A gross example of faulty group composition was a group of patients who had cystic fibrosis. All patients in the medical center were seen as needing a support group and were invited by their physicians to attend the group. The age range was from twelve to twenty-nine. There was a clash of interest between the eight members who were in junior or senior high school and the adults. The younger members needed help with their feelings about the diagnosis, the effects of the illness on their peer relationships, and responses to the knowledge that most patients die at an early age. The adults were concerned with broader issues, such as discrimination in employment, education of the public about the illness, and lack of community resources for patients. Different needs led to conflict, resolved by the young people dropping out of the group.

When a social worker consulted with the leader in charge of the group, the decision was made to divide the members into two groups, based primarily on age. The young people returned, and each group then pursued its particular goals.

The importance of group composition as a crucial element in planning for social work with groups is underscored by a study by Boer and Lantz. In comparing a group in which composition was planned with another group in which it was not planned, the authors concluded: "The groundwork of membership selection that occurs before the group, has as much importance in determining member commitment, attendance, and therapeutic results as does the ongoing group process."[54]

Number and Type of Personnel Involved

Traditionally the one-worker-to-one-client relationship has predominated, but an important issue in planning for services to a family or group is the decision whether to have one practitioner or to have coworkers with shared responsibility for giving service. Despite tradition, some workers espouse the use of more than one worker.[55]

One rationale for the use of coworkers is that this procedure improves the accuracy of assessment and the objectivity of workers. One practitioner may observe something that another misses. Workers' perceptions may become more realistic when they are tested against those of a colleague. The worker who is less active at a given time can note reactions of less verbal participants, as well as of those engaged in the immediate give and take.

A second major rationale is that coworkers enrich treatment. A division of labor between workers makes it possible for one to focus on major common themes of members while the other responds more frequently to individual concerns. Coleadership makes it possible for one worker to make demands for work while the other one provides necessary support, or one may reinforce the support given by the other. It provides more opportunities for learning new ways of communication and problem-solving, since the members can perceive how the workers communicate with each other and handle their differences.

Workers thereby serve as models for clients. If the coworkers are of different genders, they can model gender roles for members and serve as objects of identification for members of the same gender. They can also model appropriate heterosexual relations. Reed says that these ideas are, however, contradicted by evidence that male-female coleadership situations may perpetuate gender-stereotyped behaviors, even when both leaders are behaving in nonstereotyped ways for their gender.[56] In a world in which the roles of males and females are changing rapidly, the workers' own views of appropriate roles may be in conflict with those of members or with the family's cultural identity. Different perceptions exist concerning definitions of appropriate gender roles.

The rationale for the use of only one practitioner with a family or group concerns the influence of additional workers on the process.[57] With the addition of a second worker, there is much greater complexity of relationships and communication, with which each participant must cope. There are a subgroup of workers and another one of members. Each member must relate to the practitioner subsystem, as well as to each of the workers in it. With two or more workers participating, opportunities for members to participate are lessened. Each member must develop and cope with a relationship with at least two professionals, which dilutes the intensity of the worker-individual relationship and the worker-family or group relationship. The members must fathom the differences in expectations that each worker has for them and for the group. They usually identify one worker as the primary practitioner and the other as an assistant. Being an assistant is not the same as fully sharing the authority and responsibility that is implied in the coleader concept. Ethically, the members have a right to know what to expect of each practitioner and why each one is working with the group.

Any difficulties that copractitioners may have in working together are likely to be detrimental to the progress of treatment. Frequent difficulties are those of rivalry for the love and attention of the members, struggles for power to influence particular members or the group's structure and content, pressures on the workers to prove their ability and to do at least their fair share of the work, and a tendency to divert primary attention from the work of the unit to the relationship between colleagues. Too often, also, the workers do not share the same theoretical perspectives on practice, which creates confusion for clients in understanding the means being used to help them, unless these differences are discussed adequately. The members may resist the coleader situation by making unfavorable comparisons, taking sides, making one a scapegoat, pitting one against the other, giving or withholding affection from one, or projecting their feelings about the leaders onto each other.

The practical matter of cost in time and money is another factor to be considered in deciding on the number of workers assigned to a family or group. The use of two workers is more than twice as expensive as that of only one worker. Time is spent not only in individual and family or group sessions. If coleadership efforts are to be successful, the practitioners need to review together each session, work through their difficulties in roles and relationships, and engage in ongoing planning together.

The literature is rich in studies on this question.

In one study of fifty therapists in conjoint family therapy, Rice, Fey, and Kepecs found that experienced therapists gradually reached a point of diminishing returns in satisfaction with cotherapy. They came to prefer to work as the sole therapist because they considered this to be a more effective way to serve clients.[58]

In a survey of twenty-five faculty members who teach courses on practice with groups, Rothman found that 73 percent favored solo leadership for the education of students but half of them might use coleadership in practice under some circumstances.[59]

In another survey of psychologists, social workers, and psychiatrists, it was also found that the more experienced practitioners no longer preferred the coworker role.[60]

A review of literature on research on marital therapy by Gurman indicated that no support was found for the view that therapy by coworkers is more effective than treatment by a sole practitioner.[61]

Dies summarized five studies on coleadership in therapy groups and concluded that "Overall, the findings from these five studies suggest that the coleadership model may complicate the group therapeutic process and actually precipitate problems that are not evident in groups with only one leader."[62]

In a survey of residents in psychiatry, Friedman found that the quality of prior cotherapy experience seemed to be directly related to choosing one's own partner and that equal status seemed to be a more important determinant than such other factors as the gender of the coleader.[63]

Gitterman's opinion is that "the usual and most effective model for the staffing of groups is one worker who possesses substantive knowledge and practice skills."[64] The rationale for solo leadership is that it provides opportunities for more potentially intimate relationships and identifications with the worker and other members. The role of the worker in relation to members is clear to all, uncomplicated by differences in workers' perceptions of that role. Because only one person is in a formal power position in the group, the predominant power is with the members. Less time is taken in worker-to-worker communications, permitting more time for participation by members. The focus is maintained on the members' own concerns and on the process, rather than diluted by attention to the interactions between the coleaders.

More than one worker is, however, essential in some circumstances. There is often a realistic need for more than one practitioner, depending upon the size of the group, the nature of the content, and the needs and problems of the members. Often when members of other professions are involved in treatment, it is desirable that representatives of these professions participate in the sessions, at least some of the time. Such a plan makes it possible to integrate the contributions of both professions.

For example, a nurse or physician may focus on the physical needs of the patient and be responsible for the treatment of the illness, while the social worker's focus is on the psychological and social antecedents and consequences of the illness for both the patient and family. Another example of the need for more than one practitioner would be an activity group composed of children who are deficient in the ability to verbalize feelings and ideas and who require a great amount of attention within the group. Another would be a large multiple-family group, composed of several families who are also engaged in family therapy. By participating in the multiple-family group, the practitioners are able to further the plan for integrating two forms of help.[65]

The use of more than one worker, when the differences in roles are clearly defined, has potential values. One example, described by Marshall, is the use of aides to assist the social worker in activity groups of emotionally disturbed children and adolescents.[66] The functions of the aides were in the realm of child care activities with six- to eight-year-old children: Helping the members of the group on trips by driving the car while the professional worker's focus was on interacting with the members; maintaining safety; assisting with the content of the group by preparing materials, helping to select activities, arranging the room, teaching or leading a particular activity; and conducting life space interviews with particular members when their maladaptive behavior or troublesome events made this necessary. The effective use of aides requires careful selection and orientation, opportunities for observation, and participation in planning and in post-session evaluation conferences. It seems most appropriate to use more than one worker with large groups as in multiple-family therapy, with activity groups of disturbed children, and with some groups of married couples.

Duration: Brief Service/Extended Service

Although there has always been some emphasis on brief or short-term service, its use has accelerated greatly in recent years. In reality, most services have been short-term, but not necessarily planned as such. They include crisis intervention, task-centered practice, psychoeducation, advocacy, behavior modification, assisting clients through life transitions, specific problem-solving, and most forms of family treatment. Several studies have shown that short-term treatment is at least as effective as continued service.[67]

The first major study by Reid and Shyne compared short-term carefully planned treatment with extended treatment.[68] The findings were that planned short-term treatment was at least as effective as extended treatment and that at time of follow-up, gains had been sustained. The theoretical approach was in psychosocial casework, with some modifications to adapt that approach to a specified length of service. The results might have been different had the extended treatment been as carefully planned as was the time-limited service.

The advantages of short-term treatment are numerous. There are fewer unplanned terminations. A time limit discourages the often potentially destructive development of undue client dependency. It enhances a sense of hopefulness that positive changes will occur. Some people, particularly men, are thought to be more willing to participate in a time-limited service than in a longer one. Planned short-term treatment is thought to be most effective when the goals are clear and limited, as in the performance of tasks, improving communication, restoring the steady state following a crisis, making specific decisions, changing behavior in defined situations, and when the focus of the service is limited to the present time frame.

Task-centered practice is one of the best-known forms of short-term treatment and has been found to be effective in many situations. It offers a degree of specificity seldom present in other models of practice. Yet, it is evident that there are indications and contraindications for the use of this approach. A recent reevaluation of the practice cites some situations in which the approach is not suitable. The conclusion was that it is valuable for "psychologically intact clients who present relatively specific and limited problems. It is contraindicated for clients who lack the ego skills necessary to use a task-centered approach effectively, and have extensive difficulties that require long-term support and treatment."[69] The need is for accurate assessment to determine the applicability of task-centered or other brief services to the needs of clients.

Some individuals and families need continued service beyond the one-to-twelve weeks usually considered maximum for short-term service. A demand for a high degree of structure and time limits may run counter to the perspectives on time held by different ethnic groups. Cultural variations occur in preferred orientations to past, present, and future time frames. Devore and Schlesinger give the example of American Indians who need to be protected from early intimate disclosure.[70] Some people need considerable time before they are willing to share intimate thoughts and experiences and to enter into open communication with strangers.

The issue is not whether brief or longer service can be effective but rather under what circumstances each type is preferable. Numerous demonstration projects of longer term services have led to successful outcomes. These projects have included work with very troubled and disadvantaged young children, disturbed acting-out adolescents, regressed schizophrenic patients, and families with multiple problems. Certainly some people can benefit optimally from brief service; others need a longer period of time. William Meyer's view is that when clients have problems that are deeply pervasive and that influence adaptations in many spheres of their lives, long-term treatment is appropriate. "The ideal treatment for people who have been failed by human relationships is an enduring relationship that does not fail."[71] The important point is that, because there is evidence of the effectiveness of short-term treatment for some clients, there should be compelling reasons for deciding on long-term help. Unfortunately, agency policies and managed care organizations may conflict with clients' needs for continued service. It is the responsibility of clinical social workers to make efforts to influence the social context.

Clinical social workers need to understand the major issues in the planning process, including the selection of one or more modalities of practice, the make-up of the client system, the selection of practitioners, and the duration of service. They are then ready to work with their clients in the initial phase of treatment.

Ten | The Initial Phase

The means by which applicants take the first step to contact an agency or a practitioner has great influence on their use of the service. Some potential clients seek help voluntarily; others are involuntary clients.

Voluntary clients' decisions to apply for service are often the result of a number of interrelated decisions. They have already recognized that they want something which they think an agency or a private practitioner might be able to offer. The desire may be for a resource such as financial aid, adoption, foster care, or medical treatment; family planning or family life education; counseling or therapy for some personal or social problem. They may be self-referred or have been referred by another person. They may have learned about the service in varied ways. They may have learned about it through a representative of another organization, such as a teacher, employer, or judge. They may have learned about the service through the agency's publicity, as when a counseling service in a university publicizes its services to all students or when a youth-serving agency announces that it is starting a vocational exploration service for high school students and dropouts.

There has been increasing interest over the years in reaching out to prospective clients who do not seek service. In these instances, there is an active search for persons whom the worker or agency perceives to be in need of help. Reaching-out approaches are used in schools when the initial concern is usually expressed by a teacher or administrator who then tells a social worker about the pupil's needs. The child or his parents may or may not respond positively, but an agency of the community has decided that help should be offered. Cases in probation, work with delinquent gangs, and protective services in child welfare are other examples of this approach. These may become services that people want once they know about the positive intent of them, or people may be required to accept them or suffer some undesirable consequence.

Several authors make the point that a basic distinction appears between the roles of voluntary and involuntary clients. The voluntary role is assumed by persons because they hope for some benefit from the service. Initial positive motivation, however, may vary from a strong desire to some reluctance to enter into an agreement with a social worker. The involuntary role is ascribed to persons because of some other status they occupy, such as being a parolee or because of acts they are judged to have committed, such as child abuse.

Initial motivation is a transient factor. People who come with high expectations of having a need met may lose this motivation during the course of the initial sessions if the worker is not attuned to their needs, their feelings about requesting service, and their psychosocial situation. People who come with active resistance can develop motivation to use a service effectively.[1] Webb and Riley conducted research that indicates that voluntary initiation of a service is not required for successful involvement of clients.[2] Results of family-centered programs for multiproblem families, work with delinquent gangs, and services to hard-to-reach adolescents indicate that many initially unwilling clients can be reached and can make good use of social work help.[3] Other authors state that people can be changed even when initially they do not want to try, that motivation can be created.[4]

Even voluntary clients have ambivalent feelings about applying for a service. They almost always have some anxiety about a new experience: they have no way of knowing how they will be received and what will happen to them; they are hesitant about their own abilities to meet the practitioner's expectations. There is a sense of stigma attached to certain types of problems, such as a man's inability to provide for his family, certain illnesses such as epilepsy and AIDS, and such behavior as child neglect and spouse abuse. The still prevalent ethic in America that people should be independent and pull themselves up by their bootstraps makes it difficult to admit a need for help. In some cultures, the preference is for solving problems within the family.

The voluntary or involuntary aspect of service will have direct bearing on the process in the initial phase of service. It influences the length of time needed to achieve mutually acceptable goals and an effective working relationship between a worker and clients.

In addition to the voluntary or involuntary aspect of service, other matters greatly influence the use of social work services. Accessibility of needed services is essential. Being kept on waiting lists reduces motivation to use a service. One study found that applicants who had waited the shortest period of time accepted the service when appointments were offered. In another study, it was found that one-half of the applicants who had to wait nine weeks or more dropped out. Several other studies have confirmed the relationship between premature dropouts and length of waiting between sessions. Applicants who have longer waiting periods are less apt to keep their appointments. Agencies and practitioners, therefore, need to devise means for offering prompt help to those who need it.[5]

MAJOR TASKS OF PRACTITIONERS

The major focus of the clinical social worker's understanding and skills in the first sessions may be summarized as:

1. Orienting the individual or family to the agency's social context, structure, and available services.
2. Initiating a social work relationship with the individual or family and, in groups, initiating relationships among the members.
3. Clarifying the nature of the request and its suitability to the agency's service and determining the clients' eligibility.
4. Enhancing the motivation of clients to want to use an appropriate service, which requires recognition of ambivalence and resistance and the use of skills to enhance motivation.
5. Developing a preliminary contract that is arrived at through joint decisions about: (a) the nature of the needs or problems to be addressed; (b) one or more goals relevant to the clients' needs and, in family or formed groups, some common purpose; (c) the means and content to be used in working toward the achievement of the goals; and (d) the expectations and responsibilities of the clients and worker in their respective roles.

Preparation for the Interview

Social workers need to prepare for the initial interview with an individual or family. They review whatever material is available about the clients, such as telephone requests for appointments, completed application forms, or material prepared by the person referring the client. They use their knowledge about biopsychosocial functioning of people as they reflect on the characteristics of the clients as these might influence the initial interview. McQuaide, for example, describes how the practitioner, in working with Vietnamese refugees, might reflect on the emotional experiences they must have had in the flight from Vietnam and the resettlement process; the cultural shock of the difference between what they dreamed of and what exists in the new country; grief at the loss of people and things left behind; feelings about the discrimination against them, and so forth.[6] Reflection on the clients' situations and capacity for empathy are combined to make it possible for the practitioner to reach out to the clients with respect and sincerity.

Anticipatory Empathy

Practitioners use the available data for what Kadushin calls "anticipatory empathy" in an effort by the worker to consider imaginatively the clients in their situations.[7] Schwartz and Shulman have a similar idea which they call "tuning in," an effort by practitioners to get in touch with feelings and concerns that clients may have in coming for help.[8] As Devore and Schlesinger note, it is a process of reflection.[9] Within a general understanding of persons who have certain characteristics, practitioners remember that each person and family within a category is different. They consider their own feelings concerning their preliminary expectations about the person, as reflected through whatever information is available to them. Kadushin says that

> Adequate preparation increases the interviewer's confidence, diminishes anxiety, and ensures a more positive start to the interaction. Since many routine problems to be encountered in the interview are thought out and resolved in advance, the interviewer's mind is freed to deal more adequately with unanticipated problems during the interview.[10]

Setting the Stage

The success of treatment is influenced by the physical and social environment in which sessions are held. Practitioners prepare for the interview by arranging the physical setting so as to reduce the applicant's anxiety and enhance participation in the process. That is the skill of stage-setting.[11] Practitioners arrange the furniture in ways that optimize ease of communication. Comfortable chairs, places for hanging coats and leaving packages, and pleasantly furnished rooms indicate concern for the comfort of clients. The availability of amenities, such as coffee for adults and toys for children, may reduce initial anxiety. Workers need to position themselves at a suitable distance or angle in relation to clients' choice of positions.

Such seemingly minor details make a difference in the way the interview proceeds and in the applicant's satisfaction with it.

Most interviews take place in offices, but there is a renewed trend toward home visits.[12] Clients are often more comfortable, less defensive, and more accessible when met in their own homes. In selecting a meeting place, the ethics of confidentiality need to be considered. Ethnic groups vary in their attitudes toward privacy, as in the case of persons from Eastern European cultures who may be ashamed to ask for help and to have others know they are seeking it. Privacy and anonymity need to be assured.

Initiating a Relationship

An important task in the early phase of service is to achieve the quality of relationship that will make it possible for clients to have confidence in the worker's genuine concern for their well-being. Anticipatory empathy about what it means to enter into a new kind of relationship with a professional practitioner helps to establish a productive working relationship.

Sensitivity to Feelings

Most clients have some concern about their acceptability to the worker and, if in a group, to other members. The client may wonder: Will the worker like me, be interested in me, and accept me? Will I like the worker? If I am in a group, will the other members accept me and will I accept them? Will I be ignored or rejected? Who is the worker's favorite client? The fear of not being loved often runs deep and pervades much of the initial behavior of clients in new situations.

The second closely related concern is that of intimacy. The client may ask: How much will I need to disclose my thoughts and feelings? How close will we get to each other? Will my privacy be violated so that I am forced to reveal my most innermost self to another? Will the worker read my mind?

The third major concern of most clients is the issue of power and control. The client may wonder: Who will control what goes on? How much freedom will I have? How much can I determine what will happen? How dependent will I have to become to get what I yearn for? How will the information I provide be used? The clients ask these questions of themselves in many ways, but seldom in the form presented here and often through nonverbal means. The workers need to be sensitive to the clients' feelings and reactions and to be able to control their own feelings and reactions toward them.

Trust

Clients generally have little confidence in a social worker's ability to help them until they have developed some trust in the worker's genuine caring about them. Trust does not develop all at once. It develops as clients successfully test the worker's concern for them, through observing the worker's responses to their verbal and nonverbal behaviors. Achievement of trust is relatively easy or hard, depending upon the extent to which clients have developed a basic sense of trust. With an appropriate amount of support, acceptance, empathy, and authenticity from the worker, clients who have a healthy sense of trust will move rather quickly into a good working relationship with the worker. The less their ability to trust, the more difficult it will be.

Social workers convey trust by modeling, through their own attitudes and behavior, the qualities of acceptance, empathy and authenticity that were presented in chapter 6. They help clients to express their doubts about whether or not they can trust the worker and give clear and honest information about who they are and their intentions. An example is of a group.[13]

> In a first meeting of a group of fifth-grade boys, the practitioner recognized that they seemed to be suspicious about being referred to the group. Therefore, the worker said that maybe he should explain to them what the group is about and how they had gotten into it. He told them that he had met with the vice-principal, who expressed concern about the boys' school work and thought that they had the capacity to do better, and that a group could help them. The boys looked skeptical and when they did not respond to his request for comments or questions, he went on to say that he and the vice-principal thought the group would be a safe place in which to talk about some of the troubles kids often have, and do things that might help them get along better. There was another silence, but facial expressions and posture seemed to convey interest. Then he added, "Some of you seem to feel the group is some kind of punishment." The boys were verbally silent, but a couple started to giggle. The worker added, "Perhaps you don't think you can trust me." The comment identified the boys' feelings accurately. First one, then others asked such questions as: "well, are you connected with the police?" " will

you squeal to the vice-principal on us?" " will you squeal to my mother?" and, "if I mess up here, will you kick me out of the group?" Facing these doubts and finding acceptance from the worker began a gradual change from active resistance to positive motivation to be in the group.

Sensitivity to cultural differences and racial issues is crucial to the development of cross-cultural relationships, as discussed in chapter 6. Gibbs presents the need for personalized relationships with black clients, referring to this approach as an interpersonal orientation as contrasted with an instrumental or task-focused orientation to relationships.[14] She formulated a model that is similar to the personalized approach described by Solomon and Pinderhughes. She proposed that black people place a greater value on interpersonal competence than on instrumental competence.

The interpersonal orientation proposes that the development of a treatment relationship can be broken down into five microstages:

1. In the first or *appraisal* stage, the client sizes up the worker, waits guardedly for the worker to initiate the interview, and generally behaves in an aloof, reserved, or superficially pleasant manner, beneath which may be feelings of distrust, suspiciousness, or hostility. The clients are evaluating the genuineness of the worker.

2. The second or *investigative* phase is characterized by the client's checking out or testing the worker. Clients may challenge workers with questions about their backgrounds or power, in order to achieve greater equalization of power and status. The clients are judging the workers' abilities to equalize the differences in status and power

3. A third stage of *involvement* follows only if the client feels that the worker has checked out favorably. Otherwise, the client terminates prematurely. If the practitioner has checked out favorably, the client makes a positive identification with the worker, begins to disclose feelings and concerns, and attempts to establish a personal relationship with the worker, based on a perceived sense of similarity and mutuality by, for example, inviting the worker to have coffee, go to an ethnic event in the community, or contribute to an ethnic cause. This is a form of testing the degree of the worker's empathic identification with the client.

4. The fourth stage of *commitment* is one in which the client becomes committed to the relationship, drops defensive behavior, and expresses loyalty and personal regard for the worker. The worker is perceived to have demonstrated acceptance of the client as a unique individual, through empathic and supportive behaviors.

5. The final stage of *engagement* follows, in which clients involve themselves fully in the task-centered or problem-solving activities of treatment. They have tacitly acknowledged the interpersonal competence of the practitioner and are now ready to explore their problems with trust and confidence in their instrumental competence.

Anderson Franklin demonstrates the use of the interpersonal orientation in therapy with African American men, who generally have low rates of participation in therapy.[15] He discusses how socialization, cultural, gender-related, and psychosocial issues contribute to men's negative attitudes toward therapy and practitioners. Respect, genuineness, and integrity must be displayed in order to develop a trusting relationship. Trust is crucial in overcoming their healthy skepticism toward the value of therapy. He says that "providing clients with gentle, well- paced insights conveys knowledge, understanding, and empathy, all of which will strengthen the client's sense of trust in the therapist's humanity and competence" Clients need to disclose information at their own pace. "After trust is established, the empowerment process can begin" (p. 354).

The concept of interpersonal orientation to the professional relationship may be generalizable to other ethnic groups. A similar concept has been described as personalism that refers to the inclination of Latin people to relate to and trust persons, rather than institutions, and their dislike of formal, impersonal structure and organizations. The concept has many similarities also to the description of relationships in the early phases of group development, particularly with resistant adolescents, disturbed acting out children, and adults with serious mental disorders. It seems to be more typical of many clients who enter treatment than does the instrumental orientation.

Engagement: Motivation and Resistance

Engagement in the use of help requires recognition of some need or problem that is appropriate to the services offered; acceptance of some responsibility for a part in the situation; willingness to express feelings, thoughts, or experiences with a practitioner and often also with members of a family or formed group; and a decision to invest energy, time, and perhaps money in the effort. When a decision about these matters is made by clients, they are motivated to use the help that is offered.

Motivation

Motivation is the amount of pressure clients feel to change their problematic situations. The pressure stems from the perceived gap between what is and what might be and from feeling some hope of closing the gap. Clinical social workers believe that all people have the capacity for growth and positive change, which attitude is conveyed to their clients through verbal and nonverbal communication. Most people do want to feel more satisfied with their psychosocial functioning and to overcome obstacles in their environment, which desire is a positive influence on their use of a social work service.

But even within a highly positive commitment to get help for their problems, some ambivalence is present. Seldom is the desire so strong as the eager anticipation of five- and six-year-old boys and girls in a children's hospital. A play group was developed for the purpose of helping the children to reduce anxiety about their illnesses, to understand the varied procedures of treatment, and to develop relationships with other children that might sustain them through the difficult period of hospitalization. When the social worker entered the ward to invite the children to come to the group, she found poignant desire combined with apprehension about exclusion. One little boy in a wheelchair asked, "Do you want me?" in a tone that expressed both wonder and fear. A girl tugged at the worker's skirt and in a high-pitched voice asked, "Me, too; me, too?" The oldest boy asked, "Is there room for one more; is there room for me?" How different this behavior is from an adolescent boy who was referred by a judge for counseling with the admonition to "stay in counseling or go to Juvenile Hall," hardly a positive motivation toward the service.

Hope as motivation. Hope is a powerful motivating force. An increasing amount of medical research provides evidence that hope can strengthen the immune system: a determination to overcome an illness or other obstacle has a positive influence on the outcome.[16] Particular feelings can actually affect the functioning of the human body. Positive feelings contribute to healing. As is true of the body, so does hope have a positive influence on psychosocial functioning.

The amount of hope and encouragement given during and immediately following the initial interview is associated with continuation in treatment, according to Ripple. She reports that discouragement by the worker is almost always associated with discontinuance.[17] Discouragement is characterized by blandness and neutrality toward the client, no offer of hope that the situation could be improved, and no specific offer of an early second appointment. In order to want a service, a person must have some discomfort about the current situation, but also some hope that something can be done about it. From another study, Fanshel drew similar conclusions.[18] Zalba, in studying continuance in private family agencies, confirmed the finding that continuance is related to the optimism of the worker. A higher rate of continuance was associated with higher optimism about the outcome of the services. In cases in which there was both low optimism on the worker's part and great severity of client's problems, the discontinuance rate was highest.[19] In another study, Boatman found that appraised hopefulness had a discernible influence on workers' activities.[20] It is clear, then, that workers need to communicate to their clients their expectations that there can be improvement in some aspect of the psychosocial situation, so as to evoke hope in the client.

Clients motivations certainly influence their use of service, but the worker has to assume a part of the responsibility for enhancing or weakening motivation. Bounous, in a study of 106 women and their eight workers in a family service agency, found that 28 percent of the clients dropped out after only one interview, without discussing their intentions with the worker or without agreement between worker and client that discontinuance was appropriate. The worker's perceptions of client motivation tended to be inaccurate. The workers had predicted that almost none of the clients would discontinue.[21] When clients were highly motivated, the workers tended to underestimate their acceptance of counseling as a preferred means of help, the amount of responsibility they felt in relation to a problem, and the support from significant others for their getting help. They tended to overestimate the severity of problems and the clients' perceptions of the severity of the problems. These findings indicate that workers need to give more attention to a client's strengths, to focus attention on the relative value the client places on getting help at a particular time in a particular place, and on the degree to which the client is willing to assume some responsibility for changing the problem or situation.

When clients reject the idea that service will be beneficial and are not ready to engage themselves in using help, the initial phase will be prolonged. Workers can anticipate that there will be considerable denial or projection of problems on others and great ambivalence about becoming involved with the worker. Workers will need actively to enable such clients to find some goal, no matter how small, that they are willing to work toward. At the same time, they will need to deal with the ambivalence and projection that block the movement into relationship. Even though the client denies the problem, there is usually some thread of concern that the worker can pick up, such as being able to do something different enough "to get dad off your back" or to "keep you out of jail" or "to be able to get your child back." Apparent resistance to using help may be related to a pervading sense of hopelessness or despair. Some clients have problems of long standing that seem so serious to them that they have given up hope that things can be better. They believe that positive change is impossible, either because of environmental conditions, such as feeling that "you can't beat the system," or because of feelings of inadequacy to perform in the desired way. Such clients often have practical obstacles that interfere with the use of help, such as physical impairments, lack of money for child care, suitable transportation, or difficulty in arranging appointments during work hours. Workers must be able to help such clients to feel some hope that something can be better, to begin to relieve the sense of powerlessness that many poor people and members of minority groups experience. They may send a message that "Sometimes it feels hopeless but, if we work together, we can probably find ways of making it better"; and then giving them information about how they will be helped to find and use essential resources in the community.

Resistance

Resistance is a trend of forces against using the help that is offered. It consists of those attitudes and behaviors that interfere with making progress in solving problems.[22]

To be effective, social workers need to understand the multiple reasons that people have for resisting the help that is offered and often desired. It is difficult for some clients to identify with the role of client and accept help from a professional person. Clients may be reluctant to admit that they need help from an outsider. They may regard inability to cope adequately with their difficulties or to provide necessary resources for themselves as serious weakness. If they value independence more than interdependence, they believe that they should be able to act independently. If they need financial assistance or other tangible resources, they may feel humiliated and embarrassed at having to secure these through social agencies or they may feel ashamed to request a reduction in usual fees. If they have been victimized by an unjust and racist society, they may feel hostility toward agencies that are a part of that society. Some people find it difficult to accept a role as client because they associate the present experience with similar past experiences that were unpleasant. If they have had prior experience with a social agency, and were dissatisfied with the content, process, or outcome, they may not expect that it can be better this time. These are examples of obstacles to achieving a positive identity as a client.

Resistance in the early phase may be related to fear or, at least, to uncertainty about the unknown. It is natural to feel fearful about what any new endeavor will entail and hesitant about becoming involved in it. Use of professional help is a new experience for most clients so that they lack adequate knowledge of what is expected of them and what they can expect of the worker and of other members, if they are in a group. They may fear they will not be able to meet expectations and thus fail again. They may doubt that their needs and goals are appropriate to this particular situation.

Some insecurity or even psychic trauma is natural as a person meets with one or more strangers. Entering into new relationships is often particularly difficult for clients who are having difficulties in relating to other people. Anxiety about relationships varies from minimal concerns to deep paranoid terrors. Entering into a new relationship stirs up earlier conflicts about a person's acceptability to others, trust versus distrust, exposure of all of one's vulnerabilities to others, fear of being controlled, and fear of closeness and intimacy.

Evidences of resistance.   The forms that resistance takes are myriad. There may be denial that there is a problem or insistence that one can handle it alone. Resistance may be indicated by the use of time: forgetting to come, arriving late, or giving signals that indicate a desire for early ending of the session.

Resistance may be indicated by failure to follow certain procedures, such as completion of a registration or application form. It may be related to the nature of participation: refusing to answer questions even if these were appropriately asked; avoiding relevant subjects; over compliance; blaming others for one's predicament; changing the subject; monopolizing the conversation in a way that shuts out the worker or other members; bringing gifts; and using such defenses as denial, rationalization, or displacement in discussion of needs or problems. If there has been transfer of an individual or a group to a new worker, the clients are apt to show resistance through comments that compare the present worker with the former one or that test the present worker's knowledge of their situations.

An example of a client who was initially resistant to service:

Billy, a sixteen-year-old black youth, was referred to a youth-family counseling center by the local police department. Because he was involved in three auto thefts within a period of five days, the police regarded his case as one that merited attention. The social worker, a black man, was assigned to study the offense, the boy and his family, and the environmental influences affecting his behavior in order to recommend whether the family could be helped by our agency or what other plans should be made for Billy. A report from the school indicated that Billy's schoolwork is poor and that his conduct both in and out of class is unsatisfactory. Teachers report that he is sullen, defiant, and uncooperative. His choice of companions and activities is questionable. He has not, however, been in trouble with the police before this time.

Billy lives with his mother, Mrs. Grant, in a rented five-room house located in a predominantly black residential neighborhood of modest homes. His mother has worked periodically in the past, but she is now unemployed and receives AFDC payments. She has been in poor health most of her life. She is a deeply religious person and insists that Billy practice his religion seriously and engage in church activities. Soon after completing high school, Mrs. G. met and became pregnant by Billy's father. Although he refused to marry her, they lived together for several years. She reported that he beat her on numerous occasions. She left him because of his heavy drinking and irresponsibility.

Billy did not keep his first appointment and did not want to see me. I told him the court had ordered it. I arranged to meet him at school and we had our discussion in my car as I drove him home. He is average height for his age, slight in build, rather nice looking in appearance, but his face was clouded with a somewhat depressed look. Initially, he was extremely defensive and brusque. He seemed to be expecting a punitive, authoritarian approach and was acting accordingly. I told him who I was, the agency I represented, and explained why I was here. I remarked that, as he knew, the police and school were concerned about his behavior. I was here to get acquainted with him and his family and to talk with him and his mother about the difficulties they were having.

Billy relaxed slightly. I asked if there were any questions he wanted to ask me. He looked at me intently and after a long silence, said, "yeah, can I ask what the outcome of all this will be?" I said certainly, and I could understand that he must feel worried about what will happen to him because of the seriousness of what he had done. I said I wished I could tell him, but I need to know more about him and the situation before I could honestly say what my recommendation to the police would be. He said that was fair, but he hoped it wouldn't take too long because he was very nervous. When I asked about these feelings of being nervous, he said that it just felt awful not knowing what was going to happen to him. He did not think he could take being sent away and locked up for a long time. He added that it was always black kids who got sent away. I said that many kids were sent to a correctional school, but that did not mean it had to happen to him.

I said I had learned from him that he and his mother have difficulties in getting along together, and I would like to try to help both of them to work things out so that there wouldn't be these bad feelings between them. Billy remarked, with some bitterness, that his mother and relatives just did not trust him, and he gave examples of what he meant by that statement. I said he seemed to think that no one can be of much help to him, perhaps including me. He did not respond to this statement. I asked if he would be willing to try to work with me to talk more about his feelings and the things that bothered him, and to meet with me and his mother to try to find ways to get along better. He said he was willing to try anything.

In an analysis of this interview, the social worker thought he had overcome some of Billy's initial resistance that seemed to be related to his perceptions of the worker as a punitive person, the worker's power to make a recommendation about the disposition of the case to the police, a sense of hopelessness and despair, and a great lack of trust in adults. He reached out to Billy by meeting him in familiar surroundings and driving him home in his car, thus creating an atmosphere of informality. At the same time, he presented himself and his responsibility clearly. In the communication between the worker and his client, the worker observed and responded to Billy's nonverbal behavior, gave Billy opportunities to ask questions and answered them simply and honestly, explored and understood Billy's feelings and his perceptions of the problems in an accepting way, and felt and conveyed an attitude of empathy through words and manner. He offered some hope that Billy's relationship with his mother and other adults could be improved. He selectively used techniques that are most appropriate in the initial phase in the categories of support, structuring, exploration, education, and clarification of purpose and roles. He gained considerable information that will be helpful in formulating a biopsychosocial assessment as a basis for a viable treatment plan. The major problem at this time seems to be dysfunctional interpersonal relations at home and school.

Most new clients, like Billy, are not completely motivated to use a service. Even when they apply voluntarily they begin with considerable ambivalence. They simultaneously have antithetic emotions and attitudes. It is natural for people to have mixed feelings about other people and situations; they come to new experiences both wanting and fearing them. It is anxiety- provoking to find one's way through a maze of customs and procedures that are specific to a particular kind of service. In order to gratify some of their desires, clients have to deny others. Being a client requires giving as well as receiving, and it requires some degree of involvement of self in the process. In group situations, the demand for giving as well as receiving is perhaps even greater than in the one-to-one relationship.

Children and adolescents are often reluctant to discuss difficulties at home or at school because they are dependent upon their parents, guardians, and school personnel. They fear that what the worker tells other adults will be used against them: they fear collusion between the worker and other adults. Work with children almost always involves work with the significant adults in their lives. Full confidentiality cannot be promised, but it is reassuring to the child to be told the worker will be talking with certain adults, the reasons for doing so, and what kind of information will be discussed and what will not be discussed. As workers prepare to work with a child alone, as part of a family, or as a member of a group, they can imaginatively reflect on what it would be like "to walk in the child's moccasins." They can reflect on the possible mood when the child comes to the first session: fear of being seen as bad or sick; fear of losing control of their feelings; doubt about a strange new adult who is neither a teacher, doctor, parent, relative, nor recreation leader. As they get started with children, a simple statement introducing themselves and explaining what they will be doing together tends to reduce anxiety and prepare children for their part in the process.

As workers sense evidences of anxiety, they can reassure the client by universalizing the experience, for example, by telling the child: this is a place where lots of children come and when they first come, many don't know what will happen and it feels scary to them. The response, "yeah," leads to exploring, for recognizing and responding to the child's feeling is crucial. Inviting the child to ask questions about the worker's initial statement often leads to personal questions about the worker's status and interests. The worker usually gives the sought-for information directly and briefly rather than requesting reasons for the question or turning it back to the child. Children want to know and need to know something about workers, if they are to admit them into their lives.

When trust is established, children are able to express some of their deep concerns. An example is David, a Chinese boy with a Caucasian stepmother.[23] He had been referred by a family therapist, following hospitalization after a suicide attempt. He also has juvenile diabetes. In the traditional Chinese family, work, education, achievement, and self control are highly valued. A white male therapist had been working with David, who grew increasingly resistant and the therapist acknowledged that he and David "were stuck." The new social worker was able to demonstrate empathy, warmth, and interest in David. She had explained to him how he was referred to her, what she knew about him, and that he would decide whether he wanted to continue with her. The record reports:

> After a brief pause and cautiously, David asked whether I knew his stepmother was white. I said I had known that and I thought perhaps that bothered him some. He agreed tentatively, and went on to say angrily that "she just took over, just moved right in" after his father had sent his mother to a mental hospital. . . . He talked about his mother, saying he wasn't sure what had happened to her. I said it was very hard not to be sure, it seemed there might be lots that he was not sure about. . . In the reflective silence, I told him that so many unsure ideas could make one upset, confused, and even angry. We sat quietly for a moment as I watched David's discernible struggle to take in my thoughts. I added then that David had told me he resented his white stepmother: I, too, was white. David grinned a bit sheepishly and asked whether I knew about zebras, bananas and oreos. I said I did. David grinned again and listened alertly as I commented that he would have to decide how I was on the inside, and whether he could trust me, such things take time. I invited David to make his own judgment.

Resolving ambivalence.   Resistance and positive motivation often exist side by side. In group situations, pregroup interviews are used to help prospective members to resolve ambivalence, facilitate attendance, and clarify goals and expectations.

Research findings indicate that there are important benefits of pregroup interviews. In a controlled experiment comparing sixteen groups whose members had interviews with an equal number without interviews, Meadow concluded that the pregroup interview is a useful tool in facilitating attendance and developing clarity of purpose and expectations.[24] From his own research and a review of studies on the subject, Yalom concluded that evidence from a compelling body of research demonstrates that systematic preparation of patients for group therapy facilitates the patients' course in that therapy and supports the efficacy of advance preparation of the group.[25]

The following illustration presents excerpts from a taped interview with a recently discharged patient from a mental hospital.[26] The patient was referred to a group in a community setting by her psychiatrist, who had talked with the group worker and provided her with information about the patient's schizophrenia and current state of psychosocial functioning. She needed to break out of her social isolation, enhance her self-esteem, and develop skills in relating to other people.

Mrs. Mayhew arrived early for her appointment with the social worker, who greeted her, invited her to take off her coat and find a comfortable chair. The worker said she understood that Mrs. M. was here to learn about the mental health group and decide whether or not she wanted to become a member. Mrs. M. responded with "uh-uh-yes." The worker gave information briefly about the purpose, composition, and content of the group, stopping frequently to ask Mrs. M. if she understood. The response was always "uh-huh." She listened intently, with nonverbal gestures indicating extreme anxiety.

WORKER: Sometimes people feel uncomfortable about being interviewed.

MRS. M. (laughing): That's me.

WORKER: Yes, most people do at first. Could you tell me what you think of your doctor's suggestions about the group

MRS. M.: Well . . . (pause) I just came here because the doctor arranged the interview, so I'm here. . .

WORKER: Uh-huh. . .

MRS. M.: And I do want him to think I'm trying.

WORKER: Well, I know that he thinks that the group would help you and that being with other people will improve your health.

MRS. M.: That's what he told me.

WORKER: But, you're not sure you want to try it.

MRS. M.: Well . . . when you tell me about the group, it makes me feel a little dazed . . . (silence)

WORKER: A little dazed?

MRS. M.: Yes—that's how I think I feel.

WORKER: Can you tell me more about that feeling?

MRS. M.: I'll try. What will happen to me in the group? It'll be so confusing—so strange—all so new.

WORKER: It will feel that way at first all right—but I'll be there to help you feel more comfortable.

MRS M.: Like here today?

WORKER: Yes—you're not as anxious now as when you first came in, are you?

MRS M.: No. No. Could you tell me again what we'll be doing in the group—what it will be like?

WORKER: Certainly. (W. explains what the purpose of the group is, how it can help, who will be in it, and what the content of the sessions will be.)

MRS M.: So, we'll hash over each others' problems?

WORKER: Well—yes. But not only that. It's also what's going on in your daily lives—how you can get along living in the community—and learning social skills.

MRS. M.: I guess I need that. There are no lectures, then?

WORKER: No, but what do you think about that?

MRS. M.: Well—if there were, I could just listen—I wouldn't have to talk.

WORKER: You won't be forced to talk until you're ready.

MRS. M. (sigh of relief)

(MRS. M. asked questions about when the group would meet, whether there would be a fee, how many members there would be, whether the group would do other things, to which questions the worker gave answers and tried to determine the meaning of the questions to Mrs. M.)

MRS. M.: Well, yes, I just don't know. It seems rather . . . (inaudible)—just to be around people who are sick like me—it'll be almost like being back in the hospital again. That's scary.

WORKER: It's true that all members of the group have been in mental hospitals, but that does not mean they do not have many abilities and good qualities. They all want to make it in the community and they're in the group because we think they can make it in the community—and the group can help them with that.

MRS. M.: Well—I want to make it, too.

WORKER: That's something you have in common with the others. The group can help you to enjoy being with other people and getting along well with them. That's what it's for.

MRS. M.: When your whole life has been disrupted like mine has been, I just don't feel any satisfaction with anything or anybody.

WORKER: Would you like to?

MRS. M.: Oh yes, I would, but it seems so hopeless.

WORKER: Hopeless—that's a scary feeling.

MRS. M.: Yes. (silence) Could the group help?

WORKER: I feel quite sure that it can and your doctor feels it can, too.

MRS. M.: That's what he said.

WORKER: But you still feel unsure about it.

MRS. M.: Well—it's so scary to have to meet new people.

WORKER: Yes, it is. But you'll have help with that. You'll be surprised how helpful members can be to each other.

MRS. M.: I've always been shy about meeting people.

WORKER: And that's what the group is for . . .

MRS. M.: Maybe I should try it—all my life—getting out and making friends—I haven't been able to—I haven't been able to.

WORKER: Would you like to learn to do that?

MRS. M. (sigh): You think I could?

WORKER: Yes, I do—in the group.

MRS. M.: Well, I'll give it a try.

WORKER: Good. (Then W. gives information about the importance of not just dropping out after first meetings and of giving the group a real try for at least two months and answers more questions about the conduct of the group and other members.)

MRS. M.: If you think I should come next Tuesday, I'll be here. Both you and my doctor seem to want me in the program.

WORKER: And I hope you'll soon feel that you really want to be in it, too.

MRS. M.: Well, I do want to come, but I know I'll feel like a sore thumb sticking out all over.

WORKER: That's not a pleasant feeling, but you're not like a sore thumb with me.

MRS. M.: It's not so hard to talk with you now (smiling).

WORKER: You're not nearly as anxious as when you first came in here, and after you get used to the group, you won't be so anxious there either.

MRS. M.: I will come to the group on Tuesday. (There followed discussion of transportation; a visit to the meeting room; an introduction to the receptionist; an invitation to call the worker if Mrs. M. had any more questions that need answering.)

MRS. M.: Goodbye and thank you. I'll see you Tuesday.

In this situation, the social worker agreed with the psychiatrist's judgment that Mrs. Mayhew could make appropriate use of a particular group. There are instances, however, in which the decision is that any group, or a particular group, is inappropriate for the client at this time. When practitioners have doubts about the group's suitability, they share these doubts directly with the person. For example, in the case of Mrs.

M., a simple "maybe you are not ready for the group now" or "I think I see that you need something different from what the group could offer" may suffice, and then the worker follows up with eliciting the responses to such a statement. The response would tend to confirm or disconfirm the worker's judgment. When the decision is not to admit a person to the group, the worker sensitively, with empathy, explores and responds to the person's feelings about the decision, whether or not it is jointly made. The important point is that an alternative be offered—the search for a more appropriate group, or an offer of individual or family help, or a different type of service through referral within the agency or elsewhere.

Resistance to family therapy.   A member of a family who initiates a request for service may resist involving other members of the family in the service. They may fear that family secrets will be revealed, that members who differ from them may retaliate against them, they are convinced that the problem lies within one member of the family. Freeman points out that one of the first tasks of the practitioner is to reframe a problem as one of the family.[27]

Doherty and Baird provide a series of principles aimed at getting all members of the family to the initial session.[28] The first principle is to simply and confidently state that all members of the family are expected to come to the meeting. The second principle is to communicate a sense of urgency about assembling the family. The practitioner may note, for example, that family involvement is the only way that the problem can be resolved. A third principle, when there is hesitation to involve the family, is to ask for the help of family members to understand the one who is thought to have the problem. Other members are necessary to help the worker to gain necessary understanding of the defined client. The final principle is to declare the limits of the practitioner's ability to help unless the family is involved. Such a declaration is often a reality. Most people will respond to the worker's minimum requirement for helping with the problem—namely, a family meeting. Nelsen gives an example from a community mental health center.[29]

> Mrs. Williams began the call rather nervously giving her name, explaining that the receptionist had given her mine, and saying she would like to make an appointment for her son. I replied that I would certainly like to help. Would she mind telling me a little more about the situation? She went on to say that Jimmy, ten, has always been a quiet child with only a few friends but now he seems even more withdrawn, and she and her husband are worried. I asked

how Jimmy acts with his folks and whether he has brothers and sisters. Mrs. Williams said he almost seems afraid of his parents, especially her husband, and of his older brother, too. I asked how she decided to call this setting and she said a neighbor had been helped here in the past. This is the first time the family has sought help of this sort.

I asked more questions about the family, learning that Jimmy's big brother, Mike, is fourteen, and that no one else lives with the family. Then I said that when a child Jimmy's age is having trouble, we like to start off by meeting with the whole family. Mrs. Williams said, "Oh" in some kind of choked off way and there was a short silence. I wondered if she had questions about this. She said she thought she might be asked to come in to give information about Jimmy but not that anyone else would be. I replied that from what she had said, her husband is worried about Jimmy and his brother Mike is probably aware of the situation, too. Everybody, including Jimmy, is probably unsure of the best thing to do. Seeing everyone could help us all understand better what's happening and begin to plan what to do. What did she think?

In addition to the voluntary initial motivation for service, other matters greatly influence the use of social work services. accessibility of needed services is essential. Being kept on waiting lists reduces motivation to use a service. One study found that applicants who had waited the shortest period of time accepted the service when appointments were offered. In another study, it was found that one half of the applicants who had to wait nine weeks or more dropped out. Several other studies have confirmed the relationship between premature dropouts and length of waiting between sessions. Applicants who have longer waiting periods are less apt to keep their appointments. Agencies and practitioners, therefore, need to devise means for offering prompt help to those who need it.[30]

Self-awareness. There is a tendency for social workers to regard all objections or opposition from clients as negative. Hamilton has cautioned that the client may not want some aspects of the service for many good as well as poor reasons.[31] The worker needs to evaluate the meaning of the defenses against involvement in treatment; they may indeed be reactions to inappropriate means used by the social worker or to the worker's own fears or insensitivities to the needs and abilities of individuals or groups. Clients from cultures different from the workers may be motivated to have help, but have a different view of the process. Levine notes that one major cause of group resistance occurs when the worker has directly, or through a sub- system, forced his will on the group without negotiations with members. He notes that most resistance represents a power struggle between the worker and one or more members.[32]

Social workers, as well as clients, have some ambivalence about undertaking a new case. They have some fears and doubts that are similar to those of clients. They may feel uncertain about whether or not they can be helpful to a particular individual or group. They may be concerned about how clients will perceive and evaluate them and whether or not they will accept them. They may fear that they will encounter unmanageable resistance, especially if a client is not self-referred. They may be so engrossed in what appears to be serious pathology that they feel hopeless about the client's ability to use help. They may fear acting out behavior on the part of the clients, as in excessive aggression. They may expect that some clients will make overwhelming dependency demands on them.

Learning to handle retaliatory resistance is an important key to a beginning relationship. To some extent, resistance constitutes a rejection of the worker. In seeming to act against what a worker has to offer, the client stirs up feelings of annoyance or frustration. If resistance is not understood and dealt with, it is natural for the client to retaliate. A client, for example, avoids the worker by failing to keep an appointment; the worker avoids discussing this default. A client keeps changing the subject; the worker fails to keep the focus on the topic. When a worker knows a client is lying, the worker may retaliate by failing to challenge the client, or even by drawing the client out to further fabrication and trying to trap him or her. There is a tendency to avoid directness because of fear of provoking hostility. If a worker understands the feelings that are aroused by a client's behavior, she or he can challenge it in a nonpunitive and nonaccusatory manner. Being direct is essential, but it is not to be confused with being directive.[33]

Contracting

One major focus of the initial phase is development of a partnership between the social worker and an individual, family, or group in which all parties have a common understanding of the enterprise in which they are engaged. Many recent writers refer to this task as contracting between a worker and a client system. Siporin defines a contract:

> A contract is a consensual, mutual agreement, and acceptance of reciprocal obligations and responsibilities, with a promise to perform certain tasks

and to deliver certain goods within some time period. Usually there is also a sanction or penalty for failure to perform expected behaviors; the penalty may be to terminate the relationship, pay back the goods, or pay damages. A contract has the effect of providing authority to take certain actions, including to do something to or for the other party of the agreement. A contract is usually written and often enforceable by law[34]

Remember, clients must give their informed consent to the contract.

Perlman states that the social worker and client form "a pact that is the basis of ongoing productive partnership between client and agency."[35] The worker gives information; affirms what the client expects and what the agency can offer; clarifies the conditions for working together and the responsibilities of each to the endeavor. Other writers similarly emphasize that the working agreement sets forth the goals of the service, the needs or problems to be addressed, the reciprocal roles of worker and client system, the model or theoretical orientation of the practice, and the unit or system through which service will be given.[36] Such mutual agreements are fundamental in determining the direction, structure, and nature of the service. But flexibility is necessary if working agreements are to be tools in treatment. Flexibility makes it possible to redirect efforts, as appropriate to the needs of clients or according to changing environmental circumstances. There is a danger that if an initial contract is formal and very explicit, it can become a "corrupt one," as when the initially stated goals of clients are specified in the contract and conceal more important unavowed ones.[37]

A tentative working agreement is derived from shared experience in exploring the client's needs and situations. Its major values are that it gives both the worker and the client a sense of involvement and participation, and it signifies mutual commitment and responsibility. It provides a common frame of reference for the participants so that each one is clear about what is expected of self and others. It provides a foundation for periodic review of progress and next steps. Congruence among the parties to the agreement leads to effective functioning, and failure to achieve congruence promotes maladaptation and hinders directed activity. With the rise of incongruities, individuals are working at cross-purposes, and the worker's efforts tend to be diluted and diverted. Congruence allows a worker and clients to establish and sustain a working alliance. Contracting needs to be viewed as an on-going process rather than as a series of static agreements. It is a transactional process of negotiating agreements.

Problems and Goals

The purpose for which people engage in a joint venture is a propelling motivation and a necessary condition for successful action. John Dewey has stated clearly the meaning of the word "aim," used synonymously with goal or purpose: "An aim denotes the result of any natural process brought to consciousness and made a factor in determining present observation and choice of ways of acting."[38] He also explains:

> Since we do not anticipate results as mere intellectual onlookers, but as persons concerned in the outcome, we are partners in the process which produces the result. . . .The net conclusion is that acting with an aim is all one with acting intelligently. To foresee a terminus of an act is to have a basis upon which to observe, to select, and to order objects and our own capacities. (pp. 102–3)

He makes clear that goals cannot be completely determined in advance.

> The aim as it first emerges is a mere tentative sketch. The act of striving to realize it tests its worth. If it suffices to direct activity successfully, nothing more is required, since its whole function is to set a mark in advance, and at times a mere hint may suffice. But usually—at least in complicated situations—acting upon it brings to light conditions which had been overlooked. This calls for revision of the original aim; it has to be added to or subtracted from. An aim must, then, be flexible; it must be capable of alteration to meet circumstances.(p. 104)

In the early phase, social workers attempt to clarify the purposes for which they are able to offer service. Oxley notes that to begin with clients where they are means understanding their hopes and expectations. When clients come to see a worker, they have some idea, however vague and general, about the agency where they are making their request for assistance or which they have been sent by another person. The clients' initial expectations about the purpose may be based on knowledge, rumors, or attitudes that seeking service is degrading or that it is respectable. These ideas influence the statements they make about the reasons for coming or being sent to this particular place. Clients are deeply concerned with determining if they can get some particular needs met and under what conditions. It is not their responsibility initially to understand the agency's function and to gear their requests accordingly.[39] It is the worker's responsibility to clarify what help can be given in relation to what the client desires.

Workers do not determine the purpose or goals for the clients; they explore with them their reasons for seeking assistance or having been referred by someone else. To clarify goals they must seek expression of perceived needs, problems and aspirations. Goals are clearly related to the resolution of one or more problems identified by the clients and which are suitable to social work intervention. Some clients are so overwhelmed by stress that they have difficulty identifying problems. They need help to sort out and order their concerns. Frank gives an example:

Mrs. O. came for a first appointment, citing a range of serious concerns. Her words tumbled one upon the other, topics shifted rapidly, her face was flushed, and she appeared breathless. Each problem cited would eventually need exploration but the therapist attended to her need to stave off chaos: "There seem to be many things troubling you. Perhaps it would be useful if we tried to sort them out so you can see what you want to approach first."[40]

The intervention suggests a future order, preserves autonomy, and at the same time, attends to current needs.

Goals are hoped-for solutions to the problems of clients or to their need for enhancement in some area of functioning, as perceived by them and the worker. The presenting request may or may not be the one that is most crucial to a client's welfare or that can be dealt with through social work practice. Wants and needs are not necessarily synonymous. A common example is a request by a parent for correction of a child's behavior, when the need is for changes in family relationships and inter-action. A request by a hospital patient for a particular service may be a device for seeking assistance with more complex problems, some of which may not be clear to the client. People have goals which they avow. They have others of which they are aware but which they do not express until they sense trust in the worker and the situation; and they have some important goals of which they are not initially aware but which become clear to them as they explore their situation. It is impossible to make an agreement about goals of which the applicants are not aware; they cannot make a choice unless they know what the alternatives are. Self-determination is much more complicated than asking clients what they want and using that as the aim of service.

Following exploration of problems and goals, clients usually are able to verbalize with what concerns they would like help. Toward the end of the first session, for example, an adolescent girl said, "You've already helped me to know that I really want an abortion, but I think my mother suspects that I'm pregnant and I just don't know what to do about that. Could you help me with that?"

In another situation, a psychiatrist was working with a thirteen-year-old and suggested that the parents also needed help, Mrs. Jerrow accepted referral to a mental health clinic, but her husband absolutely refused to seek any kind of help whatsoever. Their marriage was severely threatened. When the practitioner asked whether Mrs. J. felt that there could then be no help unless her husband participated, which was certainly the best plan, Mrs. J. said "No." She wondered if that approach were practical. The worker answered that it would be better to get help, not to try to change her husband, but to think about her own part in the relationships and communication with her son and husband. Mrs. J. replied, "Well, that's what I really meant. I'd like to work on that."

Practitioners need to check out their understanding of the clients' messages about their problems and goals. Some examples might be as follows:

> To a couple, "You seem to agree that you'd like to find ways to discipline Janie other than scolding and spanking. That will require you to think about the relationships and communication patterns in the family, as well as alternative forms of discipline. Is that what you've agreed to do?"
> Or, to a young woman of Mexican American background, with strict parents who hold to traditional norms of behavior: "You've talked about conflict at home, especially with your father. Is that what you want to work on?" The reply: "Yes, I want to be able to live my own life but I don't want to hurt my parents too much."
> And, in a group of homeless women, "Do I understand that you really want to try to get out of the shelter and find a place of your own to live in?" The reply: "You've said it!" "What about the rest of you? Do you agree that that's what this group should be for?"

In order to clarify problems and goals with clients, the social worker needs to communicate with acceptance and empathy, listen to the client's latent as well as manifest messages, accurately assess the client's behavior, and act in relation to this understanding. These skills in communication are applicable to all facets of the interaction process. Realistic goals depend upon common knowledge of the situation and possible alternative outcomes.

In groups, realistic goals depend also upon understanding both the avowed and unavowed goals of each member. Individuals make statements about their goals, they also give the worker clues as to what they desire through what they talk about and how they respond to messages from others. In groups, most members search for common concerns and experiences as they discuss their reasons for coming, and gradually they relate their own particular goals to a common purpose.

When a family comes for aid, it is usually because a problem is described as that of one member—often a child or a spouse. The family often does not regard the need as some type of change in the functioning of the family system. In such instances, there is lack of congruence between the worker and clients about the problems and the purposes of the service. The worker, therefore, has the task of redefining the client as the family, recognizing that all members are involved. As Freeman says, "the struggle between the family and the therapist to define the problem is the heart of the first stage of family therapy."[41] Workers use their influence to reorient the family to the idea of improvement in family functioning, as distinguished from individual or subgroup functioning.

Work with young children also poses special difficulties. They rarely have a conscious desire for help. The need is recognized by a parent, nursery school teacher, or doctor; sometimes even with little cooperation from the parents. Children do know, however, that they are in trouble or "bad," and they are exceedingly anxious until they know the reasons for being brought to an agency. They can understand the purpose of the service, if it is described simply, clearly and accurately in terms they can understand. After an initial period of defensiveness, they are usually relieved to know and make good use of the service.

Several studies have been made on the use of purpose in social work practice. Failure to clarify goals is a source of problems in ongoing treatment.

Based on a study in six family service agencies, Schmidt found that when workers made a purposeful effort to formulate objectives and communicated these to clients, a high proportion of clients accurately perceived and agreed with the objective. When workers did not specify objectives, the majority of the clients did not understand how interviews were intended to benefit them. There was incongruence between the goals of the worker and the client. The goals of clients were more often related to concrete resources, while those of workers were more abstract and psychological in nature.[42]

In another study, Raschella found that clients served in outpatient mental health centers were less likely to drop out prematurely when there was a high degree of congruence between worker and client in the specification of the goals of service.[43]

Levinson reviewed sixty-one articles on social work with groups and found that the major goal of the practitioner was often some change in individual behavior, even though collective effort to change the clients' environment was often needed. When purposes of members and workers were in accord, the groups tended to operate optimally to achieve their purposes. When the worker ascribed the purposes for the group, these tended to be rejected by the members, leading to dissolution of the group.[44]

Expectations

Clarification of the expectations that clients have concerning the behavior of each in their respective roles is an important determinant of the outcome of the service. A major concern of new clients is finding an appropriate role in relation to the worker and other participants, if any. They have questions about whether or not they want to and can do what is expected of them and whether or not they made the right decision to apply for service. In order to clarify expectations, practitioners explore with the client how the worker's expectations fit with the client's expectations. The worker needs to orient the clients to what it means to be a client in this particular situation, and the clients need to respond to these messages from the worker, expressing their feelings about them and understanding of them as they relate to the situation. As messages are exchanged, the nature of the client's expected participation becomes clarified, leading to mutual understanding of each other's part in the process.

As in other areas of practice, lack of knowledge about cultural norms by workers may limit the clients' initial participation in the process of working toward mutual expectations. Clients may expect, as is probable in the Japanese culture, that they should give only polite answers to questions, suppress strong feelings, be indirect in their patterns of speech, and be apologetic for the slightest lapse.[45] If social workers do not understand the values on which such behavior is based, they are apt to interpret these behaviors as resistance rather than as efforts to behave appropriately in an ambiguous situation. If workers are able to understand the meaning of the behavior, they can respect it, listen attentively to the client, and gradually reduce the ambiguity in the situation for the client.

Another obstacle to achieving mutual understanding of role expectations, often unrecognized by workers, is conflict concerning power. Clients need to come to understand the nature and extent of the worker's legitimate authority, and the worker needs to come to understand the client's need to control or to submit to the worker's power. Clients may attempt to control the process and content in many ways, as for example, by using either silence, long monologues that are difficult to interrupt, or coming in late and/or leaving early. In families, there may be the struggle of one member to control the messages sent or the behavior of others or to expect the worker to control the process of communication or the behavior of members. In formed groups, there is often a struggle for power among the members or between the worker and the group.

Whether it pertains to individual, family, or peer group, the usual initial pattern is for the clients to accede to the worker's authority; then challenge some aspects of it; and gradually develop an appropriate balance of control in the worker-client interaction. There is almost always some testing of the extent of the worker's ability to control or to relinquish control to the clients. This struggle is prolonged when workers are ambivalent about their responsibilities or fearful of losing control of the situation. When clients discover that they have both rights and responsibilities to participate freely within certain agreed-upon parameters, both the relationship and the motivation for change are enhanced.

The desired and the actual content of interviews, family, or group sessions may be a matter about which clients and workers are in agreement, or there may be misperceptions by clients of what they are expected to talk about or to do and what they prefer to do. The content provides the focus for the interchange between worker and client. New clients have many questions about what they will be expected to do or talk about.

In beginning with clients, exploration about what they prefer to discuss or to do provides a natural base for understanding their primary concerns and their readiness to deal with particular issues. Rosen and Lieberman studied the relevance of content to expectations of clients. The purpose of the research was to discover "the extent to which the content of an interactive response is perceived by a participant to be relevant to, and in agreement with, his own definition and expectations of the content to be dealt with in the treatment relationship."[46] The major finding was that there is need for clear worker and client orientation to the purpose of the interview which assists the worker to keep the interview focused on relevant content. Thus, content is directly related to purpose.

In a study of two groups of adoptive parents, there was consensus that the topics most preferred by members were legal procedures in adoption, knowledge about parent-child relationships, information for children that they were adopted, and the reasons for placing a particular child with particular parents. It was found to be important for the workers to initiate and maintain appropriate focus on topics that clients deemed to be important. It was suggested that attrition is related to the extent to which clients' expectations about content are met.[47]

Policies and procedures that govern the clients' participation in treatment need to be clarified. Often they are in the nature of the organization's policies concerning the nature of assessment, payment of fees, confidentiality and its limits, informed consent, attendance, recording of sessions, and expected duration of treatment. There may also be rules about expected behavior such as smoking, drinking, bringing guests, leaving the room, or use of supplies. Clients should, of course, be informed about these policies and rules, understand the reasons for them, and have a right to object to them: they become a part of the contract between the practitioner and clients. The rules that are established should be firmly related to the situation, rather than based on the arbitrary use of authority.

Research clearly supports the importance of setting mutually agreed-upon expectations. In the first one or two meetings, much of the content concerns mutual expectations. In a study, Leonard Brown found that discussion of expectations leads to congruence between worker and members on their attitudes toward the group.[48] They share similar perceptions concerning the experience. Workers of groups in which agreement was highest initiated the discussion of expectations in the first meeting. These workers helped the members stay with the topic and dealt with their resistance to clarifying expectations. They were able to pick up and respond to nonverbal cues indicating that a member might be ready to react to something said earlier. They were able to recognize and encourage expressions of feelings about the experience. In contrast, in those groups in which agreement was low, the workers were less likely to initiate the topic and to deal with it in early sessions. In one group of parents, for example, it was never clarified whether the group would focus on personal or family problems of members or engage in social action. The major conclusion of Brown's study was that developing mutual expectations as early as possible is significantly related to the effectiveness of group functioning and member satisfaction.

Clarity and consensus about expectations not only prevent discontinuance but also have a positive effect on progress in problem solving. In a study, Garvin found that when workers accurately perceived the expectations of members, their responses tended to be more appropriate and there was significantly greater movement in problem-solving than in instances in which workers did not perceive the members' expectations correctly.[49]

Developing a working agreement between worker and clients assumes that social workers perceive accurately the clients' expectations of the worker's role. In her research, Clemenger found that one important intermediate goal is achieved by the worker during the beginning phase: workers develop accurate assessments of the way that clients perceive their roles. Such assessment is essential to the selection of appropriate means for help. She also found that accuracy of assessment was reduced when the clients were mentally ill and distorted reality, which made it difficult for workers to understand how the patients perceived them. Accurate assessment was also impaired when workers viewed the behavior of certain members to be negative; when they thought of members in stereotyped terms, such as passive-resistant, noncommunicative, or domineering. The tendency to stereotype distorts the worker's skill in assessment. Generally, however, most workers are able to communicate the components of their roles quite accurately to clients, and clients are able to perceive them accurately.[50]

In another research project, Rhodes studied the extent to which fifteen pairs of practitioners and clients in a hospital agreed upon expectations for each other.[51] He found moderately high agreement on most items. Clients, however, desired more direction, friendship with the worker, concrete advise, and shorter term service than did practitioners. Practitioners did not develop full mutuality in contracting. Lima, Rodriguez, Eisenthal, and Lazare, in a similar study, found a high degree of agreement between workers and clients with the exception that clients had greater desire for more limit setting and insight.[52]

Effects of Working Agreement on Outcomes

There is support from research for the principle that mutual agreement between worker and clients concerning goals, roles, and content is fundamental in determining the direction and quality of the service.

Several studies have compared clients who continue in service with those who discontinue when the worker judges continuation to be desirable. In one of the first major studies, Ripple and associates found that factors associated with a high discontinuance rate were: the worker's irrelevant or minimal effort to clarify the problems; low perceptiveness and lack of sensitivity to the clients' presentation of their problems and situations; inadequacy or absence of explanations of agency services; and an incompatible or opposed view of the problem vis-à-vis the clients. When there was agreement about purpose and realistic expectations of help, there was a very high rate of continuance. The most decisive factor was clarity of expectations and mutual agreements.[53] Several other studies tend to confirm the principle that clarification and agreement about expectations are essential ingredients in continuance.

In a survey of research in the field of family service, Briar found that factors associated with continuation were adequacy of communication between client and worker, client's attribution of responsibility for the problem to self rather than to others; and the appropriateness of the client's attitudes and expectations regarding the worker and treatment. His conclusion was that "the degree of congruence between the worker and client in their definitions of the client's situation has been found to be strongly associated with continuance in all studies that have examined the factor."[54]

Continuation in treatment.   Effective contracting is essential if clients are to continue in treatment long enough to achieve their goals. Major factors in discontinuance, as cited earlier, have been found to be:

1. Lack of hope, combined with discomfort with the present situation;
2. Lack of explicit attention to the formulation of goals;
3. Lack of congruence between the worker and client on several factors, including: (a) worker-client role expectations; (b) levels of help or modalities that clients wanted or needed; (c) perceptions of problems and ways to deal with them;
4. Lack of effective communication by not providing feedback to clients that their messages were received;
5. Lack of focus on content relevant to the clients' perceptions of their needs; and
6. Long waiting periods between appointments.

These findings attest to the great importance of the contracting process.

The Plan for Service

The plan for service is based on the preliminary assessment, knowledge about modalities and structures of service, and the achievement of a contract covering goals, problems, roles, and content. An example follows.

Annette, a sixteen-year-old girl of Italian Catholic background, came to a free clinic because she was pregnant and did not know where to turn for help; she was in a mess and just did not know what to do. Exploration of the inquiry brought out the facts that she was not married, lived with her mother, age thirty-seven; and her father, age forty-two; two brothers, ages fourteen and ten; and two sisters, ages twelve and seven. Both parents were Italian immigrants and naturalized citizens who spoke English well. They had strict standards for their children's behavior, including Annette's dating. Mr. D. was a carpenter; Mrs. D., a housewife. Annette was in the eleventh grade in a Catholic school.

Annette explained that when she thought she might be pregnant, she went to her doctor, who promised not to tell her parents but advised her to do so herself. He suggested that she go into a maternity home and give up the baby for adoption. He offered to help with these arrangements. She was very upset at the time and just did not want to do what the doctor suggested—at least she didn't think so. She said that this was the most embarrassing thing that had ever happened to her. She went to the clinic because it was near her school and she saw a poster about the clinic, which said it gave confidential pregnancy counseling. She had walked around the block several times before getting up enough nerve to go in.

The boyfriend with whom she had sexual intercourse denied any responsibility for her pregnancy. He was twenty years old and a college student. She thought they really loved each other and she went too far one night: "It was an awful thing to have done and here I am pregnant and it's the only time I've had sex." When she told him she was pregnant, there was a big fight between them, after which he insisted he would never see her again, saying, "It's your baby and your problem—don't put it on me."

She dared not tell her parents because she knew they would disown her forever. Furthermore, she would be expelled from school as soon as her condition became known. She did well in school and had hoped to graduate with honors and go on to college, but now "that's all over for good." She espressed these facts and ideas, with a considerable amount of gentle questioning and probing by the worker. At one point she said, "I can't believe it, but you're not lecturing me about the mess I've got myself into." Several times she burst into tears, but regained her composure when the worker accepted the tears and supported her efforts to talk about her concerns.

At the beginning of the interview, the worker had assured Annette that she had come to the right place. She assured her that whatever she told the worker would be held in confidence, unless she gave the worker permission to share information with others in her behalf. Following the exploration of the facts of the case and Annette's feelings about them, the worker reiterated that she could get pregnancy counseling at the clinic. She gave her information about the clinic and its operating procedures. In response to the worker's inquiry about what she thought she might want to happen, she burst into tears and then said, "Just what you've done—listen to me and understand—but I just don't know what I can do."

The worker outlined briefly a number of ways that some clients found help: health information and care; individual counseling; group counseling for young women who have similar concerns; and working with families of clients. To the latter, Annette shuddered and gasped, "oh, no," to which the worker assured her that this would not happen unless she came to decide it would be a good thing to do. Annette asked if the worker could give her advice as to what she should do. The worker said she could help her to think through what she wanted to do about the baby, mentioning the alternatives of abortion, raising the child herself, or adoption. Annette said, "That's exactly what I want—I just don't know what to do."

On the basis of Annette's own desires and the worker's preliminary assessment, she decided to offer individual counseling to Annette. She thought that Annette was in a state of great emotional distress, as a reaction to the pregnancy and its consequences for her family, other social relationships, and for her future plans. She was very concerned about the responses of family and friends to her situation and she was upset about her boyfriend's rejection of her. She had a great deal of anxiety, guilt, and self-blame. She seemed well-motivated to use help: even though she was very upset, she was able to communicate facts, express feelings, and identify major concerns. She demonstrated ability to enter into a relationship and to accept the worker's part in the process.

The worker explained that she would be glad to continue to talk with Annette on a regular basis, and that making a decision about the baby and her future would not be easy because there were many things to be considered. She reiterated that the final decision would need to be Annette's; mentioned some of the things they would need to talk about; and how she thought she could be helpful. Because Annette expressed a strong need to make the decision as soon as possible and the worker also thought this was very important, a plan was agreed upon for Annette to come twice a week for an hour immediately after school for the next few weeks, with the goal in mind of making a good decision about the outcome of the pregnancy. If additional time was needed, this would be possible.

In relation to this interview, social work values are evident. Belief in the dignity and worth of the individual are reflected in the worker's acceptance of Annette, treating her with respect, assuring her about confidentiality, encouraging freedom of expression, securing her consent to the plan, and individualizing the process and plan of treatment, according to mutual perceptions of Annette's needs. Social justice was exemplified by informing Annette of her right to have access to resources and to make decisions, based on knowledge concerning the goals of treatment, the outcome of pregnancy, and the modality of practice. The value of interdependence was exemplified through encouraging Annette's participation in the process and recognizing the network of social systems of which Annette is a part.

The worker's actions were based on explanatory knowledge about behavior from a biopsychosocial perspective including the ethnic and religious factors. A fuller assessment will be developed of Annette's needs, problems, and capacities as these interact with supports and limitations of the social environment. In developing an initial and flexible plan of treatment, the worker used knowledge about the major concepts of planning. She made selective use of techniques of social treatment with considerable emphasis on support, use of structure, exploration, education, and some clarification. With Annette's participation, she not only elicited appropriate information and arrived at a tentative treatment plan, she also enabled Annette to feel accepted, understood, and less anxious; to understand herself and her situation better; and to engage in a problem-solving process regarding an important decision. Thus, assessment of the person- situation configuration, initial planning, and social treatment go on simultaneously.

A number of principles of practice are proposed to guide clinical social workers in early sessions. They are to be used flexibly, with due regard for the clients' situations.[59]

PRINCIPLES OF PRACTICE

1. Social workers express clearly, simply, and explicitly their understanding of the purpose of the interview. Such statements enable the applicant to respond appropriately and allay anxiety and confusion. They solicit reactions to the statements and give additional information as it is needed.
2. Social workers are sensitive to the prospective client's situations. They elicit feelings and information, according to the person's readiness without requiring undue exposure of self.
3. Social workers assist the client to become oriented to the new situation, through offering information about the agency, available services, policies, procedures, and the roles of practitioners.
4. Social workers treat the persons as applicants until there is acceptance of a client role and an initial agreement about the nature of the service to be given. They have no right to interfere in the lives of others until permission is granted.
5. Social workers acknowledge people's ambivalence about accepting a service and becoming a client. They recognize and accept the applicant's feelings and engage the person in a problem solving process directed toward making a tentative decision about the use of a service.
6. Social workers establish a relationship that is characterized by interest in each person present, acceptance, empathy and authenticity and an attitude of hope and encouragement.

7. Social workers maximize the applicant's motivation by working to achieve an optimal balance of hope and discomfort. Realistic hope of a favorable outcome is encouraged, problems are defined as capable of resolution with effort, and realistic expectations are set.
8. Social workers take responsibility for helping the applicant to meet eligibility requirements, or to modify them when possible and when such changes are in the best interests of the potential client.
9. Social workers, in interviewing more than one person simultaneously, elicit participation by all of them. They individualize each person while searching for the common threads and similar goals.
10. Social workers, if the applicants decide to continue, engage them in a problem solving process concerning a choice of at least some short-term goal to be worked toward in the next session.

The contract between social workers and clients constitutes the plan for action. It is to be remembered that the plan is a flexible one to be changed by mutual agreement between the practitioner and clients as the needs and situations of clients change. The successful problem-solving involved in developing the contract should carry over to work in the core phase of the treatment.

Eleven | The Core Phase: Problem-Solving

No clear demarcation between phases of process is possible, but there comes a time when the worker and individual, family, or group recognize that they have reached an agreement to work together toward some mutually acceptable goals. Clients have come to a preliminary decision that the service has positive meaning for them in terms of satisfaction in the relationship and the desire to achieve a realistic purpose. They have demonstrated sufficient positive motivation to continue beyond the first sessions. In groups, there is sufficient acceptance among the members that they are able to work together with some capacity for mutual support and mutual aid. In family situations, members have accepted the worker into their family for a limited purpose and period of time. They have accepted, at least partially, a need for improvement in the structure and process within the family unit as well as perhaps in individual members and environment.

Problem-Solving: The Essential Process

The essential process used in helping clients to achieve their goals is problem-solving that has been incorporated widely into theories of social work practice. Problem-solving emphasizes reflective thinking used for coping with questions and difficulties. According to Dewey, "Active, persistent, and careful consideration of any belief or supposed form of knowledge in the light of the grounds that support it, and the further conclusion to which it tends, constitutes reflective thought."[1] It integrates feelings with rational thought processes and takes into account both conscious and unconscious elements. Emotions influence cognition and cognition influences affect. Perlman points out that "in actuality, too, problem-solving in social work probably proceeds not linearly, but by a kind of spiral process in which action does not always wait upon the completion of assessment and assessment often begins before data collection is completed."[2]

Dewey's steps provide the model for reaching some decision and action. His steps are: recognize the difficulty; define and specify the problem and the goals; consider alternative proposals for solution; decide which alternative to accept; plan a course of action for putting the decision into operation; implement the decision; and evaluate the results (pp. 72–78). These steps in the process will be illustrated by the process of making a decision to disclose or not disclose one's sexual orientation.[3]

1. *Recognize the difficulty.* Some state of doubt, hesitation, perplexity, or difficulty is recognized by the client or some other person. The practitioner may bring the difficulty to the attention of the clients, based on assessment and observation.

Stress inevitably accompanies being a homosexual person in a world that still regards heterosexuality as normal and preferred. To reduce the stress, a decision must be made as to whether or not to disclose that one is a lesbian or gay man.

> Thus, while self-disclosure is, in general, considered necessary to the formation of authentic interpersonal relationships, the potential consequences of disclosure of a stigmatized sociosexual identity frequently act as an effective deterrent to self-disclosure. One stress- producing aspect of disclosure decisions, then, may be viewed as an approach-avoidance dilemma; that is, in seeking authentic relationships, a gay person often must risk social rejection and being defined as deviant.[4]

2. *Define and specify the problem and the goals.* The process involves formulating specific questions or aspects of the problem and its component parts. The difficulty, as initially presented, may not be the problem selected for focus. In exploring the ramifications of the situation, it may become evident that there is a core difficulty underlying the stated one. Either the core problem or some facet of it may be selected for work. The process involves analysis of the problem to clarify who is concerned about the difficulty and what it means to those concerned about it. In this step, there is ventilation and exploration of feelings about the problem. If the problem is a complex one, a particular aspect might be chosen as the

immediate focus of worker-client interaction. A series of decisions is made in defining and selecting a problem.

In relation to disclosure of sexual orientation, several questions need to be considered. Does disclosure or nondisclosure threaten the person's fulfillment of economic, self-esteem, and affiliative needs? How much changes does disclosure or nondisclosure require, for example, in self-presentation, social relationships, and employment? How stress producing will disclosure be as contrasted with nondisclosure? Major problems have to do with the environmental context, including devaluation of homosexual persons, discrimination in social life, and lack of legislation to prohibit discrimination in housing, employment, and membership in groups and organizations.

3. *Consider alternative proposals for solution.* Selections for solutions are elicited from the clients or may be offered by the practitioner. Facts need to be obtained in order to assess the suitability of each proposal to the achievement of the goal. The choices to be made need to be based on realistic available alternatives. The only alternatives available are those that are within a cognitive field of experience related to past personal experiences, social and cultural characteristics, and the social and physical environment of the participants. The potential consequences of the alternatives need to be considered, even though there might be unanticipated consequences of the choices made.

Considerable reflective thinking on the meaning of the possible solution to the clients and significant others is essential in considering alternatives for action. Alternatives are based on different constellations of values, norms, resources, and role sets. Thus, some understanding of self and situation is required for analysis of alternative choices: one's attitudes, emotions, values, and norms of behavior influence decisions about which alternatives are acceptable and which are not. The possible choices are influenced by the availability of support systems in the family and community. Many blocks to problem-solving are imposed by society. There may be a lack of appropriate resources or rigid policies that deter any viable choices. Certain stigmatized groups are objects of discrimination and thereby lack power to achieve their goals. As alternatives are considered, some will be recognized quickly as either not feasible or not worth further consideration; one or more will be seen to have the potential for sound decision.

In the example of disclosure, gays and lesbians have the major choice to disclose or not to disclose their sexual orientation. But, within that major decision are others; to deny one's own sexual identity, to disclose to only a small number of friends and/or family, to other gays and lesbians, or to the general public.

4. *Decide which alternative to accept, necessitating the exclusion of other proposals, and evaluate the probable consequences of the decision.* As in all steps of the process, the result is not based only on rational thinking; unconscious factors, values, experiences, and external facts are powerful forces in choosing. Often, there is a spontaneous recognition that a particular decision seems right. Sometimes the choice is arrived at through a cognitive process of summarizing the problem and goals, the advantages and disadvantages of each alternative, and the reasons for the particular choice. Clients often need help with rethinking the proposed choice in light of their goals, the resources available, the strength of motivation to implement the decision, and the consequences of the anticipated decision.

The client who is deciding about disclosure needs to make a careful analysis of the consequences of each alternative decision for self and significant other persons. The risks need to be evaluated.

The optimal decision-making process would include (1) sufficient time to rationally assess the degree of risk in disclosure or nondisclosure and (2) an appraisal of one's internal and external resources that would mediate stress irrespective of the outcome of disclosure or nondisclosure. The person asks such questions as: "Which response will be the most rewarding for me?" "Will disclosure or nondisclosure bring out more pleasure or pain?" "How much support will I have for the decision I make?" Finally, the political meaning of one's decision to disclose or to remain undisclosed must be evaluated.

5. *Plan a course of action for putting the decision into operation and clarify the roles of worker, clients, and significant others in implementing the decision.* The plan involves clarifying the actual steps to be taken and the persons to be involved in the process.

If the decision is to remain undisclosed, one needs to consider how to reduce the stress of hiding a stigmatized and devalued position in society. When the decision is to disclose one's sexual orientation, specific decisions need to be made concerning to whom to disclose and how to send the messages in terms of content, place, and timing, and whether or not to join support groups or become politically active.

6. *Implement the decision and evaluate the results.* When an individual or group acts on a decision, another series of sub- problems need to be faced. Clients may not know how to do this effectively. A decision to seek to adopt a child, for example, requires accomplishing a series of tasks culminating in the legal adoption. A decision by a teenager to enter college requires knowing how to make application, submit necessary papers, and having a financial plan. Other clients may need instruction

and guidance in relation to their roles as parent, spouse, sibling, or employee. Some may need to know how to get out of debt through budgeting and managing their money. In some instances, the worker will refer a client to a specialized resource for help, as with vocational tests or informal and formal classes. In other instances, the worker may actively assist the client in securing the necessary information or skills. There may be a need to find an alternative way to enact the decision. Obstacles may be encountered in the abilities of the individual or group or in the environment. Once an effort to act on the decision has been made, the results need to be evaluated. There may be a sense of great success, or the results may not bear much resemblance to what was intended.

In implementing the decision concerning disclosure, a client might run into unanticipated obstacles in terms of overwhelming stress, negative responses from others, or overt discrimination. That, then, suggests a need to decide whether or not to use professional help to cope with the problems that were not anticipated.

The Social Work Role

Social workers use their knowledge and skills in assisting individuals, families, and groups to use the problem-solving process. An interview illustrates the social worker's part in efforts to resolve a family conflict.

> The Cohn family consists of Mr. C., age forty-three, an engineer; Mrs. C., age forty-one, homemaker and part- time clerk; and Bill, age seventeen, only child. During the intake interview, the presenting problem was Bill's unacceptable behavior.
>
> The problem became serious about a year ago when Bill's school grades dropped precipitously. He had done well in school up to this time and had also worked after school. Both parents complained that Bill was lying to them, had lost respect for them, and was very mean to his mother. Both parents felt that Bill was destroying their relationship with each other. Mrs. C. and Bill had frequent fights about how he spent the money he earned on his part-time job. After one of these fights, Bill had left home and stayed with a friend all night. Bill, too, was concerned about the fighting and thought his parents were too strict and restrictive.
>
> A friend suggested that the family call the Community Mental Health Center for counseling, which Mrs. C. did. Mr. C.'s goal was for Bill to quit school and join the army, where he would get the discipline he needed. Bill's goal was to stay home and graduate from

high school. Mrs. C. felt caught between husband and son. During the first two months of treatment, the goals were to achieve resolution of the conflict about Bill's immediate future and to improve the relationships and social climate of the family. The plan was for individual conferences with Bill, joint interviews with the parents, and family conferences when these seemed to be indicated.

The worker recorded: "After two months, I got three telephone calls in quick succession from all three of the Cohns. Each said it was impossible for them to live together any longer and that there had been a physical fight between Bill and Mr. C. Both parents said that their doctor had advised them to file an incorrigibility petition with the Juvenile Court. They did not want to do this, but had agreed that Bill should join the army. When in each instance, I suggested the family come in for a conference, each agreed to do this at the suggested time."

At the family interview, all three of the Cohns were quiet, expectant, and waiting for me to begin. I said I understood that the purpose of the conference was to understand the immediate crisis and then to come to some decision about Bill's future. I asked the family how it would like to begin to work on the trouble. Mrs. C. began in a short burst of whining anger, "I have tried, but (pointing to Bill) he just gets at me; for no reason at all he explodes and threatens me." Her sister and her doctor have both told her that if she keeps on getting aggravated, it will kill her. She doesn't want to make Bill leave, but she doesn't see any other way out. I commented, "Things really seem bad, then." She nodded, and tears came to her eyes.

I turned and looked at Mr. C. He began hesitantly, then forcefully said that he agreed with his wife. He talked about his own frequent stomach upsets and his doctor's advice to get the boy out of the home. I looked at Bill and asked if life at home seemed this bad for him, too. He said, in quiet anger, that he is really mixed up, he seems to be the one who's done most of the trying, but when he gets just a little out of hand, they make it worse. He wants to finish school, but since they want him out, what is there to do?

I asked if they had come here to tell me they had already reached a decision—that Bill was to leave home. No one answered me directly. There was a long silence. Mr. C. seemed uncomfortable, shuffled around, and looked at his wife. She, in turn, became tearful and talked about her helplessness in view of Bill's terrible temper. Mr. C. repeated much of what Mrs. C. had said. Then Bill very quietly asked, "What else is there to do?" I asked Bill if he wanted to enter the army. He said firmly, "No—I do not—but maybe that's the only way out." I asked the parents if they wanted me to agree that Bill's going into the army was the only way out. There was another long silence.

Mrs. C. broke the silence, saying, "I don't know. I don't know anything anymore. Look—this is my only son, but when he starts fighting with his father . . ." (Silence.) I asked, "And what happens then?" She responded, "I was caught in between and almost killed. But, of course, I want Bill home. I've worked to keep him, but he'll soon be gone anyway and I've got to live with my husband." I said, "You seem to feel that your son wants to stay but your husband wants him to leave and the whole thing is up to you." She answered in desperation, "Yes, he told me that if Bill doesn't go, he will." "I commented that was a tough position to be in and turned to Mr. C. He acknowledged that he had said that to his wife and even meant it at the time. "And I still think no child should be permitted to disrupt and destroy his parents." I said, "And this is what you feel Bill is doing." After a silence, he said, "Yes." Bill said, "You see, it is stacked against me." Neither parent replied.

I said I wondered if the parents would respond to Bill's comments. (Silence.) Then I asked, "Do you want me to say the only possibility was for Bill to leave home?" (Silence.) Mrs. C. started to cry quietly—then she said almost inaudibly that Sam (her husband) wants Bill to go and Bill wants to stay. "I just have to choose between them . . . but which one is going to hate me?" (Silence.) I asked, "And which one do you think will hate you? She said, "Maybe they both will . . . then I'll be left all alone."

I asked how this felt to Mr. C. and to Bill. Mr. C. said, "But that's silly. Bill is my son, too. It's hard to know . . . when I'm mad I want him to go, but when I sit here and think about it, I'm not sure." Looking directly at me, he said, "Remember what we talked about before—how mad I still am that I was thrown out of my home. I was denied an education." I said, "And you can't help acting toward Bill as your parents did toward you." He said "Yeah—and that's not fair to Bill . . . but I just can't seem to get over it." I asked Bill if he knew about his father's experience. He answered, "Yes, that's why I can't understand what my parents are doing and that's why I want to finish high school and even make plans to go to college."

Mrs. C. turned toward Bill and shouted, "Then, why don't you behave so it can happen?" Bill replied with anger, "Here we go again . . . here we go again . . ." Then, more softly, "But, I'm not saying I've done nothing wrong. I did get out of hand on Sunday. But most of the time I do try . . . And when I go off a little bit, you make it worse and then things just build up . . . then Dad suddenly gets into the middle of it." I asked Bill, "Are you saying that the fight usually starts with your mother over some small thing? Then you try to stop, but mother keeps it up—then father interferes and the fight between you and Dad becomes explosive? He said, "I just wish Dad would take a stand that's his own—not just follow Mom all the time." Mr. C. said "You know, in some respects, the boy is right—that's what happens." (Silence.)

I asked the group where they wanted this discussion to go: are they here still to find out how Bill can leave in a good way or how they can all live together? This time Mr. C. answered clearly, "I want Bill home." Mrs. C. said, "So do I, but things must change." At that I asked, "Who must change?" Mr. C. said, "I guess all three of us." Mrs. C. nodded.

There was a noticeable change in the atmosphere. For the first time father and son sat back comfortably in their chairs, but mother was still very tight. She said she hoped they could work it out, but wanted to know how this could be done—there had been a terrible fight. I suggested that we talk about the fight. All began to talk at once. I said it would be helpful, not only to me, but everyone, if we really began from the beginning and tried to hear what each was saying.

After a detailed review of the fight and each person's reactions to the incident, I summed up the major facts. Further elaboration was presented, after which I commented that the parents were angry and ashamed because the landlady had to intervene. Bill felt unjustly accused because it was Mr. C. who had struck the first blow, and both Mr. C. and Bill felt that Mrs. C. had triggered the actual fight. All three were silent, but seemed very thoughtful.

Then Mr. C. commented that he was thinking that they all wanted to stay together—but they couldn't go on the way they'd been. When I asked him to summarize the way it had been, he said he thought they ganged up on each other without even trying to figure out what was going wrong. Mrs. C. then broke in with further incidents of Bill's money demands, his schoolwork, and his girlfriends. It was Mr. C. who reminded Mrs. C. that Bill had a part-time job and was now doing much better in school. Mrs. C. said this was true, then repeated many of the things that worried her and concluded with, "If only they will take some worries away from me." When I questioned the "they," she said, "my husband." He said part of it was his fault—he had let his wife take most of the responsibility for Bill. Bill seemed to want him to be more of a father.

Both mother and son became immediately supportive. Bill said that he loved them both and would try to do his part in helping them to get along together. He said he wanted to try to make it with them, and Mrs. C. said perhaps she could do some things differently, too.

I asked if there was still uncertainty about wanting Bill to stay at home. Each one said he'd like to try to get along better with the others. I commented that our time was up; that they seemed to agree they wanted to try to have Bill remain at home; that they seemed to be feeling better now; but that they need to realize there would be some setbacks until they were able to make some of the changes. I arranged for another appointment with the family. Since the problem is primarily one of unsatisfactory family relationships, the major modality of treatment should be the family unit.

The problem-solving process is not complete. The family still needs to decide how to work to implement the decision and evaluate the progress made.

Interventive Skills

Analysis of the interview demonstrates the skills used by the practitioner within a relationship of apparent trust. *Support* was offered to all members of the family in that the practitioner paid attention to each one, listened carefully, expressed empathy through expressions of understanding and acceptance of a range of feelings. She used *structure* to maintain the focus on the conflict among members. Much use of *exploration* was evident in comments and questions to elicit each member's feelings and perceptions of the problem and solution, probing for details, and requesting elaboration of the messages sent. Gentle *confrontation* was used in challenging the parents about what they wanted the worker to say about the solution. *Clarification* was used frequently to secure agreement about the purpose of the interview, reflect feelings, make connections, and clarify alternative solutions. *Interpretations* were made to Mr. C. and to the family as a system. *Facilitation of the process* occurred through encouraging participation of all members, seeking for and commenting on both likenesses and differences, requesting feedback by receivers to messages sent to them.

Tension and conflict.   The problem-solving process, as illustrated in the case of the Cohn family, often deals with ways to resolve interpersonal conflict.

The view of conflict espoused here is a social psychological one, consistent with a systems approach to practice. It recognizes the need to understand the persons involved, the nature of the issues, the responses of others to the conflict, the social environment in which the conflict occurs, and the consequences of the conflict for all who are affected by it.

The word *conflict* tends to elicit frightened or hostile responses, yet conflict itself is an important ingredient in development and change. According to Buckley, "tension is seen as an inherent and essential feature of complex adaptive systems: it provides the go of the system, the force behind the elaboration and maintenance of structure."[5] Numerous social scientists agree that conflict is inevitable and has potentially functional and constructive uses, as well as dysfunctional and destructive ones.[6]

Conflict encompasses a wider range of behavior than its usual images of violent struggle and war. It occurs when at least one person feels being obstructed or irritated by one or more others. Three basic elements characterize the conflict situation: there are two or more identifiable focal units or parties to the conflict; the parties perceive incompatible differences that create frustration; and there is interaction between the parties around the differences. Conflict is the behavior as contrasted with the emotions, such as fear or hostility, that are often connected with it. At the intrapersonal level, conflict refers to contradictory, incompatible, or antagonistic emotions and impulses within a person. At the family or group level, conflicts arise out of the intrapersonal conflicts of the members, misinformation about the objective state of affairs, or differences in goals, values, and norms among the members. At times, conflict has its source in the divergence between the values and norms of one's reference groups and those of certain segments of the community. Differences in goals, values, and norms are due to differing life experiences and socioeconomic resources within a given culture and in other cultures.

The person who has learned to manage internal conflicts may well be what Sanford has called a more fully developed person than one who has never dealt with serious intrapersonal conflicts.[7] Such a person's range of coping mechanisms and adaptive behavior may be broader and more flexible, and capacity for empathy may be greatly increased. Conflict prevents stagnation, stimulates interest and curiosity, and makes possible the recognition of problems and the consequent rethinking and assessment of self. Conversely, however, intrapersonal conflicts that are too long last-ing, too severe, or too basic to the personality structure may lead to severe intrapsychic disintegration and breakdown in functioning.

At the family and group level, conflict may lead to enhanced under-standing and consequent strengthening of relationships among members because differences are aired and not allowed to remain irritatingly below the surface. Only through the expression of differences is it possible for a group to delineate its common values and interests. As areas of disagree-ment are explored, the areas of agreement become clarified. This clarity, in turn, contributes directly to the cohesiveness of the group. Social con-flict may have consequences that increase rather than decrease the group's ability to engage in successful problem-solving activities. To focus on the useful aspects of conflict is not to deny that much conflict is destructive and may lead to the disintegration of the group. Thus, the way in which members of groups recognize, resolve, and manage conflict is crucial to the very survival of the group.

Research by Baxter indicates that avoidance of conflict is the prevalent means of coping with it. The result is often an accumulation of unre-solved issues. Although avoidance may relieve tension in the short term, the long term consequence is dysfunctional.[8] The successful resolution of conflict strengthens the cohesiveness of the family or other group, re-establishes a steady state and enables the members to move toward accomplishment of their goals.

Deutsch says that the less intense the conflict, the easier it is to resolve through cooperative means. When conflict is instigated by fears or uncon-scious processes, when it threatens self-esteem, or when it concerns major issues of principle, it will be more difficult to resolve than when the oppo-site is true. As conflict accelerates, the degree of commitment to it increas-es, as does holding on to one's position. Pathogenic processes inherent in competitive conflict or distortions in perception and self-deception tend to magnify and perpetuate conflict. According to Deutsch:

> The tendency to escalate conflict results from the conjunction of three inter-related processes: (1) competitive processes involved in the attempt to win the conflict; (2) processes of misperception and biased perception; and (3) processes of commitment arising out of pressures for cognitive and social consistency. These processes give rise to a mutually reinforcing style of rela-tions that generate actions and reactions that intensify conflict.[9]

The social worker's concern goes beyond the resolution of single conflict situations to an ability to manage conflict. Since conflict is an inevitable and continuing process in human relationships, one of the worker's tasks is to help clients to develop more effective means for dealing with the process of conflict as it occurs again and again. Mutual acceptance, open communication, and respect for differences make it possible for members to become competent to deal with the conflicts so characteristic of the human condition.

Obstacles

During the initial stage, some satisfactory patterns of communication between worker and client are developed. In families and groups, patterns among the members should be adequate to develop a working agreement and satisfying enough for clients to continue. But, as the content of the sessions shifts and as increased demands for active participation are made, new difficulties arise. In other instances it may take a long time for clients to be able to communicate verbally in effective ways. Examples are in work with very disturbed children who have been verbally inaccessible or psychotic patients who have great difficulty in making themselves understood and in understanding the messages of other people.[10]

Communication

Problems in communication within the family often become obstacles to successful coping with other problems. Fear of discussing subjects that have been taboo make open communication impossible, accelerating the stress. A typical example taken from a record of practice follows:

> The case is one of Mr. Trelliss, age seventy-six, who was hospitalized with an unknown illness that later was diagnosed as terminal cancer. Since Mr. T. was quite depressed, the physician had not told him about the diagnosis, but had informed the concerned family members—his daughter and her husband with whom he lived and a twenty-five-year-old granddaughter.
>
> Being in the hospital, deepened Mr. T.'s depression. Thus, when the family visited Mr. T., any discussion of the illness was avoided. The members talked about events in the community and in their lives which they thought would cheer him up. But his mood only worsened and the interaction between Mr. T. and the other members was extremely limited. The family dreaded seeing him and felt guilty for having these feelings.
>
> The oldest daughter requested a meeting with the social worker to get suggestions for dealing with the problem. The social worker

recommended that a way be found to discuss the diagnosis with Mr. T., but family members were unwilling to go against the physician's recommendation.

With the permission of the doctor, the worker suggested a family meeting in Mr. T.'s room. After a brief transition, she opened the discussion with comments about how many patients and family members feel better if they talk about the illness. She asked if Mr. T. would be willing to say what he knew about his illness. He looked startled, paused for a minute, and then said that no one had bothered to tell him what was wrong but he knew he was going to die and that he thought he had cancer. He said he did not tell these folks about it because he did not want to worry them. Once out in the open, there were expressions of relief and both the patient and other family members could begin to find adaptive ways of coping with this dreadful situation.

In another example, Germain and Gitterman dealt with opening up communication between a mother, Ms. Greeley, and her two children, Lucia and Tony. The worker recorded:

I have begun to observe a pattern. Each time one of the children brings news home of an outside activity, in school or play, this is almost always met with derision, rejection, and always with the notion that it is completely unimportant compared to even the slightest happening in the home. Today, Ms. G. told us that Lucia and she had a big fight about Lucia's joining the choir. She then turned to me and asked if she was too tough on the kids. I said it seemed as if she felt she was. She nodded, and then told me she is only trying to protect the kids. I suggested she turn to the children, tell them the same thing, and then ask them how they felt about it. After she did this, there was silence. Ms. G. again asked how they felt about it. Lucia said, "You've got to leave us alone more, Ma." Tony said nothing, but hung his head. I asked him what he was thinking. He looked up and said, "I'm no baby." Ms. G. looked to me and told me to tell them how tough the world is. I said to her that I shared her concern about the kids, but I also felt that exposing them to some things is important, too, and that joining the choir seems harmless. She began to sob and said that she didn't want to let the kids go from her and leave her alone. Lucia reached over and took her hand, and said, "We're not going, Ma—just trying to have some fun." I pointed up how hard it is for her as a parent to see her kids growing up, but this is a part of what all parents experience. She seemed comforted by that, and told Lucia she'd think about the choir.

The worker succeeded in having Ms. G. communicate directly with the children instead of through the worker. This brought about more direct communication from the children to Ms. G.. The worker empathized with Ms. G.'s feelings, but at the same time pointed up their inappropriateness with respect to the choice. Generalizing and legitimizing her feelings gave needed support to Ms. G. in front of the children, a support overdue because her style of parenting had been the focus of attention for the past several sessions.[11]

Maladaptive Patterns of Roles

Several maladaptive patterns of behavior, often referred to as membership roles, occur in families and groups and interfere with the system's progress in problem-solving.

Scapegoat.   The role of scapegoat is one that is stressful to the person in the role and to the worker confronted with such a phenomenon. Scapegoating involves the simultaneous infliction of pain on its victims and a threat to the group's morale.[12] The members turn their aggression onto another member who becomes a symbol of some tendency or characteristic they dislike in themselves and on whom they project their hostility and thus protect themselves from recognizing their own unacceptable tendencies and free themselves from guilty feelings. It is one way to avoid conflict. When a group has a scapegoat, the steady state is maintained. The scapegoat performs a valuable function in channeling group tensions and in providing a basis for group solidarity.

The scapegoat is usually one from whom the others do not fear retaliation. When there is a scapegoat, a two-way transaction etiology is seen, at both individual and group levels. The scapegoat adapts to the situation through defensive maneuvers: the primary dynamic is often, however, the group's need to place a person in such a role.

The social workers need to understand the person or persons who scapegoat, often out of fear of their own powerlessness and fear of social rejection by higher status persons. Scapegoating may be a defense of identification with the aggressor.[13]

In a one-to-one relationship, when it becomes evident that a client has become a scapegoat in the family or other group, the worker is limited to helping the members understand what is going on in the relationship with others and the part played in provoking hostility. Some understanding may make the role more bearable and relieve the scapegoat of feelings of guilt and anger by finding an acceptable channel for the release of feelings. Since the scapegoat meets the often unconscious needs of others, the ideal situation for working with the problem is intervention in the family or group which needs to scapegoat one of its members. This is a difficult task for the worker, especially in a family because there the pattern has often been established over a long period of time. The worker finds ways to bring the tensions and conflicts into awareness and to clarify the stresses that result in the projection of hostilities onto a particular member, to clarify the pattern of relationships, and to discover alternative ways of dealing with the needs that result in the behavior. The techniques of support and exploration are used first, but confrontation is usually necessary. Gradually, the worker can move toward clarifying the meaning of behavior and trying out new behavioral patterns.

The monopolizer.　Very different from the scapegoat, the monopolizer is another common dysfunctional role, whether it occurs in the worker-client dyad, families, or preventive or therapeutic groups.[14] The role often meets the person's emotional need to maintain control and ward off anxiety in a way that, if maintained, disrupts the relationship or prevents the goals from being achieved. The person feels compelled to talk, becoming anxious when the worker or other members take over. Often the talk is repetitive ventilation of feelings or experiences.

Continuous pouring out of negative feelings, experiences, thoughts, and problems without stopping to reflect on them or trying to change the dissatisfying conditions becomes nonproductive. In situations outside the social work one, such ventilation is also harmful to the development of social relationships that are mutually beneficial. Some clients who have been able to give and take in communication revert to monopolizing when they become anxious.

Workers often become irritated with this pattern of behavior. In groups, other members develop resentment of the monopolizer. They tend to react through silent hostility, feelings of helplessness, fear of trying to change the situation, or blaming the worker. The pattern tends to be self-perpetuating since the more the monopolist talks, the more irritation of others is sensed and the more anxious the talker becomes. Monopolizers are too anxious to give up the center of the stage. The tendency to monopolize is a self-protective device. For these reasons, it is important for the worker to attend to the problem as soon as possible.

In dealing with a monopolizer, the worker's task is to interrupt the pattern of behavior, first through supportive means, such as finding something that can be acknowledged as a positive effort and then stating wanting to respond to the client's message. In a group the worker might interrupt long enough to comment that other members might like to respond. If these techniques do not work, then the worker needs to confront the monopolizer with a direct request to stop talking because the prolonged talking is not being helpful. Later the worker can help the person to deal with the anxiety or need to control that underlies the pattern of behavior. In groups, others may need help to learn to interrupt and enter into the discussion or activity.

Scapegoats and monopolizers are but two of the patterns of behavior that tend to be dysfunctional. Among the other roles with which the worker needs to be concerned are the *isolate*, who lacks psychological bonds with associates; the *clown*, who seeks acceptance by offering to be laughed at, usually with an undercurrent of contempt for self and others; and *passive-aggressive* roles. Whatever the pattern of behavior, the parts are interdependent: there is an interrelatedness between individual needs and the needs of the dyad or group in the creation and maintenance of such roles. Thus, the desirable interventions are with the systems of relationships.[15]

In intervening to change patterns of relationship that are painful to a member or that threaten the stability and progress of the group, the workers need to check their own responses to the situation. They may come to recognize that they have strong countertransference reactions. In scapegoating, for example, they may feel strongly that injustice has been inflicted on a weak victim by cruel aggressors so that they defend and protect the scapegoat. They may align themselves with the scapegoat against the group and be unable, therefore, to accept and empathize with those members and serve as mediator. Or if workers are identified with the group and its anger toward the scapegoat, they may support the group in its attack on the individual. Shulman puts it this way: the worker needs "to be with both clients at precisely the same time . . . the anger directed toward the scapegoat is often a signal of the hurt and confusion felt by the group members."[16] To remember that the scapegoat symbolizes some of the attacking members' problems with self-esteem, identity, and displaced anger helps the worker to focus interventions. As in any dysfunctional role, the problem is a result of the interaction between the person in the role and the needs of the others. The worker needs to be able to accept and empathize with all members and to focus on the common feelings and problems. As members are ready to do so, they can be helped to recognize the patterns of behavior and their common and divergent feelings and assisted in finding ways of problem- solving.

In whatever the dysfunctional role, a worker may use two major types of intervention, depending upon how well established the role. When the role is not yet firmly established, the worker may use indirect means to help the member not to get stuck in the role and to help the other members not to trap that person into a dysfunctional role. These techniques include the strong use of support, including encouraging participation of all in discussion or activity, approving a norm of acceptance and concern for each member, and using activities that involve the threatened member in positive ways.

Once a member has become stereotyped into a role, however, such interventions are insufficient. The worker needs to become active in directly confronting the group with the situation and moving the discussion toward clarifying the process that led to the establishment of such a role. They may, for example, request that the family track the sequence of interaction that led to the scapegoating of a member or to the emergence of other roles.

Roles are reciprocal: the worker needs to assess and attend to both the person in the role and the other members; both individual and group play a part in creating and maintaining the situation. The group needs, therefore, to examine its own process in efforts to change the attitudes and patterns of behavior of all the members.

Resistance

Identification with the social worker and feelings of trust and mutual acceptance provide powerful motivation for continuing in treatment. In such an atmosphere, anxieties and fears are lessened and hopefulness is increased. People are not likely to continue if they believe that some positive changes in themselves or their situations are not possible. They need to have and to believe that they have the power to achieve some change. In an earlier chapter, it was noticed that there must be hope that relief from discomfort, pain, or dissatisfaction with the current situation can occur. There must be enough discomfort with what is, for a person to desire some further development or change in the situation. Thus, the worker needs to work to maintain a balance between discomfort and hope as clients try to change in some way. Mastery of skills and situations strengthens the ego and success tends to build on success. What might have been a vicious cycle of hopelessness-failure-greater hopelessness gets replaced with a cycle of hopelessness-success-hopefulness.[17]

Even within a general atmosphere in which individual or group motivation is there, there will be times when apathy or discouragement sets
in. Clients resist efforts by the worker to help them work on difficulties
or obstacles to goal achievement. In this stage, resistance is often mobi-
lized by anxiety about the helping process itself. As the demands for
work increase, clients may find it difficult to participate. They may fear
disclosing certain secrets or highly charged experiences or become aware
of feelings and ideas that have been suppressed as these break into consciousness. Facing things in themselves that they find difficult to accept
upsets the steady state. When anxiety increases beyond a tolerable level,
people defend themselves; they resist. During this stage, resistance often
represents an effort to hold on to the familiar, fears of intimacy, and
fears of trying out alternative ways of feeling, thinking, and doing.
According to Ackerman, "it reflects the patient's need to place a fence
around the most vulnerable areas of self in an attempt to immunize the
self against the danger of reopening old psychic wounds."[18] Clients may
resist by such means as staying away or coming late, monopolizing the
discussion, remaining silent, engaging in repetitive comments or behavior, changing the subject, or telling about the past to avoid dealing with
the present.

But resistance does not occur only because of the feelings and needs of
the clients. It may be a reasonable response to workers' parts in the
process, as when they are late to meetings, when they confront members
in a punitive manner and without conveying empathy, or when their
interpretations are too numerous and even threatening.

The following example is taken from the record of a group of adult
men and women with problems in social relationships in an adult psychiatric clinic.

About halfway through the tenth session, the subject turned to religion. The discussion was more of a social conversation than an
application to the members' problems. There was very little personal investment in the subject by any of the members, and it
seemed to be a device to avoid talking about their fears.

After a while, I said, "You've been talking about religion; does
that help you to work on your difficulties?" Joe said he was just
interested in making a philosophical point—he enjoys talking about
philosophy. I asked, "Do you remember that, in our last meeting,
you shifted away from talking about yourselves to talking about
general things that didn't really seem to involve you much: aren't

you starting to do the same thing again today?" There was an uncomfortable silence.

I said, "It's been different in this group for the last two sessions." There was another uncomfortable silence. Allen broke the silence. "Who's holding back?" Everyone laughed.

Shirley said she came to this group because she was putting all her own problems on her children. I said, "Yes, and you and the others have not been working on those kinds of problems recently. What accounts for that?" There was another uncomfortable silence.

Shirley broke the silence. "You don't want to bring out the real, deep problems that are bothering you."

Leon: "It's hard to even put your finger on the real problem—I'm mixed up about that." Allen: "It's easier to talk about religion than about what I really feel. I guess it's a cover up."

Leon cracked a joke and the mood changed. The other members laughed and Leon told another joke.

I said, "Let's look at what's been going on right now. Shirley said it's hard to share the real problems; Leon, that he's not sure what these are; Allen, that he needs a cover up for what he really feels; and Susan, Barbara, and Carl haven't said a thing. Some of you were just getting close to talking about things that matter when Leon cracked a joke to take the focus off yourselves. It may feel scary to delve deeper into the feelings and relationships that contribute to your troubles."

Shirley said, "I have to agree with that." Susan said, "Me, too, what will happen to me if I tell too much? But I'm willing to try."

The social worker presented observations of the members' behavior and changes in it, used clarification in making connections between recent and current behavior, confronted the members with the fact that they were avoiding working on their problems, and requested that members try to find their own explanations for their behavior. The worker's perception of the pattern of behavior in the group's process was summarized and interpretations for consideration by the members were offered.

The major principle to guide workers is that they respect the clients' need to protect themselves and do not arouse more anxiety than can be dealt with at a given time. Clients tend to drop out if they disclose too much too soon. To advance expectations and achieve certain gains, it is necessary that some anxiety be felt; the crucial factor is whether the clients have the ego capacities to cope with the disturbed feelings.

Confrontation tends to arouse anxiety and hence resistance. What is to be conveyed is not condemnation or withholding of acceptance but a direct statement that the worker is aware that something is going on that prevents moving ahead. Such challenges bring the obstacle into the conscious awareness of the clients and make it possible for them to express their concerns and move ahead in problem-solving activities. Confrontation that strips defenses is harmful; the worker needs to allow time to provide support to the clients as they try to take in the confrontive message and then to work it through.

Interpretation often follows confrontation. Such statements about the meaning of behavior may be resisted, or they may be readily accepted. They may be resisted because the worker has expressed a truth that the client is not yet ready to recognize or because the worker has misunderstood the meaning of the situation and the interpretation is inaccurate. It is hard for anyone to face the intensity of deep feelings, and it is no wonder that clients defend themselves against such understanding until they have developed enough self-esteem to accept these aspects of themselves.

Secrecy may indicate resistance. When members keep a secret from the family or group, they are making it impossible to help. When a worker withholds information the clients are deprived of a source of help. In therapeutic groups, Balgopal and Hull explain how resistance often occurs because there are secrets between one or more members and the worker that are not revealed or discussed in group sessions. These areas of secrecy create barriers.[19] Secrecy also creates barriers in families.

Clients need strong support from the practitioner in recognizing that such resistant behavior has prevented them from working toward the goals, and practitioners need to encourage members to respond, giving realistic reassurance to reduce the threat, universalizing the problem, and encouraging a refocusing of the discussion.

During the core stage, the predominant focus of the content is on the problematic situations of the clients, as these are connected with those of others and with the general purpose of the service. The particular problems that become the focus of discussion and activity-oriented experiences are those that are primary concerns of the clients at a given time. Successful outcome usually involves work toward (1) interpersonal learning, that is some degree of improvement in affective and cognitive understanding of oneself in relation to others, (2) social competence, that is achievement of the social skills essential to the performance of vital social roles, and (3) enhancement of the environment.

Interpersonal Learning

Acquisition of more accurate perception of self in relation to other people and to the demands of the environment is a frequent task of this stage. Striving for self-understanding is based on the theoretical assumption that if people can understand how the values, emotions, patterns of behavior, and prior experiences have contributed to the current problems, they become able to distinguish which attitudes and behaviors best serve their goals. It is assumed that the more accurate the perception of inner and outer reality, the firmer the foundation for effective social functioning. Clients may come to a better understanding of their feelings and attitudes, their patterns of behavior in relation to what they are doing with other people, the reasons for the behavior and, in some instances, the influence of the past on current functioning. They may then be able to decide how to behave differently or what needs to be changed in the environment.

The worker's role is a complex one. All of the interventive skills are used differentially in helping clients achieve increased interpersonal understanding.

Sensitive Listening and Observation

In interpersonal learning, sensitive listening and observation of nonverbal behavior are essential skills. An example is of a group of parents in a child guidance clinic.

> [The meeting opened with listening to a tape on parent-child relationships.]
>
> During the time the tape was being played, Mr. Draper appeared to be fully involved. Hands, eyes, posture, body movement, and absence of whispering to others reflected his involvement. Since he had not been this intense before the tape, something was affecting him deeply. When the tape was over, he sat back for only a second, but it was long enough for a discussion to get going about children's problems. Every time he tried to get into the discussion, someone else got in first. His finger tapping, leg crossing, and squirming seemed to indicate growing anxiety. By the time he got into the discussion, the topic was only distantly related to the tape.
>
> Mr. and Mrs. Alonzo were talking about their nephew's difficulty in cub scouts. Mr. D. stated that, since he is a den master, he could help the boy if they would like. After some further discus-

sion of children's problems in clubs, I said to Mr. D., "I bet you really enjoy helping the cub scouts—it does tend to strengthen parent-child relations . . . but you know what? I have a feeling you would like to talk about something else and just haven't been able to get it into the discussion. It seemed like parts of that tape had a lot of meaning for you." Everyone perked up when Mr. D. said, "Yes, they did. There was a lot of me in that tape. I could see myself in it."

All of a sudden, the members seemed to realize that, in their excitement to talk about how the tape related to their children, they overlooked how the content might relate directly to themselves. The members were very supportive of Mr. D. as he shared some emotionally powerful experiences. That, in turn, led to discussion of other members' parts in the problems of relationships in their families.[20]

In addition to listening, the skills in practice reflected in this brief excerpt include sensitive observation of nonverbal, as well as verbal behavior; support of Mr. D.'s positive abilities in Boy Scouting; the nonthreatening use of interpretation based on observation and sensitive listening; demonstration of an empathic response to anxiety; and a refocusing of the content to the primary needs of the members. With a worker who supports the group process, the ventilation and discussion of feelings by one member evoke greater self-disclosure on the part of the others also.

Exploring Feelings

Ventilation of feelings and having them accepted is a first step toward understanding their meaning to clients. The social worker often needs to be able to accept, with empathy and objectivity, a variety of frightening feelings. An example:

Maria, a seventeen-year-old Mexican American girl who has been in serious conflict at home, particularly with her father. She looked distressed as she entered my office. She slammed her school books on the table, sat down, and did not wait for me to open the session. Breathlessly, she said, "I need to ask you: am I going crazy?" I remained silent for a brief time to see if she wanted to go on. Then I responded, "I'm sure you're not going crazy, but tell me what you're feeling that makes you wonder about that." I felt it was necessary to reassure Maria so that anxiety would not be increased, and then move to explore the related feelings and experiences.

Providing Information

Within the problem-solving process, there are times when knowledge is needed in order to further interpersonal understanding. In a group of Spanish-speaking mothers with little education, for example, the members first needed information about the school system and its expectations for children, leading to discussion of how they could help their children succeed. Later, the women became able to participate in reflective discussion about themselves, their families, and the neighborhood conditions that made life difficult. As the women brought up problems and feelings related to sex, the worker learned that they had very little accurate knowledge about human sexuality, so she provided information as the members requested it and were ready to use it. The discussion then concerned the meaning of that information to them.

Clients may lack knowledge that is essential to understanding. They may, for example, lack knowledge about what is normal development and normal reactions to events in their culture: they mistake the usual for abnormality or vice versa. When normal expectations for physical, psychological, and social development through the life cycle are not understood, what is normally expectable behavior is often regarded as deviant; or, on the other hand, problematic behavior is not recognized as such. Similarly, lack of knowledge about physical handicaps and illnesses and the effect of these on the psychosocial functioning of patients and their relatives is a common source of misconception. Lack of knowledge about sex is another frequent example. In such instances the provision of facts, according to the client's ability to accept and understand them, is necessary. The client can make the best use of the facts if there is discussion of their meaning to the clients and persons in their social network.

Reducing Misperceptions of Self

Through social work help, there can be opportunities to correct errors in one's assumptions about oneself by checking these assumptions against those of the worker, thus getting corrective feedback. In groups there is the further opportunity to test these assumptions against those of one's peers.

The attitudes toward the self with which the worker deals most frequently are the closely interrelated ones of identity and self-esteem. Erikson has pointed out that "a common feeling of having a personal identity is based on two simultaneous observations: the immediate perception of one's self-sameness and continuity in time; and simultaneous perception of the fact that others recognize one's sameness and continuity."[21]

This sense of identity involves knowledge about and acceptance of oneself. As it develops through the life cycle, it incorporates more broadly and fully many aspects that define who a person is, what one can do, and what one will become. Often, clients feel stigmatized by the nature of their illnesses or handicapping conditions, for example, mental illness, mental retardation, cancer, AIDS, delinquency, or even the "bad mother" or "bad child" label. Feelings that people have about their sociocultural backgrounds often interfere with the development of positive self-esteem.

Irrational beliefs about oneself are signs of lack of self- knowledge. A low self-image or lack of positive identity leads many clients to deprecate themselves and engage in self-defeating patterns of behavior: "I am not loved," "I can't do it," "I'm really ugly," "If you really knew me, you'd know how rotten I am." All these are messages that convey irrational beliefs about oneself. Self-evaluation is a process that influences an individual's level of self-esteem and beliefs about one's ultimate worth. Along with self-evaluation goes a process of self-definition, through which one acquires a sense of identity or beliefs about who and what one is. Both sets of beliefs are developed through relationships and experiences with other people who confirm or contradict the beliefs around which responses from others interact with one's own perceptions.[22] Identity and self-esteem influence how a person relates to others and is influenced by the person's perceptions of the responses of others.

Certain events threaten the self-esteem of even healthy egos. Report cards, civil service examinations, work evaluations, or comparisons of development between children arouse fears of failure and worries about adequacy. These events force people to find out how their performance stands in relation to their own expectations and in relation to others. Sexual adequacy is a recurrent theme in services to adolescents and adults, related to the underlying theme of sexual identity. For aged persons, forced retirement and loss of relatives and friends through death are threats to their identity and self-esteem. Conflicts in identity also often come to the fore with clarity as members come to feel some success in their achievements. For example:

A black girl, a senior in high school, has expressed a strong desire for educational success and a college degree. In a session with her counselor one day, she said, "I just cannot go to school and take that test tomorrow. I know I'll flunk it." The social worker responded, "Is there something different now than when you took the last test? You did very well then."

CLIENT: "I don't know. I've studied even harder but it's just no use."

WORKER: "Can you tell me more about that feeling?"

CLIENT: "No, but I just feel scared. I'm scared."

WORKER: "Do you have an idea about why you're more scared this time?"

CLIENT: "Not really, but I just want so badly to get that scholarship. Mrs. Gresham told me to apply for it and I know all the best kids in school will want it, too."

WORKER: I understand how badly you want that scholarship. It means a lot to you. But Mrs. G. would not have advised you to apply if she didn't think you could make it, and it's not just one scholarship. The school has many to give."

CLIENT: "You're right, but that test!"

WORKER: "You certainly want to do well in that test, but you know what? The grade on one test can't possibly make the difference in your grade point average."

CLIENT: I never thought of it that way: I'll try to take it."

Commonly held prejudices are often determinant of persons' inability to perceive themselves and others accurately. When one is prejudiced, perception is distorted. One perceives individuals as representatives of categories which have been devalued. Prejudice may be based on ethnicity, poverty, age, sex, or being on welfare, and both interferes with a person's opportunity for relationships with others and harms the others. There is usually great resistance to acknowledging that one is prejudiced; there is a tendency to deny this attitude and rationalize the reasons for one's attitude and behavior toward others. Recognition of the fact is the first step toward change. Factual information is essential but seldom sufficient to bring about changes in attitudes and behavior. Alternative techniques to be used are ventilating feelings, followed by examination of the basis for the feelings; raising questions about actual events that seem related to the prejudice; or providing experiences with the victims of prejudice. Understanding and empathy reduce prejudice. For example:

A worker led a group of black girls, all with problems in high school and from low-income families. Frequent topics of discussion were feelings of being discriminated against and feelings of prejudice toward others. In one meeting, a teacher, also black, entered the room to ask the girls if they could be less noisy. One member screamed, "Oh, I hate her; she is just prejudiced. She doesn't even stick up for her own race."

Others joined in the ventilation of feelings against teachers and white students, who were perceived as being discriminatory. Gross distortions were evident, one complaint being that no black student had ever been an officer of the student organization.

When the worker expressed understanding of the members' feelings but confronted them with the reality of the situation, including the fact that the president of the student organization was black, the girls stopped talking. After a silence, one girl grudgingly admitted, "That's true, but I just hate white kids." Later, the worker commented that the members seemed to feel as one about this. All agreed. The worker asked, "and there are no exceptions?" Two teachers were mentioned as being all right, but the expressions of hatred continued. To the two girls who expressed most of the feelings, the worker commented, "You seem to be full of hate today." The response was, "Well, yes, we've a right to." The worker acknowledged that sometimes there were reasons to feel hatred.

Gradually, the members themselves began to confront each other with the facts. One girl said, "After all, Mrs. G. (the worker) is white, too." The most vociferous of the members looked startled, and said, "Oh, no" and broke into tears, then added, "But, but, I like you." From that point, the girls began to at least make some exceptions to stereotyping people.

Note that the practitioner's skills included sensitive listening, conveying empathy, accepting the expression of feelings, naming the feelings, confronting the members' distortions of facts, encouraging feedback to the confrontation, supporting member to member confrontation, and gradually working toward clarification of reality.

Transference reactions, earlier discussed, are a special instance of distortion of perception. Clients may react to the worker or to other members in ways that were appropriate to an important person in their earlier experience but which are not appropriate in the current situation. This phenomenon is apt to be more intense in long-term than in short-term treatment and it is apt to be more intense in individual than in treatment with couples or in groups. In multiple-person situations, however, there is the added complexity of transference reactions directed toward other members of the family or group.

Making Connections

Clients are helped to understand themselves and others better by discovering connections between two events, linking the problems of one person with those of another, and linking current problems to the past. Clarifying patterns of behavior and their consequences for individual, family, or group functioning increases understanding and efforts to make change. Clarification through linking the problems of one member with those of others is illustrated in an article by Bittner:

> For example, Gary L. was a five-year-old boy who protested going to kindergarten, complaining bitterly of stomach aches. After obtaining a clean bill of health from the pediatrician, Mr. and Mrs. L. sought family counseling. Mrs. L.'s father had suffered from a chronic illness throughout her childhood, and she had constantly worried about his death. He died when Mrs. L. was nineteen years old. During Gary's infancy, Mr. L. was diagnosed as having a life-threatening illness; however, the illness was in remission, and his prognosis was good. Gary had never been told about his father's illness, although Mrs. L. admitted that she was never free from worry about her husband's health. During the course of family counseling, the worker was able to link Mrs. L.'s worries about loss and separation with Gary's identical concerns; these were symbolically enacted in his refusal to leave home for school. In addition, Mr. L. spoke for the first time about his own fears regarding his illness. Gradually, Mrs. L. began to observe her overprotectiveness toward both her son and her husband. The family ended counseling after five months of weekly sessions. At that time, Gary's symptoms had stopped and Mr. and Mrs. L. were quite pleased with his behavior[23]

The case indicates the common problem of parents' efforts to keep children from learning about the illness of a family member. Being able to see the connection between the mother's worries about loss and separation with the child's refusal to go to school opened up further communication within the family concerning attitudes and behavior in response to the illness of a member.

During the course of treatment, earlier experiences in the person's or family's past may be brought up by the client or when the worker decides it is desirable to elicit such information in order to remove an obstacle to progress. There are times when making connections between an event in the past and a present difficulty is necessary. Much talk about the past is done to ventilate anger or to justify or defend a present position or behavior. Even so, for a person to recall an important event and the related emotions may be crucial to change present feelings and behavior. For example:

Alan is an adult male who was adopted when he was four years old and now wants to find his biological parents. He became able to say that he feels abandoned and rejected by them and that, not even knowing who they are, makes him feel strange and abnormal. His current dilemma is that his wife of fifteen years has just taken a job which requires her to travel several days each month. His income is very adequate, and she does not need to work. He also worries that she will abandon him, in spite of every realistic evidence to the contrary. The early feelings of being abandoned seem to be resurging in the present. Thus, clarification of the present fears of abandonment as related to earlier events may be helpful.

The practitioner might say, for example, that "I recall that we talked about your feeling that your birth parents abandoned you. Now you worry that your wife's work will lead to abandonment. Have you thought about that?" or "The feelings you have been expressing about your wife seem similar to the ones you expressed about feeling abandoned by your birth parents. Is there any connection?" The decision to help the client find connections should be based on the assessment that the client had sufficient ego strength to do this.

Viewing behavior from a developmental perspective may help the clients to change their definitions of their own behavior or that of significant others. Looking at what precipitated a problem can help put it into perspective. The perceptions of the past events may be accurate or distorted: only if it is possible to test the reality of the events seen as traumatic can either worker or client know the facts. But the important issue is the meaning of the perceived event to the clients and its influence on their current psychosocial functioning. The worker's focus is on the influence of these events on the present attitudes, relationships, and problem-solving capacities of the individuals involved.

In family and group situations, when one member recalls historical material, workers need to assess its impact on other individuals and on the progress of the group. They need to decide whether the nature of the past experience and its influence on current functioning is such that it can be worked with in the multiple-client situation. If such persons are members of a group, it may become clear that their situations are so different from those of other members that they need individual treatment, in addition to the group. The worker also needs to decide whether a change in plans is required in order to deal with the matter. In some instances, for example, short-term treatment may need to be extended.

Interpreting Meanings

Seeking for the meaning of behavior or emotions involves bringing them into conscious awareness when they can be recalled with assistance. When the worker suggests explanations, these are related to the particular pattern of behavior, emotion, or situation—not generalized to the personality. The practitioner refrains from interpretation of unconscious processes: the focus is on conscious and suppressed material. The worker generally approaches internalized conflicts as they are manifested in social adaptation, interpersonal relationships, realistic aspects of the cultural milieu, and the realities of the living experience.

In some instances, it is helpful for clients to reflect about dynamic and developmental factors so that they learn how their emotions and thoughts work for or against them. Workers may encourage them to search for possible reasons within themselves for their feelings; they may call attention to a discrepancy between fact and feeling or recognize inappropriate behaviors. The worker may note that a pattern seems to be emerging in the way their clients feel and think about different situations, making comments to help the clients to discover the pattern. When clients are ready, the worker may interpret their use of defenses in a tentative manner. One worker said to a client, for example, that when things are hard for us, we tend to deny that this is so in order to protect ourselves. Sometimes when a client does not recognize difficult behavior, an interpretation from the worker may help. An example is a comment: "There seems to be some connection between your anger and the death of Jimmy that we need to try to understand." However, unless clients recognize the behavior as ego-alien or unprofitable, they will not seek to understand or change it.

Explaining the Problems

To carry understanding further, the practitioner helps clients to find explanations for the problematic situation. For example:

Mr. and Mrs. Bajer are a couple in conflict over ways of raising their five-year-old daughter. In the process, the worker identified a pattern of communication as one in which Mrs. B. talked loudly and long in an argumentative way, complaining about Mr. B.'s unwillingness to discuss problems at any length. Mr. B. listened, spoke very little, and made comments softly, briefly, and concisely. That made it hard for them to make decisions about their daughter.

Once the problem was identified, there was a need to account for it. How did that pattern develop? The practitioner, feeling that progress was not being made, went back to the initial interviews. She was reminded of two sets of information. One was that Mr. B. was the son of Norwegian immigrants and had lived on a farm until he went to college. Mrs. B. was the daughter of Russian Jewish immigrants; her family loved to discuss politics and argue about them. Mrs. B. loved to argue with her brother and emphasized the fact that she usually won.

There are, generally speaking, wide differences in the basic communication styles of Norwegians and Jews which, combined with difference in family life, might account partially for the Bajers' problems in communication. The second set of information was that Mrs. B. had emphasized that she was frustrated because she had not completed work on a master's degree, while her husband had completed his education and was highly successful in his work. This issue had not been explored fully because after Mrs. B. would bring it up briefly, she then changed the subject.

Here are two possible explanations for the couple's lack of progress in counseling. The practitioner decided to focus first on the communication patterns. She told the Bajers that she had noted the vastly different styles of communication that seemed, at least partially, to be rooted in the difference in their cultural backgrounds and family upbringing. She wondered if that might be related to their current problems in communication. Both partners were silent and thoughtful. Then, as if a light dawned, Mrs. B. said, "Oh, I just thought Anders was refusing to discuss things with me," and then he said he felt she was nagging him to go on and on in talking about things.

The next time that Mrs. B. mentioned her frustration in not having completed her education, the worker held the couple to a focus on that issue. Mrs. B.'s competitive feelings, combined with the cultural differences in styles of communication, were interrelated parts of what had been defined as differences in opinion about raising their child. Despite the problems, there were many positives in the marriage and the Bajers were able to move quite quickly into deciding how each wanted to change their patterns of communication and made plans for Mrs. B. to continue her education without feeling like a bad wife and mother.

In seeking for explanations of problem-causing behavior, the focus is on bringing to conscious awareness feelings and experiences that have not been recognized, but that can be recalled and acknowledged with some assistance from the worker, or in families and groups, from other members. At times, the past must be dealt with. Many clients suffer from vague memories of earlier traumatic experiences, such as the Holocaust, rape, divorce, sexual molestation, or the suicide or murder of a relative. The ghosts of the past must be brought up and coped with in the present.

Verbal communication alone is not the royal road to understanding of self in relation to environment. Actions often clarify what people are thinking, feeling, and doing. Video-taping and replaying a session may enhance awareness of both verbal and nonverbal behaviors. Role-playing may be used to help a client become more aware of repressed feelings and patterns of relationships, with the worker taking the part of a family member or the client playing both roles. In families and formed groups, various members may participate in role-playing and in its analysis and evaluation.[24]

There is some evidence from research for the idea that acquiring self-knowledge is effective. In one study, clients reported that increasing their understanding of their problem was one of the two elements of greatest importance to them during a brief service. A statistically significant correlation was found between clients' reports of increased understanding and improvement in the problem at the follow-up.[25] In another study clients rated understanding of self and others as most helpful.[26] Enhanced understanding should lead to decision-making concerning maintaining patterns of behavior that are functional and satisfying and changing those aspects of self which are self-defeating and which contribute to the misery of others.

Social Competence

A problem is not resolved until the treatment that was made is implemented. Clients often do not know how to do this: they lack social competence. Social competence is the ability to perform roles in ways that are satisfying to the person in the role and that meet the expectations of significant other persons, such as spouse, employer, teacher, or colleague.[27]

Changes in perception of self and others and failure to make decisions do not necessarily lead to effective functioning. The client needs to do something more effectively. Achievement of competence in the performance of tasks related to problems in social relationships is often a goal of practice. The worker needs to assess the extent to which persons have mastered the tasks associated with each phase of psychosocial development. In helping clients to achieve competence in the performance of particular tasks or roles, the social worker primarily uses an educational process. Goldstein differentiates the educational role of the social worker from that of the school teacher. In social work, "the learning process is primarily directed toward the acquisition of knowledge that will aid in the completion of certain tasks or in the resolution of problems related to social living."[28] In order to adapt more effectively, people need the necessary knowledge and skills. The knowledge and skills need to be appropriate to the particular characteristics and needs of clients.

The necessary skills vary with the role and the particular problems in role functioning. A decision to seek to adopt a child, for example, requires accomplishing a number of tasks relevant to application, learning about adoptive parenthood, and culminating in the legal adoption. A decision by teenagers to go to college requires that they have a plan for financing education and know how to apply for admission to those colleges whose eligibility requirements are met. Other clients may need instruction and guidance in relation to their roles as parents, spouses, siblings, students, or employees. Some may need to know how to get out of debt through budgeting and managing their money. They often need knowledge about community resources and skills in communicating with representatives of agencies and organizations that have the resources.

The theoretical assumption underlying work toward enhanced knowledge and skills is that the ego is strengthened as a person develops effective means of communication, and enhances accuracy of their perceptions of self and situation. It is also strengthened as people have confidence in their abilities to perform roles in ways that are personally satisfying and that meet reasonable expectations of others. Mastery of tasks leads to self-esteem. The ability to think needs to be tested in the crucible of experience. It is especially important to have opportunities to master tasks in areas in which a person has previously been found lacking.[29] Thus, in social work, help in developing competence is related to the problems of the clients. It is thought that "social competence leads to increased ego strength which, in turn, enhances capacity to cope with conflict and anxiety. Increased coping capacity may then lead to increased competence."[30]

Self-esteem is a necessary ingredient of social competence. Many clients are burdened by a sense of low self-esteem. Often, they have been the victims of the negative valuations of others; have been discriminated against because of the race, sexual orientation, or gender; or have been labeled as deviant. They have had innumerable experiences with failure in family, education, work, or friendship roles. Heap writes that: "Such low self-esteem is self-nourishing, since it conditions the expectations and behavior with which new situations are met and thereby maintains the likelihood of new failure. It also frequently inhibits clients from risking new encounters at all and causes their withdrawal into a stultifying but protective passivity."[31] In working toward the aim of self-esteem, it is particularly important that the members achieve a sense of success in whatever they are doing. The shift from an attitude of "I can't" to "I'll try" to "I can" is a powerful motivator for success in social functioning.

Task-centered practice, as formulated by Reid and associates may be appropriately used with some clients individually, as part of families, or in groups.[32] The focus is on task performance, that is, a sequence of actions that people must follow in order to improve their functioning in a particular social situation.

Changes in task-centered practice over the years relate it more closely to problem-solving. It has become a specific model within problem-solving, best suited to clients whose problems are neither pervasive nor deep-seated.[33] Performance of tasks is one important way of helping people to develop social competence. The growth in the use of education as a major component of service has been tremendous in recent years.

Educational activities are used for both preventive and therapeutic functions. There are a large number of educational groups for parents or for relatives of patients, usually short- term in structure. One recent example by Wayne and Feinstein illustrates the use of short-term groups for parents of children who had identified problems in school. Two types of groups were organized: activity and discussion.[34] For some parents, activity groups were judged to be most suitable. These tended to be people who were less verbal and more cautious about verbalizing feelings or foreign- born parents who were still struggling to learn the English language. Many mothers who joined the activity groups were suffering from feelings of apathy and isolation. In a safe and supportive environment, communication flows between verbal and nonverbal modes of expression and moves from superficial to meaningful levels. The social workers concluded that Erikson's concept of mastery as the key task in latency was found just as relevant to adults who had been underachievers and who were suffering from low self-esteem.[35] In addition to activities, common concerns about parenting and school were discussed, decisions were made, and solutions to mutual problems were sought.

Demonstration, role-playing, and rehearsal are common tools used to prepare clients for dealing with difficult situations. Planning with the client to try something out, then report back, evaluate the effort, and plan next steps, helps to build confidence to try new ways of dealing with stressful situations.

Participating actively and responsibly in the effort to change one's behavior is a step in building competence and confidence. The worker maintains a relationship, encourages the client to try out new patterns of behavior, and offers support for experimentation with new behavior that may prove rewarding. In groups, mutual support from members is an additional dynamic.

In his research on family therapy with families living in urban slums, Minuchin and associates discovered the value of the use of tasks within a treatment session to help members deal with conflict among two or more members.[36] The practitioner actively guides members in learning how to observe the process that is going on among other members and instructs family members in role playing in order to learn new and unfamiliar ways of dealing with conflict. These action-oriented techniques are accompanied by identification of intrapersonal and interpersonal obstacles that emerge as new efforts to solve conflicts are attempted. The intent of such role playing is "to induce a vivid awareness of hidden patterns and underlying motivations while at the same time providing an opportunity to find new ways of attacking a problem" (p. 269).

Enhancing the Social Environment

A major obstacle to successful problem-solving is lack of environmental opportunities and resources or inability to use available resources. Social workers are uniquely qualified to deal with problems in the fit between client, family, and the environment. A major responsibility is to enable families to make use of resources in the community that will aid in the client's and family's well-being; and to negotiate collaborative relationships with members of other professions and organizations.[37] Many problems are not reflective of individual or family pathology but of problems in the complexity and maldistribution of health and welfare delivery systems, making knowledge about and access to needed resources difficult for almost anybody.

A living system requires constant transaction with its environment in order to maintain differentiation and impede entropy. Inadequate opportunities for interchange tend to isolate individuals and families from the larger social structure and to cut them off from inputs of an economic, educational, and social nature.[38] Food, clothing, shelter, and transportation are essential to physical survival; so, too, are social relationships that nurture and support developmental processes. Social relationships can become more satisfactory and adaptive patterns can change positively in response to favorable experiences. A harsh physical environment, too limited a cultural milieu, and inadequate social and educational opportunities create obstacles for a person. Gross social pathology, denial of civil rights, unhealthy and unfair employment practices, and racial segregation or other forms of group isolation affect the personality and its coping capacities. When the difficulty is between a person and a depriving environment, efforts must be made to change the particular part of the social system so that it can support, rather than impede, the person's efforts toward more effective functioning. Reducing environmental stress enables a person or a family to regain a satisfactory steady state, and the provision of more adequate opportunities contributes to psychosocial development.

Stresses occasioned by lack of adequate resources or unpleasant physical environments, as well as inadequate knowledge and skills, are obstacles to the achievement of their goals by families. Reducing environmental stress is one way to assist individuals and families to regain a dynamic steady state, and the provision of more adequate opportunities contributes to the psychosocial development of the clients.

Some clients and other members of their families will reach out to find and use resources when they know what is available and how to make application for material aids or services. But many families need more help than that. They may fear how they will be accepted and received by the persons providing the resource; they may not have the anticipated financial resources; or they may be too immobilized by stress to take initiative in reaching out to the providers. Helen Perlman gives examples of patients who have the medicine but also have serious doubts about taking it and of a special training class that was found for a neurologically damaged child whose mother failed to get him there.[39] Such people may need help to express and clarify their feelings, think about the value of the service offered, consider the conditions for the use of the resource, and work through their ambivalence about using the service. For example, a client may both want and still resist moving from a wheelchair to crutches, and the family may or may not support that move, thus needing considerable help in relation to the decision.

Modifying environmental obstacles requires that the social worker move into one or more systems in the client's social network. Such work is "a goal-directed process, undertaken after (a) an evaluation of the social environment and (b) an assessment of the individual's specific capacities, needs, and desires have been formulated."[40] It requires the differential use of knowledge and skills in practice. It requires, however, the specification of goals and procedures that are appropriate for influencing people who are not in roles of client or patient. They are rather potential supporters and helpers.

In chapter 12, on the provision of multiple services to meet the needs of clients, further attention will be given to the roles of social workers in their work with significant persons in clients' environments.

Twelve | Multidimensional Services

Many clients of clinical social workers are helped to solve a problem through carefully selected, planned, and time-limited individual, family, or group modalities. Many other clients have multiple, interacting problems that require a range of services. They may need some combination of individual, couple, family, or group treatment, including the provision of human and material resources in the client's environment. The practitioners' role is the selection, monitoring, coordination and evaluation of these services is an integral part of clinical practice, as contrasted with a separate case management role. Their work is with, not for, clients every step of the way. At times, these resources may be the most crucial ones in improving the clients' psychosocial functioning.

Multiple Problems

Multiple personal, interpersonal, cultural, and environmental factors interact in the emergence of the social problems that are present in our country today. Certain categories of people are especially vulnerable to biological, psychological, and social deterioration without appropriate help. They have need for accessible, comprehensive, and integrated sets of services. Among the at-risk populations are:

1. Members of racial or minority ethnic groups, particularly African Americans, Haitians, Hispanics, and Native Americans who are poor in disproportionate numbers, suffer from the deprivations that accompany life in poverty and from the effects of devaluation by society, discrimination, powerlessness, and poor neighborhood conditions. They often have

severe financial, housing, health, mental health, educational, and employment difficulties.[1]

2. Those with a chronic or terminal illness or disability are found in all population groups.[2] Although each medical or psychiatric condition has its own particular symptoms, degree of severity, prognosis, and set of psychosocial challenges, there are common problems connected with living with an illness or disability. Their conditions are often accompanied by major financial burdens, disruptions in family life, and serious psychosocial problems. In some diseases, stigma, prejudice, and discrimination add to the patient's and family's distress.

3. Recent immigrants and refugees comprise another vulnerable segment of the population.[3] Physical and social dislocation and relocation are highly stressful experiences. Cultural dissonance, intergenerational strains, language difficulties, inadequate finances, low employment opportunities, prejudice, and discrimination make life in their chosen country extremely difficult, even though preferable to remaining in their former countries.

4. Neglected and abused children are a most serious expression of family stress and breakdown.[4] These children have problems in functioning at home, in school, and in the community. They often are separated from their families of origin and require placement in new living environments. That results in problems of separation and adaptation to new strange caretakers and communities. Family violence, especially toward women, is closely related to child abuse.

5. Many individuals and families are suffering from the effects of the raging drug epidemic.[5] This American tragedy has produced multidimensional problems for the abuser and members of the abuser's family. There are both specific and general problems of drug-dependent adults, youth, increasing numbers of younger children, and perinatally exposed and HIV-infected infants. Members of families of drug abusers who do not use drugs, especially children and adolescents, tend to develop a range of serious psychosocial problems.

Multiple Services

Multidimensional problems require multiple services. An example is of services required by clients suffering from AIDS.[6] It has been proposed that these patients need some combination of professional individual, family, and group treatment; long-term support groups for patients and their families; crisis intervention, often episodic in nature; referral to social and health resources; advocacy for accessible, appropriate and dignified care; and coordination of services. In addition, preventive services should be provided for current clients, their families, and the general public in the form of education about the causes of the disease, the means of acquiring it, safer sex, the effects of illness on the lives of people, and whatever else can be done to prevent the spread of HIV infection.

Over and over again, the contemporary writings on these multidimensional problems assert that interventive strategies must be multidimensional, informed by a biopsychosocial framework that reflects a systems perspective.[7]

Crisis Intervention

Multidimensional services often encompass crisis intervention within a broader plan of service, or crisis intervention may be the only help needed by an individual or family. Crisis intervention is a form of the biopsychosocial approach to practice, making full use of the problem-solving process in time-limited treatment. It has been defined by Parad, Selby, and Quinlan as:

> a process for actively influencing the psychosocial functioning of individuals, families, and small groups during a period of acute disequilibrium. . . . A person is in a state of crisis when an emotionally hazardous situation, so interpreted by the person(s) involved, creates stress which becomes unbearable at the point when some precipitating event places demands on the person(s) for coping resources not readily available. A severe anxiety state sets in, and is not easily dispelled because of lack of effective problem-solving means . . . habitual coping means do not suffice.[8]

A crisis is precipitated by a hazardous event. The precipitating event may be a disaster such as a flood, hurricane, earthquake, or fire; or a threatening experience such as rape, attempted suicide, diagnosis of a life-threatening illness, hospitalization, separation, divorce, or death of a loved one. The hazardous event may be perceived as a threat to important life goals, security, or affectional needs. The person or family becomes increasingly anxious, uncomfortable, and confused. The state of crisis is temporary, characterized by signs of confusion and emotional upset which immobilize the ego's problem-solving abilities and interfere with other aspects of daily living. The crisis of one member of a family has an impact on the other members, disrupting the functioning of the family unit.

First developed as a service to individuals, crisis intervention is now practiced with family units when there is a collective crisis or when the crisis of one member is upsetting to the others as well. It is also used with formed groups whose members share the experience of being in a state of crisis.

The major goals of crisis intervention are to lessen the stress and to help clients and significant others mobilize and use their capacities, interpersonal skills, and social resources for coping adaptively with the effects of the stressful event.

Treatment

Early accessibility to treatment is considered essential. When people are in a state of crisis, it is thought that they are especially susceptible to well-timed and well- focused help. Golan says that "a small amount of help appropriately focused, can prove to be considerably more effective than more extensive help at periods of less emotional accessibility."[9] The total length of time between the initial blow and the final resolution varies widely, depending upon the severity of the hazardous event, the capacities of the clients, the tasks that have to be accomplished, and the available supports.

The social worker's activities usually consist of the following:

1. Study the precipitating events and their meaning to the client, members of the client's family, and significant others. Clarification of the what, when, where, and how of the event enhances the client's cognitive functioning.

One important factor in the successful resolution of a crisis is the nature and quality of the information received by the patient and family. The intensity of a crisis is reduced through education. Frye notes that "the basic, underlying principle is that families cope better when they understand events and are encouraged to channel anxiety into positive, participating activities."[10]

2. Encourage the expression of emotions that have been stirred up by the event. Clients in a state of crisis display much anxiety and a range of other emotions, depending partly on their previous ways of coping with stress and partly on the nature of the event. Anger, hopelessness, depression, guilt, or remorse are accepted by the practitioner with empathy, which helps the clients to understand and master them and simultaneously to be able to work on problems created by the event.

3. Explore the means by which clients have tried to cope with the stress and assess their usefulness. Resolving a crisis depends upon giving up or reducing the use of inadequate coping devices, such as the defenses of denial, rationalization, projection of blame onto others or to self, and isolation.

4. Discover and use appropriate resources. Many families need help to discover and use resources that can provide emotional support or health and welfare resources. The clients can be helped to engage in problem-solving concerning the help they need, who can help them, and how they will access the resources.

5. Consider alternative means of coping with the problems that are associated with the hazardous event, and decide on particular goals that clients wish to achieve to restore the steady state. Support the clients' efforts to cope in new ways and make viable decisions through the problem-solving process.

Crisis intervention is thought to be appropriate to people of all ages, ethnic groups, and social classes. The only requirements are that clients must be in a state of crisis or be influenced by family members or another significant person who is in a state of crisis, be willing to seek or be referred for help, and be able to sustain a relationship with a practitioner for a brief period of time.[11] The service is carried on in many settings in all fields of practice. It is frequently used in the field of health, including mental health, when the precipitating events are diagnoses of life threatening illnesses or those that are stigmatized, serious accidents, premature births, babies born with deformities, separation, placement in nursing homes, or death of a loved one. In family/children's services, the precipitating events tend to be related to abandonment; battering of women, children or elderly persons; divorce; loss of child custody; unemployment; and homelessness. In occupational social work, severe stress may accompany being fired or laid off, poor evaluations, and problems from outside that are brought into the work place.

Disasters are hazardous events that have an impact on many people simultaneously. Houston and Robey give the following description:

> Disasters are defined as calamitous events, especially those occurring suddenly and causing great damage to property and hardships for human beings. The stresses of a major disaster are most often shared directly or indirectly by the community. A family is not alone in its suffering. Experiences can be evaluated relative to the losses of others. Family members often jointly experience the terror-filled moments of impact and extended period of clean-up, in contrast with victims of rape or distant war. Roles within the family may be very different when members are responding to a shared event. Disorganization of the family system can be swift and dramatic during a disaster. Widespread social disruption accompanies disasters. It reduces the family's access to outside resources and throws the family back on its own resources.[12]

The social worker's activities, as previously described, are applicable to work with victims of disasters. There are additional emphases, however.

There is greater attention to education concerning the nature, extent, and severity of the disaster; finding ways to reunite families; encouraging participation in community efforts to rehabilitate property; and helping clients to deal with loss of jobs and community facilities, destruction of kin and friendship networks, and to cope with "red tape" and the bureaucratic disaster relief organizations. Disaster work illuminates the need for multiple services: counseling to resolve individual and family crises; group work to provide support and mutual aid in resolving personal and interpersonal problems; referrals to secure concrete aids or medical help; and participation in community efforts to rebuild damage and provide social networks. Reaching-out approaches are essential.

Referral and Resource Consultation

Many clients need to have the benefit of health, education, and welfare resources. The social worker may refer clients to supportive networks or to other health and social agencies for help with needs that cannot be met within the agency. Referrals to employment agencies, work-training programs, health and medical care, recreational and educational opportunities, or religious organizations should be part of treatment if clients are to be helped to function at more nearly their full capacity.

Some writers refer to this service as a brokerage role in which the worker serves as a link between a client and a resource. Solomon has broadened the concept of the role to that of resource consultant, which is the preferred term because a consultant directs attention to the clients' capacity to use their personal resources and skills in the effort to achieve their own goals.[13] The provision of resources in the form of financial assistance, housing, and health care, is crucial, but the trick is to provide them in such a way that they do not reinforce dependency and powerlessness. Solomon explains, "The resource consultant role is defined here much more broadly than that of resource dispenser or resource provider; it involves linking clients to resources in a manner that enhances their self-esteem as well as their problem-solving capacities" (p. 346). The client's participation in the process is extensive: consultants offer their knowledge and expertise to the client.

Use of the Resource

The effective use of a resource requires that clients have a great deal of knowledge and skill. Essentially, the consultants share their knowledge, offer encouragement, and give advice that is essential to the client's decision to use a resource. Effective consultation requires that workers have assessed the clients' needs for particular resources, and that they have accurate information about available resources and the conditions for their use.

Workers then need to call the clients' attention to, and give appropriate information about, the alternative resources that might be available to them in solving a problem or providing opportunities to enrich their own lives or the lives of members of their families. They need to clarify their reasons for suggesting a resource and to work with whatever ambivalence clients may have about it. They need to engage the clients in the problem-solving process toward making a decision to use a resource and selecting the most appropriate one. Clients, and often their families, should be prepared as fully as possible to know how to proceed in making application to the agency or organization and meeting its eligibility requirements and intake procedures. They should be prepared to make optimal use of the resource. Workers may also need to consult with the responsible person in the receiving agency, with the full knowledge and consent of the client, in order to assist that person to aid the client in becoming eligible for and using the service. Workers can thus pave the way for clients, without taking away from the clients' use of their own skills in getting a desired resource.

In the use of resources, the major emphasis is to provide additional resources, often not within the province of the social worker's agency, which will enrich the lives of clients and provide additional opportunities for them. The nature of the resources may be as varied as a special library, tutoring, a music class, recreational activity, employment service, provision of a Big Sister or Big Brother, or a leadership training group. In working with families, for example, children can often benefit from a camp or day care experience so that, in a supportive and nurturing environment, they can take advantage of opportunities for making friends, developing competence in activities that facilitate normal developmental processes, and find relief from an unbearable burden at home or in the neighborhood. Other types of groups, such as Scouts, Camp Fire Boys and Girls, and those under the auspices of community centers, are designed to enhance social development through the provision of interpersonal and social experiences. Likewise, referrals of adults to informal classes for learning new activities that might become hobbies, such as cooking, sewing, photography, or camping, can be sources for the development of self-esteem, social relationships, and new interests in life. Referrals to cultural, civic, and political organizations may provide an opportunity for clients to give to others, thereby enhancing their self-esteem and sense of power.

Advocacy

Case advocacy covers activities through which the practitioner strives to secure a service or benefit to which clients are entitled, but which they have been unable to secure by their own efforts. It covers situations in which clients are discriminated against owing to race, ethnicity, religion, sexual orientation, or gender. It covers situations in which policies have a serious adverse effect on the client's welfare and there is a clear need to plea for an exception to the policy.

Case advocacy can perhaps be most accurately defined as "partisan intervention on behalf of an individual client or identified client group with one or more secondary institutions to secure or enhance a needed service, resource, or entitlement."[14] It is not a simple action of demanding that a client be given something. Far from it. A study by McGowan supports the view that advocacy is a complex, skilled process.[15] Her study found that (1) the choice of this strategy is influenced by the objectives, the nature of the problem, the sanction for advocacy, the channel agent and target systems; (2) the primary determinants of the action are the practitioner's resources and the receptivity of the target system, and (3) the use of communication and mediation rather than power are emphasized in the range of resources and techniques that are used.

The decision to use advocacy, then, is based on the problem- solving process. The nature of the problem is clarified; the goals are specified; the advantages and disadvantages of different alternatives are pursued; the nature of the client's participation in the process is clarified and mutually-agreed to; the possible positive and negative consequences of the action are weighed. The client has the right to determine the action to be taken.

Becoming an advocate for a client is often desirable, but requires that the practitioner be clear about the ethical judgments and skills that are necessary.[16] Situations that workers encounter often present ethical dilemmas as to what types of actions are most appropriate. In order to make an appropriate decision concerning advocacy, social workers need to be aware of their own biases, including a tendency to want to do for other people rather than work with them, and a need to exploit clients in pursuing their own political causes. They need to make an accurate assessment of the client's needs and capacities, the effect of the action on the client's ability to function effectively, and alternative means to solve the problem. The worker, with a strong desire to help a client to receive a benefit, needs to remember the client's rights to choose and to decide that they want to take the risks that are involved. Informed consent is essential every step of the way with the clear understanding that, although a positive outcome is hoped for, it cannot be guaranteed. Realistic hope, as contrasted with false hopes, is a motivation toward successful implementation of a plan to intervene.

With skill in the use of relationship and communication applied to persons in powerful roles, the practitioner is often able to influence the other persons to cooperate in resolving a client's justifiable complaint. They need to be able to listen to the other's point of view and rationale for the situation, rather than accusing or blaming the other of injustice. It is possible that the client has misunderstood or misinterpreted the decision. It is possible that the collateral did not have sufficient knowledge of the client's situation. When it is clear that the client's case is justified, then efforts to reconsider the decision are appropriate.

An example of successful advocacy is presented by Woods and Hollis:

A sixteen-year-old boy, Jonathan, had been periodically suspended from school for cutting classes and for displaying a surly attitude toward teachers. He disliked the academic program and wanted to be transferred to a special vocational program to train in automobile mechanics, for which he had a special gift. The school authorities, however, who were clearly angry, were unwilling to refer him to this program, which would cost the school district money, because they assumed from his behavior that he would be a poor risk. After learning this, the worker was able to help Jonathan recognize that his attitude contributed to the school's unyielding position. Subsequently a conference at the school was arranged by the worker. Jonathan participated and, with the worker's support, was able to speak for himself; he explained his unhappiness with his present program and apologized for his behavior. The worker's expression of confidence in Jonathan's seriousness about vocational training was instrumental in tipping the balance, and the transfer was approved. Months of direct work, in which the worker encouraged Jonathan's strengths preceded mediation with the school. Had the worker intervened prematurely, before Jonathan was willing to share in the responsibility for the problem, the work undoubtedly would have backfired.[17]

Successful intervention with decision-makers is based on accurate information about entitlements, policies, and procedures and accurate information about efforts previously made by the client. When a decision against the client has been made, the practitioner and client may appeal to review boards, governmental agencies, or legislators. Legislators can often intervene in behalf of their constituents, as exemplified in the following situation.

> A young woman with a serious chronic illness could no longer tolerate the traditional methods of treatment. A new treatment, not yet approved by the Food and Drug Administration, had been found effective in every experimental test thus far. Based on his study, her physician thought the new treatment showed great promise for his patient. He was unsuccessful in convincing the FDA that he could use it. In a conference with the physician, the social worker suggested that she thought the patient's senator might be able to intervene with the FDA. The worker prepared a first draft of a letter, which was revised by the client and physician, signed by all three of them, and sent to the senator. It did not take long for the physician to get approval to use the new treatment.

There are groups of lawyers and organizations who are interested in protecting the rights of people, to whom the practitioner can refer a client. These organizations can provide services that go beyond what an individual worker or agency can do alone. Conclusion: advocacy is an integral part of clinical social work, involving work with the client and others simultaneously.

Use of Social Supports

Clients need support from significant people in order to work toward their goals. Gottlieb's empirically derived definition is that "Social support consists of . . . verbal and/or nonverbal information or advice, tangible aid, or action that is proffered by social intimates or inferred by their presence and has beneficial emotional or behavioral effects on the recipient."[18]

A support system is one in which significant others help the individuals to mobilize their personal resources; provide the material means and skills that are essential to improve the situation; and provide emotional support for efforts to cope with the problems. According to Caplan, "kinship and friendship are the most important types of primary social relationships, which can be used as support systems."[19]

Values of Support

The support of the participants in the practice situation is important, but it is seldom sufficient. The social worker needs to take into account the extent to which the environment provides support for a client. In one study of adolescent probationers, reconviction rates were significantly related to lack of support at home, work, or school, and to crime contamination. Those with the greatest difficulties in the environment were least likely to show satisfactory achievement.[20] In an earlier study in a family service agency in which adults had interpersonal conflicts, continuance in treatment was strongly associated with support of the clients' efforts by other people. If other people were indifferent or opposed to the clients' efforts, clients were less likely to continue.[21] Thus, a frequent task for the social worker is to seek support from significant others in enhancing the motivation of clients in the use of service.

In the field of family and child welfare, Tracy and Whittaker reviewed studies which indicate that when family members and friends provide psychological and material resources, people are in better physical and emotional health and are better able to adapt to stressful life events than are those with fewer supports.[22] The findings indicate that there is a positive relationship between the availability of social resources and parenting behaviors and attitudes and parent-child interactions.

In the health field, Ell and Northen provide convincing evidence of the salutary effects of social supports in recovery from illness and the outcomes of rehabilitation.[23] Social support from significant others enhances adaptation to illness by assuring patients that they are cared for, valued, and have access to tangible resources.

Social Networks

Networks are composed of people and relationships and are systems of mutual aid. They provide opportunities for social relationships beyond the family. In one study by Gottlieb of the social networks of low-income mothers, it was found that their membership in networks provided a variety of social supports, including companionship, emotional support and to, a lesser extent, goods or services and advice or guidance. Networks, however, created tension or conflict in 13 percent of the cases. Networking generates the exchange of resources through "tapping one's own connections and the connections that branch outward from them."[24] Mutual aid and self-help groups usually provide support to their members. People often join such groups through their on-going contacts in networks. Participation in such groups, in turn, may lead to changes in the network. Existing social networks may provide access to new ties with peers who share similar interests, life conditions, or circumstances. They are a primary source for making friends.

Social networks vary in size, subgroups, stability, composition, and connectedness. Interaction may be more or less frequent and intense, unidirectional or mutual. The research indicates that many are supportive, but some are not. Some members may be preoccupied or self-centered, or members may be in conflict with other members. Some networks reinforce deviance as in drug-oriented networks or delinquent gangs. Some may force conformity to their norms: peer pressure is a powerful influence. Some may have rigid boundaries that isolate and exclude some persons from entry. The network relationships that are truly supportive are those that are characterized by close proximity, frequency of interaction, mutual trust, similar norms, and reciprocity.

Roles for social workers. When meeting with a network or a subsystem of the network face-to-face, practitioners are working with a group. The tasks of the practitioner who thinks in terms of networks are: to mobilize the network as a source of support for clients; to maintain an effective network or one of its parts or repair an ineffective network; to manage tension or conflict among the parts; to seek to add a new cluster to an impoverished or incomplete network; and to disengage clients from maladaptive affiliations with members of the network.

Self-Help and/or Support Groups

Self-help and mutual aid have existed since primitive times. Groups and associations of many kinds have always been characteristic, too, of American society. Alexis de Toqueville wrote about this tendency in 1832, in a book entitled *Democracy in America*, in which he analyzed democracy as a working principle of society and of government. He said:

> Thus, the most democratic country on the face of the earth is the one in which men have, in our time, carried to the highest perfection the art of pursuing in common the object of their common desires and have applied this new science to the greatest number of purposes. Among democratized nations, people become powerless if they do not learn voluntarily to help one another. . . . Feelings and opinions are recruited, the heart is enlarged, and the human mind is developed only by the reciprocal influence of man one upon another. . . . As soon as several of the inhabitants of the United States have taken up an opinion or a feeling which they wish to promote in the world, they look out for mutual assistance; and as soon as they have found one another out, they combine into groups: from that moment, they are no longer isolated men.[25]

Before modern group work existed, groups were organized for numerous purposes. Trefethen, for example, described how women in the nineteenth century formed groups under many names to give them strength to fight for women's rights or to "serve as each other's refuge from difficulties at home or, for half, at work."[26]

The terms self-help and support group are used interchangeably; the focus on members doing for themselves distinguishes these groups from those with professional leaders. There has been a resurgence of interest in self-help groups in social work, particularly in the fields of health, family service, child welfare, and mental health. The primary purposes for which these groups are organized tend to be:

1. To control what is perceived to be undesirable behavior or conditions, as in groups to control weight, smoking, alcoholism, drug abuse, and gambling.
2. To provide information and instrumental aid about the matter of concern through the use of speakers, audio-visual media, and discussion.
3. To provide support and aid from peers in coping with stress related to the problem of concern.
4. To be a source for the development of informal interpersonal relationships and networks.
5. To achieve changes in conditions outside the group in order to achieve better public understanding of the condition or to change deleterious policies and procedures.
6. To combat discrimination and enhance self-esteem when members feel stigmatized owing to their gender, race, ethnicity, sexual orientation, or diseases that carry stigma.[27]

Some social workers have tended to glorify such groups and to expect miracles from them. Indeed, there are powerful and potentially beneficial processes in groups upon which the self-help movement builds. Many groups make use of the helper-therapy principle which asserts that mutual aid benefits both the giver and receiver; they attempt to maximize a system of peer support; and they enhance motivation through belief in the power of people, individually and collectively, to achieve their goals. Above all, perhaps, they build on the common need for human interaction and relatedness. At their ideal best, they offer friendship and experiential empathy.

The reality is that there is no assurance that members will indeed benefit from the group experience.

The potential casualties for some members arise from a combination of qualities of individuals who are members of the groups, rather than from the intent of some members to destroy others.[28] Group structures and processes are not necessarily healing or constructive in their effects. The group purpose, composition, expectations, and content may not be in harmony with the goals and needs of particular individuals: without such congruence, it is unlikely that an individual will benefit. Indeed, some will be harmed by membership in a group that is inappropriate for them.

Professional Responsibilities and Guidance

Social workers often serve as a linkage by connecting traditional services, clients, and support groups to each other.[29] They may provide knowledge of groups available in the community, refer clients to appropriate groups, and accept referrals from them. It was noted earlier, however, that referral is a very complex process that goes beyond simply giving information about available resources. Modern ecosystems theory demonstrates the importance of a complementary fit between the person and the new situation. Social workers must have an adequate assessment of the person and of the strengths and limitations of the proposed group in order to determine the appropriateness of the group for a particular client.

Social workers who organize and develop support groups are undertaking major leadership responsibilities. The danger is that they may dominate the group and interfere with the mutual aid process. To avoid dominance over the group, practitioners should work in partnership with members of the target population to insure that adequate indigenous leadership, direction, and participation will develop from within the group itself. Recent studies indicate that groups often benefit from the early support and leadership of professionals and that professional persons have been responsible for beginning many of the groups.

A common role for social workers is that of consultant. In such a role, workers provide information, guidance, expert knowledge, and technical assistance to the group's own selected leaders. In so doing, they do not take over the leadership of the group, but take direction from the needs and requests of the group's own leaders and membership. The clinical social worker and lay leader can be mutually reinforcing and complementary, rather than isolated from each other.

Not all groups need professional leaders, many do not. Professional help is usually necessary when the members have psychological and social problems beyond the need for support and mutual aid, when the goals include personal problem-solving, or when the group structure and process is inimical to the group's achieving its goals. Professional help is probably not necessary when the purpose of the group is to offer strong peer supports and sociability within a structure that provides clear, but somewhat flexible, norms for individual and group behavior. There is evidence that most groups attract and hold a highly selective membership composed of the more highly educated and less disadvantaged members of our communities. Rather than attracting people who do not use professional services, they consist of populations similar to those who use professional health and social services. Thus, support groups are not competitive with, but complementary to, professional services. The challenge for social workers is to develop groups that will appeal to more of the disadvantaged populations.

Self-help should not be a substitute for needed professional services. The belief that self-help is adequate leads to a tendency to blame the victim and expect people to pull themselves up by their own bootstraps. Individuals are expected to change through their own efforts. And, many times they do. But too great dependence on self-help may result in failure of social work and health organizations to develop programs to meet the needs of people when professional services are indicated, and to avoid or resist bringing about necessary legislative and other environmental changes.

Most clients receive social work services while living in their own homes, but there are occasions when a change in a living environment is essential to their health and welfare. New environments are often provided for children who need placement in foster, adoptive or institutional settings and for people for all ages who need long term hospital, rehabilitative, or nursing care. When moving from one living environment to another, they are in a period of transition that creates stress for them and their families

Changes in Living Environments

A major life transition is defined by Golan as "a process of change, moving an individual from one relatively stable state through an interval of strangeness and uncertainty on the way to a new stable state."[30]

Relocation is one of life's typical and severe sources of stress. Such stressful situations, according to Maas, "call for altered patterns of interaction between persons and their social contexts."[31] Such stressful events tax people's coping capacities.

Placement

Provision of new environments through placement of clients away from their own homes is a highly skilled service that usually involves the worker in making fateful decisions about the environment of a client and the welfare of all parties to the process.[32] It involves the physical and emotional separation of persons from one natural life situation, often a family, and their adjustment to a new environment. In a sense the client is moving out of one group and into another one. It is an anxiety-producing experience for all concerned.

The social worker may be a resource consultant, helping voluntary clients to find a suitable retirement community, temporary foster home, residential school, nursing home, or camp. In other instances, however, workers have considerable power to select the home or facility and to monitor the process. They often have the power to accept or reject adoptive applicants or foster parents and to select the person to be placed in a particular home or facility. The placement may be compulsory by court order. Working with the person being placed and both the old and new family, or institution, involves a direct counseling service, of which helping the person to use the resource and helping others to make it effective are integral parts.

In child welfare, too often placements are unsatisfactory for the child and/or the foster family.

Ed was a fourteen-year-old Mexican American Catholic boy who, since age nine, had been placed with his older brother in three foster homes and two residential homes for boys. The first three placements had been in predominantly Mexican American working-class neighborhoods with Mexican American families with parents old enough to have been the boy's grandparents. Although there were no serious problems, the foster parents all thought they were unable to continue to care for the boys. The first residential home was in a predominantly non-Hispanic neighborhood, under Protestant auspices, where the boys experienced considerable cultural conflict. The second residential home placement, a boys' lodge in an affluent community, provided a high standard of living for its residents, some of whom are Mexican American.

After placement, the older boy settled in and seemed to adjust well. The younger one, Ed, did not. In a short time he rejected the placement; he was especially upset at being identified as a "lodge boy." As the placement failed, his school adjustment and performance declined rapidly; behavior and affect disturbances soon indicated progressive emotional upset. Within a few weeks he ran away. When he was picked up by the police, he refused to return to the facility; therefore, he was taken to juvenile hall and transferred from the supervision of the child welfare agency to the probation department. At juvenile hall, where he was diagnosed as clinically depressed, the examining psychiatrist recommended in-patient care at a psychiatric unit for adolescents. While Ed was on the waiting list for hospitalization, he remained at juvenile hall where the staff reported that his condition was worsening. They said that he did not relate to much around him, and he wept a lot. The staff hoped for an early opening in a treatment facility, but after several weeks none had materialized.

Quite apart from the clinical plan, the child welfare agency, which had been apprised of Ed's condition by probation staff, acquired a newly licensed foster family. The family was Mexican American and Catholic, but unlike Ed's previous foster parents, the parents in this family were well within the age range to be the parents of a fifteen-year-old. A review of the licensing record and a subsequent home visit indicated that their potential parenting capabilities and interests appeared to correspond well with Ed's needs as these had been evaluated before his emotional decline.

After a weekend preplacement visit, Ed said he wanted to "take a chance" with this family, though he commented, "I wonder what will happen to take those people away from me?" Therefore, by his decision, he was placed with this newly licensed family in lieu of the planned, but indefinitely delayed, hospitalization, and the case was transferred from the probation department back to the child welfare agency. By now, he was fifteen and in the tenth grade. Recognizing that there were many factors that would pose obstacles to the success of this placement (the many foster family placement failures, his current emotional state, his age, and the foster family's inexperience) Ed, the foster parents, and the child welfare worker were in frequent contact and consultation. After an uncertain beginning, Ed was rather quickly incorporated into the family, which included two young sons, ages three and five, and an active, involved, very accepting extended family. His school performance quickly improved and he began to make friends. By the time he graduated from high school, he often referred to "me and my family"; his school achievement was satisfactory, and he had developed good peer ties. This placement went well from the beginning.

At the family's invitation, the social worker attended Ed's graduation. Immediately after graduation, which was about four months following Ed's eighteenth birthday, the agency terminated board and care payments, all contacts and services. With the agency's blessings, but with no help, the foster family and Ed acted on their own assumption that he would remain with them. The foster parents gave him a car for graduation; he already had a part-time job; and in the fall he enrolled in the nearby community college. During his first year in college, he not only did well academically but also became a campus leader[33]

This case clearly demonstrates the importance of selecting placements that are a good fit between the child's needs and the new environment and the need for frequent contacts between the practitioner, child, and foster family.

In child welfare, out-of-home placement of children is usually a last resort when children have been neglected or physically or sexually abused and efforts at rehabilitation of the family have failed. Other children need long-term hospitalization or residential treatment. Rejection or abuse of elderly relatives, inability to care for seriously ill family members, or loss of housing are other reasons for needing alternative living arrangements.

The goals of placement and also of discharge planning are stated in similar ways. Predominant is the concept of providing a good fit between the person and environment. According to Coulton, "person-environment fit refers to the degree of congruence or correspondence between the individual's needs, capacities, and aspirations and the resources, demands, and opportunities characteristic of the environment."[34] What Hartmann calls an "average predictable environment" is essential to growth.[35] Assessment of adaptiveness can be determined only in relation to the environment.

The removal of children from their families has been preceded by unsettling and often pathological experiences that made placement necessary. The continuity and security essential for psychological growth and mastery have been threatened. The selection of a new residence that meets a particular child's needs is a crucial, but often neglected, responsibility of the practitioner.

The process of placement involves the clinical social worker in numerous activities.

1. Meeting with the child's family to provide information about the decision and the reasons for making it; accepting and responding to their feelings about removal of the child; clarifying their questions; and offering a package of services to enable the family to become able to have the child returned; and, if accepted, developing a plan and contract for each service.
2. Meeting with the child to inform and clarify the decision for removal; dealing with the feelings and questions about separation from the family; and preparing the child for entry into the foster home or other form of residence.

3. Selecting the placement facility that best fills the child's age, gender, race, ethnicity, religion, intelligence, physical and mental health, and special needs. The match between the child's and family's characteristics partially determine the child's potential adaptation to the new environment. The caretakers' demographic characteristics, attitudes, interests, and capacities as they interact with those of the child are important factors in successful placement. The conditions and location of the new neighborhood may or may not provide for suitable peer affiliations, activities, and resources to meet the child's needs.

4. Preparing the caretakers for the entry of the child into the new living situation and working out a plan of services for the child within the home and through the use of community resources.

5. Planning for consultation to caregivers to help them meet the child's needs and assure that the child is safe, well cared for, making progress, and maintaining appropriate ties with family members.

Planning for Discharge or Transferal

Planning for transferring a person, such as a patient or resident in an institution, from the hospital or other setting, requires a high degree of professional competence. Most publications on discharge planning are limited to patients in hospitals, where it is clear that effective discharge planning is critical to the patient's health and the family's welfare. It is also important to the hospital from a fiscal point of view: practitioners face pressures of time limits in expediting the earliest possible discharge.[36] If the planning process is not adequate, the length of stay may increase when that is not desirable. The patient may be released to an inappropriate level of care, require readmission to the hospital, or suffer the loss of gains made during the period of hospitalization. In addition, the hospital may increase its risk of liability if discharge planning is inappropriate to the needs of the patient.

Alternatives to home care are numerous and may be more appropriate for the patient than efforts to maintain the patient in a home setting. Depending upon the goals and the medical-social situation, the decision may be placement in some type of residential facility. In addition to assessment of the patient-family-community interaction, careful attention needs to be given to the proposed residence itself in order to assure a good fit of the patient with the new environment. Foster homes, retirement communities with assisted living arrangements, or board and care homes may meet the needs of some clients.

The discharge planning function is described by the Committee on Discharge Planning of the Society for Hospital Social Work Administrators of the American Hospital Association as follows:

> Successful discharge planning is a centralized, coordinated, interdisciplinary process that ensures a plan for continuing care for each patient. It reflects both the patient's and family's internal and external social, emotional, medical and psychological needs and assets. It recognizes that the transition from the hospital is often more threatening than the actual hospitalization and a plan must be developed to both provide for a continuum of care and address the patient's immediate needs following discharge. It is the clinical process by which health care professionals, patients, and families collaborate to ensure that patients have access to services that enable them to regain, maintain, and even improve the level of functioning achieved in the hospital.[37]

A report by a social work intern provides an example of an inappropriate discharge concerning an eighty-four-year-old patient with terminal cancer.

She had lived alone since the death of her husband two years prior. She was too ill to return home and refused to move to a nursing home; she felt she still needed hospital care. When the case was presented at a team meeting, the social worker recommended that the patient be allowed to remain in the hospital, at least until a conference could be held with the daughter and son who, along with the patient, could be involved in planning for the patient's discharge from the hospital. The physician, supported by the nurse, insisted that a nursing home placement be found immediately because the patient could not go home and could not remain in the hospital.

The worker tried to help the patient choose between two nursing homes, but the patient did not want to go to either of them. In desperation, the worker selected what she considered to be the best of the two placements and told the patient there was simply no alternative. Under protest, the patient was transferred to the nursing home. The next day, the social worker at the nursing home called to say the patient was too ill for the level of care provided in the nursing home. Then the patient was sent back to the hospital and died a few days later. The daughter and son expressed much anger that they had not been involved in the shift from the hospital. Because of her relative lack of experience and pressure from the physician and nurse, the social worker had compromised her own professional values and judgment.

How different the foregoing situation was from another one, reported by Simmons:

> Following hospitalization, a sixty-eight-year-old woman was discharged on a routine basis, without adequate assessment of the suitability of her return home to live with her son. After a period of time, the son called the hospital's case management program requesting the names of convalescent hospitals in order to place his mother. Her need for care was so great that it required the son to come home from work to care for her four times daily, threatening his employment and disrupting his personal life, which was hard on both of them. The social worker suggested a home visit to identify the problems and help mother and son consider the best solution to the problem.
>
> Assessment identified an extremely low income, lack of knowledge of eligibility for in-home health care, hazards to good nutrition, an untreated gout condition, and a lack of transportation to the physician's office. But there was also a good relationship between mother and son and a desire to find out what was best for both of them. A planning session resulted in a decision, supported by the physician, to attempt in-home care. A variety of services were mobilized including personal care, Meals on Wheels, a lifeline emergency response system, physical therapy, and transportation to the physician's office. Along with stabilization of medications and treatment of gout, the enrichment of social support also proved stimulating. As a result, what seemed like a hopeless case transformed itself into a predictably safe in-home care arrangement with which both mother and son were extremely satisfied.[38]

Return home is often the choice that is made by families, particularly with the increased emphasis in health care on preventing institutionalization and the increased availability of home health care. Basic to the success of this plan is a thorough assessment of the family unit in its broader physical and social environment and changes in family functioning that are bound to occur with the return of the patient. When a patient returns home and still needs some assistance with the tasks of daily living, the burden of care and concern for the patient falls largely on the family. Before making the decision final, the family needs to acquire understanding of the impact of the illness or disability and any long-term consequences on family life.

When home care is the preferred choice of the patient and family, the social worker's task is not completed. There is need to monitor the plan to assure its continued suitability. As situations change, the original decision needs to be renegotiated.

Nursing homes are suitable and necessary in many instances. When it is necessary to move to a nursing home, stress tends to increase for both the patient and the family. A considerable amount of stigma is attached to placement in nursing homes, and families often feel guilty and frustrated in not being able to take adequate care of a family member. The high cost also creates serious problems for families. Nursing home care is improving; it is possible to select one suitable to the client's needs. Patients and families need considerable help in making such a decision.

Intervention.   Social workers' interventions consist of all of the sets of skills used in clinical social work, with a focus on relocation of patients from the medical facility to their own home or to an alternative residence, or from their own home to another setting.[39] The major tasks for the social worker are both socioemotional and instrumental in nature. Based on the assessment of the client-family-environment interaction, the tasks are to:

1. Analyze the implications of the assessment for making and implementing a plan and explore for additional information when indicated.
2. Involve appropriate personnel in providing adequate, appropriate information about the medical situation and the purpose and rationale for discharge at a given time.
3. Facilitate the participation of the family, including the patient, to the fullest extent possible in deciding upon and implementing a post-discharge plan.
4. Use a family problem-solving process to make decisions about the patient's relocation.
5. Provide counseling services to the patient and family members who have problems in psychosocial functioning so that the discharge plan will likely be effective.
6. Assist the family to implement the plan, making use of specialized knowledge, instruction in caretaking skills, and use of community resources.
7. Assure the patient and family that there will be adequate follow-up in monitoring, evaluating and, when indicated, changing the plan.

Collaboration

Collaboration is defined by Carlton as "interdisciplinary practice by two or more practitioners from two or more fields of learning and activity, who fill distinct roles, perform specialized tasks, and work in an interdependent relationship toward the achievement of a common purpose."[40]

Social workers enhance the psychosocial functioning of clients by conferring with significant others—those persons in the ecosystem who have or can have special meaning for the client's well-being. Such people have a part in creating or exacerbating the problem or they have some means to assist the client's coping efforts. The purpose of the conference may be to influence the other persons to change their attitudes and behavior toward the client so as to secure change in the client's situation, to enhance the worker's own effectiveness, or to find a better solution to a problem than the social worker alone is able to find.

Social workers may meet with representatives of other organizations which serve the same client to plan for dividing responsibilities among them and finding ways to coordinate their services for the client's benefit. They may meet with teachers, principals, parents or foster parents, judges, or industrial personnel. They may provide them with pertinent information about the client and make suggestions that can bring about a positive change in the relationship between the client and other person. They may successfully suggest a change in environment for the client, such as reassignment to a less pressured job or special class, or a new cottage in a residential center. They may report on the client's improved motivation or progress, thereby setting in motion a chain reaction in the client's favor. Professional ethics requires that these activities take place with the informed consent of the client. If workers engage in such efforts in a spirit of mutual benefit, they will discover that the significant others make valuable contributions to their own knowledge and skills.

Teamwork is a primary means of collaboration which involves the working together of two or more persons to make decisions about services to a client.[41] Its basic purpose is to organize and integrate the work of practitioners from more than one discipline or with different roles and responsibilities in social work. For example, physicians, social workers, nurses and other health personnel meet regularly to contribute to assessment, coordination of medical and psychosocial treatment, and discharge planning. In other settings, the team members may be educators, lawyers, or personnel managers. Successful collaboration requires, according to Falck, a commitment to the values, ethics, and usefulness of one's own profession;[42] a positive attitude toward a holistic approach to practice; a recognition that all components of practice are interdependent; and appreciation of the expertness of the other participants.

An example of the social worker's role in collaboration with a physician is presented by Conway:

At one of these conferences (the) physician asked me rather definitely to order a wheelchair for a patient whom I felt could not use it. In my most frank, honest, and straightforward manner I said I could not do that. Dead silence covered the room and it was obvious that I needed to respond. I could not tell him, a physician, what to do and neither could I say whether or not the patient needed the wheelchair medically. I could say, however, from my standpoint as a social worker, that she could not use it from a social standpoint. She was severely disabled with arthritis and needed help in all that she did including getting to and from the bed or chair or toilet to the wheelchair, and there was no one to help her do this. Her husband was past seventy-five, a severe cardiac himself, and somewhat senile. She had no other human supports. She also had little if any financial supports available. I told him again that I could not tell him what to do as a physician but that I could not use the patient's or the community's money for an item (that) in my best judgment . . . I knew would not be useful. . . . He agreed with me and we began to consider alternative plans for the patient.[43]

That example illustrates the practitioner's strong identity with social work, confidence in her knowledge, ability to relate to the physician with acceptance and respect, and knowledge of the rights and competence of members of other professions. That example also illustrates in a small way the generic principles of collaboration proposed by Dana:

1. Acceptance of the need to begin where one's colleagues are.
2. Respect for differences in values, knowledge, and problem-solving styles and capacities.
3. Willingness to share one's own knowledge, values, and skills even when they may conflict with the knowledge,   values,   and   skills that others hold to.
4. Willingness to work through, rather than avoid, conflicts.
5. Willingness to change or modify the definition of the problem to be addressed, or the means of addressing it, on the basis of new insights derived from the perceptions and interpretations that other practitioners hold of both the problem and ways of dealing with it.
6. Ability to use group process as a means for meeting the salient demands of collaborative practice, for distinguishing between the performance of the collaborative role by social workers and the performance by collaborators from other professions and disciplines, and for transmitting social work knowledge.[44]

It is imperative that social workers understand the goals, functions, and structure of each discipline and the problems with which it deals. They need to be clear about their own contribution to the team's efforts and be able to explain it to the other members. They need to be able to recognize their own and others' feelings of differential status, competitiveness, and turf; and be able to participate effectively in the resolution of interdisciplinary conflicts. There is a considerable amount of overlapping among the helping professions, but more than enough work for all. Acceptance, empathy and genuineness are as important in work with significant others as in work with clients. The quality of relationships among personnel have a great influence on the satisfaction and progress of clients.

Case Management

Although case management is an unfortunate term because clinical social workers do not manage their clients or providers of resources, it is an important component of practice.[45] There is general agreement that case management includes at least these five functions: assessment, planning, linkage, monitoring, and advocacy. Clinical social work, as indicated in this book, includes these functions as an integral part of practice, rather than as a separate role. Research by Florentine and Grusky indicated by case managers perform a variety of therapeutic functions along with the organizational linchpin function. The functions performed, in order of frequency, were supportive therapy, crisis intervention, client advocacy, individual therapy, referral or linking, and group therapy.[46] The biopsychosocial systems orientation encourages the provision of multiple, accessible, and integrated services to meet the needs of particular individuals, families, and groups. The final section of this chapter will demonstrate how these functions are carried out by a creative social worker for a therapeutic purpose.

Corrective Emotional Experiences

Many clients have had devastating experiences in their families, social networks, and neighborhoods which are sources of problems in psychosocial functioning. In addition to treatment by the social worker, they require additional supportive and corrective experiences in relationships with other people. Levy presents a community-based approach to clinical services for children of parents who abuse drugs. The approach, however, is applicable to work with children with many different types of needs and problems.

Based on his review of research on children of substance abusers, Levy concluded that "it is apparent that the needs of children of substance abusing parents are complex and multifaceted. It is apparent that these children are at-risk for developing a range of deleterious biopsychosocial conditions with differing severities of dysfunction. The developmental pathways that produce such dysfunctions are as yet unexplored, but they are most likely multiple and interacting."[47]

A central issue in working with these children is that parental functioning has been inadequate, owing to their substance abuse and perhaps other problems as well. Levy suggests, therefore, that a primary therapeutic task is to provide corrective emotional experiences for the children. This concept, first developed by Alexander and French, has generally been limited to the clinician's relationship with clients characterized by positive regard, empathy, and genuineness.[48] Levy proposed that the concept be expanded to encompass "all relationships that may directly help to overcome emotional difficulties."[49]

Levy's review of research indicates that in cases where parental functioning is compromised, alternative caretakers can make the difference between successful and pathological functioning" (pp. 2–4).

Alternative caretakers should be sensitive to the meaning that deleterious experiences hold for these children, and learn to respond in ways that therapeutically counter existing maladaptive patterns. They should be knowledgeable about the nature of substance abuse, be able to be consistent, and to communicate directly and clearly, and be genuinely invested in the child. They should be able to be noncompetitive with parents in order to prevent loyalty conflicts for the child. It is preferable to develop supports that most approximate children's natural environments as they are often less disruptive to the milieu and are inherently less stigmatizing. For example:

Pedro was a fourteen-year-old Puerto Rican boy who was referred to a child guidance clinic by a school counselor because "he was missing school, his grades were very low, and he seemed to have a lot on his mind." As he did not know how to take public transportation to the clinic, and no one was available to accompany him, it was arranged that the social worker initially see Pedro at a local community center.

At the first interview, Pedro complained of stomach aches (no organic basis was subsequently found), stated that he had few friends, and reported that he was teased by peers. A community worker reported that Pedro lived with his maternal grandfather and older brother. She reported that his mother died five years ago from a drug overdose. He never met his biological father. She stated that his primary caretaker had been his maternal grandmother, who died, one year prior to referral, from cancer. His older brother was an intravenous drug user who, though working as a truck driver, may have started stealing from the family to support his habit. His grandfather, the current head of household, was reported to be an alcoholic and in poor health.

During the next several sessions, Pedro confirmed all of this information, and said that he had to miss school because his grandfather needed to go to numerous medical appointments. He needed Pedro to accompany him because Pedro's grandfather spoke little English. Pedro also said that he wanted to make sure that his grandfather kept his appointments. His grandfather consented to Pedro's treatment.

It was clear from this data and Pedro's further statements that he was clinically depressed. In addition, he was overburdened by the demands of caring for his ailing grandfather, coping with an older brother whose behavior was growing increasingly out of control, and by the more commonplace demands of school and peers. He was also coping with the losses of his mother and maternal grandmother. He desperately craved nurturance, and believed that those who cared for him would not prove to be trustworthy. He said he expected that things would go from bad to worse, though he had difficulty articulating what this meant to him. He had few sources of support, and those that were available were not currently in a position to provide him with what he needed.

As treatment progressed, the social worker learned how deeply rooted Pedro was in his neighborhood. While he had no close friends or other contacts, he clearly felt secure because people knew who he was and he was familiar with the various shopkeepers and neighborhood personalities there. The social worker began to realize that the community worker who had provided family history might function as an alternative caretaker. She knew the family because she lived in the neighborhood, and was genuinely concerned about Pedro. She also was quite aware of substance abuse, as she has been in recovery for nine years. The worker discussed the possibility that she help Pedro by becoming an informal "big sister/aunt," that she talk weekly with the social worker about her work with Pedro and any other problems that may arise. The community worker became more and more involved with Pedro, nurturing him and monitoring his well being.

The counselor at Pedro's school agreed to monitor Pedro's progress at school and look for additional sources of support. Upon consultation with the social worker, the counselor met with Pedro's teachers to help them to become more invested in Pedro and to respond in a more empathic manner toward him.

Pedro and the worker identified another older brother who lives across town. He did not use drugs, was employed in a stable job, and had a wife and two young daughters. With permission, the social worker contacted this brother. He stated that he had broken off contact with his family of origin because he was disgusted with all the drug use. He was concerned about Pedro's well-being and, after several contacts, agreed to invite Pedro regularly to dinners and family outings.

These new sources of support were helpful in several ways. First, they provided Pedro with new, direct sources of nurturance and instrumental support. They also evoked deep emotional responses in Pedro, which became the focus of therapeutic work with the social worker. Finally, they helped monitor Pedro's precarious status and helped ensure his well-being.

When Pedro's grandfather died (of alcoholic liver disease) and his brother left the family home, these caretakers took care of Pedro until a more long-term placement was arranged. The social worker engaged the child welfare worker and consulted with her so that she could find an appropriate foster home. The foster home was in Pedro's neighborhood, so that he had access to the community worker, his teacher, and the social worker. The social worker consulted with Pedro's new foster parents to help them to provide corrective emotional experiences for Pedro. While his brother was unable to have Pedro live with him, he increased the number of days per week that he saw Pedro.

It should be noted that the social worker regularly consulted with all of these caretakers and helped them to understand Pedro's behavior and to respond therapeutically. It should be clear that much therapeutic benefit can be derived by integrating community-based resources into clinical treatment. Clinical social work, with its person-in-environment perspective, can work to foster corrective emotional experiences with significant others as an important treatment component for clients of all ages, not just children. As Levy said, "Such an approach is at the heart of clinical social work."[50]

Thirteen | Termination and Transition

Termination is a dynamic and vital process in social work.[1] It is more than a symbol of the end of treatment: it is an integral part of the process. If properly understood and managed, it becomes an important force in integrating changes in feeling, thinking, and doing. These changes, though, are of little value to the clients until they can apply the benefits gained in everyday relationships and achievements. Social work treatment is always time limited. Treatment beyond the point that the person's natural growth can be resumed may interfere with the natural potential for growth and lead to continuing dependency.[2] What happens when it comes time to terminate may make a critical difference as to the nature and extent of gains that will endure. If clients are helped to face the meaning of the social work experience and to leave it with a sense of achievement, they may well be prepared to use what they have learned in their roles and relationships in the community. They may be more able to cope with the other separations that will confront them through life.[3]

Ending an experience needs to be done in such a way that professional values are implemented. Ideally, individuals have entered into a relationship in which they have been helped to achieve their goals, felt that they have been treated with acceptance and respect, and encouraged to participate actively in the process and make their own decisions, with due regard for the welfare of self and others. A somewhat intimate and interdependent relationship has been achieved with the practitioner. In families and groups, in addition to each individual's relationship with the worker, the members have found mutual acceptance and respect and have participated actively in a process of mutual aid and interdependency. As

Yalom said in reference to groups, "termination is thus more than an extraneous event in the group; it is the microcosmic representation of some of the most crucial and painful issues of all."[4] And Balgopal and Vassil point out that the termination stage is marked by a "transition from the rhythm of work to disengagement and preparation for the future. Earlier themes of loss, dependency, and ambivalence are revisited and co-exist with feelings of satisfaction and recognition of limited but worthy accomplishments."[5]

The decision to terminate and the process of ending make use of the knowledge essential to the biopsychosocial system approach to practice. A worker-client system has been formed and sustained for the purpose of achieving particular goals. Now, the knowledge about biopsychosocial functioning in environments is used to help the worker-client system to break up in a way that benefits the clients. Particularly useful are perspectives on the life cycle that incorporate the concepts of loss and separation related to the significance of social relationships to people in each phase of development, and that explain the ways that the ego defends itself against, copes with, and masters the experience.[6] When faced with loss or separation, the steady state is upset. There are certain expectable emotional and behavioral reactions to the threat of loss. The feelings of loss are also accompanied by satisfactions with the social work experience and a resulting sense of positive achievement and competence to face the challenges of social living without the assistance of a social worker. The nature and intensity of the reactions to termination depend upon many circumstances, such as length of service, reasons for termination, past experiences of clients with loss and separation, and the extent of meaningful relationships and supports in the environment.

If termination is to be a meaningful and growth-producing experience, the social worker has a number of important instrumental goals to achieve during the final phase of service. These are to help the clients to:

1. Evaluate the progress they have made, acknowledge the realistic gains, and accept the fact that the experience is ending.
2. Resolve the ambivalence about leaving the relationship with the worker and, in the case of formed groups, with the other members, resolving the conflict between acknowledgment of progress and giving up a meaningful relationship and experience.
3. Work toward stabilizing and strengthening the gains that have been made.
4. Set priorities for work on pressing problems or tasks that are still unfinished and that seem crucial to the clients' progress.

5. Use the social work experience as a frame of reference for continued efforts toward achievement, through tying this experience more directly to their subsequent life tasks and relationships.
6. Make transitions toward new experiences, such as follow-up sessions or referrals, as indicated.

Reasons for Termination

Planned Termination

Termination occurs for a number of reasons, some of them planned as an integral part of treatment, and some of them unplanned or unanticipated. Ideally, termination occurs when a person, family, or group no longer needs the professional service. Clients are terminated when a defined purpose has been achieved. When planned termination occurs, a social worker and client have made a judgment that sufficient progress has been made to enable the person or family to continue to consolidate the gains without the help of the worker and sometimes also without the help of a group. All people have problems in social living, but usually they can cope with the problems with the support and help of families, friends, and other significant people in the community. It is unrealistic and generally unhelpful to continue service until a total "cure" has occurred or until clients have achieved an ideal state. The challenge is to predict that sufficient progress has been made so that the client or family can maintain the gains and possibly also continue to progress without social work help. The process of termination itself is an important part of treatment.

During the planning process, the worker and individual, family, or group had agreed upon an anticipated length of service, usually with flexibility to shorten or extend the time as needed. Sometimes the nature of the service determines the approximate number of sessions, planned and understood from the beginning. This is typical of crisis intervention, parent or family life education programs, task-centered practice, and services to patients who are to be hospitalized for a fairly predictable length of time.

In a study that Fox, Nelson, and Bolman made of thirty- three clients and their eleven social workers in family service agencies,[7] it was observed that termination was planned in approximately two-thirds of the cases. In the majority of these cases, the social worker and client concurred in the decision to terminate; clients were actively involved in discussing the ending; and plans were made to end gradually. The workers purposefully tried to use the termination phase for therapeutic purposes. The main reasons given for ending were that the goals had been achieved, clients were ready to function independently, or additional sessions would result in limited productivity. These were middle-class clients who were generally satisfied with the social worker and the outcome of service.

Unplanned Termination

In one-third of the cases in the study, termination was not planned. In these cases, the situation and outcome were quite different. These clients who withdrew tended to be of lower socioeconomic status whose decision to use the service had not been fully voluntary. They either felt they had achieved what they wanted or, more often, were dissatisfied with the service: there were problems in worker-client interaction; lack of agreement concerning goals and expectations; or lack of open communication between worker and client. Thus, there were earlier cues that should have alerted the worker to problems of motivation and communication.

Termination may occur due to certain factors in the clients and their use of service. There are times when little progress has been made. Recognition of this state should result in reevaluation of the plan for service and the development of one more suitable to the clients' goals, needs, and capacities. If neither worker nor client can work out a shift in focus that is acceptable to both of them as a basis for further work together, termination occurs. There are times when entropy takes over: a group disintegrates before the goals have been achieved, due to loss of members or unresolvable problems in the group's structure or process. There are times when clients need to withdraw from treatment because they are unable to meet the minimum expectations for behavior.

Bolen, writing about termination in a residential treatment center, has indicated that early termination of an individual is sometimes necessary.[8] Even though institutions are geared to allow for a wide range of problematic behavior during the course of treatment, there are limits to what behavior can be tolerated. Extremely aggressive or assaultive behavior, for example, usually falls outside the acceptable boundaries. The possibility of danger to self or other clients may require the transfer of such a person to another setting which is considered to be better equipped to handle the behavior.

Other factors often contribute to unplanned termination. Changes in individual or family situations often result in premature termination: for example, a move to a new community, a change in work or school schedules, a long illness, the removal of a child from treatment by the parent, lack of continued eligibility for service, or other situations over which the worker and the agency have no control.

Another set of reasons includes those over which the client system has no control, occasioned by changes initiated by the worker or other person in the agency. The worker may leave the agency for a variety of reasons. Occasionally the worker's own needs may motivate terminating a case when the client is not ready. Fox and associates note that workers may precipitate termination: "When the child does not get well fast enough, when the transference becomes negativistic, or when a family's goals differ from the worker's goals, the result may be felt as a narcissistic wound and lead to discontinuance of treatment."[9] The solution to such problems lies in enhancing the worker's self-awareness and abilities in assessment and evaluation. These situations are, in a sense, failures of workers—not clients.

Follow-up of absences is essential in order to understand the reason for dropping out of treatment, to assess the clients' needs and situations and, when indicated, to help them to return. After all, people cannot be helped if they do not come. Some highly competent practitioners almost never have drop-outs, because they have skill in planning, assessing, and preparing prospective clients for the experience. They also have confidence in the value of social work help, which gets transmitted to the clients. They have skill in selecting and using the appropriate supportive or challenging skills at a given time.

Terminations occur at times in situations over which neither the client nor the worker have any control. Termination is forced. Practitioners may, for example, be transferred from one assignment to another, or financial exigencies may force the ending of services before the clients are ready to terminate. According to Schaffer and Pollak, in such situations, more intense emotions are stimulated in both the worker and client; each one's disappointment, anger, or other feeling influences the other.[10] Their behavior may follow parallel lines.

Reactions to Termination: The Clients

The ending of a meaningful experience stirs up a variety of feelings and reactions. Just as clients had feelings of anticipation and dread at intake, so do they have strong feelings about ending. Schiff says:

> Of all the phases of the psycho-therapeutic process, the one which can produce the greatest amount of difficulty and create substantial problems for patient and therapist alike is the phase of termination. It is at this time when

the impact of the meaning in affective terms of the course of therapy and the nature of the therapist-patient relationship is experienced most keenly, not only by the patient but also by the therapist.[11]

The major theme is separation and loss. It is the reawakening of old losses in the present that makes this phase useful for modifying conflicted emotions, stabilizing gains, and motivating further progress in whatever time remains.

Ambivalence

Doubt, hesitation, and unresolved tugs between positive and negative feelings are characteristic of the termination phase. Most terminations contain elements of both happiness and sadness. Clients may recognize the progress they have made or feel badly because they have not achieved their vision of the ideal outcome. They may want to move on to other relationships and experiences without being dependent upon the worker or a group; yet they may also want to continue the gratifications received through the relationship with the worker. In groups, gratification also comes from a sense of belonging to a system that has provided mutual support and stimulation for positive changes in self and situation. Clients may feel good about the prospects of termination one day and then feel despair another day.

The mixture of positive and negative feelings is described by Blanchard in work with young children:

> If the therapeutic relationship has had any real meaning the child will naturally have ambivalent feelings in ending it. It is sad to say goodbye to someone who has been loved for a while and to whom one feels grateful, but it is a satisfaction to become independent of help and to be freed from the obligation to keep appointments that sometimes interfere with other interests and activities. Moreover, the child has been brought to the clinic because the parent was dissatisfied with him. If, at the ending, the parent is better satisfied, this adds to the child's happiness in the termination of treatment, which becomes proof that the parent is no longer dissatisfied with him. So, the desirable aspects of ending may well outweigh the regrets.[12]

Although all persons will have their own particular feelings and reactions concerning termination, certain themes have been identified which give clues for understanding what is happening and what to do about it. Writers on both work with individuals and work with groups liken the termination process to the initial phase in terms of the number of diversity of reactions by clients. A typical statement is that of Garland, Jones, and Kolodny. "Anxiety over coming together that was experienced in earlier stages, now is felt in relation to moving apart and breaking the bonds that have been formed."[13] Considerable agreement is found among the writers that the termination stage has several sub-phases of emotional reactions to the final event. Whether in individual or group services, the most common reactions seem to be denial, anger, grief over loss or separation, flight or early detachment, regression, and fears for the future.

Denial

When confronted with the reality of termination, clients frequently deny that termination is imminent or that the experience has been of value to them. Denial serves as a defense against facing the impending separation and the feelings of loss and anxiety associated with it. Clients may deny that they were told that the relationship would not last indefinitely. They may protest that they are not ready to leave or even that problems are worse than ever. Sometimes denial is more subtle. Some evidences of denial may be long atypical silences when termination is mentioned; numerous references to loss scattered throughout the interview or group discussion; or changing the subject when the worker tries to explore the meaning of separation to the individual or members of a group. A variation of the usual denial maneuvers may be exaggerated independence, which is not an accurate reflection of the person's level of functioning. A person may act stoical and need to appear strong when confronted with the loss. These reactions, too, are defenses against acceptance of the anticipated loss. In groups, the denial may be expressed through superficially greater cohesiveness than before: the group strengthens its bonds against the threat of the worker or agency.

Anger

Angry reactions often overlap with denial. Clients may react with anger to what they perceive as abandonment, rejection, or punishment. There may be what Schiff calls the "unspoken rebuke": aimed at the worker for leaving the client.[14] Anger may be expressed in such phrases as: "So, you're kicking me out"; "I guess you never did care"; "It doesn't matter—I never did get help here anyhow"; or a simple, "So what?"

For example, here is a worker's interview with a fifteen-year-old girl Susie, who had been talking about how much better things were going for her in school now. There was much recognition by both Susie and her worker that her behavior at school had improved and that her relationships at home seemed better also.

> Toward the end of the interview, the worker said she wanted to bring up something with Susie for her to think about so they can discuss it more fully next week. Susie asked, "What is it?" The worker said,"I think we should talk about your not coming here any more after summer vacation begins." In a startled voice, Susie asked, "B-b-but why?" The worker said that they had talked about how much better things were for her now. She thought Susie was almost ready to get along without social work help now. Susie said, "Ohh— I still need you—things really aren't good at all." Then, and after a long silence, "So—you're just like everyone else after all." To the worker's query about in what ways, the response was, "Letting me think you really care about me when you really don't." Then she cried.

This incident illustrates the sudden disruption of a trusting relationship with a client who had previously been deprived of positive relationships with her parents and other adults.

Loss and Separation

A major theme in the termination phase is that of loss and separation, both in terms of feelings among the participants in the social work service and also in terms of opportunities to work on old conflicts about loss and separation. As Bywaters says, "closure is an opportunity to choose, face, and accept separation and to experience the survival of loss and evidence of new strength and mastery."[15] The desire for dependency is reactivated and there is a need to retest relationships, as was done in earlier phases. To the extent that a worker or members of a group become loved and valued by a client, the client will feel a deep sense of loss and will need to mourn the loss. Thus, as Bowlby indicates, "separation anxiety is the inescapable corollary of attachment behavior."[16] When clients face the reality of their feelings about the loss that is inherent in termination, they react with expressions of sadness and engage in reflective thinking about the situation.

Regression

Regression to earlier patterns of behavior is one frequent reaction to the reality of separation; negative symptoms that had been alleviated may reoccur. Through the reemergence of symptoms, clients attempt to prove that they still need the service as much as ever. Dependency on the worker may increase. In groups, eruption of previously settled conflicts may occur. The conflict between the acknowledgment of improvement and the fear of the loss of the worker's love and attention can end in an explosion of problematic behavior. A child who has stayed in school and improved in his relationships with teachers and peers may suddenly become a truant or get into a serious fight with another pupil. A father who had long since given up abusive behavior toward his wife may strike out at her again in a fit of anger. A young adult may sass his employer and endanger his job. Green reports that:

> I have known children with a six- and seven-year history of enuresis who dried up during several months of treatment, but who often had bad lapses during the ending phase. When assured that no one was trying to get rid of them, many of these youngsters could talk about how many more visits they would like to have. Some would say impulsively that they would come forever, or a thousand times. Yet, in a surprisingly short time, they could whittle that down to two or three visits and be free of neurosis in the same short time.[17]

Another example is of an inexperienced worker and a nine-year-old boy who had been brought to a child guidance clinic because he was stealing frequently.

> His symptoms had been gone for several months, and he was ready to terminate. On their last day together, the worker took him to his favorite place for ice cream. There, for the first time in the worker's presence, he stole something. The worker was unprepared for this behavior and had no understanding of it. She felt upset, angry, and helpless. The little boy knew it, but neither one of them knew what was going on.[18]

In such instances, the flare-up is an indication of trouble over terminating a relationship that has been important to a client. It serves as a means whereby the client can test the worker again, as was done in the initial phase. It is a need to ascertain whether the worker really does care about clients and what happens to them.

Flight

Early detachment from the experience is another pattern of behavior that occurs when clients are anxious about the termination. Clients often respond to the fact of termination through flight—coming late or missing sessions. Such clients seem impelled to break off the relationship themselves, as if to say, "I'll leave you before you leave me." When children in a residential treatment center or in foster care are ready to return to their families, which they have longed for, they may run away so as not to face separation from the social worker and the foster parents. They may do this to provoke people into rejecting them so that they can prove that they really did not care about them. Usually they return within a few days, but feel great anxiety about how they will be received. If they are received back with understanding and empathy, they are able to move on to effective coping with terminations. People who have been hurt badly through earlier relationships are particularly sensitive to evidences of being rejected. They are easily triggered into withdrawal if they have a glimmer that they might be hurt again.

Frequency of Reactions

These feelings and reactions are not typical of all clients, but they have been observed frequently. The nature and intensity of the feelings will vary with the personal characteristics and experiences of the clients. Usually the greater the difficulties that clients have had in prior experiences with separation and relationships, the stronger will be their feelings about ending, providing the social work experience has been a truly meaningful one for them. Since social workers serve many people with disturbed human relationships, there is likely to be trouble during the termination phase.[19]

General agreement is found in the literature on both socialization and psychosocial treatment groups that emotional reactions to termination occur. The findings come from analysis of process records or tape recordings of practice. Research was conducted by Lewis, who studied fourteen treatment and ten socialization groups, predominantly of adolescents but also including a fewer number of groups for children and adults. The groups met weekly for an average of one year and were led by social workers with graduate degrees. The study confirmed the presence of the major categories of emotional reactions in the groups, although not all groups were characterized by all reactions.[20] In another research study, Lackey also confirmed the presence of multiple emotional reactions to termination.[21]

A study by Kramer found that 49 percent of the clients reported feelings of loss, while the other emotional reactions were much less frequent.[22] Fortune conducted research on termination, based on questionnaires with fifty-nine social workers in Virginia. Almost all of the clients had some negative responses, but she concluded that the reactions during the termination stage are more positive than negative.[23] Clients often expressed a sense of maturity, relief, confidence, and a sense of achievement. There were fewer emotional reactions, as would be expected, from clients in short-term than those in longer term treatments.

The expression of such feelings as anger, sadness, abandonment, or denial are not to be regarded as negative. Having the opportunity to express them, have them accepted, and then working them through is a positive growth-promoting experience, tending to result in a realistic evaluation of the helping experience. The amount of pain experienced seems to be related to the intensity of the attachment between a practitioner and client and whether or not clients have developed other intimate relationships with family members or friends in the community. It would be expected, for example, that Pedro, whose case was presented in the last chapter, would have a deep sense of loss when his worker leaves, but that would be lessened by the other meaningful relationships that he now has.

Expressions of Positive Emotions

The literature places heavy emphasis on the painful feelings and problematic behavior that tend to accompany work toward termination. It is to be remembered that there is also the positive side of the ambivalence, and in many situations this side predominates, There is, perhaps, always some sense of loss in leaving an experience that has been helpful in important ways or to which clients have contributed much of themselves and their skills. It has been suggested by Schwartz that in groups, "the resistance to endings seems to be marked by a general reluctance to tear down a social structure built with such difficulties, and to give up intimacies so hard to achieve."[24] There is, also, however, anticipation of the ending, as is true of certain other experiences in life such as graduation or leaving the parental home. Some clients have highly positive reactions to termination, such as, "I really think I'm ready"; "You've been wonderful' " or "I never thought a group could be this great." Feeling competent to cope more effectively with life's challenges and having confidence in one's ability to do so are richly rewarding and are accompanied by feelings of satisfaction and hope. These feelings and reactions are often the outcome of working through the positive and negative feelings and making constructive moves toward new experiences and relationships.

For many clients the termination phase is characterized predominantly by positive feelings toward the relationship and a sense of goal achievement. They come to work on a problem which is brought to a satisfactory resolution. An example is a couple who wanted to work through a marital conflict and did so successfully. The couple felt great warmth toward the social worker and expressed appreciation for her services. Their own improved relationship with each other was a great gain for them, so that the loss of the worker was not perceived as a devastating one.

Another example is of work with a chronic elderly patient and his family to develop a discharge plan satisfactory to all concerned. There were serious conflicts among family members about the most desirable plan for there was a need for members to face changes in family roles and circumstances and to consider the effect of these changes on each member. A suitable plan was implemented which was satisfactory to all parties. Termination was a natural conclusion to the problem-solving process, but there was still a need to review the work together, acknowledge its completion, and say goodbye to the worker in appropriate ways.

Reactions to Termination: The Practitioner

The process of termination involves the feelings and reactions of the social worker as well as the client. Facing termination stirs up feelings about both the client's and the worker's role in the process. If an individual or group has made considerable progress, it is natural that workers will feel pleased about the gains and about their contributions to the progress. The workers may, however, be apprehensive as to whether the clients will be able to make it on their own. It is natural, too, that they will feel some sense of loss, for it is not easy to separate from persons whom one has helped within a meaningful relationship. Clients are apt to test the workers' confidence in their ability to stand alone, and thus workers must come to grips with learning that they are important to the clients and that they need to sanction and encourage the clients' independence. The extent to which the worker and client are able to cope with the separation process is a major determining factor in the client's ability to use ending an experience for further growth.[25]

Woods and Hollis have emphasized the importance of the practitioners' need to be alert to their own feelings about termination. As indicated earlier, the emotions expressed by clients can be used for positive growth.[26] Levinson said it this way:

If the therapists see separation and termination not as a matter of growth but as a traumatic event for the patients, then they will find themselves acting in a variety of ways to postpone the eventual day of termination. Subsequently, this delay will retard the patients' progress toward finding new solutions to old problems. . . . Simply put, patients cannot take steps away from a therapist holding back from moving on.[27]

In other cases, if practitioners have worked hard with clients and little progress has been made, their self-confidence may be threatened and they may become irritated with, and disappointed in, the clients. These feelings can lead to premature termination. Similar reactions can occur when clients, in myriad ways, stir up feelings of hostility, irritation, or anxiety in workers. Workers often defend themselves by labeling the clients as hopeless or lacking capacity for further gains. Working with such clients is difficult for both client and worker. If the workers' own feelings toward such a client cannot be modified, the client may need to be transferred to another resource.

Factors Influencing Termination

Duration of Service

It was noted earlier that feelings and reactions toward termination vary from person to person, depending upon the intensity of the worker-client relationship and the client's prior experience with separation and relationships. There are other factors as well that influence the termination process. One is the purpose of the service. Therapeutic services are apt to be more intense and more permeated with problems in relationships than are preventive services which aim to facilitate the positive psychosocial functioning of people who do not usually have serious problems; hence, they are more able to anticipate and work through termination without intense emotion or negative reactions. In task-oriented interviews or groups, the fact that the participants are there to work toward some defined tasks means that somewhat less emphasis is placed on the socioemotional dynamics of the experience. This does not mean that there is not a sense of loss of relationships at ending such an endeavor. It does not mean that feelings of satisfaction or dissatisfaction are not stirred up, including the possibility of anger at the worker or the group that more was not accomplished.

The duration of the service influences the content of the ending process to some extent. Generally, short-term services of up to four months are offered to clients where problems are less severe and less chronic than the problems of clients who are offered long-term treatment. This means that the impact of termination will usually be less upsetting to these clients than to those in longer term treatment. But short-term services are not less meaningful to the clients. Although there has not been time to develop and test the durability of relationships, the greater specificity of the goals and the problems may enhance the development of a strong bond between worker and client system. The limited duration may itself be a factor in motivating very intensive work on mutually understood problems which makes clients aware of the meaning of the service to them.

In crisis intervention, which is by definition a brief service, the resolution of the crisis or at least a return to a previous steady state provides a natural time for termination which has been built in from the beginning. Little attention has been given to the ending phase of crisis intervention. Rapoport, however, emphasizes that "in brief treatment, termination needs to be dealt with explicitly."[28] Since the length of treatment is discussed in the initial interview, the ending process is anticipated from the beginning. Because of the partialized and specifically defined goal and the assumption that the state of crisis is a time-limited phenomenon, the minimum goal is achieved within a period of several weeks. It must be remembered, however, that clients in an acute state of crisis do not always grasp the idea of brief service. A client is bound to have feelings toward a worker who has been helpful in restoring equilibrium, reducing unbearable anxiety, and enhancing understanding of the crisis situation and its meaning to those in the situation. One of the powerful dynamics in crisis intervention is the experience that there are people available—a worker or a group—who reach out to help at a time when one's own coping capacities are inadequate. Thus, the relationships between worker and client, or member and member, are very meaningful. Since many crises involve loss of some kind, it is essential that clients learn better ways to handle the loss of the worker or the group. Working through the termination phase can thus contribute to better facing and coping with future losses.

It has been suggested that in open-ended groups in which membership changes frequently, intensity of relationships and strong cohesion tend not to develop. If this be true, then it would be expected that termination would be less imbued with strong emotions than in other situations.[29] The important point is that social workers have the sensitivity and the knowledge to make an accurate judgment about the meaning of themselves and often also of other members to a client and that they use this understanding in the termination process, whether the service has been brief or long.

Modality of Practice

There are differences in termination, depending on whether the client is an individual, a family, or a group. In the dyadic relationship of worker to client, the primary emotions are related to separation from the worker and the particular service. In work with families, the family continues as a unit; it is the worker who terminates the relationship with the family. Each member of the family will have his or her own particular feelings and reactions to the termination, ranging from relief, to acceptance, to intense feelings of anxiety and loss. The worker has meant something different to each of them, but there is also a core family reaction to termination. In working with these reactions, the family's capacities for group problem-solving can be strengthened and their improved relations can be supported. In terminating with families, the primary issue seems to be the family's sense that it can now "make it on its own," and continue to use what was learned in treatment when it recognizes problems in the future.

In formed groups, members may terminate at different times. In open-ended groups there is a more or less regular entering and leaving of members. Even in closed groups, some members may be ready to leave before the others. In either instance, a member leaves a group that is going to continue. When this occurs the one leaving will have mixed feelings about it, but so too will the other members. The one who is leaving may display any of the feelings and reactions previously described. Those who remain may feel a deep sense of loss of a valued member; or they may feel guilty or angry because they are not yet ready to leave. The fact that one member is ready for termination may provide hope and enhanced motivation for the others. In other instances, it points up the slower progress of the others, who may react with a sense of discouragement or failure. Feelings of rivalry and competition may be aroused, supplanting the sense of cooperation and mutual aid that previously prevailed. Those who remain may feel apprehensive about new members who fill the vacancy left by the departing member. They also may react to the fact that, with the loss of a member, the system's steady state is disrupted. The remaining members have to readapt to a changed situation.

When a new person enters the group, both the group and the newcomer worry about whether they will be acceptable to each other. If the members are not helped to resolve the varied feelings, they tend to project onto the new arrival the anger which is left over from the experience of loss, taking out on the newcomer the feelings they had not worked through earlier. With skillful help from the worker, every new termination provides an opportunity for clients to prepare for the time of their own termination; thus, there are both hazards and opportunities as the remaining members face their feelings and come to understand their reactions to frequent terminations.

In closed groups, in addition to the separation of a client from a worker, there is the separation of the members from one another. There is also the dissolution of a social system that has meaning to the members. In some instances, the major anxiety is related to the threatened loss of the group, not just the worker. A study by Scheidlinger and Holden found that the major separation anxiety was expressed in regard to the threatened loss of the group as an entity, rather than to the loss of the worker.[30] More of the total personality is probably invested in counseling and therapeutic groups than in task-centered groups, but there is a sense of loss in ending the latter type of group if members have worked well together or an important goal has been achieved.[31] As one member of a prerelease group in a mental hospital expressed it to the worker, "I came to say good-by to you again. It's hard to do this and hard to leave after such a long time here." Then, following the worker's comments, "Yes, I know," the patient continued, "But leaving our group is hardest of all." After another supportive comment by the worker, "But it's easier knowing others are facing the same things, trying to make a go of life outside." In such instances, it would be important for the worker to help the client to say these things in the group, too. The group which is being dissolved is a meaningful reference group and a vehicle for social gratification for its members, which fact creates additional anxieties and resistances to termination, but the dissolution of a group is also an overt symbol that the progress that has been made is sufficient for the members to manage without the group. People internalize meaningful experiences, so, in this sense, the group becomes a part of them, influencing their values and norms of behavior in other situations.

The Role of the Social Worker

In the termination phase, social workers have many tasks to perform. With the client's participation, they evaluate the clients use of the service and assess their readiness to end. They inform the client system that termination should be discussed. They then help each person to resolve ambivalent feelings, set priorities for the use of the remaining time, deal with the application of learnings to social living, and plan for desirable follow-up services.

Termination, as a phase in the social work process, is related to the agreed-upon goals, the nature of the client's needs, what has gone before in the helping process, and the client's hopes and plans for the future. The complexity of the process is illustrated by the following example.

Mrs. Swift is a thirty-eight-year-old, well-educated, white professional woman, who was married to a man who is a multiple drug abuser and actively committed to a drug culture lifestyle. At time of intake, Mrs. Swift had a multitude of problems in psychosocial functioning: severe anxiety and other emotional reactions to stressful situations, great dissatisfaction with her own ability to develop and maintain satisfying social relationships, and feelings of being overwhelmed by marital and other interpersonal conflicts. She identified herself as "crazy" and a deviant; felt inadequate to give up what she called "a hippie lifestyle" and alcohol, and to take responsibility for her own decisions and behavior. She used denial and projection to defend herself against facing and coping with self-defeating attitudes and behavior. She was overweight, due to compulsive consumption of sweets.

The client's own goals for treatment were to give up her self-destructive behavior, gain a sense of self-worth and adequacy, and make important decisions about her marriage and other social relationships. Prior to her application to the family service agency, she had joined Alcoholics Anonymous and Overeaters Anonymous, groups which provided considerable support for her motivation to control her eating and drinking. She recognized, however, that she also needed counseling. It was clear to the worker that despite the overwhelming problems, the client had many positive personal qualities, ego strengths, and motivation to change her attitudes and behavior.

The agreed-upon plan for service was a flexible one, with recognition that relatively long-term treatment might be indicated, and that a combination of individual and group modalities would be tried. The worker recognized that the client would need a great deal of support, but would also need to develop some understanding of herself in relation to other people. This understanding would be used in making decisions about her marriage and other options in her life and in developing satisfying relationships with people who share her new values and desired lifestyle. In the first three months, personal interviews were used; then these were combined with experience in a small therapy group led by the worker. Following the termination of group therapy, individual sessions were continued in order to help the client assess her progress, make further gains, and prepare for termination.

[The social worker recorded]:

Mrs. Swift has been in treatment for about two years. During treatment, she developed a strong positive relationship with me, characterized by great dependency needs. Gradually, she came to feel that I accepted her fully and empathized with her: a sense of mutual trust and positive regard has developed between us.

As we worked together, the client was able to recognize that she had made much progress. She has remained sober throughout the course of treatment and continues to be active in Alcoholics Anonymous and Overeaters Anonymous. She rather rapidly lost forty pounds and has maintained her ideal weight for the past year. She has separated from her husband and has filed for divorce, extricating herself from what was a destructive marriage and a lifestyle with which she no longer identifies. She has worked out conflicts in relationships with members of her family and developed a supportive network. Her phobic anxiety reactions have almost disappeared, and she has come to understand their purpose and to be able to assert herself more affirmatively. She has maintained herself in her own apartment. During the past weeks, discussion has more often focused on her growing ability to try out new positive experiences. For the first time recently, she telephoned me—not for the usual reassurance, but to report a very positive experience. The time to terminate treatment is approaching.

Due to the intensity of the therapeutic relationship and the central themes of dependence and abandonment in the client's life, terminating will be difficult. But it will also be a real opportunity for her to solidify further the gains that have been made and experience a positive ending of a significant relationship as well as a new beginning in living without my support and help. There will be much pain for her in facing and working through the termination phase.

I began on termination by reminding Mrs. Swift of the progress she has been reporting and suggested that counseling need not continue much longer. I suggested that it might be a good idea if she began to come every other week instead of once a week. She had many reactions to this statement. She talked about knowing that she was getting ready to end, but expressed great uncertainty about her ability to get along without me. She resisted the change in frequency of sessions. She would, for example, call me to request additional appointments. She begged for reassurance that she would not be forced to quit before she was ready. She anticipated the pain of separation, but she also rejoiced in her new-found confidence. I remained supportive and assured her that she could set the final date.

After the client expressed feelings of comfort with the new schedule of appointments, I again brought up termination. This decision followed a review of the client's progress and changes made, which she herself initiated. I restated her belief that she was ready to work on terminating, to which she agreed. I asked her if she could set a date, explaining the significance of ending well and the reason for setting a date ahead of time.

She set a date, two months away. Together we marked the remaining five sessions on a calendar. The client again expressed the fear of leaving and recounted previous endings that had not been good. She expressed anxiety about being on her own and feared that, without me, she would go back to her old self-destructive habits. We needed to spend time working on these fears. She came to recognize that the gains she has made are real and that her new-found abilities to express and understand her feelings and to know how to go about working on problems would make a return to drinking and other unsatisifying behavior unnecessary. Besides, she now has new friends who can give her support and she can also give much to them.

I shared my own feelings of sadness at ending and my very positive feelings about the client and the work we have done together. She responded, "We're really a great team." Although this case has not terminated yet, we are well into the process, a process that is planned, structured, and purposeful. This process not only encapsulates an exciting opportunity to review and solidify the gains made during the course of work, it also provides for the client a positive, growth- enhancing separation from a valued person, along with the recognition and maintenance of an integrated self. It is a separation with love.

Dealing with Feelings

It has been noted that many clients have ambivalent feelings about terminating the helping process, to which the clinical social worker responds with acceptance and empathy. Referring to long-term therapy, Lackey writes that termination has a painful component for both the client and the worker, even when there is mutual agreement and successful completion of the therapy. She said, "It is difficult to relinquish a helping relationship which has acquired a meaning of its own, independent of the client's problem which was the original reason for its existence."[32] Facing termination may even precipitate a crisis for some clients. Crisis inter-

vention then becomes the treatment of choice: understanding the precipitating event of the threatened loss, encouraging ventilation and clarification of feelings, and problem-solving. One example is of work with a
client individually and in a group.

> Cathie, age seventeen, had a series of losses in her life. The immediate
> crisis was a boyfriend's decision not to marry her and to break off the
> relationship. Cathie was pregnant. She was placed in a group of ado-
> lescents whose purpose was to assist the members to resolve an imme-
> diate crisis, using the support and contributions of other members as
> well as of the worker. The goals for Cathie were to have emotional
> support to express and clarify feelings and to reduce anxiety, to under-
> stand the situation and her part in it, and to clarify what decisions she
> needs to make. In individual service, the focus was to make a decision
> about whether to bring the pregnancy to term or to have an abortion.
> When the latter decision was made, the worker helped Cathie to cope
> with her feelings about the baby, the desertion of her boyfriend, and
> fears of doctors and surgery. Medical time limits put great pressure on
> Cathie and the worker. A great deal of help was given through the
> group, but individual sessions were required around the specific deci-
> sion to abort and plans for implementing that decision.
>
> When the worker reminded Cathie that termination from both
> individual and group help was imminent, Cathie reacted with mas-
> sive denial. The denial was not broken until the end of her last ses-
> sion in the group when the worker asked Cathie to say good-bye to
> the group. She reacted first with shock and then with great emo-
> tional expression of sadness and grief, mixed with considerable
> anger at the worker for sending her away. Because there was not
> time for her to work through these feelings in the group, the work-
> er scheduled additional interviews to enable Cathie to face the expe-
> rience of loss and to help her move on to carry out the plans she had
> made for her immediate future.

When the client is a child, West has used activities as a way of letting
the child and therapist let go of each other without jeopardizing the therapeutic outcome.[33] Preparation for separation becomes an integral part
of the process.

> To help the child resolve the transference, she was told that next
> week will be the last time and that she will be missed. She sat close
> to me while we ate and I said we could have a party next week if she

liked. The child responded, "We could have the story." "What story," I asked. "The one we were writing about my coming here." "That's a good idea," I said. Children understand the use of stories, photographs, and play to resolve difficulties.

Elbow describes the use of memory books, an activity in which the worker encourages children to write or draw pictures that depict their views of the problems or issues, what they did in the meetings with the worker, and what was gained from the treatment.[34] That book is then used in the termination phase to summarize the experience.

A major task of the social worker during this phase is to encourage the ventilation of ambivalent feelings about the termination. This process clears the air so that clients can evaluate the experience realistically. If ambivalent feelings are worked through, the client's energies are released for further work on problems or tasks. Clients can learn how to handle loss and separation through the experience they have in terminating a social work service. Fox and associates note: "The manner in which the therapeutic relationship is brought to a close will heavily influence the degree to which gains are maintained; failure to work through the attitudes and feelings related to the ending of therapy will result in a weakening or undoing of the therapeutic work."[35]

In groups that are open-ended, some members may terminate before the others do. When one member is leaving a group, the worker understands that this change influences each of the remaining members and the functioning of the group. The steady state is upset. If members do not bring it up, a collective sense of denial may be operating. The worker needs to introduce the subject and explore its meaning to the members. A universalizing comment is often effective, for example, such as that people usually feel sad when someone is leaving, followed by asking them to discuss this topic. Usually, members are relieved when the issue is brought out into the open. Such discussion is invaluable to terminating members who perceive the meaning that their leaving has for them and for others. People with long histories of damaged self-esteem find it extremely difficult to imagine that they have really helped others. The painful disruption of relationships during termination is eased for such persons when they understand not only that they are ready to leave, but also that they will be missed.

Review of Process and Progress

Along with ventilation of feelings and at least partial resolution of ambivalence, the worker engages clients in a review of their progress in relation to agreed-upon goals and relevant to their particular situation. They may ask the clients to discuss symptoms or particular behaviors that were of concern to them, and to present their ideas about changes made in attitudes, achievements, and relationships, including the relationship with the worker and/or other members. The workers share with the clients their own assessment of the changes clients have made.

A common theme during the last sessions is review of the experience and an evaluation of the extent to which clients feel they have benefitted from, or been disappointed in their progress. It is important that clients be helped to recognize and accept their part in the progress. Then they can understand that they can use some of these understandings and skills in their roles outside the social work experience.

A group of Spanish-speaking mothers who were immigrants from Mexico had agreed to meet for approximately fifteen weeks, the length of the semester of the school their children attended. The purpose of the group was to learn more about education and life in this country in order to enhance their roles as wives and mothers so their children could improve their academic and social competence in school. The practitioner, a Spanish-speaking second-year student, after reviewing the progress that members had made, recorded:

> Once the reserves were down and trust had come, the leap to relating comfortably in and out of the group sessions seemed very sudden. Several members reported that they had enrolled in English classes, driver education, or conferred successfully with school personnel concerning the needs of their children. There was car-pooling, giving of rides, sharing of telephone numbers. As the members began to feel some power over their own lives, the group tackled serious problems of members: financial difficulties, marital conflict, child and wife abuse, problems in relationships with children and school officials, and cultural conflicts.
>
> During the last month, I directed the content of the group toward unfinished areas of concern. At the beginning of one meeting, I reminded the members that we had only three meetings left. When Juanita reported an important achievement, and then said, "I did not have the trust to try before," Corita said, "I think we have all learned to trust and assert ourselves." Then Elena said to me, "But it is so sad, for soon you will leave us." I answered, "With sadness, for I have come to care for each of you and you will soon be ready for our ending." Elena had spoken the heretofore unspoken words.

During the next session, I asked what specific issues that we had left unfinished would they like to discuss today. Elena said, "We have a thousand things—a thousand things." I responded, "You are really concerned because this group is ending." She said, "I can't talk about it now." But this elicited a spate of comments from others about their feelings; anger at me for leaving them and fears of making it on their own predominated. Mixed in with these expressions were examples of positive changes in themselves and their situations.

On the last day, the ladies came into the room carrying trays, pots, and utensils, and it became apparent to me that they had gotten together on their own and planned a meal. I expressed surprise and delight, and they responded with great pleasure. When the members took their usual chairs, Corita said they ought to talk before brunch. When no one else responded, I said that it would be helpful if they could discuss their feelings about the group—the positive and negative parts and whatever progress they thought they had made. Each one compared herself as she thought she was in the first meeting with today. Corita, for example, said, "When I came I felt like this," placing her hand about a foot from the floor. "Now I feel free and proud. I am no longer afraid; he has learned about the children because I've taught him what you said, *maestra* . . ." Juanita's eyes filled with tears as she told us she had found peace of mind, faith in herself, and capacity to live her own life so that her children would not suffer. She said she had applied for a community aide job, finally having enough belief in herself to do this . . . Lupe shyly spoke of having gained so much in learning about the individuality of each child and how she has gained friends here. . . .

After each member had spoken, I reviewed the progress that I thought had been made in the group, with emphasis on how they had slowly become cohesive, given each other hope, shared very painful experiences, and found they were not alone or unique, and thus could give strength to each other. . . I said that I, too, had learned from working with them. . . When I paused, Maria said, "There's one more thing." She proudly came forward with a plaque in Spanish which says:

> Mary.
> Thank you for helping us to be
> better spouses and mothers
> woman to woman.

I was overwhelmed and had difficulty expressing my thanks and appreciation. Lupe took some pictures of the group: then we feasted, socialized, and said good-bye. The members had planned to continue as an informal group, and they invited me to come to their meetings any time.

The social worker concluded her record with the statement that some colleagues have questioned whether Spanish-speaking people living in the barrio will respond to group treatment. Her answer was:

> That they can make effective use of a group experience is what really excites me! . . . Finally, these ladies made me aware of the natural perceptiveness and sensitivity which have made them able to bear the indignities that life has presented them. It was a humbling experience for me to see them bloom in self-awareness and self-esteem.

Evaluation of progress and identification of remaining problems was a natural, ongoing component of the content of the group.

When groups, such as the mothers' group, have had a particularly satisfying experience in working together, the members may desire to continue on a friendship basis after the original purpose has been achieved.[36] Such a decision by a group usually means that it has changed its purpose to that of a social group that continues without the assistance of a social worker. Although the members remain together, they still need to face the changes and deal with the separation from the worker and often also from the agency. Many self-help and support groups have started with some members who participated in a therapeutic or educational group and then desired to maintain relationships with people with whom they shared a particular need.

In families and other groups, practitioners need to accept the fact that there will be differences in progress made and that the criteria for judging progress are different for each person. This is so because, in addition to family or group goals, there are different goals for each member. It is also so because of differences in age, sex, developmental phase, severity of problems, and so forth. They need to explain such differences to the group, and to accredit the real, even though different, progress made by each. They need to give special help to members who feel disappointed and, if realistic, give encouragement that progress can still be made. In focusing on an individual, they need to be sensitive to what is going on with other members.

As individuals or groups evaluate their experiences, workers need to be secure enough to listen to, and respond non- defensively to, criticisms of their part in the process. Such criticisms may or may not be valid, but they provide feedback for use in evaluating their own performance, which can contribute to understanding of the use of oneself in practice. They need also to be comfortable in accepting genuine praise.

> One social worker in a hospital described her work with a family and its physician following the death of the oldest daughter, who had undergone minor surgery. The physician, who had been close to the family and who had reassured the members that there would be no danger in the surgery, was devastated by the death, as was the family, At the end of the very long session with the worker, the physician reached out to the worker, hugged her, and said, "I really love you—you've done so much for me." The family members gave similar expressions of appreciation. The practitioner, feeling confident that she had, indeed, been helpful, and being able to both give and receive positive feelings, was able to accept this praise and derive pleasure from it.

An important part of the workers' activity is to recognize and acknowledge the progress that has been made and to explore with the clients the specific work they have done to bring about the changes. Another activity is to express one's own enjoyment and satisfaction in the clients' increasing strength to manage their affairs better. This requires that workers be in touch with their own feelings about the relationship with clients so that their own resistances to termination do not make it difficult to convey these positive feelings.

Problem Resolution

As clients review what has happened to them, it is often discovered that some serious concerns were touched on from time to time but not dealt with adequately. Now, under the need to use the remaining time profitably, means for coping with this unfinished business may be found. Clients also often need to improve their problem-solving competence and to gain skills necessary for meeting the expectations that significant others will have for them in the near future.

The worker may engage clients in discussion or action-oriented experiences to help them stabilize the gains they have made. These activities tend to be oriented to the network of systems in the community of which the clients are a part. Further discussion of new ways of decision-making and action and of ways to apply the acquired understandings and skills help clients to distinguish between effective and less effective ways of meeting their needs. There tends to be talk or action about ways in which the gains can be applied to varied social situations. There often is a desire to repeat earlier experiences, either those that were gratifying or those in which failure was experienced in some way. Through such recapitulation, the clients confirm their judgments that they are now more able to deal with problematic situations. Resources in the community are often discussed or used in order to foster the transition from social work help.

The workers support clients' efforts to develop or strengthen new relationships and to find new roles in the community through which they can test and use their recently acquired knowledge and skills. They accredit their developing interests and are pleased when these take precedence over the treatment sessions. Hamilton said that: "The painful aspects of terminating a helpful relationship are diminished by the clients' own growing sense of strength, by a comforting feeling of improvement because of the channelizing of his activities into ego building and enlarged social activities and interests with the realization of the worker's continuing good will and the fact that he can return to the agency if necessary."[37] And Siporin has said that "the interventive system should be terminated in ways that link the client to the natural helping system of the community and that enable the client to continue to have access to its resources."[38]

Transition

During the termination stage there is often work to be done with others in behalf of the client system. Parents may have some anxiety about whether their child will be able to maintain the gains made. They need to be consulted and helped to consider the meaning of the social work service to them so that they can help the child to continue to progress. In residential settings or hospitals, other staff need to be notified about, or participate in, the actual decision about termination, depending upon the circumstances.

Social workers need to present and clarify the nature of any continuing relationship they may have with individuals, their families, or with a group. They make plans with the client to be available if problems are encountered, to follow up with interviews for the purpose of evaluating the outcome of service, or for reunions with a family or group. They make clear, when possible, that they will be available to clients who feel it necessary to return. It is becoming usual for workers to offer some form of follow-up to clients who may simply want to review the use they have made of the service. This issue should be addressed flexibly in terms of individuals' and families' desires to use such follow-up services.

Clients who have been hospitalized or placed in foster homes, residential treatment centers, or correctional facilities often need some continuous service to help them in their adaptation to family and community life. The ideal situation is for the same worker to continue, but usually a different one is assigned for aftercare responsibilities. In such instances, the new worker needs to work with these clients about the meaning of the change of workers to them. Whether these clients return to their own families or to another type of residence, they have an adjustment to make in adapting to and performing their social roles. Both client, family members, and other caretakers need to be prepared for the ambivalence and difficulties in readjustment.

At other times, clients may be referred to another service for a different kind of help. The case is transferred or reassigned to another agency or to another worker within the same agency, Transfer is indicated under several circumstances. Some clients may need and want further help, but the present worker is unable to continue; the clients need and want a particular type of service that is not available in the present agency; the clients and worker have reached an impasse in their work together; or a group is so seriously malstructured or malfunctioning that the defects cannot be remedied by the worker. Although ambivalent, many clients are willing to be transferred to another worker or agency. The decision to transfer is a mutual one between client and worker.

Clients who are transferred are often reluctant to begin with a new worker and sometimes also a new agency. It feels to them like starting all over again. It is really not so, however, because clients are different from what they were when they began with the present worker. It needs to be explained that it should be easier for them to move to another helping situation because they have learned a great deal in the present one.

Termination itself occurs at the end of the last session. When the time for ending comes, workers help the clients to say good-by in meaningful ways. They assure the clients that their interest in them does not stop because the service is terminating. They express hope that the new strengths and learnings from the social work experience will provide a foundation for each person's continued coping with everyday problems of living. They suggest that clients should be able to continue to use the knowledge and skills throughout their lives. There is often a summary of the experience and a ritual to formalize the breaking of ties. The ritual may be as simple as shaking hands, saying good-by, and wishing each other well. When social workers feel that the service to an individual, family, or group has been successful, they will have grown; for, in a sense, workers benefit as much from the clients as the clients do from them. They teach them how to be better practitioners. What they learn from working with a particular client system should make it possible for them to give even better service to the next individual or group.

Fourteen | Evaluation

Evaluation of the client's progress is essential. The appraisal of the quality of the service and the person's use of it is an ongoing process. Evaluation involves a capacity to make sound judgments in relation to the agreed-upon goals. The ultimate test of the effectiveness of social work practice is the extent to which the persons who were served have made positive changes toward the goals that were set with them. The progress or retrogression of clients is appropriately made in relation to their particular characteristics, background, problems, and needs rather than in relation to fixed or uniform standards. This view is in accordance with the values of social work: it is in opposition to many evaluative research studies in the human service professions which have used the same tests or measurements to evaluate the success or failure of service, regardless of difference in client conditions, type of service provided, and agreed-upon goals.

In some instances, notably work with families or other groups that will continue to exist when the social work service is terminated, the concern is with changes in the structure and interacting processes of the group, as well as changes in the individuals who are part of the group. If goals for each individual and the family have been developed, evaluated, and modified periodically, they naturally become the criteria against which progress is evaluated.

Numerous reviews of evaluation research in social work practice have been made, the later ones indicating generally positive outcomes.[1] Clinical social workers have a strong commitment to be helpful to their clients. In addition to their own desires to be effective and accountable, external demands for accountability are increasing.[2]

The demands come from clients, third-party payers, and regulatory and legal bodies, each of which may have different requirements. The growth of managed care requires that practitioners meet the reporting requirements of insurance agencies, health maintenance organizations, and such governmental programs as Medicare and Medicaid. To meet these demands, a suitable system of recording is essential.

Recording

Evaluation of outcome is dependent upon accurate records of practice.[3] The records prepared by clinical social workers should promote the quality of service as well as the evaluation of outcomes. A good record enhances the delivery of services, providing data for the worker's reviews of the course of treatment, facilitating communication among members of teams, and providing the necessary information for use in supervision, consultation or peer review. In keeping with ethical principles, clients must give their informed consent to whatever use is made of their records.

Content of Records

The content of records varies with the purpose for which they are kept. For example, records of incidents of the process between worker and clients serve educational purposes. Statistical records of clients' characteristics, number of clients served, and duration of treatment serve administrative purposes. Other types of records about clients or social workers serve evaluation and research purposes. For purposes of evaluation of outcome, records usually include the following areas of content:

1. Face sheet. The face sheet includes identifying information about the clients and significant others, such as age, gender, ethnicity, religion, occupation, education, and family constellation. It provides immediate clues for identifying the needs of clients. An example is that ethnicity and religion alert the practitioner to possible cultural values and norms. As an adjunct to the face sheet, ecomaps, genograms, or sociograms may add to the practitioner's quick grasp of the client and the social context that influences behavior, opportunities, and obstacles.

2. A summary of the assessment of the client and situation, as presented in chapter 8. When expectations for third-party payers must be met, it is usually necessary to make an accurate diagnosis of mental disorder, using the latest edition of the *Diagnostic and Statistical Manual*. It is necessary to make a clear statement of

maladaptive behaviors and environmental obstacles. What matters is the constellation of biological, psychological, sociocultural, and environmental aspects of the problems to be addressed. Client strengths and environmental opportunities are also important.

3. An enunciation of the short-term and long-term goals of treatment that have been agreed upon between the practitioner and clients. These goals comprise the base for evaluation. They may include changes in the attitudes, relationships, or behavior of individuals; changes in the family's or groups functioning as a system and changes in the environment.

4. The treatment plan should flow logically from the assessment. It generally includes the specific goals to be sought, anticipated duration of treatment, one or more modalities of practice to be used, provision of resources, and collaborative activities.

5. Progress notes that are expressed in terms of changes in clients related to the interventions of the practitioner, and summaries of referrals, consultation, or collaboration.

6. Summaries of periodic evaluations with clients concerning problems or progress in moving toward the achievement of goals.

7. A summary of the final evaluation, with information about the extent to which the client is in agreement with it.[4]

The information noted in records should be as objective, factual, and relevant as possible. The social work practitioner should keep in mind that the client and others may have legitimate access to records via proper procedures. Those who may wish to have access include consultants, supervisors, or other health care providers; schools; third-party payers; family members; attorneys; and the courts. The practitioner who keeps such records and follows ethical principles will have the information necessary to evaluate the outcome of service and also meet the usual requirements of peer review and quality assurance procedures.

Philosophies of Science

The philosophy of science preferred by a profession influences the plan for evaluating the results of treatment. For almost two decades, controversy has swirled within the profession concerning the selection of a philosophy of science to guide evaluation and research. A large number of writers about social work practice or research identify themselves as logical positivists and empiricists.[5] They emphasize the importance of restricting the profession's knowledge base, evaluation methods, and research findings to those that satisfy requirements of proof, developed through experimental research and the use of quantitative data. From Orcutt's historical review of philosophies of science, it is clear that this philosophy dominated scholarship until the middle of this century and that many social work researchers accepted empirical and quantitative methods as the only valid form of research.[6] According to this view, evaluation needs to be based on controlled experiments.

Social workers who espouse logical positivism evaluate practice through group experimental method or quasi-experimental research designs. More recently, emphasis has turned to single subject designs.[7] These designs were borrowed from behavioral psychology, along with the practice of behavioral modification in the 1970s. Several researchers point out that single subject designs are most appropriate with behavioral and task-centered models of practice, although efforts have been made to apply them to other types of practice.[8]. A recent conference on clinical social work research contains reevaluations of the strength and weakness of single subject designs in social work practice for varied situations.[9]

An alternative paradigm is accepted by those social workers who reject logical positivism in favor of a humanistic or phenomenological philosophy of science.[10] Hermeneutics, the science of interpretation and explanation, attempts to synchronize intuitive inquiry with objectivity. The view is that, in order to understand phenomena, the need is to think not in terms of direct relations between cause and effect, but in terms of circular and reciprocal relations among parts of the whole. Subjective as well as objective reality can be studied. Knowledge is discovered, not only through experimental research, but through numerous means of inquiry, often referred to as qualitative research. Included are case studies, direct observation, content analysis, use of client and worker judgments, and clients' own stories. There are many valid ways of knowing.

Most of the arguments have focused on services to individuals, but an analysis of twelve theoretical approaches to work with groups in 1976 concluded that the strongest disagreement among the writers concerned the selection of an appropriate philosophy of science.[11] Many social work theorists occupy a middle stance, being comfortable with both viewpoints by asserting that the approach to be used depends upon the nature of the problem to be solved.

In the biopsychosocial systems approach, it is recognized that there is a difference between evaluation of outcome as an integral part of concluding practice and evaluation of outcome for formal research purposes. Both qualitative and quantitative measures may be used in ascertaining the extent to which clients have achieved their goals.

Evaluation as a Component of Treatment

In one important sense, evaluation is an integral part of the practice of clinical social work. What a worker does at any time is based on assessment of what has gone before as that affects further work toward goal achievement. The worker reflects on and engages the clients in discussion of progress and obstacles to further progress. An example from a group of couples who had severe marital problems follows.

> Esther changed the mood with a statement that while she has a long way to go, this group had helped her and her husband more than earlier therapy had. When Katherine asked her about this, she replied, "Well, it's something when six people land on you at one time; boy, that really made an impression on me; it was a painful process and I wouldn't want to go through it again. But I lived through it because you all seemed to like me and care about me." Her husband said that he agreed—it was good to be able to talk things over with people who had marital problems, too, even though not identical with theirs. There was further discussion of the ways the group had helped them. There was also presentation of things that were not going well, so that ventilation of feelings, problem-solving, and review and evaluation were interspersed during this meeting.

Another example is of practice that took place within a counseling service of an Employee Assistance Program.

> Mrs. Dublek commented that things were so much better now. She had resolved the conflict with her supervisor and they had worked out a new plan that both of them were happy with, and her boss had commended her for a piece of work she had done. I said that seemed to have accomplished one of her major goals for which she should be congratulated. She acknowledged my praise with pleasure. Then she said, "but" and was silent. I asked, "but what?" She replied that she still didn't feel really accepted by her colleagues, especially the men, and she presented more details about the problem. I asked her if she'd like to work on that next. She asked if I thought that could be done within the three weeks left until our time was up. I assured her that it was possible, but that I could extend the time if it seemed indicated.

As the date for termination approaches, social workers often suggest that an evaluation take place in a more planned way. They may suggest that they take time to review what progress has been made, what the client hoped would be better by coming here, and how things are now. For example:

> During a session with Mrs. Pelling, she said, "It was awful whcn I first came. I was afraid that you would tell me you were going to take my child away. But you didn't. You said you'd work with me to see if I could learn to become a better mother, but I'd have to do my part." I asked, "And what was to be your part?" In reply, "I decided I needed to learn to discipline Jennie without hurting her, find out why she wouldn't go to school, and get her there. And I did it, didn't I?" I said, "Yes, and you were also going to get health care for her, weren't you?" In reply, "Yes, and the doctor says she's in good health now. Wow, that was a lot of work, wasn't it? I feel I've come a long, long way. I'm a different person now and besides, I've made new friends. And I have a surprise. I'm going to get married to a wonderful man who'll make a very good dad for Jennie. They like each other and I'm very happy about that."

After further discussion in this vein, the practitioner reviewed the agreed-upon goals one at a time, asking Mrs. P. to decide how well the goal had been achieved and adding her own opinion to the evaluation. The aim was to have the client evaluate her own progress to the extent possible, rather than doing it herself. That is a way of empowering clients.

Evaluation of the progress of clients is made more precise and easier for the worker if some plan is developed for tracing changes in the client's psychosocial functioning, including changes in the environment as these relate to goal achievement. Some measurements can be used for this purpose.

Measurements

Agreement between the client's and the worker's judgments about the changes that have been made, based on a careful review of the available information, generally constitutes the basis for appraising the success or failure of the treatment. Reports of clients are considered important indicators of change; so, too, are expert judgments of workers. In addition to the use of judgments of practitioners and individuals, families, or groups, there are times when it is desirable to use measurement tools to test changes in the clients' functioning. Some of these tools do not intrude negatively on the helping process and clients find satisfaction in participating in their use. When selecting one or more measurement tools, a major obstacle is the large number of available ones and the small number that are useful in a particular situation. Hudson and Thyer suggest guidelines for selecting measurements for application to practice.[12] Measures should be selected for their suitability to the particular problems of clients that are being addressed; they should be reliable and valid; and they should be short, easy to administer, easy for clients to understand, and easy to score and interpret.

Three major types of measures are available to help clinical social workers to accurately evaluate the client's use of the service. Russell has classified them as: standard rapid assessment instruments; individualized rapid assessment instruments; and measurement of client satisfaction.[13]

1. *Standardized rapid assessment instruments.* These measures are usually in the form of paper and pencil self-report scales or indices designed to measure a variety of problems of clients. Hudson developed a package of these scales for use by social workers, which have been found to be reliable and valid. Levitt and Reid have also developed a similar set of such scales.[14]

2. *Individualized rapid assessment instruments.* As contrasted with standardized measures, self anchored scales may be more appropriate for use in clinical social work when a standardized scale does not accurately portray a particular client's problems. These scales can be constructed quickly by the practitioner and used easily. The best-known of these scales is the one for ascertaining and listing the goals for practice, called Goal Attainment Scaling and the Problem-Oriented Recording device for monitoring the progress made by clients in relation to particular problems.[15] Both of these scales are individualized for clients, relatively easy to use, and do not interfere with the ongoing client-worker relationship or treatment.

3. *Measurements of client satisfaction.* The voice of the consumer is regarded by many practitioners as a necessary component of evaluation, as discussed by Maluccio, by Rehr, by Sainsbury, and by Garber, Brenner, and Litwin.[16] These measures are in the form of questionnaires and interviews that range from securing the opinion of clients on one or two issues to in-depth interviews that elicit clients' perceptions of the outcome.

Clinical social workers often participate in formal research evaluations of outcome, in addition to their direct practice. In such research, they have the responsibility to make sure that the research procedures pose no risk for clients and that they are conducted with full respect for confidentiality and informed consent. The goals on which the results are measured must be clearly those that are relevant for particular clients and the treatment plan and interventions used. Only then can the results of such research be valid.

Research on Process

Research on evaluation of outcome has generally given inadequate attention to the nature and effectiveness of the social worker's interventions. Practice that is based on research is presumed to be more effective than that which is not. A substantial body of research has accumulated that at least suggests what it is that brings about changes in the psychosocial functioning of clients and their environmental circumstances.

Orcutt has summarized the research on direct practice up until the early seventies to determine the major types of research that have contributed to understanding the helping process. These include:

1. Case studies, including their use in evaluative research.
2. Prediction of continuance or discontinuance in treatment.
3. Classification of treatment procedures or interventions.
4. Evaluation of outcome and effectiveness.
5. Development of models of practice.
6. Interpersonal dynamics and strategies in family and group treatment.
7. Surveys of services.
8. The use of clinical judgment.[17]

Russell, in a survey of recent research, has added:

1. Studies of the clinical process, including entry and engagement; decisions to seek help and barriers to entry; differential use of skills and procedures; negotiating contracts between workers and clients; and duration and structure of intervention.
2. Interventions and evaluation of treatment with special client populations and modalities of practice.[18]

In addition to the findings from these reviews, research has made a contribution to understanding motivation and resistance, the essential components of planning, the nature of assessment, the termination process, comparative studies of the effectiveness of practice with individuals, families and groups, and the appropriate use of models of practice. In this book, findings from research have been woven into the discussion of concepts and principles of practice.

Competence of Social Workers

Clients and practitioners engage in a process whereby both clients and workers influence the outcome of the service. It is, therefore, essential to evaluate the practitioner's competence in performing a particular service.

It is competence that counts: values, purposes, and knowledge need to be translated into effective performance. The provision of high-quality services to people is a complex endeavor. Competent practitioners have a mastery of knowledge they can draw upon in the moment-to-moment communication with their clients. They act in accordance with professional values and the purposes of social work. They exercise sound judgment in the use of techniques within the processes of planning, assessing, directly intervening, and intervening through the environment. They facilitate the achievement of tasks that are typical of each phase of the helping process. They keep current with the theory and research on practice so that, to the extent possible, their actions are based on principles that are derived from research.

The use of guidelines for the analysis of skill are useful in helping workers assess their own competence and then use supervision, consultation, and study to further enhance their skill. The characteristics of a competent practitioner concern values, the knowledge foundation, planning, intervention in psychosocial helping, and termination.

Values

Translated into ethical principles, values guide actions. Competent practitioners need to have great sensitivity to their own personal and cultural values as these are similar to, or different from, those of the clients, those espoused by the employing organization, and those expressed by dominant segments of the community. They are aware of the ethical principles of the profession and evaluate their own behavior in relation to them. They recognize conflicts in values and use a problem-solving process in making decisions about acting in relation to the conflicts. They follow ethical principles concerning such matters as informed consent, confidentiality, privacy, self-direction, maximum participation, choice of treatment procedures, and discriminatory policies and practices.

Purpose and Problems

Competent practitioners are clear about the mission of the profession and give help within the profession's purposes. Social work has always had concern for individuals in their interpersonal relationships and in encounters with their environment. Workers help clients to identify the problems that are amenable to social work intervention and to clarify mutually acceptable goals. Changes are often desired in individuals' attitudes, perceptions, and behavior toward themselves and others, and to changes in the structure and dynamics of families and groups. Changes are often desired also in the environment in order to provide the necessary resources and a nurturing social milieu. Most frequently, the sought-for changes are in the interrelationships of person-group-situation. The general purpose is translated into more specific goals for each client. The function of the practitioner may be to promote opportunities for the enhancement of potential, to prevent problems in psychosocial relations, or to remedy existing problems that interfere with the achievement of goals.

Foundation of Knowledge

The activities of competent practitioners are based on a body of knowledge that is consistent with values and purpose. No single source of theory is adequate to explain the complex intrapsychic, interpersonal, and societal processes that influence the adequacy of a person's, family's, or group's functioning at a given time. In order to help people with their social needs and problems, it is necessary to have a broad perspective that incorporates knowledge about the interrelationships among biological, psychological, and sociocultural influences on individual and group functioning.

An ecological systems perspective combined with knowledge of biopsychosocial functioning offers a framework of concepts that aid the practitioners in understanding the relationships between people and their environments. The model of the open organismic system helps practitioners to understand the organization, interdependence, and integration of the parts and the effects of inner and outer stresses and strains that threaten adaptive capacities. Human systems are perceived as complex, goal-directed, and adaptive units in constant interaction with other social systems. Competent practitioners make use of knowledge in all of the major interrelated processes of practice—assessment, planning, social treatment, and evaluation. Knowledge is for use.

Assessment

Competent practitioners can assess accurately the client system-situation configuration. They make assessments in order to understand and appraise an individual, family, or other small group, in its social situation. A preliminary assessment is an essential prerequisite for planning what should be done to enable a system to improve its functioning or to effect changes in its environment, or both.

The biopsychosocial perspective guides practitioners' focus in exploring the situation with the client system. To achieve an accurate appraisal of the meaning of the facts that have been secured, workers make appropriate use of sources of information, classifications of psychosocial needs and problems, and criteria for judging the adequacy of biopsychosocial functioning in particular environments. They are able to organize the data and assess their significance for the functioning of both the individuals and the social systems with which they interact.

Planning Individualized Services

Competent practitioners engage in effective planning, a process by which decisions are made about the nature of the services and resources to be made available to particular individuals, families, or groups. Although it is an ongoing process, certain decisions need to be made prior to or during the initial sessions. These decisions concern the social context of service; the general needs, problems, and goals of clients that will serve as an initial focus of content; the unit of attention or type of client system which is most appropriate to the particular situation, and the structure of the service. If family or group service is being planned, practitioners attend to the criteria for group composition, the size and structure of the group, and their primary role in the group. Practitioners need to understand the concepts and principles that guide their decisions. In an important sense, planning is a problem-solving process in which social workers use their professional knowledge to make decisions about a plan of service to be negotiated with particular clients. The preliminary plan is a flexible one, to be changed as the clients' needs and goals become clear.

Social Treatment

Competent practitioners are those who use themselves in ways that truly are adapted to particular clients' needs, requiring large doses of sensitivity, self-awareness, flexibility, and creativity. No words can convey adequately the complex process of social treatment—that complex constellation of attitudes and feelings, thought processes, and skills that is the worker's contribution to the clients' efforts to achieve their goals. The goals are achieved through the acquisition of new or enhanced attitudes, knowledge, perceptions, and behaviors and through changes in environmental conditions.

Competent practitioners have mastered clusters of skills that are used within a therapeutic relationship and supportive milieu. They are able to develop and sustain relationships with clients and with other significant persons in their behalf. They have enough self-esteem and interpersonal competence to reach out and engage people in interacting with them and with other people. They can bridge social distance through their attitudes of acceptance, empathy, and genuineness and through knowledge of the common ground that underlies age, socioeconomic, and ethnic differences. In addition to relationship building, these clusters of skills are support, structuring, exploration, clarification, education, advice, and facilitation of interaction. Verbal communication is an important medium for help, but so too are action-oriented experiences. Appropriate use of particular media and techniques is dependent upon understanding the theory on which they are based, the values they have for achieving particular outcomes, and the phase in the helping process. Although the skills are generic, they require differential application. Basically, it is not the techniques per se that effect changes, but rather the judicious way they are used, based on self-awareness and self-discipline and on cumulative understanding of the person-family or group-environment system.

Facilitating the Process

Competent clinical social workers understand the special characteristics of each of the major phases of practice and use interventions that are appropriate to the particular phase.

The major tasks to be achieved in the initial phase are initiating relationships, developing a contract, and establishing patterns of effective communication. When the social workers and the individual or group recognize they have reached an acceptable working agreement or contract, the clients are ready to move into the core phase of work toward defined goals. In helping clients to achieve their goals, workers simultaneously pay attention to the maintenance and further development of the worker-client system and to the problems and tasks that are essential to progress. In the termination phase, competent practitioners help clients to acknowledge the positive and negative feelings and resolve their ambivalence about leaving the relationship with the worker and, in the case of formed groups, with the other members. They help clients to evaluate the progress they have made, acknowledge the realistic losses and gains, and accept the fact that the experience is ending. They help clients to set priorities for work on unfinished problems or tasks that seem central to their progress, and refer them to appropriate resources in the community.

The skills of social workers must be buttressed by sound knowledge from the relevant biological, psychological, and social sciences, and from knowledge derived from practice, wisdom, and studies of actual practice. Curti has said that:

> I believe that we should make room in our outlook for tested knowledge about human nature and social behavior. But if we are wise, we shall also provide for the revision of this knowledge—for what we know, or think we know, is not the last word. And I am equally convinced that we should find out how to make more constructive use of the knowledge that we have[19]

That is a task for clinical social work. Knowledge is for use in helping clients to achieve their desired goals within the mission of their chosen profession, social work.

Notes |

One | Evolution of Clinical Social Work

1. Stewart, "From the President."
2. University of Southern California, Transcript, *Faculty Newsletter*.
3. Eisenhuth, "The Theories of Heinz Kohut and Clinical Social Work Practice"; Carlton, *Clinical Social Work in Health Settings*, p. 5; Lustman, "Development of Research in a Clinical Social Work Service"; Stewart, "From the President."
4. Hathway, "Twenty-Five Years of Professional Education for Social Work"; Johnson, "Development of Basic Methods of Social Work Practice and Education"; Richmond, *What Is Social Case Work?*
5. Kasius, ed., *A Comparison of Diagnostic and Functional Casework.*
6. Bartlett, "Toward Clarification and Improvement of Social Work Practice"; Boehm, "The Nature of Social Work."
7. For discussions of applicability of systems theory to social work practice, see Auerswald, "Interdisciplinary versus Ecological Approach"; Compton and Galaway, *Social Work Processes*, pp. 97–110; Freeman, "Social Work with Families"; Hartman, "To Think About the Unthinkable"; Hearn, *Theory Building in Social Work*; Hearn, ed., *The General Systems Approach*; Janchill, "Systems Concepts in Casework Theory and Practice"; Rubin, "General Systems Theory"; Stein, *Systems Theory, Science, and Social Work.*
8. An early major effort was the work of Friedlander, ed., *Concepts and Methods of Social Work.* More recent formulations have been those of Compton and Galaway, Germain and Gitterman, Goldstein, Carol Meyer, Pincus and Minahan, Nelsen, Siporin, Smalley, Turner, and Whittaker. See Bibliography.
9. Bartlett, *The Common Base of Social Work Practice*, pp. 141–42; Bertha C. Reynolds, *Learning and Teaching in the Practice of Social Work*; Gertrude Wilson, *Group Work and Case Work.*
10. Carol Meyer, "Direct Practice in Social Work," p. 413; Middleman and

Goldberg, "Social Work Practice with Groups," p. 916. Berry, in "Confrontation at the National Conference on Social Welfare," presents deetailed information about chaos in one organization.

11. Fischer, "Is Casework Effective?"

12. Jackson, "Clinical Social Work: Definition, Status, /Knowledge, and Practice."

13. Board of Behavioral Science Examiners, *Laws Relating to Registered Social Workers. . .* , pp. 5–7.

14. Jackson, "Clinical Social Work."

15. Helen Harris Perlman, "Confessions, Concerns, and Commitment of an Ex- Clinical Social Worker."

16. Pinkus et al, "Education for the Practice of Clinical Social Work at the Master's Level," p. 254.

17. Ewalt, ed., *Toward a Definition of Clinical Social Work.*

18. Jerome Cohen, "Nature of Clinical Social Work."

19. NASW. 1987. National Council on the Practice of Clinical Social Work, *The Expanded Definition of Clinical Social Work*, p. 1.

20. Florence Lieberman/Leiberman, *Clinical Social Workers as Psychotherapists.* p. 17.

21. Lurie, "A Warning to Clinicians," p. 4.

22. Rosenblatt and Waldfogel, eds., *Handbook of Clinical Social Work*, "Introduction," p. xxvii.

23. Turner, *Social Work Treatment*, p. 84.

24. Coyle, "Some Basic Assumptions about Social Group Work," p. 89.

25. Pinderhughes, *Understanding Race, Ethnicity, and Power*;
Heller, *Power in Psychotherapeutic Practice*, p. 30.

26. Solomon, *Black Empowerment*, pp. 28–29.

27. Turner, *Psychosocial Therapy*, pp. 5–12.

28. Jerome Cohen, "Nature of Clinical Social Work"; Ewalt, *Toward a Definition of Clinical Social Work.*

29. Papell, Personal Memorandum.

30. Norton, "The Dual Perspective."

31. William Gordon, "Social Work Revolution or Evolution."

32. Carol Meyer, *Social Work Practice*, p. 28.

33. Baker, "Toward Generic Social Work Practice," p. 195.

34. National Association of Social Workers, *NASW Guidelines on the Private Practice of Clinical Social Work*, p. 17.

35. Getzel, "AIDS."

36. Brown and Weil, eds., *Family Practice.*

37. Carol Meyer, ed., *Clinical Social Work in the Ecosystems Perspective.*

Two | The Social Context

1. Cook, "Population: Some Pitfalls of Progress," p. 42.

2. Dies, Man's Nature and Nature's Man, pp. 2–3.

3. Hazen and Trefil, "Ecological Literacy," p. 26.

4. Coyle, *Social Process in Organized Groups*, p. 19.

5. Bronfenbrenner, *The Ecology of Human Development*.

6. Winett, "Ecobehavioral Assessment in Health Life Styles."

7. Germain, "Social Context of Clinical Social Work."

8. Towle, "Social Casework in Modern Society."

9. P.L. 94–142, *Education for All Handicapped Children Act*; P.L. 96–272, *Adoption Assistance and Child Welfare Act of 1980*.

10. NASW, *Guidelines on the Private Practice of Clinical Social Work*.

11. APA, *Diagnostic and Statistical Manual of Mental Disorders*.

12. Yalom, *Inpatient Group Psychotherapy*, p. x.

13. Proshansky, Ittelson, and Rivlin, eds., *Environmental Psychology*, p. 18.

14. Bartlett, *Analyzing Social Work Practice by Fields*.

15. Carol Meyer, "Direct Practice in Social Work," pp. 417–18; NASW, "Specialization in the Social Work Profession."

16. Major books on social work in health include: Bartlett, *Social Work Practice in the Health Field*; Bracht, *Social Work in Health Care*; Carlton, *Clinical Social Work in Health Settings*; Ell and Northen, *Families and Health Care*; Germain, *Social Work Practice in Health Care*; Wallace, Goldberg, and Slaby, *Clinical Social Work in Health Care*.

17. Mental health services are integrated into references on social work practice, including those on psychotherapy. See, for example, Florence Lieberman, *Clinical Social Workers as Psychotherapists*; Rosenblatt and Waldfogel, *Handbook of Clinical Social Work*; Woods and Hollis, *Casework*.

18. Examples of major books in the field are: June Brown et al, *Child, Family, Neighborhood*; June Brown and Weil, eds., *Family Practice*; Hartman and Laird, *Family-Centered Social Work Practice*; Tolson and Reid, eds., *Models of Family Treatment*; Whittaker, *Caring for Troubled Children*.

19. Some major references for occupational or industrial social work are: Akabas and Kurzman, eds., *Work, Workers, and Work Organizations*; Masi, *Designing Employee Assistance Programs*; McGowan, *Trends in Employee Counseling*; Reynolds, *Social Work and Social Living*; Thomlinson, ed., *Perspectives on Industrial Social Work Practice*.

20. Ozawa, "Development of Social Services in Industry."

21. Constable and Flynn, *School Social Work*; Hancock, *School Social Work*; Allen-Meares, Washington, and Welsh, *Social Work Services in Schools*; Sarri and Maple, eds., *The School in the Community*; Winters and Easton, *The Practice of Social Work in Schools*.

22. NASW, *Guidelines on the Private Practice of Clinical Social Work*; Matorin et al., "Private Practice in Social Work."

23. Jayartne, Davis-Sacks, and Chess, "Private Practice May Be Good for Your Health and Well-Being."

24. Jayartne, Siefert, and Chess, "Private and Agency Practitioners: Some Data and Observations."

25. Arches, "Social Structure, Burnout, and Job Satisfaction," p. 206.

26. Simmons, "A Philosophical Perspective on Social Work Administration."

27. Hartman, "Social Worker-in-Situation."

28. Glasser and Garvin, "An Organizational Model," p. 87.

29. Pincus and Minahan, *Social Work Practice*, p. 115.

30. For a detailed discussion, see Germain and Gitterman, *The Life Model of Social Work Practice*, pp. 297–339.

31. Shimer, *This Sculptured Earth*, p. 1.

32. Cousins, *Head First*.

33. Horn, "Hospitals Fit for Healing."

34. Hall, *The Hidden Dimension*, p. 173; Hartford, *Groups in Social Work*, pp. 167–81; Seabury, "Arrangement of Physical Space."

35. Ell, "Social Networks, Social Support, and Health Status"; Hartman and Laird, *Family-Centered Social Work Practice*, pp. 114–21; Whittaker, Garbarino, and Associates, *Social Support Networks*; Selby, "Support Revisited."

36. Pinderhughes, *Understanding Race, Ethnicity, and Power*, p. 71; Solomon, *Black Empowerment*, pp. 141–42.

37. Devore and Schlesinger, *Ethnic-Sensitive Social Work Practice*; Pinderhughes, *Understanding Race*; Solomon, *Black Empowerment*.

38. Solomon, *Black Empowerment*, p. 45.

39. Sotomayor, "Language, Culture, and Ethnicity," p. 196.

40. Toth, "New Ties to the Old Country."

41. Cornett, "Toward a More Comprehensive Personology."

42. Marla Williams, "Taking Charge," p. 21.

43. Cornett, "Toward A More Comprehensive Personology."

44. Major classifications of social class are: Hollingshead and Redlich, *Social Class and Mental Illness*; Warner, *Social Class in America*. Devore and Schlesinger discuss social class in *Ethnic-Sensitive Social Work Practice*. See also Duberman, *Social Inequality*.

45. Milton M. Gordon, *Human Nature, Class, and Ethnicity*, p. 134.

46. Greer. "Remembering Class."

47. Lieberman, "Clients' Expectations, Preferences, and Experiences of Initial Interviews in Voluntary Agencies," p. 152.

48. Spiegel, "An Ecological Model with an Emphasis on Ethnic Families."

49. Kluckhohn and Strodtbeck, *Variations in Value Orientations*, p. 89.

50. Spiegel, "An Ecological Model," p. 142.

51. Anderson, "Group Work with Families: A Muticultural Perspective."

52. McAdoo, *Black Families*.

53. Longres, *A System Approach to Human Behavior*, pp. 149–52.

54. Solomon, *Black Empowerment*.

55. Germain, *Human Behavior in the Social Environment*, pp. 52–53.

56. U.S. Dept. of Labor, *A Report on The Glass Ceiling Initiative*, p. 2; U.S. Dept. of Labor, *Pipelines of Progress*.

57. Horwitz and Brandel, "The Struggle Continues."

58. Germain, *Human Behavior in the Social Environment*, pp. 258–60.

59. Moses and Hawkins, *Counseling Lesbian Women and Gay Men*.

60. Pinderhughes, "Power, Powerlessness, and Practice."

Three | Theoretical Perspectives

1. Chin, "The Utility of Systems Models and Developmental Models for Practitioners," p. 207.

2. Germain, *Social Work Practice*, pp. 7–8.

3. Hearn, "General Systems Theory and Social Work," p. 335.

4. von Bertalanffy, "General Systems Theory and Psychiatry," p. 1100.

5. Greene, "General Systems Theory"; Carol Meyer, *Clinical Social Work in an Ecosystem Perspective*; Schwartz, "Between Client and System."

6. For discussion of these concepts, see Greene, "General Systems Theory"; Freeman, *Techniques of Family Therapy*; Longres, *A Systems Approach to Human Behavior*; Stein, "The Systems Model and Social Systems Theory."

7. Parad, Selby, and Quinlan, "Crisis Intervention," p. 306.

8. Buckley., *Sociology and Modern Systems Theory*, p. 79.

9. Stein, "The Systems Model and Social System Theory," p. 134.

10. Hare, *Handbook of Small Group Research*, p. 9.

11. Erikson, *Childhood and Society*.

12. Erikson, *The Life Cycle Completed*.

13. Erikson, *Identity and the Life Cycle*, p. 162.

14. Greene, "Eriksonian Theory," pp. 97–98.

15. Maas, *People and Contexts*.

16. Bronfenbrenner, *The Ecology of Human Development*.

17. Piaget and Inhelder, *The Psychology of the Child*.

18. Vourlekis, "Cognitive Theory for Social Work Practice," pp. 28–29.

19. Gilligan, *A Different Voice*.

20. Gilligan, *A Different Voice*; Konopka, *The Adolescent Girl in Conflict*; Golan, *The Perilous Bridge*; Mishne, *Clinical Work with Adolescents*; Schlosberg, *Counseling Adults in Transition*.

21. Longres, *A Systems Approach to Human Behavior*.

22. Mailick and Vigilante, "Human Behavior in the Social Environment."

23. Pollak, "A Family Diagnosis Model"; Rhodes, "A Developmental Approach to the Life Cycle of a Family"; Terkelsen, "Toward a Theory of the Family Life Cycle."

24. For a summary of group development, see Northen, *Social Work with Groups*, pp. 173–84.

25. Lewin, *Field Theory in Social Science*, pp. 239–40.

26. Moreno, *Who Shall Survive?*; Jennings, *Leadership and Isolation*.

27. Homans, *The Human Group*.

28. Ackerman, *Treating the Troubled Family*; Bion, *Experiences in Groups*; Durkin, *The Group in Depth*; Freud, *An Outline of Psychoanalysis*; Freud, *Group Psychology and the Analysis of the Ego*; Redl and Wineman, *Controls from With-*

in; Scheidlinger, *Psychoanalysis and Group Behavior*; Scheidlinger, *Focus on Group Psychotherapy*; Yalom, *Theory and Practice of Group Psychotherapy*.

29. Taylor, "Schizophrenia: Fire in the Brain," p. 259.

30. APA, Task Force on DSM-IV, *DSM-IV Options Book*, p. B-15.

31. Saleebey, "In Clinical Social Work Practice, Is the Body Politic?"

32. Saleebey, "Biology's Challenge to Social Work."

33. Eda Goldstein, *Ego Psychology and Social Work Practice*, pp. xiv-xvi.

34. Hartmann, *Ego Psychology and the Problem of Adaptation*, p. 24.

35. Holmes and Raye, "The Social Readjustment Rating Scale."

36. Woods and Hollis, *Casework*, pp. 34–35.

37. Mailick, "The Short-Term Treatment of Depression of Physically Ill Hospital Patients."

38. Goodman, "Presumed Innocent."

39. Carlton, *Clinical Social Work in Health Settings*, p. 9.

40. Bowlby, "Separation Anxiety."

41. Gilligan, "Adolescent Development Reconsidered," p. 7.

42. Sanville, "Theories, Therapy, Therapists," p. 84.

43. Imre, "The Nature of Knowledge in Social Work," p. 43.

44. Falck, "Aspects of Membership"; Kernberg, *Object Relations Theory and Clinical Psychoanalysis*; Kohut, *The Restoration of the Self*; Mahler, *The Psychological Birth of the Human Infant*.

45. Grunebaum and Solomon, "Toward a Peer Theory of Group Psychotherapy"; Grunebaum and Solomon, "Peer Relationships, Self Esteem, and the Self."

46. Hartford, *Groups in Social Work*, pp. 202–6; for fuller discussion of triads, see Caplow, *Two Against One*.

47. Hartman and Laird, *Family-Centered Social Work Practice*. p. 68.

48. Phillipa, *Essentials of Social Group Work Skill*, p. 25.

49. Schutz, *Interpersonal Underworld*.

50. Pinderhughes, "Empowerment for Our Clients and for Ourselves"; Pinderhughes, "Teaching Empathy, Ethnicity, Race, and Power at the Cross-Cultural Treatment Interface"; Pinderhughes, *Understanding Race, Ethnicity, and Power*.

51. Bronfenbrenner, *The Ecology of Human Development*.

52. For discussions of transference in groups, see Durkin, *The Group in Depth*, pp. 139–70 and 183–97; Levine, *Group Psychotherapy*, pp. 160–64; Scheidlinger, *Psychoanalysis and Group Behavior*, pp. 80–85; Yalom, *Theory and Practice of Group Psychotherapy*, pp. 199–212.

53. Jerome Cohen, "Social Work and the Culture of Poverty," p. 5.

54. Merton, *Social Theory and Social Structure*," pp. 233–34.

55. Chau, "Social Work Practice: Toward a Cross-Cultural Practice Model."

56. Jack Rothman, "Analyzing Issues in Race." For a similar statement see Solomon, *Black Empowerment*.

57. Sotomayor, "Language, Culture, and Ethnicity in the Developing Self Concept."

58. Locklear, "American Indian Myths."

59. June Brown, "Social Services and Third World Communities," p. 27.

60. Mendes, "Some Religious Values Held by Blacks, Chicanos, and Japanese Americans."

Four | Values, Ethics, and Malpractice

1. Rokeach, *The Nature of Human Values*, p. 4.

2. Montagu, *The Cultured Man*, p. 13.

3. Silberman, "A New Strain for Social Work," p. 9.

4. Younghusband, *Social Work and Social Change*, p. 106.

5. Falck, "Aspects of Membership."

6. For fuller discussion of this issue, see Kitano and Sue, "The Model Minorities"; Kluckhohn, "Family Diagnosis"; Mendes, "Religious Values of Blacks, Chicanos, and Japanese Americans."

7. Konopka, "All Lives Are Connected to Other Lives," p. 109.

8. Pray, *Social Work in a Revolutionary Age*, p. 278.

9. Charles S. Levy, *Social Work Ethics*, p. 14.

10. NASW, *Code of Ethics*, p. 2.

11. Charles S. Levy, *Social Work Ethics*, p. 15.

12. NASW, *Code of Ethics*, p. 3.

13. Ibid. For an excellent discussion, see Phi Kappa Phi, *Biomedical Ethics and the Bill of Rights*.

14. Barker, "Just Whose Code of Ethics Should the Independent Social Worker Follow?"

15. Jack Rothman, "Client Self Determination: Untangling the Knot."

16. Kassel and Kane, "Self Determination Dissected."

17. Weil and Sanchez, "The Impact of the Tarasoff Decision on Clinical Social Work Practice."

18. Abramson, "Enhancing Patient Participation," p. 154.

19. Reamer, *Ethical Decisions*, pp. 100–110.

20. NASW Commission on Education, *The School Social Worker and Confidentiality*, p. 2.

21. Charles S. Levy, *Social Work Ethics*, p. 142.

22. Sample, "Message to the University Community," p. 6.

23. Kurzman, "The Ethical Base for Social Work in the Workplace."

24. Sample, "Message to the University Community," p. 7.

25. Harold Lewis, *The Intellectual Base of Social Work Practice*, p. 97.

26. Ryan, "Cultural Factors in Casework with Chinese Americans," p. 338; Humphreys, "Valedictory Address," p. 3.

27. Linzer, "Resolving Ethical Dilemmas in Jewish Communal Services," p. 105.

28. Conrad, "Ethical Considerations in the Psychosocial Process."

29. Reamer, *Ethical Dilemmas*, pp. 36–37.

30. Kurland and Salmon, "Self-Determination: Its Use and Misuse," p. 107.

31. Dworkin, "To Certify or Not to Certify."

32. Reamer, *Ethical Dilemmas*, pp. 67–76.

33. Parry, "Informed Consent: For Whose Benefit?" p. 537.

34. Adler, "Truth Telling to the Terminally Ill," p. 160.

35. Hafferty, "Whose Files are They Anyway?"

36. *Seattle Post Intelligencer*, "A Bad Ruling for Child Services."

37. Reamer, *Ethical Dilemmas*, pp. 13–20.

38. Dewey, *Democracy and Education*; Lindeman, *The Roots of Democratic Culture*.

39. Reamer, *Ethical Dilemmas*, p. 227.

40. Linzer, "Resolving Ethical Dilemmas."

41. Holland and Kilpatrick, "Ethical Issues in Social Work," p. 141–42.

42. B. E. Bernstein, "Malpractice"; Besharov and Besharov, "Teaching About Liability"; Watkins and Watkins, "Negligent Endangerment."

43. Cohen and Marino, *Legal Guidebook in Mental Health*.

44. Besharov and Besharov, "Teaching About Liability."

45. Black, *Black's Law Dictionary*, p. 71.

46. NASW, *Code of Ethics*, and NASW, *Standards for the Practice of Clinical Social Work*.

47. Applebaum, *Informed Consent: Legal Theory and Clinical Practice*; Reamer, "Informed Consent in Social Work."

48. Kagle, "Teaching Social Work Students About Privileged Communication"; Knapp and Van de Creek, "Privileged Communication in the Health Professions"; Kermani and Weiss, "AIDS and Confidentiality: Legal Concept and Its Application"; Gail L. Perlman, "Mastering the Law of Privileged Communication"; Reynolds, "Threats to Confidentiality."

49. Jones and Alcabes, "Clients Don't Sue: The Invulnerable Social Worker."

50. Besharov, "The Vulnerable Social Worker: Liability for Serving Children and Families."

51. Sharfstein, Towery, and Milowe, "Accuracy of Diagnostic Information Submitted to an Insurance Company."

52. Alexander, "Professionalization and Unionization."

53. Kutchins, "The Fiduciary Relationship," p. 107.

54. Landers, "AIDS Deepens Duty-to-Warn Dilemma."

55. Kurzman, "Managing Risk in the Workplace."

56. Saltzman and Proch, *Law and Social Work Practice*.

57. Cohen and Moreno, *Legal Guidebook in Mental Health*.

58. Houston and Northen, "Reducing Risks and Enhancing Practice," p. 21.

Five | Communication

1. For applications of communication theory to social work practice, see William Brown, "Communication Theory and Social Casework"; Davis, "Human Communication Concepts and Constructs"; Nelsen, *Communication Theory and Social Work Practice*; Satir, *Conjoint Family Therapy*; Polansky, *Ego Psychology and Communication*.

2. Northen, *Social Work with Groups.* pp. 22–23

3. Nelsen, *Communication Theory and Social Work Practice*, p. 2.

4. Shaw, *Group Dynamics*, p. 137.

5. Sereno and Mortenson, *Foundations of Communication Theory.* p. 8.

6. Weiner, *The Human Use of Human Beings*, p. 33.

7. Day, *Communication in Social Work*, p. 3.

8. Ruesch and Kees, *Nonverbal Communication*, pp. 190–93.

9. Imre, "The Nature of Knowledge."

10. Polansky, *Ego Psychology and Communication*, p. 187.

11. Deutsch, "The Role of Social Class in Language Development and Cognition," pp. 78–88; Siller, "Socioeconomic Status and Conceptual Thinking," pp. 365–67; Bernstein, "Language and Social Class," p. 27.

12. Lee, "The Helping Professional's Use of Language Describing The Poor."

13. Major references on nonverbal communication include: Argyle, *Bodily Communication*; Burgeon et al., *Nonverbal Communication*; Kadushin, *The Social Work Interview*, pp. 268–99; Malandro and Banker, *Nonverbal Communication*; Richmond, McCroskey, and Payne, *Nonverbal Behavior in Interpersonal Relations*.

14. Borenzweig, "Touching in Clinical Social Work."

15. Spiegel, "The Ecological Model," pp. 134–56.

16. Hall, *The Hidden Dimension*; Hartford, *Groups in Social Work*, pp. 181–90.

17. Hall, *The Hidden Dimension*, p. 70.

18. Germain, *Human Behavior in The Social Environment*, p. 32.

19. Nelsen, "Communication Theory and Social Work Treatment," p. 225.

20. Northen, *Social Work with Groups*, pp. 78–84.

21. For references on affective ties and interpersonal relations, see Durkin, *The Group in Depth*; Northen, *Social Work with Groups*, pp. 25–28; Scheidlinger, *Psychoanalysis and Group Behavior*, pp. 131–45.

22. Northen, *Social Work with Groups*, p. 22.

23. Ell and Northen, *Families and Health Care*, pp. 148–49.

24. Nakama, "Japanese Americans' Expectations of Counseling."

25. Kadushin, "The Racial Factor in the Interview."

26. Shulman, *The Skills of Helping Individuals, Families, and Groups*, pp. 147–50.

27. In addition to the references cited, the following authors have presented problems in communication: Hepworth and Larsen, *Direct Social Work Practice*, pp. 75–87; Kadushin, *The Social Work Interview*, pp. 20–22; Seabury, "Communication Problems in Social Work Practice."

28. For a fuller discussion of evaluation of communication, see Riskin and Faunce, "An Evaluative Review of Family Interaction Research"; Luthman with Kirschenbaum, *The Dynamic Family*, pp. 35- 43, 65–80.

29. Northen, *Social Work with Groups*, pp. 216–18.

30. Satir, *Conjoint Family Therapy*.

31. Garvin, "Group Process: Usage and Uses in Social Work Practice."

32. Satir, *Conjoint Family Therapy*, pp. 63–90.

Six | The Professional Relationship

1. Helen Harris Perlman, *Relationship, the Heart of Helping People*, pp. 1, 22.

2. Winnicott, "Casework Techniques in Child Care Services," pp. 135–54.

3. Rogers, "The Necessary and Sufficient Conditions for Therapeutic Personality Change." p. 96.

4. Kadushin, *The Social Work Interview*, pp. 49–53.

5. Shulman, *The Skills of Helping Individuals, Families, and Groups*, pp. 126–27.

6. Konopka, *Social Group Work*, p. 78.

7. Quoted in Katz, *Empathy: Its Nature and Uses*, p. 1.

8. Quoted in Raines, "Empathy in Clinical Social Work," p. 59.

9. Hepworth and Larsen, *Direct Social Work Practice*, pp. 95–99.

10. Polombo, "The Psychology of Self."

11. Cousins, *Head First*.

12. Kolodny, "Retrospective on Reaching Out," pp. 165–66.

13. Truax and Carkhuff, *Toward Effective Counseling and Psychotherapy*, pp. 47–56; Barrett-Lennard, "Dimensions of Therapist Response."

14. Truax and Carkhuff, *Toward Effective Counseling and Psychotherapy*, p. 160.

15. Ripple, Alexander, and Polemis, *Motivation, Capacity, and Opportunity*. pp. 76–77.

16. Sainsbury, *Social Work with Families*.

17. Beck and Jones, *Progress in Family Problems*, p. 8.

18. Mullen, "Casework Communication."

19. Papers of other studies by psychologists are presented by Hepworth and Larsen, *Direct Social Work Practice*, p. 100.

20. Russell, *Clinical Social Work*, p. 53.

21. Robert Dies, "Clinical Implications of Research on Leadership in Short-Term Group Psychotherapy," pp. 32–35.

22. Elliott, "Hospitality as a Professional Virtue."

23. Fischer, *Effective Casework*; Lieberman, Yalom, and Miles, *Encounter Groups*.

24. Larsen and Hepworth, "Skill Development Through Competency Based Education."

25. Truax and Carkhuff, *Toward Effective Counseling and Psychotherapy*, p. 161.

26. Hobbs, "Sources of Gain in Psychotherapy."

27. Buckley, "The Concept of Confiding Ties."

28. Pigors, "Leadership or Domination."

29. Major references on power are Pinderhughes, *Understanding Race, Ethnicity and Power*; Solomon, *Black Empowerment*.

30. Phil Brown, "Black Social Workers in Private Practice."

31. Hammond, "Cross-Cultural Rehabilitation."

32. Cooper, "A Look at the Effect of Racism in Clinical Work"; Kadushin, "The Racial Factor in the Interview."

33. Chestang, "The Issue of Race in Casework Practice."

34. Stiles et al., "Hear It Like It Is," for a discussion of racial barriers in the relationship.

35. Velasquez et al, "A Framework for Establishing Social Work Relationships Across Racial Lines."

36. Ignacio Aguilar, "Initial Contacts with Mexican-American Families."

37. Hammond, "Cross-Cultural Rehabilitation."

38. Nakama, "Japanese Americans' Expectations of Counseling."

39. Solomon, *Black Empowerment*, p. 211.

40. Ho and McDowell, "The Black Worker-White Client Relationship."

41. Donna Franklin, "Differential Clinical Assessments"; Franklin, "Does Client Social Class Affect Clinical Judgments?"; Franklin, "Race, Class, and Adolescent Pregnancy."

42. Maki, "Countertransference with Adolescent Clients of the Same Ethnicity."

43. Kadushin, "The Racial Factor in the Interview."

44. Calnek, "Racial Factors in the Countertransference."

45. Kadushin, "The Racial Factor in the Interview," p. 182.

46. Solomon, *Black Empowerment*, p. 211.

47. Kadushin, *The Social Work Interview*, pp. 323–25.

48. Ibid., pp. 320–23.

49. Gilligan, "Adolescent Development Reconsidered."

50. For discussions of transference and countertransference, see Woods and Hollis, *Casework*, pp. 208–13; Mendes, "Countertransference and Counterculture Clients"; Durkin, *The Group in Depth*, pp. 159–70, 183–97; Levine, *Group Psychotherapy*, pp. 160–64; Scheidlinger, *Psychoanalysis and Group Behavior*, pp. 80–85.

51. Helen Harris Perlman, *Relationship, the Heart of Helping People*, pp. 74–84.

52. Levine, *Group Psychotherapy*, pp. 160–64.

53. This example is in Northen, *Social Work with Groups*, p. 262.

54. Wasserman, "Ego Psychology."

55. Gareffa and Neff, "Management of the Client's Seductive Behavior."

56. Imhof, "Countertransference and the EAP Counselor," p. 64.

57. Buehler, *Values in Psychotherapy*, p. 1.

58. Konopka, *Social Group Work*, p. 94.

59. Solomon, *Black Empowerment*, p. 236.

60. Wellisch, "On Stabilizing Families with an Unstable Illness."

61. Sprung, "Transferential Issues in Working with Older Adults"; Waller-stein, "Transference and Countertransference in Clinical Intervention with Divorcing Families."

Seven | Intervention

1. For a similar categorization, see Carlton, *Clinical Social Work in Health Settings*, pp. 118–23; Reid, *The Task-Centered System*.
2. Carol Meyer, "The Search for Coherence," pp. 5–34.
3. Selby, "Supportive Treatment"; Selby, "Support Revisited."
4. Hepworth and Larsen, *Direct Social Work Practice*, p. 120.
5. Hollis, *Casework*, p. 93.
6. Yalom, *The Theory and Practice of Group Psychotherapy*, p. 72.
7. Reid and Epstein, *Task-Centered Casework*, p. 151.
8. Hollis and Woods, *Casework*, p. 243.
9. Kadushin, *The Social Work Interview*, pp. 180–201.
10. Solomon, *Black Empowerment*.
11. Kane, "Editorial Thoughts on Parent Education," p. 12.
12. Reid and Epstein, *Task-Centered Casework*, p. 177.
13. Mayer and Timms, *The Client Speaks*.
14. Reid and Shapiro, "Client Reactions to Advice."
15. Sainsbury, *Social Work with Families*.
16. Davis, "Advice Giving in Parent Counseling."
17. Lieberman, Yalom, and Miles, *Encounter Groups*, pp. 371- 73.
18. Videka-Sherman, *Harriet M. Bartlett Practice Effectiveness Project: Final Report*, p. 327.
19. A similar formulation is given by Kadushin, *The Social Work Interview*, pp. 173–74.
20. Overton and Tinker, *Casework Notebook*, p. 65.
21. Hallowitz et al., "The Assertive Counseling Component of Therapy."
22. Nadel, "Interviewing Style and Foster Parents' Verbal Accessibility."
23. Hepworth and Larsen, *Direct Social Work Practice*, pp. 406–08.
24. Solomon, *Black Empowerment*, p. 311.
25. Schon, *The Reflective Practitioner*, p. 20.
26. Saari, "Clinical Social Work Treatment: How Does It Work?" p. 56.
27. Ibid.; Woods and Hollis, *Casework*, incorporate this concept in their categories of reflective discussion of pattern dynamics and developmental factors, pp. 135–46, 288–89.
28. Heinz, "A Comparison of Patients' Reports on Psychotherapeutic Experience with Psychoanalytic, Nondirective, and Adlerian Therapies."
29. Hutten, "Short-term Contracts IV Techniques," p. 17.
30. Segal, "Focused Problem Solving," p. 216.
31. Middleman and Wood, *Skills in Direct Practice in Social Work*, p. 82.
32. Robert A. Brown, "Feedback in Family Interviewing."
33. Konopka, *Social Group Work*, p. 128.

34. Robert R. Dies, "Clinical Implications of Research on Leadership in Short-Term Group Psychotherapy," p. 50.

35. Lieberman, Yalom, and Miles, *Encounter Groups*.

36. Gitterman and Shulman, *Mutual Aid Groups in the Life Cycle*; Shulman, *The Skills of Helping Individuals, Families, and Groups*; Tracy and Whittaker, "The Evidence Base for Social Support Interventions in Child and Family Practice."

37. Lieberman, Yalom, and Miles, *Encounter Groups*.

Eight | Assessment

1. Addams, *Twenty Years at Hull House*, p. 123.

2. Mary E. Richmond, *Social Diagnosis*, p. 357.

3. Lee, "Letter to H. Northen."

4. Vigilante and Mailick, "Needs-Resource Evaluation in the Assessment Process," p. 35.

5. Carol Meyer, *Assessment in Social Work Practice*, p. 17.

6. Reid, *The Task-Centered System*, pp. 35–38; Reid and Shyne, *Brief and Extended Casework*; Reid and Epstein, *Task-Centered Practice*.

7. In their classifications of problems, the following authors include a similar category: Ripple, Alexander, and Polemis, *Motivation, Capacity, and Opportunity*, pp. 22–34; Helen Harris Perlman, *Persona*, pp. 193–227; Reid and Epstein, *Task-Centered Casework*, pp. 41–49.

8. Orcutt, "Family Treatment of Poverty Level Families," p. 92.

9. A classification of role problems has been developed by Karls and Wandrei, "PIE: A New Language for Social Work."

10. Jenkins and Norman, *Filial Deprivation in Foster Care*.

11. In Reid, *The Task-Centered System*, this category is used.

12. Gilligan, "Adolescent Development Reconsidered," p. 5; Konopka, *The Adolescent Girl in Conflict*; Whittaker, "Causes of Childhood Disorders."

13. This is a category in Reid, *The Task-Centered System*.

14. This category has been used by Mullen, "Casework Treatment Procedures as a Function of Client Diagnostic Variables."

15. Ell and Northen, *Families and Health Care*, pp. 25–54.

16. Devore and Schlesinger, *Ethnic-Sensitive Social Work Practice*; Pinderhughes, *Understanding Race, Ethnicity, and Power*.

17. Chau, "A Model of Practice with Special Reference to Ethnic Minority Populations."

18. For good discussions of this subject, see Rothman, "Analyzing Issues in Race and Ethnic Relations"; Solomon, *Black Empowerment*; Locklear, "American Indian Myths"; Fong, "Assimilation and Changing Social Roles of Chinese Americans."

19. This is a category in Reid, *Task-Centered Practice*.

20. For classifications of problems in groups, see Garvin and Glasser, "The Bases of Social Treatment"; Bradford, Stock, and Horowitz, "How to Diagnose Group Problems"; Pincus and Minahan, *Social Work Practice*, pp. 230–38.

21. APA, *Diagnostic and Statistical Manual of Mental Disorders, III-R*.

22. APA Task Force on DSM-IV, *DSM-IV Options Book*.

23. For discussion of this issue, see Carol Meyer, *Assessment in Social Work Practice*, pp. 94–100; Northen, "Assessment in Direct Practice"; Woods and Hollis, *Casework*, pp. 260–68.

24. Fishman "Therapy for Children," p. 54.

25. Turner, *Adult Psychopathology*; Janet Williams, "A Comprehensive Approach to Diagnosis"; Woods and Hollis, *Casework*, pp. 263–64.

26. Hobbs, "The Future of Children"; Schur, "Labeling Deviant Behavior"; Toch, "The Care and Feeding of Typologies and Labels."

27. Reid, *The Task-Centered System*.

28. Harold Lewis, *The Intellectual Base of Social Work Practice*, p. 197.

29. Kutchins and Kirk, "DSM-III and Social Work Malpractice."

30. Carol Meyer, *Social Work Practice: The Changing Landscape*; Middleman and Goldberg, *Social Service Delivery*.

31. Tufts, *Group Work with Young School Girls*.

32. Schwartz, "Private Troubles and Public Issues."

33. Goldstein, "Questions and Answers"; Mary E. Richmond, *Social Diagnosis*.

34. Couch, *Joint and Family Interviews in the Treatment of Marital Problems*, p. 53–54.

35. Churchill, "Social Group Work"; Sundel, Radin, and Churchill, "Diagnosis in Group Work."

36. King, "Diagnostic Activity Group for Latency Age Children."

37. Siporin, *Introduction to Social Work Practice*.

38. For examples of measuring instruments, see Ell and Northen, *Families and Health Care*, pp. 111–18; Hudson, *The Clinical Measurement Package*; Levitt and Reid, "Rapid Assessment Instruments in Social Work Practice"; Toseland and Rivas, *An Introduction to Group Work Practice*.

39. Hartford, *Groups in Social Work*, p. 196.

40. Carol Meyer, *Assessment in Social Work Practice*.

41. Hartman and Laird, *Family-Centered Social Work Practice*, pp. 215–30.

42. Carol Meyer, *Assessment in Social Work Practice*, pp. 118–20.

43. Hamilton, *Theory and Practice of Social Casework*, p. 214.

44. Detailed outlines have been offered by Compton and Galaway, *Social Work Processes*; Goldstein, *Social Work Practice: A Unitary Approach*; Pincus and Minahan, *Social Work Practice: Model and Method*; Siporin, *Introduction to Social Work Practice*.

45. Helen Harris Perlman, *Social Casework*, p. 164; Somers, "Problem-Solving in Small Groups," p. 365.

46. Harold Lewis, "Reasoning in Practice."

47. Hartmann, *Ego Psychology and the Problem of Adaptation*, p. 24.

48. Hollis, *Casework*, pp. 260–68.

49. Rutter, *Helping Troubled Children*, p. 41.

50. Martinez, "Community Mental Health and the Chicano Movement."

51. Pinderhughes, *Understanding Race, Ethnicity, and Power*; Solomon, *Black Empowerment.*

52. Goldberg, "The Normal Family."

53. The studies to which Goldberg refers are those of Young and Wilmott, *Family and Kinship Ties in East London*; Shaw, "Impressions of Life in a London Suburb"; Bott, *Family and Social Networks.*

54. Pollak, "Social Determinants of Family Behavior."

55. Goldberg, "The Normal Family," p. 26.

56. Konopka, *Social Group Work*, p. 94.

57. Startz and Cohen, "The Impact of Social Change on the Practitioner."

58. Harold Lewis, "Reasoning in Practice," pp. 9–10.

59. Solomon, *Black Empowerment*, p. 301.

Nine | Issues in Planning

1. Rosen, Proctor, and Levine, "Planning and Direct Practice."

2. Hancock et al., "Direct Practice with Individuals and Families."

3. Carol Meyer, *Social Work Practice*, p. 167.

4. Kurland, "Planning: The Neglected Component of Group Development," p. 173.

5. Main, "Selected Aspects of the Beginning Phase of Social Group Work."

6. Hancock et al., "Direct Practice with Individuals and Famillies."

7. See, for example, Carol Meyer, *Social Work Practice: The Changing Landscape*; June Brown et al., *Child/Family/Neighborhood.*

8. Boyd-Franklin, *Black Families in Therapy*. Many of the articles in Gitterman, ed., *Handbook of Practice with Vulnerable Populations*, use multisystems approaches to treatment of serious problems.

9. Pincus and Minihan, *Social Work Practice*, p. 58.

10. Toseland and Siporin, "When to Recommend Group Treatment,." p. 197.

11. Baruch Levine, *Group Psychotherapy*, pp. 10–12.

12. Beck, "Research Findings on the Outcomes of Marital Counseling," p. 159.

13. Pincus and Minahan, *Social Work Practice*, p. 201.

14. Beck, "Research Findings on the Outcomes of Marital Counseling."

15. Gurman, "The Effects and Effectiveness of Marital Therapy."

16. Macon, "A Comparative Study of Two Approaches to the Treatment of Marital Dysfunction."

17. Luthman and Kirschenbaum, *The Dynamic Family*, p. 13.

18. Group for the Advancement of Psychiatry, *The Field of Family Therapy.*

19. Phil Brown, "The Wisdom of Family Therapists."

20. Goldenberg and Goldenberg, *Family Therapy*, p. 151.

21. Helen Harris Perlman, "Identity Problems, Role, and Casework Treatment."

22. Ell and Northen, *Families and Health Care.*

23. Yalom, *The Theory and Practice of Group Psychotherapy.*

24. Solomon, *Black Empowerment*, pp. 352–54.

25. Abels and Abels, "Social Group Work's Contextual Purposes"; Goldstein, *Social Learning and Change*; Hartford, "Working Papers: Toward a Frame of Reference for Social Group Work." For numerous other authors who subscribe to this view, see Northen "Selection of Groups as a Preferred Modality of Practice."

26. Goldstein, *Social Learning and Change*, p. 185.

27. Caple, "Preventive Social Work Practice."

28. McBroom, "Socialization through Small Groups."

29. Germain and Gitterman, *The Life Model of Social Work Practice*.

30. Parad, Selby, and Quinlan, "Crisis Intervention in Families and Groups."

31. Feldman, "Work and Career Health Histories"; Fisher, "The Hospitalized Mentally Ill Patient"; Johnson and Hart, "Neurological Disorders"; Scheidlinger, *Focus on Group Psychotherapy*.

32. Russell, *Clinical Social Work*, p. 113.

33. Sherman, "The Choice of Group Therapy for Casework Clients," p. 179.

34. Mervis, "Commentary"; Northen, "Social Work with Groups in Health Settings."

35. Lane, "Psychiatric Patients Learn a New Way of Life"; O'Brien et al, "Groups vs. Individual Psychotherapy with Schizophrenics"; Smolar, "Schizophrenic Disorders"; Woods, "Personality Disorders."

36. APA, *Diagnostic and Statistical Manual of Mental Disorders—III-R*.

37. Turner, *Adult Psychopathology*.

38. See articles in Gitterman, ed., *Handbook of Social Work Practice*.

39. Getzel, "AIDS."

40. June H. Brown and Marie Weil, eds., *Family Practice*.

41. Gitterman, ed., *Handbook of Social Work Practice with Vulnerable Populations*.

42. Kadushin, *The Social Work Interview*, pp. 254–60.

43. Solomon, *Black Empowerment*, pp. 299–315.

44. June H. Brown, "Child Welfare in Transition." pp. 5–22.

45. Tolson, "Conclusions Toward a Metamodel for Eclectic Family Practice."

46. Ell and Northen, *Families and Health Care*.

47. Wells and Dezen, "The Results of Family Treatment Revisited," p. 252.

48. Northen, *Social Work with Groups*, pp. 122–27.

49. Redl, "The Art of Group Composition," p. 79.

50. Levine, *Group Psychotherapy*, pp. 13–14.

51. Garvin and Reed, "Gender Issues in Social Work," p. 17.

52. Daley and Koppenaal, "The Treatment of Women."

53. Carlach and Martin, "Sex Composition and Intensive Group Experience."

54. Boer and Lantz, "Adolescent Group Therapy Membership Selection," p. 179.

55. One entire issue of a journal deals with the issue of coleadership, *Social Work with Groups* (Winter 1980), vol. 3, no. 4. Each author presents many references on

the subject. For an excellent analysis of the positive and negative aspects of coleadership, see Galinsky and Schopler, "Structuring Co-leadership," pp. 51–63.

56. Reed, "Women Leaders in Small Groups."

57. Middleman, "Co-Leadership and Solo Leadership."

58. Rice, Fey, and Kepecs, "Therapist Experience and Style."

59. Rothman, "Studies of Patterns of Leadership."

60. Group for the Advancement of Psychiatry, *The Field of Family Therapy.*

61. Gurman, "Effects and Effectiveness of Marital Therapy."

62. Dies, "Clinical Implications of Research on Leadership," p. 59.

63. Friedman, "Co-Therapy: A Behavioral and Attitudinal Survey."

64. Gitterman, "Delivering a New Group Service, " p. 68.

65. Leichter and Schulman, "The Family Interview as an Integrative Device."

66. Marshall, "Use of Aides in Activity Group Treatment."

67. Epstein, "Brief Group Therapy"; Orlinsky and Howard, "Process and Outcome in Psychotherapy"; Reid, *The Task-Centered System*; Reid and Epstein, *Task-Centered Practice*; Reid and Shyne, *Brief and Extended Casework.*

68. Reid and Shyne, *Brief and Extended Casework*, p. 151.

69. Kanter, "Reevaluation of Task-Centered Social Work Practice," p. 242.

70. Devore and Schlesinger, *Ethnic-Sensitive Social Work Practice.*

71. William Meyer, "In Defense of Long-Term Treatment," p. 577.

Ten | The Initial Phase

1. Briar and Miller, *Problems and Issues in Social Casework*, p. 110; Compton and Galaway, *Social Work Processes*; Pincus and Minahan, *Social Work Practice.*

2. Webb and Riley, "Effectiveness of Casework with Young Female Probationers."

3. Overton and Tinker, *Casework Notebook.*

4. Briar and Miller, *Problems and Issues in Social Casework*, p. 98; Siporin, *Introduction to Social Work Practice*, ch. 8

5. Levine, "A Short Story on the Long Waiting List"; Beck, "Patterns in Use of Family Agency Services"; Lake and Levinger, "Continuance Beyond Application Interviews at a Child Guidance Clinic."

6. McQuaide, "Working with Southeast Asian Refugees."

7. Kadushin, *The Social Work Interview*, p. 104.

8. Schwartz, "Between Client and System," pp. 186–88; Shulman, *The Skills of Helping*, pp. 56–57.

9. Devore and Schlesinger, *Ethnic-Sensitive Social Work Practice*, pp. 170–72.

10. Kadushin, *The Social Work Interview*, p. 106.

11. Middleman and Wood, *Skills for Direct Practice in Social Work*, pp. 45–58.

12. Whittington, "The New Friendly Visitors."

13. The example is taken from Northen, *Social Work with Groups*, pp. 189–90.

14. Gibbs, "Treatment Relationship with Black Clients."

15. Anderson Franklin, "Therapy with African American Men."

16. Cousins, *Head First*; Siegel, *Love, Medicine, and Miracles.*

17. Ripple, "Factors Associated with Continuance in Casework Service."

18. Fanshel, "A Study of Caseworkers' Perceptions of Their Clients."

19. Zalba, "Discontinuance During Social Service Intake."

20. Boatman, "Caseworkers' Judgments of Clients' Hope."

21. Bounous, "A Study of Client and Worker Perceptions in the Initial Phase of Casework Marital Counseling."

22. Northen, *Social Work with Groups*, p. 197.

23. Cooper, "David, The First Hour in the Assessment and Treatment of an Adolescent."

24. Meadow, "The Preparatory Interview"; Meadow, "The Effects of a Client-Focused Pre-Group Preparation Interview."

25. Yalom, *The Theory and Practice of Group Psychotherapy*, pp. 295–96.

26. This example is taken from Northen, *Social Work with Groups*, pp. 167–70.

27. Freeman, *Techniques of Family Therapy.*

28. Doherty and Baird, "Forming a Therapeutic Contract that Involves the Family."

29. Nelsen, *Family Treatment*, pp. 71–73.

30. Levine, "A Short Story on the Long Waiting List"; Wolkon, "Effecting a Continuum of Care."

31. Hamilton, *Psychotherapy in Child Guidance*, pp. 134–36; Siporin, *Introduction to Social Work Practice.*

32. Levine, *Group Psychotherapy.*

33. For a good discussion, see Overton and Tinker, *Casework Notebook*

34. Siporin, *Introduction to Social Work Practice*, p. 208.

35. Helen Harris Perlman, *Social Casework*, pp. 149–52.

36. Maluccio and Marlow, "The Case for the Contract."

37. Beall, "The Corrupt Contract."

38. Dewey, *Democracy and Education*, p. 110.

39. Oxley, "The Caseworker's Expectations and Client Motivation."

40. Frank, "Discussion of Anna Ornstein's Paper."

41. Freeman, "Phases of Family Treatment."

42. Schmidt, "The Use of Purpose in Casework Practice."

43. Raschella, "An Evaluation of the Effect of Goal Congruence."

44. Levinson, "Use and Misuse of Groups."

45. Nakama, "Japanese Americans Expectations of Counseling."

46. Rosen and Lieberman, "The Experimental Evaluation of Interview Performance of Social Workers."

47. Gentry, "Initial Group Meetings: Member Expectations and Information Distribution Process."

48. Leonard N. Brown, "Social Workers' Verbal Acts and The Development of Mutual Expectations with Beginning Client Groups."

49. Garvin, "Complementarity of Role Expectations in Groups."

50. Clemenger, "Congruence Between Members and Workers on Selected Behaviors of the Role of the Social Group Worker."

51. Rhodes, "Contract Negotiation in the Initial Stage of Casework."

52. Lima, Eisenthal, and Lazare, "Perception of Requests in Psychotherapy: Patient and Therapist."

53. Ripple, Alexander, and Polemis, *Motivation, Capacity, and Opportunity.*

54. Briar, "Family Services, " p. 27.

55. Several similar principles are set forth by Siporin, *Introduction to Social Work Practice*, pp. 98–106.

Eleven | The Core Phase: Problem-Solving

1. Dewey, *How We Think*, p. 6.

2. Helen Harris Perlman, *Social Casework*, p. 91.

3. Moses and Hawkins, *Counseling Lesbian Women and Gay Men*: see also Brooks, *Minority Stress and Lesbian Women.*

4. Moses and Hawkins, *Counseling Lesbian Women and Gay Men.*

5. Buckley, "Society as a Complex Adaptive System," p. 500.

6. Cooley, *Social Process*, p. 59; Coser, *The Functions of Social Conflict*; Deutsch, *Resolution of Conflict*, p. 352.

7. Sanford, *Self and Society*, p. 33.

8. Baxter, "Conflict Management," p. 38.

9. Deutsch, *Resolution of Conflict*, p. 352.

10. See, for example, Ganter, Yeakel, and Polansky, "Retrieval from Limbo"; Lane, "Psychiatric Patients Learn a New Way of Life."

11. Germain and Gitterman, *The Life Model of Social Work Practice*, p. 242.

12. Anstey, "Scapegoating in Groups," pp. 51–63; Powdermaker and Frank, *Group Psychotherapy*, pp. 137, 162–63; Scheidlinger, "On Scapegoating," pp. 131–43; Shulman, "Scapegoats, Group Workers," pp. 37–43; Toker, "The Scapegoat as an Essential Group Phenomenon," pp. 320–32.

13. Mishne, *Clinical Social Work with Adolescents*, p. 348.

14. Hartford, *Groups in Social Work*, pp. 216–18.

15. Northen, *Social Work with Groups*, pp. 240–50.

16. Shulman, *The Skills of Helping*, pp. 268–69.

17. Solomon, *Black Empowerment*, p. 236.

18. Ackerman, *Treating the Troubled Family*, p. 88.

19. Balgopal and Hull, "Keeping Secrets," pp. 334–36.

20. This example is taken from Northen, *Social Work with Groups*, pp. 275–76.

21. Erikson, "Identity and the Life Cycle," pp. 118–64.

22. Bennis, "Introduction," Part II, pp. 207–11.

23. Bittner, "Therapeutic Mother-Child Groups," p. 23.

24. For use of activity-oriented experiences, including tasks, see Hartman and Laird, *Family-Centered Social Work Practice*, pp. 213–25; Northen, *Social Work with Groups*, pp. 78–97; Reid, *The Task-Centered System.*

25. Ewalt, "A Psychoanalytically Oriented Child Guidance Center."

26. Reid, "Process and Outcome in Treatment of Family Problems."

27. For categories of role problems, see Karls and Wandrei, *PIE: A New Language for Social Work.*

28. Goldstein, *Social Work Practice*, p. 101.

29. Dewey, *How We Think.*

30. Rae-Grant, Gladwin, and Bower, "Mental Health, Social Competence, and the War on Poverty," p. 660.

31. Heap, *Process and Action in Work with Groups*, p. 93.

32. Reid, *The Task-Centered System*; Reid and Epstein, eds., *Task-Centered Practice*; Reid and Epstein, *Task-Centered Casework.*

33. Russell, *Clinical Social Work*, pp. 103–6.

34. Wayne and Feinstein, "Group Work Outreach to Parents by School Social Workers."

35. For Erikson's description of this stage, see Erikson, *Childhood and Society*, pp. 258–61.

36. Minuchin et al., *Families of the Slums.*

37. Ell and Northen, *Families and Health Care*, pp. 67–68. See also Solomon, *Black Empowerment*, on role of resource consultant, pp. 346–47; Woods and Hollis, *Casework*, pp. 154- 67.

38. Among the books giving considerable attention to the influence of environment on psychosocial functioning are: Germain, ed., *Social Work Practice*; Germain, *Human Behavior in the Social Environment*; Germain and Gitterman, *The Life Model of Social Work Practice*; Hepworth and Larsen, *Direct Social Work Practice*; Reynolds, *Social Work and Social Living*; Woods and Hollis, *Casework.*

39. Helen Harris Perlman, *Relationship: The Heart of Helping People.*

40. Grinnell, "Environmental Modification," p. 38.

Twelve | Multidimensional Services

1. For detailed statistics on these problems, see June Brown, "Child Welfare in Transition," pp. 9–13; see also Pinderhughes, *Understanding Race, Ethnicity, and Power*; Solomon, *Black Empowerment*; Wilson, *The Truly Disadvantaged.*

2. Ell and Northen, *Families and Health Care*; Carlton, *Clinical Social Work in Health Settings*, pp. 28–46; Moos, *Coping with Physical Illness.*

3. Drachman and Shen-Ryan, "Immigrants and Refugees" provides an overview of the problems of immigrants and refugees. See also Land, Nishimoto, and Chau, "Interventive and Preventive Services for Vietnamese Refugees."

4. June Brown, "Child Welfare in Transition," pp. 13–20; McGowan and Meezan, "Child Welfare"; Videka-Sherman, "Child Abuse and Neglect."

5. Hanson, "Alcoholism and Other Drug Addictions."

6. Getzel, "AIDS."

7. See, for example, June H. Brown et al., *Child, Family, Neighborhood*; Levy, "A Community-Based Approach to Clinical Services for Children of Substance

Abusers"; Mailick and Jordan, "A Multi-Modal Approach to Collaborative Practice in Health Settings." Gitterman, ed., *Handbook of Social Work Practice*, includes numerous articles that specify the need for multidimensional services.

8. Parad, Selby, and Quinlan, "Crisis Intervention with Families and Groups," pp. 105–6.

9. Golan, "Crisis Intervention," p. 365.

10. Frye, "Brain Injury and Family Education Needs," p. 182.

11. Parad, Selby, and Quinlan, "Crisis Intervention with Families and Groups."

12. Houston and Robey, "Use of Groups in Disasters," p. 2.

13. Solomon, *Black Empowerment*, pp. 346–47.

14. McGowan, "Advocacy," p. 92.

15. McGowan, "The Case Advocacy Function in Child Welfare Practice."

16. National Association of Social Workers, "Ad Hoc Committee on Advocacy Report."

17. This example is taken from Woods and Hollis, *Casework*, p. 168.

18. Gottlieb, "Using Social Support," p. 28.

19. Caplan, *Support Systems in Community Mental Health*, p. 216.

20. Davies, "The Assessment of Environment in Social Work Research."

21. Ripple, Alexander, and Polemis, *Motivation, Capacity, and Opportunity*, pp. 203–20.

22. Tracy and Whittaker, "The Evidence Base for Social Support Intervention."

23. Ell and Northen, *Families and Health Care*, pp. 15–54.

24. Gottlieb, ed., "Using Social Support."

25. de Toqueville, *Democracy in America*, 2:107, 109.

26. Trefethen, "Circles of Strength."

27. Derived from Katz and Bender, *The Strength in Us: Self-Help Groups*; Lieberman, Borman, et al, *Self-Help Groups for Coping with Stress*.

28. Galinsky and Schopler, "Warning: Groups May Be Dangerous"; Schopler and Galinsky, "When Groups Go Wrong."

29. Much of this section is based on Whittaker, Garbarino, and Associates, *Social Support Networks*, pp. 120–29.

30. Golan, *The Perilous Bridge*, p. 3.

31. Maas, *People and Contexts*, p. 3.

32. June H. Brown, "Family Practice: The Model and Its Application," pp. 43–48. This chapter contains a large number of relevant references.

33. Ibid., pp. 64–76. Here, Brown presents a much more detailed study of the family of which Ed was a member.

34. Coulton, "A Study of Person-Environment Fit Among the Chronically Ill," p. 5.

35. Hartmann, *Ego Psychology and The Problem of Adaptation*, p. 35.

36. Ell and Northen, *Families and Health Care*, pp. 191–95.

37. Cochrane et al, "Discharge Planning," p. 3.

38. Simmons, "Planning for Discharge with the Elderly," p. 70.

39. Ell and Northen, *Families and Health Care*, pp. 199–206.

40. Carlton, *Clinical Social Work in Health Settings*, p. 129.

41. Brill, *Teamwork: Working Together in The Human Services*; Kane, "The Interdisciplinary Team as a Small Group."

42. Falck, "Interdisciplinary Education and Implications for Social Work Practice," p. 36.

43. Conway, "The Why and How of Relationships for the Social Worker in a Health Care Setting," pp. 45–46.

44. Dana, "The Collaborative Process," p. 193.

45. Rothman, "A Model of Case Management"; Weil, Karls, and Associates, *Case Management in Human Service Practice*.

46. Florentine and Grusky, "When Case Managers Manage the Seriously Ill."

47. Levy, "A Community-Based Approach to Clinical Services for Children of Substance Abusers," p. 14.

48. Alexander and French, *Psychoanalytic Therapy*.

49. Levy, "A Community-Based Approach."

50. Levy, "A Community-Based Approach," p. 45.

Thirteen | Terminition and Transition

1. The number of articles on termination has been increasing. By 1978 Beit-Hallahmi Lackey located twenty-eight articles—twelve with individuals, ten with groups, four with a combination of individuals and groups, and only two with families. See Beit-Hallahmi Lackey, "Termination: The Crucial Stage of Social Work."

2. Hamilton, *Theory and Practice of Social Casework*, p. 236.

3. Hartford, *Groups in Social Work*, p. 53.

4. Yalom, *The Theory and Practice of Group Psychotherapy*, p. 373.

5. Balgopal and Vassil, *Groups in Social Work*, p. 212.

6. Erikson, *Identity, Youth, and Crisis*, pp. 99–141.

7. Fox, Nelson, and Bolman, "The Termination Process."

8. Bolen, "Easing the Pain of Termination," pp. 519–27.

9. Fox, Nelson, and Bolman, "The Termination Process," p. 55.

10. Schaffer and Pollak, "Listening to the Adolescent Therapy Group."

11. Schiff, "Termination of Therapy," p. 80.

12. Blanchard, "Tommy Nolan," p. 92.

13. Garland, Jones, and Kolodny, "A Model for Stages of Development in Social Group Work," pp. 57–58; Stempler, "A Group Work Approach to Family Group Treatment."

14. Schiff, "Termination of Therapy," p. 81.

15. Bywaters, "Ending Casework Relationships," p. 337.

16. Bowlby, "Separation Anxiety," p. 102.

17. Green, "Terminating the Relationship in Social Casework," p. 11.

18. Bolen, "Easing the Pain of Termination of Adolescents."

19. Fox, Nelson, and Bolman, "The Termination Process," p. 64.

20. Lewis, "Examination of the Final Phase."

21. Lackey, "Termination: The Crucial Stage of Social Work."

22. Kramer, "The Therapist's View of Termination in Open- Ended Psychotherapy."

23. Fortune, "Grief Only? Client and Social Worker Reactions to Termination"; Fortune, Pearling, and Rochelle, "Reactions to Termination."

24. Schwartz, "Between Client and System," p. 192.

25. Moss and Moss, "When a Caseworker Leaves an Agency," p. 437.

26. Woods and Hollis, *Casework*, pp. 451–52.

27. Levinson, "Termination of Psychotherapy: Some Salient Issues," p. 484.

28. Rapoport, "Crisis Intervention as a Mode of Brief Treatment," p. 302. See also Webb, "A Crisis Intervention Perspective on the Termination Process."

29. MacLennan and Felsenfeld, *Group Counseling and Psychotherapy with Adolescents*, pp. 108–9.

30. Scheidlinger and Holden, "Group Therapy of Women with Severe Character Disorders."

31. Hartford, "Group Methods and Generic Practice," p. 70.

32. Lackey, "Termination: The Crucial Stage of Social Work," p. 66.

33. West, "Ending or Beginning: A Discussion of the Theory and Practice of Termination Procedures in Play Therapy."

34. Elbow, "The Memory Book: Facilitating Termination with Children."

35. Fox, Nelson, and Bolman, "The Termination Process," p. 53.

36. Hartford, *Groups in Social Work*, p. 89.

37. Hamilton, "Theory and Practice of Social Casework," p. 81.

38. Siporin, *Introduction to Social Work Practice*, p. 341.

Fourteen | Evaluation

1. Numerous surveys of evaluation research in social work have been made: see Blythe and Briar, "Direct Practice Effectiveness."

2. Kutchins and Kirk, "DSM-III and Social Work Malpractice"; NASW, *NASW Guidelines on the Private Practice of Clinical Social Work*.

3. Kagle, "Recording in Direct Practice"; Kagle, *Social Work Records*.

4. NASW, *NASW Guidelines on the Private Practice of Clinical Social Work*.

5. Videka-Sherman and Reid, "Symposium: Epistomology for Clinical Social Work."

6. Orcutt, *Science and Inquiry in Social Work Practice*, pp. 24–48.

7. Reid, "Research in Social Work."

8. Russell, *Clinical Social Work*, pp. 102–8.

9. Videka-Sherman and Reid, *Advances in Clinical Social Work Research*.

10. Orcutt, *Science and Inquiry*, pp. 112–18. For a recent article, see Tyson, "A New Approach to Relevant Scientific Research for Practitioners."

11. Northen and Roberts, "The Status of Theory," pp. 373–78.

12. Hudson and Thyer, "Research Measures and Indices in Direct Practice."

13. Russell, *Clinical Social Work*, pp. 108–10.

14. Hudson, *The Clinical Measurement Package*; Levitt and Reid, "Rapid Assessment Instruments in Social Work Practicee."

15. Beinecke, "PORK, SOAP, STRAP, AND SAP"; Kiresuk and Sherman, "Goal Attainment Scaling."

16. Maluccio, "Perspectives of Social Worker and Clients on Treatment Outcomes"; Rehr, "The Consumer and Consumerism"; Sainsbury, "Client Studies," and Garber, Brenner, and Litwin, "A Survey of Patient and Family Satisfaction."

17. Orcutt, *Science and Inquiry*, pp. 153–174.

18. Russell, *Clinical Social Work*, pp. 81–93.

19. Curti, *Probing Our Past*, p. 170.

Bibliography |

Abels, Sonia Leib and Paul Abels. "Social Group Work's Contextual Purposes." In Sonia Leib Abels and Paul Abels, eds., *Social Work with Groups: Proceedings 1979 Symposium*, Louisville, Ky., Committee for the Advancement of Social Work with Groups, 1981.

Abramson, Julie S. "Enhancing Patient Participation: Clinical Strategies in the Discharge Process. *Social Work in Health Care* (1990), 14(4):153–72.

Ackerman, Nathan. *Treating the Troubled Family*. New York: Basic Books, 1966.

Addams, Jane, *Twenty Years at Hull House*. New York: Macmillan, 1910.

Adler, Susan. "Truth Telling to the Terminally Ill: Neglected Role of the Social Worker." *Social Work* (March 1989), 34(2):158–60.

Aguilar, Ignacio. "Initial Contacts with Mexican-American Families." *Social Work* (May 1972), 17(3):66–70.

Aguilera, Donna C. *Crisis Intervention*. 6th ed. St. Louis, Mo.: Mosby, 1990.

Akabas, Sheila H. and Paul A. Kurzman, eds. *Work, Workers, and Work Organizations*. Englewood Cliffs, N.J.: Prentice-Hall, 1982.

Alexander, Franz and Thomas French. *Psychoanalytic Therapy: Principles*. New York: Ronald Press, 1946.

Alexander, Leslie B. "Professionalization and Unionization: Comparable After All." *Social Work* (November 1980), 25(6):476–82.

Allen Meares, Paula A., Robert O. Washington, and Betty L. Welsh. *Social Work Services in Schools*. Englewood Cliffs, N.J.: Prentice-Hall, 1985.

American Association of University Women: Educational Foundation. *How Schools Shortchange Girls*. Washington, D.C.: AAUW, 1992.

APA (American Psychiatric Association). *Diagnostic and Statistical Manual of Mental Disorders, III-R*. Washington, D.C.: APA, 1987.

APA. Task Force on DSM-IV. *DSM-IV Options Book: Work in Progress*. Washington, D.C.: APA, 1991.

APA. *DSM-IV: Diagnostic and Statistical Manual of Mental Disorders.* 4th ed. Washington, D.C.: American Psychiatric Press, 1994.

Anderson, Joseph D. "Group Work with Families: A Multicultural Perspective." In Kenneth L. Chau, ed., *Ethnicity and Biculturalism: Emerging Perspectives of Social Work.* New York: Haworth Press, 1991.

Anstey, Mark. "Scapegoating in Groups: Some Theoretical Perspectives and a Case Record of Intervention." *Social Work with Groups* (Fall 1982), 5(3):51–62.

Applebaum, P. S. et al. *Informed Consent: Legal Theory and Clinical Practice.* New York: Oxford University Press, 1987.

Arches, Joan. "Social Structure, Burnout, and Job Satisfaction." *Social Work* (May 1991), 36(3):202–6.

Argyle, Michael. *Bodily Communication.* 2d ed. London: Routledge and Kegan Paul, 1988.

Auerswald, Edgar H. "Interdisciplinary versus Ecological Approach." *Family Process* (September 1968), 9(3):202–15.

Baker, Ron. "Toward Generic Social Work Practice—a Review and Some Innovations." *British Journal of Social Work* (Summer 1975), 5(2):193–215.

Balgopal, Pallassana R. and R. F. Hull. "Keeping Secrets: Group Resistance for Patients and Therapists." *Psychotherapy: Theory, Research, and Practice* (Winter 1973), 10(4):334–36.

Balgopal, Pallassana R. and Thomas V. Vassil. *Groups in Social Work: An Ecological Perspective.* New York: Macmillan, 1983.

Barker, Robert L. "Just Whose Code of Ethics Should the Independent Practitioner Follow?" *Journal of Independent Social Work* (Summer 1988), 2(4):21–28.

Barrett-Leonard, G. T. "Dimensions of Therapist Response as Causal Factors in Therapeutic Change." *Psychological Monographs* (1962), 73(3):entire issue.

Bartlett, Harriet M. *Analyzing Social Work Practice by Fields.* New York: NASW, 1961.

Bartlett, Harriet M. *The Common Base of Social Work Practice.* New York: NASW, 1970.

Bartlett, Harriet M. "Toward Clarification and Improvement of Social Work Practice: The Working Definition." *Social Work* (April 1958), 3(2):3–9.

Baxter, Leslie A. "Conflict Management: An Episodic Approach." *Small Group Behavior* (February 1982), 13(1):23–42.

Beall, Lynette. "The Corrupt Contract: Problems in Conjoint Therapy with Parents and Children." *American Journal of Orthopsychiatry* (January 1972), 42(1):77–81.

Beck, Dorothy Fahs. *Patterns in Use of Family Agency Services.* New York: Family Service Association of America, 1962.

Beck, Dorothy Fahs. "Research Findings on the Outcomes of Marital Counseling." *Social Casework* (March 1975), 56(3):159–81.

Beck, Dorothy Fahs and Mary Ann Jones. *Progress in Family Problems.* New York: Family Service Association of America, 1973.

Beinecke, Richard H. "PORK, SOAP, STRAP, and SAP," *Social Casework* (November 1984), 65(9):554–58.

Bernstein, Basil B. "Language and Social Class." *British Journal of Sociology* (1960), 11:23–30.

Bernstein, B. E. "Malpractice: Future Shock of the 1980s." *Social Work* (May/June 1981), 62(3):175–81.

Bernstein, Saul, ed. *Explorations in Group Work*. Boston: Milford House, 1973.

Berry, Margaret E. "Confrontation at the National Conference on Social Welfare." *Social Service Review* (December 1989), 63(4):639–56.

Besharov, Douglas J. and Susan H. Besharov. "Teaching About Liability" *Social Work* (November/December 1987), 32(4):517–23.

Besharov, Douglas J. and Susan H. Besharov. *The Vulnerable Social Worker: Liability for Serving Children and Families*. Washington, D.C.: NASW. 1985.

Bion, Wilfred F. *Experiences in Groups and Other Papers*. London: Tavistock, 1961.

Bittner, Ruth. "Therapeutic Mother-Child Groups: A Developmental Approach." *Social Casework* (March 1984), 65(3):154–61.

Black, H. D. *Black's Law Dictionary*. Rev. ed., St. Paul: West Publishing, 1990.

Blanchard, Phyllis. "Tommy Dolan." In Helen Witmer, ed., *Psychiatric Interviews with Children*, pp. 59–92. New York: Commonwealth Fund, 1946.

Blythe, Betty J. *Measurement in Direct Social Work Practice*. Newbury Park, Calif.: Sage, 1989.

Blythe, Betty J. and Scott Briar. "Direct Practice Effectiveness." In National Association of Social Workers, *Encyclopedia of Social Work*, pp. 399–408. 18th ed.; Washington, D.C.: NASW, 1987.

Board of Behavioral Science Examiners. *Laws Relating to Registered Social Workers, Licensed Clinical Social Workers, Marriage, Family, and Child Counselors and Educational Psychologists*. Sacramento, Calif.: Department of Consumer Affairs, 1977, 5–7.

Boatman, Frances L. "Caseworkers' Judgments of Clients' Hope: Some Correlates Among Client-Situation Characteristics and Among Workers' Communication Patterns." D.S.W. dissertation, Columbia University, 1975.

Boehm, Werner W. "The Nature of Social Work." *Social Work* (April 1958), 3(2):10–18.

Boer, Annette K. and James E. Lantz. "Adolescent Group Therapy Membership Selection." *Clinical Social Work Journal* (Fall 1974), 2(3):172–81.

Bolen, Jane K. "Easing the Pain of Termination for Adolescents." *Social Casework* (November 1972), 53(9):519–27.

Borenzweig, Herman. "Touching in Clinical Social Work." *Social Casework* (April 1983), 64(4):238–42

Bott, Elizabeth. *Family and Social Networks: Roles, Norms, and Extended Relationships in Ordinary Urban Families*. 2d ed. New York: Free Press, 1971.

Bounous, Ronald C. "A Study of Client and Worker Perceptions in the Initial Phase of Casework Marital Counseling." Ph.D. dissertation, University of Minnesota, 1965.

Bowlby, John. "Separation Anxiety." *International Journal of Psychoanalysis* (1960), 41:89–113.

Boyd-Franklin, Nancy. *Black Families in Therapy: A Multisystems Approach*, New York: Guilford Press, 1989.

Bracht, Neal F. *Social Work in Health Care: A Guide to Professional Practice*. New York: Haworth Press, 1978.

Bradford, Leland, Dorothy Stock, and Murray Horowitz. "How to Diagnose Group Problems." In Leland Bradford, ed., *Group Development*, pp. 37–50. Washington, D.C., National Training Laboratory, National Education Association, 1962.

Briar, Scott. "Family Services." In Henry S. Maas, ed., *Five Fields of Social Service: Reviews of Research*. pp 9–50. Washington, D.C.: NASW, 1966.

Brill, Naomi. *Team Work: Working Together in the Human Services*. Philadelphia: Lippincott, 1976.

Bronfenbrenner, Urie. *The Ecology of Human Development: Experiments by Nature and Design*. Cambridge, Mass: Harvard University Press, 1979.

Brooks, Virginia R. *Minority Stress and Lesbian Women*, Lexington, Mass.: Lexington Books, 1986.

Brown, June H. "Child Welfare in Transition," pp. 3–22, and "Family Practice: The Model and Its Application," pp. 43–48. In June H. Brown and Marie Weil, eds., *Family Practice: A Curriculum Plan for Social Services*. Washington, D.C.: Child Welfare League of America, 1992.

Brown, June H. "Social Services and Third World Communities." *Social Work Papers* (1974), 12:23–26.

Brown, June H. et al. *Child/Family/Neighborhood: A Master Plan for Social Service Delivery*. New York: Child Welfare League of America, 1982.

Brown, June H. and Marie Weil, eds. *Family Practice: A Curriculum Plan for Social Services*. Washington, D.C.: Child Welfare League of America, 1992.

Brown, Leonard N. "Social Workers' Verbal Acts and the Development of Mutual Expectations with Beginning Client Groups." D.S.W. dissertation, Columbia University, 1971.

Brown, Phil. "Black Social Workers in Private Practice: Challenges and Dilemmas." *Journal of Independent Social Work* (1990), 5(1):53–67.

Brown, Phil. "The Wisdom of Family Therapists." *Clinical Social Work Journal* (Fall 1990), 18(3):293–300.

Brown, Robert A. "Feedback in Family Interviewing." *Social Work* (September 1973), 18(5):52–59.

Brown, William. "Communication Theory and Social Casework." In Herbert S. Strean, ed., *Social Casework: Theories in Action*, pp. 246–66. Metuchen, N.J.:Scarecrow Press, 1971.

Buckley, Miranda. "The Concept of Confiding Ties: Implications for Social Work Research and Practice." *Journal of Social Work Practice*. (November 1986), 2(3):60–76.

Buckley, Walter. *Sociology and Modern Systems Theory*. Englewood Cliffs, N.J.: Prentice-Hall, 1967.

Buckley, Walter. "Society as a Complex Adaptive System." In Walter Buckley, ed., *Modern Systems Research for the Behavioral Scientist*. Chicago: Aldine, 1968.

Buehler, Charlotte. *Values in Psychotherapy*. New York: Free Press, 1962.

Burgeon, Judy et al. *Nonverbal Communication: The Unspoken Dialogue*. New York: Harper and Row, 1988.

Bywaters, Paul. "Ending Casework Relationships (2)." *Social Work Today* (August 1975), 6(10):301–4.

Calnek, Maynard. "Racial Factors in the Countertransference: The Black Therapist and the Black Client." *American Journal of Orthopsychiatry* (January 1970), 40(1):39–46.

Caplan, Gerald. "Recent Developments in Crisis Intervention and the Promotion of Support Services." *Journal of Primary Prevention* (Fall 1989), 10(1):3–26.

Caple, Frances. "Preventive Social Work Practice: A Generic Model for Direct Service on Behalf of Children." Ph.D. dissertation, University of Southern California, 1982.

Caplow, Theodore. *Two Against One: Coalitions in Triads*. Englewood Cliffs, N.J.: Prentice Hall, 1968.

Carlach, Charlene J. and Patricia Yancey Martin. "Sex Composition and Intensive Group Experience." *Social Work* (January 1977), 22(1):27–32.

Carlton, Thomas Owen. *Clinical Social Work in Health Settings: A Guide to Professional Practice with Exemplars*. New York: Springer, 1984.

Caroff, Phyllis and Mary L. Gottesfeld, eds. *Psychosocial Studies*, New York: Gardner Press, 1987.

Chau, Kenneth L. "A Model of Practice with Special Reference to Ethnic Minority Populations." In Marie Weil, Kenneth L. Chau, and Dannia Sutherland, eds., *Theory and Practice in Social Group Work: Creative Connections*. Binghamton, N.Y,: Haworth Press, 1992.

Chau, Kenneth L. "Social Work Practice: Towards a Cross-Cultural Practice Model." *The Journal of Applied Social Sciences*. (Spring/Summer 1990), 14(2):249–76.

Chess, Wayne A. and Julia M. Norlin. *Human Behavior and the Social Environment*. Boston: Allyn and Bacon, 1988.

Chestang, Leon W. "The Issue of Race in Casework Practice." In *Social Work Practice, 1972*, pp. 114–26, New York: Columbia University Press, 1972.

Chin, Robert. "The Utility of Systems Models and Developmental Models for Practitioners." In Warren G. Bennis, Kenneth D. Benne, and Robert Chin, eds., *The Planning of Change*, pp. 201–14. New York: Holt, Rinehart & Winston, 1962.

Churchill, Sallie R. "Social Group Work: A Diagnostic Tool in Child Guidance." *American Journal of Orthopsychiatry* (April 1965), 35(3):581–88.

Clemenger, Florence. "Congruence between Members and Workers on Selected Behaviors of the Role of the Social Group Worker." D.S.W. dissertation, University of Southern California, 1965.

Cochrane, et al. "The Role of the Social Worker in Discharge Planning" Chicago, Ill. American Hospital Association, 1985.

Cohen, Jerome. "Nature of Clinical Social Work." In Patricia L. Ewalt, ed., *Toward a Definition of Clinical Social Work*, pp. 23–31. Washington, D.C.: NASW, 1980.

Cohen, Jerome. "Social Work and the Culture of Poverty." *Social Work* (January 1964), 9(1):3–11.

Cohen, Ronald J. and William E. Marino. *Legal Guidebook in Mental Health*. New York: Free Press, 1982.

Compton, Beulah Roberts and Burt Galaway, eds. *Social Work Processes*. 2d ed. Homewood, Ill.: Dorsey Press, 1979.

Conrad, Ann. "Ethical Considerations in the Psychosocial Process." *Social Casework* (December 1988), 69(10):603–10.

Constable, Robert and J. P. Flynn. *School Social Work: Practice and Research Perspective*, Homewood, Ill.: Dorsey Press, 1983.

Conway, Joan Bonner. "The Why and How of Relationship for the Social Workers in a Health Care Setting." *Journal of the Otto Rank Association* (Winter 1979/80), 14:40–49.

Cook, Robert C. "Population: Some Pitfalls of Progress." In Sylvan Kaplan and Everlyn Kivy-Rosenberg, eds., *Ecology and the Quality of Life*. Springfield, Ill.: Charles E. Thomas, 1973.

Cooley, Charles. *Social Process*. New York: Scribners, 1918.

Cooper, Shirley A. "David: The First Hour in the Assessment and Treatment of an Adolescent." *Child and Adolescent Social Work* (Fall 1988), 5(3):218–28.

Cooper, Shirley A. "A Look at the Effect of Racism on Clinical Work." *Social Casework* (February 1973), 54(2):76–84.

Cornett, Carlton. "Toward a More Comprehensive Personology: Integrating a Spiritual Perspective into Social Work Practice." *Social Work* (March 1992), 37(2):89–102.

Coser, Lewis A. *The Functions of Social Conflict*. Glencoe, Ill.: Free Press, 1956.

Couch, Elsbeth Herzstein. *Joint and Family Interviews in the Treatment of Marital Problems*. New York: Family Service Association of America, 1969.

Coulton, Claudia. "A Study of Person-Environment Fit Among the Chronically Ill." *Social Work in Health Care* (Fall 1979), 5(1):5–17.

Cousins, Norman. *Head First: The Biology of Hope*. New York: Dutton, 1989.

Coyle, Grace L. *Social Process in Organized Groups*. New York: Smith, 1930.

Coyle, Grace L. "Some Basic Assumptions About Social Group Work." In Marjorie Murphy, ed., *The Social Group Work Method in Social Work Education*, pp. 88–105. New York: Council on Social Work Education, 1959.

Curti, Merle. *Probing Our Past*. New York: Harper and Row, 1955.

Daley, Barbara Sabin and Geraldine Suzanne Koppenaal. "The Treatment of Women in Short-Term Women's Groups. pp. 343–55. In Simon H. Budman, ed., *Forms of Brief Therapy*. New York: Guilford Press, 1984.

Dana, Bess. "The Collaborative Process." In Rosalind S. Miller and Helen Rehr, eds., *Social Work Issues in Health Care*. Englewood Cliffs, N.J.: Prentice-Hall, 1983, 181–220.

Davies, Linda. "Professional Autonomy Revisited." *Canadian Social Work Review* (Summer 1989). 6(2):186–202.

Davies, Martin. "The Assessment of Environment in Social Work Research." *Social Casework* (January 1974), 55(1):3–12.

Davis, Inger P. "Advice-Giving in Parent Counseling." *Social Casework* (June 1975), 56(6):343–47.

Davis, L. Jeannette. "Human Communication Concepts and Constructs: Tools for Change as Applied to Social Work Practice." D.S.W. dissertation, University of Southern California, 1976.

Davis, Larry E. and Enola Procter. *Race, Gender, and Class: Guidelines for Practice with Individuals, Families, and Groups*. Englewood Cliffs, N.J.: Prentice-Hall, 1989.

Day, Peter R. *Communication in Social Work*. Oxford: Pergamon Press, 1972.

Dean, Ruth Grossman and Margaret L. Rhodes. "Ethical Clinical Tensions in Clinical Practice." *Social Work* (March 1992), 37(2):128–32.

de Anda, Diane. "Bicultural Socialization: Factors Affecting the Minority Experience." *Social Work* (March/April 1984), 29(2):101–7.

De Tocqueville, Alexis. *Democracy in America*. Vol. 2. New York: G. Dearborn, 1838.

Deutsch, Morton. *The Resolution of Conflict*. New Haven, Conn.: Yale University Press, 1973.

Deutsch, Morton. "The Role of Social Class in Language Development and Cognition." *American Journal of Orthopsychiatry* (January 1965), 35(1):78–88.

Devore, Wynetta and Elfrieda G. Schlesinger. *Ethnic-Sensitive Social Work Practice*. St. Louis: C. V. Mosby, 1981.

Dewey, John. *Democracy and Education*. New York: Free Press (paper ed.), 1966.

Dewey, John. *How We Think*. Boston: Heath, 1910.

Dies, Lee P. *Man's Nature and Nature's Man: The Ecology of Human Communication*. Ann Arbor: University of Michigan Press, 1955.

Dies, Robert R. "Clinical Implications of Research on Leadership in Short-Term Group Psychotherapy." In Robert F. Dies and K. Roy MacKenzie, eds., *Advances in Group Psychotherapy*, pp. 27–78. New York: International Universities Press, 1983.

Dobrin, Arthur. "Ethical Judgments of Male and Female Social Workers." *Social Work* (September 1989), 34(5):451–55.

Doherty, William J. and Macaran A. Baird. "Forming a Therapeutic Contract that Involves the Family." In W. J. Doherty and M. A. Baird, eds., *Family Therapy and Family Medicine*. New York: Guilford Press, 1983.

Drachman, Diane and Angela Shen-Ryan. "Immigrants and Refugees." In Alex G. Gitterman, ed., *Handbook of Social Work Practice with Vulnerable Populations*, New York. Columbia University Press, 1991.

Duberman, Lucille. *Social Inequality: Class and Caste in America.* New York: Lippincott, 1976.

Durkin, Helen. *The Group in Depth.* New York: International Universities Press, 1964.

Dworkin, Joan. "To Certify or Not to Certify: Clinical Social Work Decisions and Involuntary Hospitalization." *Social Work in Health Care* (1988), 13(4):81–98.

Eisenhuth, Elizabeth. "The Theories of Heinz Kohut and Clinical Social Work Practice." *Clinical Social Work Journal* (1981), 9(2):80–90.

Elbow, Margaret. "The Memory Book: Facilitating Terminations with Children." *Social Casework* (March 1987), 68(3):180–83.

Ell, Kathleen. "Social Networks, Social Support, and Health Status: A Review," *Social Service Review* (March 1984), 58(1):33–49.

Ell, Kathleen and Helen Northen. *Families and Health Care: Psychosocial Practice.* New York: Aldine DeGruyter, 1990.

Elliott, Martha W. "Hospitality as a Professional Virtue." *Social Casework* (February 1984), 69(2):109–12.

Epstein, Norman. "Brief Group Therapy in a Child Guidance Clinic." *Social Work* (July 1970), 15(3):33–48.

Erikson, Erik H. *Childhood and Society.* 2d ed. New York: Norton, 1963.

Erikson, Erik H. *Identity and the Life Cycle.* New York: Norton, 1959.

Erikson, Erik H. *Identity, Youth, and Crisis.* New York: Norton, 1968.

Erikson, Erik H. *The Life Cycle Completed,* New York: Norton, 1982.

Ewalt, Patricia L. "A Psychoanalytically Oriented Child Guidance Center." In William J. Reid and Laura Epstein, eds., *Task-Centered Practice,* pp. 27–49. New York: Columbia University Press, 1977.

Ewalt, Patricia L., ed. *Toward a Definition of Clinical Social Work; Conference Proceedings.* Washington, D.C. NASW, 1980.

Falck, Hans S. "Aspects of Membership: On the Integration of Psychoanalytic Object-Relations Theory and Small Group Science." *Social Thought* (Winter 1980), 6(11):17–26.

Falck, Hans S. "Interdisciplinary Education and Implications for Social Work Practice." *Journal of Education for Social Work* (Spring 1977), 13(2): 30–37.

Fanshel, David. "A Study of Caseworkers' Perceptions of Their Clients." *Social Casework* (December 1958), 39(10):543–51.

Feldman, Frances Lomas. *Work and Cancer Health Histories.* Oakland, Calif.: California Division, American Cancer Society, 1980.

Fischer, Joel. *Effective Casework Practice: An Eclectic Approach.* New York: McGraw-Hill, 1978.

Fischer, Joel. "Is Casework Effective? A Review." *Social Work* (January 1978), 18(1):5–20.

Fisher, Dena. "The Hospitalized Terminally Ill Patient: An Ecological Perspective." In Carel B. Germain, ed., *Social Work Practice: People and Environments.* New York: Columbia University Press, 1979.

Fishman, Katherine Davis. "Therapy for Children." *Atlantic Monthly* (June 1991), pp. 47–65.

Florentine, Robert and Oscar Grusky. "When Case Managers Manage the Seriously Ill: A Role Contingency Approach." *Social Service Review* (March 1990), 64(1):79–93.

Forder, Anthony. "Social Work and System Theory." *British Journal of Social Work* (Spring 1976), 6(1):23–34.

Fortune, Anne E. "Grief Only? Client and Social Worker Reactions to Termination." *Clinical Social Work Journal* (Summer 1987), 15(20):159–71.

Fortune, Anne E., Bill Pearlingi, and Cherie D. Rochelle. "Reactions to Termination of Individual Treatment." *Social Work* (March 1992), 37(2):171–78.

Fox, Evelyn, Marion Nelson, and William Bolman. "The Termination Process: A Neglected Dimension in Social Work." *Social Work* (October 1969), 14(4):53–63.

Frank, Margaret G. "Discussion of Anna Ornstein's Paper: `Supportive Psychotherapy: A Contemporary View,' " *Clinical Social Work Journal* (Spring 1986), 14(1):31–38.

Franklin, Anderson J. "Therapy with African American Men." *Families in Society: The Journal of Contemporary Human Services* (June 1992), 73(6):350–55.

Franklin, Donna L. "Differential Clinical Assessments: The Influence of Class and Race." *Social Service Review* (March 1985), 59(1):44–61.

Franklin, Donna L. "Does Client Social Class Affect Clinical Judgments?" *Social Casework* (September 1986), 67(7):424–32.

Freeman, David S. "Phases of Family Treatment." *The Family Coordinator* (July 1976), 25(3):265–70.

Freeman, David S. *Techniques of Family Therapy*. New York: Jason Aronson, 1981.

Freud, Sigmund. *Group Psychology and the Analysis of the Ego*, London: International Psychoanalytical Press, 1922.

Freud, Sigmund. *An Outline of Psychoanalysis*. Rev. ed. New York: Norton, 1949.

Friedlander, Walter A., ed. *Concepts and Methods of Social Work*. Englewood Cliffs, N.J.: Prentice-Hall, 1958.

Friedman, Barry. "Co-therapy: A Behavioral and Attitudinal Survey of Third Year Psychiatric Residents." *International Journal of Group Psychotherapy* (April 1973), 23(2):228–34.

Frye, B. A. "Brain Injury and Family Education Needs." *Rehabilitation Nursing* 7:27–29.

Galinsky, Maeda and Janice H. Schopler. "Structuring Co-leadership." *Social Work with Groups* (Winter 1980), 3(4):51–63.

Galinsky, Maeda J. and Janice H. Schopler. "Warning: Groups May Be Dangerous." *Social Work* (March 1977), 22(2):89–94.

Ganter, Grace, Margaret Yeakel, and Norman A. Polansky, *Retrieval from*

Limbo—the Intermediary Group Treatment of Inaccessible Children. New York: Child Welfare League of America, 1967.

Gareffa, Domenic N. and Stanley A. Neff. "Management of the Client's Seductive Behavior." *Smith College Studies in Social Work* (February 1974), 44(2):110–24.

Garland, James A., Hubert E. Jones, and Ralph Kolodny. "A Model for Stages of Development in Social Work Groups." In Saul Bernstein, ed., *Explorations in Group Work*, pp. 17–71. Boston: Boston University School of Social Work, 1965; Milford House, 1973.

Garvin, Charles D. "Complementarity of Role Expectations in Groups: the Member-Worker Contract." In *Social Work Practice, 1969*, pp. 127–45. New York: Columbia University Press, 1969.

Garvin, Charles D. "Group Process: Usage and Uses in Social Work Practice." In Paul H. Glasser, Rosemary Sarri, and Robert Vinter, eds., *Individual Change Through Small Groups*, pp. 209–32. New York: Free Press, 1974.

Garvin, Charles D. and Beth Glover Reed. "Gender Issues in Social Work: An Overview." *Social Work with Groups* (Fall/Winter 1983), 6(3/4):3–19.

Gentry, Martha. "Initial Group Meetings: Member Expectations and Information Distribution Process." Ph.D. dissertation, Washington University, 1974.

Germain, Carel B. *Human Behavior in the Social Environment*. New York: Columbia University Press, 1991.

Germain, Carel B. "Social Context of Clinical Social Work." In Patricia L. Ewalt, ed., *Toward a Definition of Clinical Social Work*, pp. 54–65. Washington, D.C.: NASW. 1980.

Germain, Carel B. *Social Work Practice in Health Care*. New York: Free Press, 1984.

Germain, Carel B., ed. *Social Work Practice; People and Environments; An Ecological Perspective*. New York: Columbia University Press, 1979.

Germain, Carel B. and Alex Gitterman, *The Life Model of Social Work Practice*. New York: Columbia University Press, 1980.

Getzel, George S. "AIDS." In Alex Gitterman, ed., *Handbook of Social Work Practice with Vulnerable Populations*. New York: Columbia University Press, 1991.

Gibbs, Jewelle Taylor. "Treatment Relationships with Black Clients: Interpersonal vs. Instrumental Strategies." In Carel B. Germain, ed., *Advances in Clinical Social Work Practice*, pp. 184–95. Washington, D.C.: NASW, 1985.

Gilligan, Carol. "Adolescent Development Reconsidered." *The Tenth Annual Gisela Komopka Lecture* (May 1987), St. Paul: University of Minnesota.

Gilligan, Carol. *A Different Voice: Psychological Theory and Women's Development*. Cambridge, Mass.: Harvard University Press, 1982.

Gitterman, Alex. "Delivering a New Group Service: Strategies and Skills." In Alex Gitterman and Lawrence Shulman, eds., *Mutual Aid Groups and the Life Cycle*. Itasca, Ill.: Peacock, 1986.

Gitterman, Alex, ed. *Handbook of Social Work Practice with Vulnerable Populations*. New York: Columbia University Press, 1991.

Gitterman, Alex and Lawrence Shulman, eds. *Mutual Aid Groups, Vulnerable Populations, and the Life Cycle.* New York: Columbia University Press, 1994.

Glasser, Paul H. and Charles D. Garvin. "An Organizational Model." In Robert W. Roberts and Helen Northen, eds., *Theories of Social Work with Groups,* pp. 75–115. New York: Columbia University Press, 1976.

Golan, Naomi. "Crisis Intervention." In National Association of Social Workers, *Encyclopedia of Social Work,* pp. 360–72. 18th ed.; Washington, D.C.: NASW, 1987.

Golan, Naomi. *The Perilous Bridge: Helping Clients Through Mid-Life Transitions.* New York: Free Press, 1986.

Goldberg, E. "The Normal Family: Myth and Reality." In Eileen Younghusband, ed., *Social Work with Families,* pp. 11–27. London: Allen & Unwin, 1965.

Goldenberg, Irene and Herbert Goldenberg. *Family Therapy: An Overview.* 2d ed. Monterey, Calif.: Brooks/Cole, 1985.

Goldstein, Eda G. *Ego Psychology and Social Work Practice,* New York: Free Press, 1984.

Goldstein, Howard. "Q & A." *Families in Society* (February 1991), 72(2):121–22.

Goldstein, Howard. *Social Learning and Change.* Columbia: University of South Carolina Press, 1981.

Goldstein, Howard. *Social Work Practice: a Unitary Approach.* Columbia: University of South Carolina Press, 1973.

Goodman, Susan. "Presumed Innocent." *Modern Maturity* (December 1991–January 1992), pp. 25–28.

Gordon, Milton M. *Human Nature, Class, and Ethnicity.* New York: Oxford University Press, 1973.

Gordon, William E. "Social Work Revolution or Evolution." *Social Work* (May/June 1983), 28(3):181–83.

Gottlieb, Benjamin H., ed. "Using Social Support to Protect and Promote Health." *The Journal of Primary Prevention* (Fall/Winter 1987), 8(1/2):49–70.

Gould, Gary M. and Michael L. Smith, eds. *Social Work in the Workplace.* New York: Springer, 1988.

Green, Rose. "Terminating the Relationship in Social Casework." Unpublished paper, School of Social Work, University of Southern California.

Greene, Roberta R. "Eriksonian Theory: A Developmental Approach to Ego Mastery" and "General Systems Theory." In Roberta R. Greene and Paul H. Ephross, *Human Behavior Theory and Social Work Practice,* pp. 79–104 and 227–60. New York: Aldine DeGruyter, 1991.

Greer, Colin, ed. *Divided Society: The Ethnic Experience in America.* New York: Basic Books, 1974.

Grinnell, Richard M. and Nancy S. Kyte. "Environmental Modification: A Study." *Social Work* (May 1974), 20(3):313–18.

Group for the Advancement of Psychiatry, Report #78. *The Field of Family Therapy* (March 1970), 7:531–644.

Grunebaum, Henry and Leonard Solomon. "Peer Relationships, Self-Esteem, and the Self." *International Journal of Group Psychotherapy* (October 1987), 37(4):475–513.

Grunebaum, Henry and Leonard Solomon. "Toward a Peer Group Theory of Group Psychotherapy, I." *International Journal of Group Psychotherapy* (January 1980), 30:(1):23–50.

Gurman, Alan S. "The Effects and Effectiveness of Marital Therapy: A Review of Outcome Research." *Family Process* (June 1973), 12(2):145–70.

Hafferty, William. "Whose Files Are They Anyway?" *Modern Maturity* (April/May 1991), pp. 58–69.

Hall, Edward T. *The Hidden Dimension*. Garden City, N.Y.: Doubleday, 1966.

Hallowitz, David et al. "The Assertive Counseling Component of Therapy." *Social Casework* (November 1967), 48(9):543–48.

Hamilton, Gordon. *Psychotherapy in Child Guidance*. New York: Columbia University Press, 1974.

Hamilton, Gordon. *Theory and Practice of Social Case Work*. 2d ed. New York: Columbia University Press, 1951.

Hammond, D. Corydon. "Cross-Cultural Rehabilitation." *Journal of Rehabilitation* (September/October 1971), 37(5):34–36.

Hancock, Betsy L. *School Social Work*. Englewood Cliffs, N.J.: Prentice-Hall, 1982.

Hancock, Helen et al. "Direct Practice with Individuals and Families." Course Syllabus, Miami, Fla., Barry University School of Social Work, 1991.

Hanson, Meredith. "Alcoholism and Other Drug Addictions." In Alex Gitterman, ed., *Handbook of Social Work Practice with Vulnerable Populations*. New York: Columbia University Press, 1991.

Hare, A. Paul. *Handbook of Small Group Research*. 2d ed. Hew York: Free Press, 1976.

Hartford, Margaret E. *Groups in Social Work*. New York: Columbia University Press, 1971.

Hartford, Margaret E., ed. *Working Papers Toward a Frame of Reference for Social Group Work*. New York: NASW, 1964.

Hartman, Ann. "Social Worker-in-Situation." *Social Work* (May 1991). 36(3):195–96.

Hartman, Ann. "To Think About the Unthinkable." *Social Casework* (October 1970), 51(8):467–74.

Hartman, Ann and Joan Laird. *Family-Centered Social Work Practice*. New York: Free Press, 1983.

Hartmann, Heinz. *Ego Psychology and the Problem of Adaptation*. New York: International Universities Press, 1958.

Hathway, Marion E. "Twenty-Five Years of Professional Education for Social Work—and a Look Ahead." *The Compass* (June 1946), 27(5):13–18.

Hazen, Robert M. and James Trefil. "Ecological Literacy: Exploring the Web of Knowledge," *Nature Conservancy* (July/August 1991), pp. 24–29.

Heap, Ken. *Process and Action in Work with Groups: The Preconditioning for Treatment and Growth.* New York: Pergamon Press, 1979.

Hearn, Gordon. "General Systems Theory and Social Work." In Francis J. Turner, ed., *Social Work Treatment: Interlocking Theoretical Approaches.* 2d ed. New York: Free Press, 1979.

Hearn, Gordon. *Theory Building in Social Work.* Toronto: University of Toronto Press, 1958.

Hearn, Gordon, ed. *The General Systems Approach: Contributions Toward an Holistic Conception of Social Work.* New York: Council on Social Work Education, 1968.

Heine, R. W. "A Comparison of Patients' Reports on Psychotherapeutic Experience with Psychoanalytic, Nondirective, and Adlerian Therapists." Ph.D. dissertation, University of Chicago, 1950.

Heller, David. *Power in Psychotherapeutic Practice.* New York: Human Services Press, 1985.

Hepworth, Dean H. and Jo Ann Larsen. *Direct Social Work Practice.* Homewood, Ill.: Dorsey Press, 1982.

Ho, Man Keung and Eunice McDowell. "The Black Worker-White Client Relationship." *Clinical Social Work Journal* (Fall 1973), 1(30):161–67.

Hobbs, Nicholas. *The Futures of Children: Categories, Labels, and Their Consequences.* San Francisco: Jossey-Bass, 1975.

Hobbs, Nicholas. "Sources of Gain in Psychotherapy." *American Psychologist* (October 1962), 17(10):741–47.

Holland, Thomas F. and Allie C. Kilpatrick. "Ethical Issues in Social Work: Toward a Grounded Theory of Professional Ethics," *Social Work* (March 1991), 36(2):138–45.

Hollingshead, August B. and Frederick C. Redlich. *Social Class and Mental Illness: A Community Study.* New York: Wiley, 1958.

Hollis, Florence. *Casework: A Psychosocial Therapy.* 2d ed. New York: Random House, 1972.

Holmes, Thomas H. and Richard H. Raye. "The Social Readjustment Rating Scale." *Journal of Psychosomatic Research* (1967), 11:213–18.

Homans, George. *The Human Group.* New York: Harcourt-Brace, 1950.

Horn, Miriam. "Hospitals Fit for Healing." *U.S. News and World Report* (July 22, 1991), pp. 48–50.

Houston, Mary Kay and Helen Northen. "Reducing Risks and Enhancing Practice: A Framework for Teaching About Malpractice." Paper presented at the Annual Program Meeting, Council on Social Work Education, February 1993.

Houston, Mary Kay and Barbara Robey. "Use of Groups in Disasters: Trauma and Loss." Paper presented at the Florida Association for the Advancement of Social Work with Groups, April 1993.

Hudson, Walter. *The Clinical Measurement Package.* Homewood, Ill.: Dorsey Press, 1982.

Hudson, Walter W. and Bruce A. Thyer. "Research Measures and Indices in

Direct Practice." In National Association of Social Workers, *Encyclopedia of Social Work*, pp. 487–98. 18th ed.; Washington, D.C.: NASW, 1987.

Humphries, Griffith. "Valedictory Address." School of Social Work, University of Southern California, May 1989.

Hutten, Joan M. "Short-Term Contracts IV. Techniques: How and Why to Use Them." *Social Work Today* (August 1976), 6(20):614–18.

Hutten, Joan M. *Short-Term Contracts in Social Work*. London: Routledge & Kegan Paul, 1977.

Imhof, John. "Countertransference and the EAP Counselor." *EAP Digest* (July/August 1987), 7(5):63–77.

Imre, Roberta Wells. "The Nature of Knowledge in Social Work." *Social Work* (January/February 1984), 29(1):41–45.

Imre, Roberta Wells. "What Do We Need to Know for Good Practice?" *Social Work* (May 1991), 36(3): 198–200.

Jackson, Josephine A. "Clinical Social Work: Definition, Status, Knowledge, and Practice," Ph.D. dissertation, Institute of Clinical Social Work, California, 1979.

Janchill, Sister Mary Paul. "Systems Concepts in Casework Theory and Practice," *Social Casework* (February 1969), 50(2):74–82.

Jayartne, Srinika, K. Siefert, and Wayne A. Chess. "Private and Agency Practitioners: Some Data and Observations." *Social Service Review*, (June 1988), 62(2):324–36.

Jayartne, Srinika, Mary Lou Davis-Sacks, and Wayne A. Chess. "Private Practice May Be Good for Your Health and Well-Being." *Social Work* (May 1991), 36(3):193–222.

Jenkins, Shirley. *The Ethnic Dilemma in Social Services*. New York: Free Press, 1981.

Jenkins, Shirley and Elaine Norman. *Filial Deprivation and Foster Care*. New York: Columbia University Press, 1972.

Jennings, Helen Hall. *Leadership and Isolation: A Study of Personality in Interpersonal Relations*. New York: Longmans Green, 1950.

Johnson, Arlien. "Development of Basic Methods of Social Work Practice and Education." *Social Work Journal* (July 1955), 36(3):109–13.

Johnson, Harriet C. and Edmund J. Hart. "Neurological Disorders." In Francis J. Turner, ed. *Adult Psychopathology: A Social Work Perspective*, pp. 73–118. New York: Free Press, 1984.

Jones, James A. and Abraham Alcabes. "Clients Don't Sue: The Invulnerable Social Worker." *Social Casework* (September 1989), 70(7):414–20.

Kadushin, Alfred. "The Racial Factor in the Interview." *Social Work* (May 1972), 17(3):88–98.

Kadushin, Alfred. *The Social Work Interview*. 3d ed. New York: Columbia University Press, 1990.

Kagle, Jill Doner. "Recording in Direct Practice." In National Association of Social Workers, *Encyclopedia of Social Work*, pp. 463–67. 18th ed.; Washington, D.C.: NASW, 1987.

Kagle, Jill Doner. *Social Work Records.* Homewood, Ill.: Dorsey Press, 1984.

Kagle, Jill D. "Teaching Social Work Students About Privileged Communication." *Journal of Teaching in Social Work* (1990), 4(2):49–65.

Kane, Rosalie A. "Editorial: Thoughts on Parent Education." *Health and Social Work* (February 1981), 6(1):1–4.

Kane, Rosalie A. "The Interprofessional Team as a Small Group." *Social Work in Health Care* (Fall 1975), 1(1)19–32.

Kanter, Joel S. "Reevaluation of Task-Centered Social Work Practice." *Clinical Social Work Journal* (1983), 11(3):229–44.

Karls, James M. and Karin E. Wandrei. "PIE: A New Language for Social Work." *Social Work* (January 1992), 37(1):80–86.

Kasius, Cora, ed. *A Comparison of Diagnostic and Functional Casework.* New York: Family Service Association of America, 1950.

Kassel, Suzanne L. and Rosalie A. Kane. "Self-Determination Dissected." *Clinical Social Work Journal* (Fall 1980), 8(3):161–78.

Katz, Alfred H. and Eugene Bender. *The Strength in Us: Self-Help Groups in the Modern World.* New York: New Viewpoints, 1976.

Katz, Robert L. *Empathy, Its Nature and Uses.* New York: Free Press, 1963.

Kermani, Ebrahim J. and Bonnie A. Weiss. "AIDS and Confidentiality: Legal Concept and Its Application in Psychotherapy." *American Journal of Psychotherapy* (January 1989). 43(1):25–31.

Kernberg, Otto F. *Object Relations Theory and Clinical Psychoanalysis.* New York: Jason Aronson, 1976.

King, B. L. "Diagnostic Activity Group for Latency Age Children." In Community Service Society of New York, *Dynamic Approaches to Serving Families,* pp. 55–67. New York: CSS, 1970.

Kiresuk, Thomas J. and Robert E. Sherman. "Goal Attainment Scaling: A General Method for Evaluating Comprehensive Mental Health Progress." *Community Mental Health Journal* (December 1968). 4(6):443–53.

Kitano, Harry and Stanley Sue. "The Model Minorities." *Journal of Social Issues* (1973), 29(2):1–9.

Kluckhohn, Florence R. "Family Diagnosis: Variations in the Basic Values of Family Systems" *Social Casework* (February 1958), 39(2):66–69.

Kluckhohn, Florence R. and Fred L. Strodtbeck. *Variations in Value Orientations.* Evanston, Ill.: Row Peterson, 1961.

Knapp, Samuel and Leon VandeCreek. *Privileged Communication in the Health Profession.* New York: Von Nostrand Reinhold, 1987.

Kohut, Heinz. *The Restoration of the Self.* New York: International Universities Press, 1977.

Kolodny, Ralph. "Retrospective on Reaching Out: Boston's Late Department of Neighborhood Clubs." In James Garland, ed., *Group Work Reaching Out: People, Places, and Power.* Binghamton, N.Y.: Haworth Press, 1993.

Konopka, Gisela. "All Lives Are Connected to Other Lives." In Marie Weil, Kenneth L. Chau, and Dannia Sutherland, eds., *Theory and Practice in Social*

Group Work: Creative Connections. Binghamton, N.Y.: Haworth Press, 1992.

Konopka, Gisela. *The Adolescent Girl in Conflict.* Englewood Cliffs, N.J.: Prentice-Hall, 1966.

Kramer, Sidney A. "The Termination Process in Open-Ended Psychotherapy: Guidelines for Clinical Practice." *Psychotherapy* (1986), 23:526–31.

Kramer, Sidney A. "The Therapist's View of Termination in Open-Ended Psychotherapy." Ph.D. dissertation, University of Chicago.

Kurland, Roselle. "Planning: The Neglected Component of Group Development." *Social Work with Groups* (Summer 1978), 1(2):173–78.

Kurland, Roselle and Robert Salmon. "Self Determination: Its Use and Misuse in Group Work Practice and Social Work Education." In David F. Fike and Barbara Rittner, eds., *Working from Strengths: The Essence of Group Work.* Miami, Fla.: Center for Group Work Studies, 1990.

Kurzman, Paul A. "The Ethical Base for Social Work in the Workplace." In Gary M. Gould and Michael L. Smith, eds., *Social Work in the Workplace.* New York: Springer, 1988.

Kurzman, Paul A. "Managing Risk in The Workplace." In Richard L. Edwards and John A. Yankey, eds., *Skills for Effective Human Services Management.* Silver Springs, Md.: NASW Press, 1991.

Kutchins, Herb. "The Fiduciary Relationship: The Legal Basis for Social Workers' Responsibilities to Clients." *Social Work* (March 1991), 36(2):106–13.

Kutchins, Herb and Stuart A. Kirk. "DSM-III and Social Work Malpractice." *Social Work* (May/June 1987). 32(3):213–20.

Lackey, Mary Beit Hallahmi. "Termination: The Crucial Stage of Social Work." D.S.W. dissertation, University of Southern California, 1981.

Land, Helen, Robert Nishimoto, and Kenneth Chau. "Interventive and Preventive Services for Vietnamese Refugees." *Social Service Review* (September 1988), 62(3):468–84.

Landers, Susan. "AIDS Deepens Duty-to-Warn Dilemma." *NASW News* (January 1992), p. 3.

Lane, Dorthea. "Psychiatric Patients Learn a New Way of Life." In National Association of Social Workers, *New Perspectives on Services to Groups,* pp. 114–23. Washington, D.C.: NASW, 1961.

Larsen, Jo Ann and Dean H. Hepworth. "Skill Development Through Competency-Based Education," *Journal of Education for Social Work* (Winter 1978), 14(1):73–81.

Lee, Judith A. B. "The Helping Professional's Use of Language Describing the Poor." *American Journal of Orthopsychiatry* (October 1980), 50:580–84.

Leichtor, Elsa and Gerda Schulman. "The Family Interview as an Integrative Device in Group Therapy with Families." *International Journal of Group Psychotherapy* (July 1963), 13(3):335–45.

Levine, Baruch. *Group Psychotherapy, Practice, and Development.* Englewood Cliffs, N.J.: Prentice-Hall, 1979.

Levine, Rachel. "A Short Story on the Long Waiting List," *Social Work* (January 1963), 8(1):20–22.

Levinson, Helen M. "Use and Misuse of Groups." *Social Work* (January 1973), 18(1):66–73.

Levinson, Hilliard L. "Termination of Psychotherapy: Some Salient Issues." *Social Casework* (October 1977), 48(8):480–89.

Levitt, John L. and William J. Reid. "Rapid Assessment Instruments in Social Work Practice." *Social Work Research and Abstracts* (Spring 1981), 17(1):13–20.

Levy, Alan. "A Community Based Approach to Clinical Services for Children of Substance Abusers." *Child and Adolescent Social Work Journal*. In press.

Levy, Charles S. *Social Work Ethics*. New York: Human Sciences Press, 1976.

Lewin, Kurt. *Field Theory in Social Science: Selected Theoretical Papers*. Dorwin Cartwright, ed. New York: Harper 1951.

Lewis, Benjamin F. "An Examination of the Final Phase of a Group Development Theory." *Small Group Behavior* (December 1978), 9(4):507–17.

Lewis, Harold. *The Intellectual Base of Social Work Practice: Tools for Thought in a Helping Profession*. New York: Haworth Press, 1982.

Lewis, Harold. "Reasoning in Practice." *Smith College Studies in Social Work* (November 1975), 46(1): 1–12.

Libassi, Mary Frances. *Psychopharmocology in Social Work Education*. Council on Social Work Education, Washington, D.C., August 1990.

Lieberman, Florence. "Clients' Expectations, Preferences, and Experiences of Initial Interview in Voluntary Social Agencies." D.S.W. dissertation, Columbia University, 1968.

Lieberman, Florence. *Clinical Social Workers as Psychotherapists*. New York: Gardner Press, 1982.

Lieberman, Morton A., Leonard D. Borman, and Associates. *Self-Help Groups for Coping with Crisis: Origins, Members, Processes*. San Francisco: Jossey-Bass, 1979.

Lieberman, Morton A., Irvin D. Yalom, and Matthew B. Miles. *Encounter Groups: First Facts*. New York: Basic Books, 1973.

Lima, Kristine, R. Rodriguez, Sherman Eisenthal, and Aaron Lazare. "Perception of Requests in Psychotherapy: Patient and Therapist." *Journal of Social Service Research* (Winter 1981), 4(2):51–68.

Lindeman, Eduard C. *Social Discovery*. New York: Republic, 1924.

Linzer, Norman. "Resolving Ethical Dilemmas in Jewish Communal Services," *Journal of Jewish Communal Service* (Winter 1986), 6(1):105–17.

Locklear, Herbert H. "American Indian Myths." *Social Work* (May 1972), 17(3):72–80.

Loewenberg, Frank M. *Religion and Social Work Practice in Contemporary American Society*. New York: Columbia University Press, 1988.

Longres, John F. *Human Behavior in the Social Environment*. Itasca, Ill.: Peacock, 1990.

Lum, Doman. *Social Work Practice and People of Color: A Process-Stage Approach*. Monterey, Calif.: Brooks/Cole, 1986.

Lurie, Abraham. "A Warning to Clinicians: Stake Out Turf." *NASW News* (1985), 30:4.

Lustman, Claire R. "Development of Research in a Clinical Social Work Service." *Social Work* (July 1959), 4(2):77–83.

Luthman, Shirley with Martin Kirschenbaum. *The Dynamic Family.* Palo Alto, Calif.: Science and Behavior Books, 1974.

Maas, Henry S. *People and Contexts: Social Development from Birth to Old Age.* Englewood Cliffs, N.J.: Prentice-Hall, 1984.

McAdoo, Harriette P. *Black Families.* 2d ed. Newburg Park, Calif.: Sage, 1988.

McBroom, Elizabeth. "Socialization Through Small Groups." In Robert W. Roberts and Helen Northen, eds., *Theories of Social Work with Groups,* pp. 268–303. New York: Columbia University Press, 1976.

McGowan, Brenda G. "Advocacy." In National Association of Social Workers, *Encyclopedia of Social Work,* pp. 89–95. 18th ed.; Washington, D.C.: NASW, 1987.

McGowan, Brenda G. "The Case Advocacy Function in Child Welfare Practice." *Child Welfare* 1978, 57(5):275–84.

McGowan, Brenda G. *Trends in Employee Counseling.* Elmsford, N.Y.: Pergamon Press, 1984.

McGowan, Brenda G. and William Meezan, eds. *Child Welfare: Career Dilemmas, Future Directions.* Itasca, Ill.: Peacock, 1983.

MacLennan, Beryce W. and Naomi Felsenfeld, *Group Counseling and Psychotherapy with Adolescents.* New York: Columbia University Press, 1968.

Macon, Lilian. "A Comparative Study of Two Approaches to the Treatment of Marital Dysfunction." D.S.W. dissertation, University of Southern California, 1975.

McQuaide, Sharon. "Working with Southeast Asian Refugees." *Clinical Social Work Journal* (1989). 17(2):165–176.

Mahler, Margaret S. et al. *The Psychological Birth of the Human Infant.* New York: Basic Books, 1975.

Mailick, Mildred D. "The Short-Term Treatment of Depression of Physically Ill Hospital Patients." *Social Work in Health Care* (Spring 1984), 9(3):51–61.

Mailick, Mildred D. and Florence W. Vigilante. "Human Behavior and the Social Environment: A Sequence Providing the Theoretical Base for Teaching Assessment." *Journal of Teaching in Social Work* (Fall/Winter 1987), 1(2): 23–48.

Mailick, Mildred D. and Pearl Jordan. "A Multi-Modal Approach to Collaborative Practice in Health Settings." *Social Work in Health Care* (Summer 1977), 2:445–52.

Main, Marjorie White. "Selected Aspects of the Beginning Phase of Social Group Work." Ph.D. dissertation, University of Chicago, 1964.

Maki, Mitchell T. "Countertransference with Adolescent Clients of the Same Ethnicity," *Child and Adolescent Social Work Journal* (April 1990), 7(2):135–46.

Malandro, Loretta A. and Larry Barker. *Non-Verbal Communication.* Reading, Mass: Addison-Wesley, 1982.

Maluccio, Anthony N. "Perspectives of Social Workers and Clients on Treatment Outcome." *Social Casework* (1979), 60:394–401.

Maluccio, Anthony N. and Wilma D. Marlow. "The Case for the Contract." *Social Work* (January 1974), 19(1):28–36.

Marshall, Eldon. "Use of Aides in Activity Group Treatment." *Social Work With Groups* (Winter 1978), 1(4):333–34.

Martinez, Cervando. "Community Mental Health and the Chicano Movement." *American Journal of Orthopsychiatry* (July 1973), 43(4):595–610.

Masi, D. *Designing Employee Assistance Programs*. New York: American Management Association, 1984.

Matorin, Susan et al. "Private Practice in Social Work: Readiness and Opportunity." *Social Casework* (January 1987), 68(1):31–37.

Mayer, John E. and Noel Timms. *The Client Speaks: Working Class Impressions of Casework*. New York: Atherton, 1970.

Meadow, Diane A. "The Preparatory Interview: A Client-Focused Approach with Children of Holocaust Survivors." *Social Work with Groups* (Fall/Winter 1981), 4(3/4):135–45.

Mendes, Helen. "Countertransference and Counterculture Clients." *Social Casework* (March 1977). 58(3):159–63.

Mendes, Helen. *Some Religious Values Held by Blacks, Chicanos, and Japanese Americans: Their Implications for Casework Practice*. Monograph #4. Boulder, Colo.: Western Interstate Commission on Higher Education, 1974.

Merton, Robert K. *Social Theory and Social Structure*. Glencoe, Ill.: Free Press, 1949.

Meyer, Carol H. *Assessment in Social Work Practice*. New York: Columbia University Press, 1993.

Meyer, Carol H., ed. *Clinical Social Work in the Eco-Systems Perspective*. New York: Columbia University Press, 1983.

Meyer, Carol H. "Direct Practice in Social Work: Overview." National Association of Social Workers, *Encyclopedia of Social Work*, pp. 409–22. 18th ed.; Washington, D.C.: NASW, 1987.

Meyer, Carol H. *Social Work Practice: The Changing Landscape*. New York: Free Press, 1976.

Meyer, Carol H. *Social Work Practice: The Urban Crisis*. New York: Free Press, 1970.

Meyer, Carol H. "The Search for Coherence." In Carol H. Meyer, ed., *Clinical Social Work in the Eco-Systems Perspective*, pp. 5–34. New York: Columbia University Press, 1983.

Meyer, William S. "In Defense of Long-Term Treatment: On the Vanishing Holding Environment." *Social Work* (September 1993), 38(5):571–78.

Middleman, Ruth R. and Gale Goldberg Wood. *Skills for Direct Practice in Social Work*. New York: Columbia University Press, 1990.

Middleman, Ruth R. and Gale Goldberg. *Social Service Delivery: A Structural Approach to Social Work Practice*. New York: Columbia University Press, 1974.

Middleman, Ruth R. and Gale Goldberg. "Social Work Practice with Groups." In National Association of Social Workers, *Encyclopedia of Social Work*, pp. 714–20. 18th ed.; Washington, D.C.: NASW, 1987.

Miller, Rosalind S. and Helen Rehr, eds. *Social Work Issues in Health Care.* Englewood Cliffs, N.J.: Prentice-Hall, 1983.

Minuchin, Salvador et al. *Families of the Slums.* New York: Basic Books, 1967.

Mishne, Judith Marks. *Clinical Work with Adolescents.* New York: Free Press, 1986.

Montagu, Ashley. *The Cultured Man.* Cleveland: World, 1958.

Moos, Rudolph. *The Human Context: Environmental Determinants of Behavior.* New York: Wiley, 1976.

Moreno, Jacob L. *Who Shall Survive? A New Approach to the Problem of Human Interaction.* Washington, D.C.: Nervous and Mental Disease Publishing Co., 1934.

Moses, A. Alefin and Robert O. Hawkins. *Counseling Lesbian Women and Gay Men: A Life Issues Approach.* St. Louis, Mo.: Mosby, 1982.

Moss, Sidney Z. and Miriam S. Moss. "When a Caseworker Leaves an Agency: The Impact on Worker and Client." *Social Casework* (July 1967), 48(7):433–37.

Mullen, Edward J. "Casework Communication." *Social Casework* (November 1968), 49(6):546–551.

Mullen, Edward J. "Casework Treatment Procedures as a Function of Client-Diagnostic Variables." D.S.W. dissertation, Columbia University, 1968.

Munoz, Faye. "Pacific Islanders: A Perplexed, Neglected Minority." *Social Casework* (March 1976), 57(3):179-84

Nadel, Robert M. "Interviewing Style and Foster Parents' Verbal Accessibility." *Child Welfare* (April 1967), 46(4):207–13.

Nakama, George. "Japanese Americans' Expectations of Counseling: An Exploratory Survey." D.S.W. dissertation, University of Southern California, 1980.

NASW (National Association of Social Workers). "Ad Hoc Committee on Advocacy Report." *Social Work* (April 1969), 14(2):16–22.

NASW. *Code of Ethics.* Washington, D.C.: NASW, 1980. Revised 1993.

NASW. *NASW Guidelines on the Private Practice of Clinical Social Work.* Washington, D.C.: NASW Press, 1991.

NASW. *NASW Standards for the Practice of Clinical Social Work.* Washington, D.C.: NASW Press, 1989.

NASW. Commission on Education. *The School Social Worker and Confidentiality,* Washington, D.C.: NASW Press, 1991.

National Council on the Practice of Clinical Social Work. *The Expanded Definition of Clinical Social Work.* Washington, D.C.: NASW, 1989.

Nelsen, Judith C. *Communication Theory and Social Work Practice.* Chicago: University of Chicago Press, 1980.

Nelsen, Judith C. *Family Treatment: An Integrative Approach.* Englewood Cliffs, N.J.: Prentice-Hall, 1983.

Northen, Helen. "Assessment in Direct Practice." National Association of Social Workers, *Encyclopedia of Social Work*, pp. 171–83. 18th ed.; Washington, D.C.: NASW, 1987.

Northen, Helen. "Psychosocial Practice in Small Groups." In Robert W. Roberts and Helen Northen, eds., *Theories of Social Work with Groups*, pp. 116–52. New York: Columbia University Press, 1976.

Northen, Helen. "Selection of Groups as the Preferred Modality of Practice." In Joseph Lassner, Kathleen Powell, and Elaine Finnegan, *Social Group Work: Competence and Values in Practice*, pp. 19–34. New York: Haworth Press, 1987.

Northen, Helen. *Social Work with Groups*. 2d ed. New York: Columbia University Press, 1988.

Northen, Helen. "Social Work With Groups in Health Settings: Promises and Problems." In Gary Rosenberg and Helen Rehr, eds., *Advancing Social Work Practice in the Health Care Field*, pp. 107–21, New York: Haworth Press, 1983.

Northen, Helen and Robert W. Roberts. "The Status of Theory." In Robert W. Roberts and Helen Northen, *Theories of Social Work With Groups*. pp. 373–78. New York: Columbia University Press, 1976.

Norton, Dolores. "The Dual Perspective." In Dolores Norton, ed., *The Dual Perspective: Inclusion of Ethnic Minority Content in Social Work Curriculum*. New York: Council on Social Work Education, 1978.

O'Brien, C. P. et al. "Groups vs. Individual Psychotherapy with Schizophrenics." *Archives of General Psychiatry* (1972), 27:474–78.

Orcutt, Ben A. "Family Treatment of Poverty Level Families." *Social Casework* (February 1976). 58(2):92–100.

Orcutt, Ben A. *Science and Inquiry in Social Work Practice*. New York: Columbia University Press, 1990.

Overton, Alice and Katherine Tinker. *Casework Notebook*. St. Paul, Minn.: Greater St. Paul Community Chests and Councils, 1957.

Oxley, Genevieve G. "The Caseworker's Expectations and Client Motivation." *Social Casework* (July 1966), 47(7):432–37.

Ozawa, Martha A. "Development of Social Services in Industry." *Social Work* (November 1980), 25(6):464–70.

Papell, Catherine P. "Suggested Revisions to NASW Definition of Clinical Social Work." Memorandum to H. Northen, October 3, 1992).

Parad, Howard J., Lola G. Selby, and James Quinlan. "Crisis Intervention with Families and Groups." In Robert W. Roberts and Helen Northen, eds., *Theories of Social Work with Groups*, pp. 304–30. New York: Columbia University Press, 1976.

Parry, Joan K. "Informed Consent: For Whose Benefit?" *Social Casework* (November 1981), 62(3):537–54.

Perlman, Gail L. "Mastering the Law of Privileged Communication: A Guide for Social workers." *Social Work* (1988). 33(5):425–29.

Perlman, Helen Harris. "Casework Is Dead." *Social Casework* (January 1967), 48(1):22–25.

Perlman, Helen Harris. "Confessions, Concerns, and Commitment of an Ex-Clinical Social Worker." *Clinical Social Work Journal* (Fall 1974), 2(3): 221–29.

Perlman, Helen Harris. "Identity Problems, Role, and Casework Treatment." *Social Service Review* (September 1963), 37(3):307–18.

Perlman, Helen Harris. *Persona. Social Role, and Personality*. Chicago: University of Chicago Press, 1968.

Perlman, Helen Harris. *Relationship, the Heart of Helping People*. Chicago: University of Chicago Press, 1979.

Perlman, Helen Harris. *Social Casework: A Problem-Solving Process*. Chicago: University of Chicago Press, 1957.

Phi Kappa Phi. "Biomedical Ethics and the Bill of Rights." Entire issue. *National Forum* (Fall 1989), 69(41):2–48.

Phillips, Helen U. *Essentials of Social Group Work Skill*. New York: Association Press, 1957.

Piaget, Jean and Barbel Imholder. *The Psychology of the Child*. New York: Basic Books, 1969.

Pigors, Paul. *Leadership or Domination*. Boston and New York: Houghton-Mifflin, 1935.

Pincus, Allen and Anne Minahan. *Social Work Practice: Model and Method*. Itasca, Ill.: Peacock, 1973.

Pinderhughes, Elaine B. "Empowerment for Our Clients and for Ourselves." *Social Casework* (June 1983), 64(6):331–38.

Pinderhughes, Elaine B. "Power, Powerlessness, and Practice." In Sylvia Sims Gray, Ann Hartman, and Ellen S. Saalberg, eds., *Empowering the Black Family*. National Child Welfare Training Center. Ann Arbor, University of Michigan, School of Social Work, 1985.

Pinderhughes, Elaine B. "Teaching Empathy: Ethnicity, Race, and Power at the Cross-Cultural Treatment Interface." *American Journal of Social Psychiatry* (1984), 4(1):5–12.

Pinderhughes, Elaine B. *Understanding Race, Ethnicity, and Power*. New York: Macmillan, 1989.

Pinkus, Helen et al. "Education for the Practice of Clinical Social Work at the Master's Level: A Position Paper." *Clinical Social Work Journal* (Winter 1977), 5(4):251–68.

Polansky, Norman A. *Ego Psychology and Communication: Theory for the Interview*. New York: Atherton Press, 1971.

Pollak, Otto. "A Family Diagnosis Model," *Social Service Review* (March 1960), 34(1):1–50.

Pollak, Otto. "Social Determinants of Family Behavior." *Social Work* (July 1963), 8(3):95–101.

Polombo, Joseph. "Clinical Issues in Self Psychology." In Phyllis Caroff and Mary L. Gottesfeld, eds., *Psychosocial Studies*, pp. 54–80. New York: Gardner Press, 1987.

Powdermaker, Florence B. and Jerome D. Frank. *Group Psychotherapy: Studies in Methodology of Research and Therapy*. Cambridge, Mass.: Harvard University Press, 1953.

Pray, Kenneth L. M. *Social Work in a Revolutionary Age*. Philadelphia: University of Pennsylvania Press, 1949.

Proshansky, Harold M., William H. Ittelson, and Leanne G. Rivlin, eds. *Environmental Psychology: Man and His Physical Setting*. New York: Holt, Rinehart, and Winston, 1970.

Rae-Grant, Quentin A. F., Thomas Gladwin, and Eli M. Bower. "Mental Health, Social Competence, and the War on Poverty." *American Journal of Orthopsychiatry* (July 1966), 36(4):652–64.

Raines, James C. "Empathy in Clinical Social Work." *Clinical Social Work Journal* (Spring 1990), 18(1):57–72.

Rapoport, Lydia. "Crisis Intervention as a Mode of Brief Treatment." In Robert W. Roberts and Robert H. Nee, *Theories of Social Casework*. Chicago: University of Chicago Press, 1970.

Raschella, Gerald. "An Evaluation of the Effect of Goal Congruence between Client and Therapist on Premature Client Dropout from Therapy." Ph.D. dissertation, University of Pittsburgh, 1975.

Reamer, Frederic G. *Ethical Dilemmas in Social Service*. 2d ed. New York: Columbia University Press, 1990.

Reamer, Frederic G. "Informed Consent in Social Work." *Social Work* (September/October 1987), 32(5):425–29.

Redl, Fritz. "The Art of Group Composition." In Suzanne Schulze, ed., *Creative Group Living in a Children's Institution*, pp. 76–96. New York: Association Press, 1951.

Redl, Fritz and David Wineman. *Controls from Within*, Glencoe, Ill.: Free Press, 1951.

Reed, Beth Glover. "Women Leaders in Small Groups: Social-Psychological, Psychodynamic, and Interactional Perspective." *Social Work with Groups* (Fall/Winter 1983), 6(3/4):35–42.

Rehr, Helen. "The Consumer and Consumerism." In Rosalind S. Miller and Helen Rehr, eds., *Social Work Issues in Health Care*, pp. 20–73. Englewood Cliffs, N.J.: Prentice-Hall, 1983.

Reid, William J. "Process and Outcome in Treatment of Family Problems." In William J. Reid and Laura Epstein, eds., *Task-Centered Practice*, New York: Columbia University Press, 1977.

Reid, William J. "Research in Social Work." National Association of Social Workers, *Encyclopedia of Social Work*, pp. 474–87. 18th ed.; Washington, D.C.: NASW, 1987.

Reid, William J. *The Task-Centered System*. New York: Columbia University Press, 1978.

Reid, William J. and Laura Epstein. *Task-Centered Casework*. New York: Columbia University Press, 1972.

Reid, William J. and Laura Epstein, eds. *Task-Centered Practice*. New York: Columbia University Press, 1977.

Reid, William J. and Barbara L. Shapiro. "Client Reactions to Advice." *Social Service Review* (June 1969), 43(2):165–73.

Reid, William J. and Ann W. Shyne. *Brief and Extended Casework*. New York: Columbia University Press, 1969.

Reynolds, Bertha C. *Learning and Teaching in the Practice of Social Work*. New York: Farrar & Rinehart, 1942.

Reynolds, Bertha C. *Social Work and Social Living*. New York: Citadel Press, 1951.

Reynolds, Mildred M. "Threats to Confidentiality." *Social Work* (April 1976), 21(2):108–13.

Rhodes, Sonya. "A Developmental Approach to the Life Cycle of the Family," *Social Casework* (May 1977), 58(5):301–11.

Rhodes, Sonya L. "Contract Negotiation in the Initial Stage of Casework." *Social Service Review* (March 1977), 51:125–40.

Rice, David G., William F. Fey, and Joseph G. Kepecs. "Therapist Experience and Style as Factors in Co-Therapy." *Family Process* (March 1972), 11(1):1–12.

Richmond, Mary E. *Social Diagnosis*. New York: Russell Sage Foundation, 1917.

Richmond, Mary E. *What Is Social Case Work?* New York: Russell Sage Foundation, 1922.

Richmond, Virginia P. James C. McCroskey, and Steven K. Payne. *Nonverbal Behavior in Interpersonal Relations*. Englewood Cliffs, N.J., Prentice-Hall, 1987.

Ripple, Lilian. "Factors Associated with Continuance in Casework Service." *Social Work* (January 1957), 2(1):87–94.

Ripple, Lilian, Ernestina Alexander, and Bernice W. Polemis. *Motivation, Capacity, and Opportunity: Studies in Casework Theory and Practice*. Chicago: School of Social Service Administration, University of Chicago, 1964.

Riskin, Jules and Elaine E. Faunce. "An Evaluative Review of Family Interaction Research," *Family Process* (December 1972), 11(4):365–456.

Roberts, Robert W. and Helen Northen, eds. *Theories of Social Work with Groups*. New York: Columbia University Press, 1976.

Rogers, Carl R. "The Necessary and Sufficient Conditions for Therapeutic Personality Change." *Journal of Consulting Psychology* (1957), 21(1):95–103.

Rokeach, Milton. *The Nature of Human Values*. New York: Free Press, 1973.

Rosen, Aaron, Enola K. Procter, and Sheila Livne. "Planning and Direct Practice." *Social Service Review* (June 1985). 59(2):161–77.

Rosen, Aaron and Dina Lieberman. "The Experimental Evaluation of Interview Performance of Social Workers." *Social Service Review* (September 1972), 46(3):395–412.

Rosenblatt, Aaron and Diana Waldfogel, eds. *Handbook of Clinical Social Work*. San Francisco: Jossey-Bass, 1983.

Rothman, Beulah. "Study of Patterns of Leadership in Group Work Field Instruction." *Social Work with Groups* (Winter 1980), 3(4):11–17.

Rothman, Jack. "A Model of Case Management: Toward Empirically Based Practice." *Social Work* (1991), 36(6):520–29.

Rothman, Jack. "Analyzing Issues in Race and Ethnic Relations." In Rothman, ed., *Issues in Race and Ethnic Relations*, pp. 24–37.

Rothman, Jack. "Client Self-Determination: Untangling the Knot," *Social Service Review* (December 1989), 63:(4):598–612.

Rothman, Jack, ed. *Issues in Race and Ethnic Relations.* Itasca, Ill.: Peacock, 1977.

Rubin, Gerald K. "General Systems Theory: An Organismic Conception for Teaching Modalities of Social Work Intervention." *Smith College Studies in Social Work* (June 1973), 43(3):206–29.

Ruesch, Jurgen and Welden Kees. *Nonverbal Communication: Notes on the Visual Perception of Human Relations.* Berkeley: University of California Press, 1956.

Russell, Mary Nomme. *Clinical Social Work: Research and Practice.* Newbury Park, Calif.: Sage Publications, 1990.

Rutter, Michael. *Helping Troubled Children.* New York: Plenum Press, 1975.

Ryan, Angela Shen. "Cultural Factors in Casework with Chinese Americans." *Social Casework* (June 1985), 66(6):337–40.

Saari, Carolyn. *Clinical Social Work Treatment: How Does It Work.* New York: Gardner Press, 1986.

Saari, Carolyn. *The Creation of Meaning in Clinical Social Work.* New York: Guilford Press, 1991.

Sacks, Jerome. "Action and Reflection Work with a Group of Homeless People. *Social Work with Groups* (1991), 14(3/4).

Sainsbury, Eric. "Client Studies : Their Contributions and Limitations in Influencing Social Work Practice." *British Journal of Social Work* (December 1987), 17(6):635–44.

Sainsbury, Eric. *Social Work with Families.* London: Routledge & Kegan Paul, 1975.

Saleebey, Dennis. "Biology's Challenge to Social Work: Embodying the Person-in-Environment Perspective." *Social Work* (March 1992), 37(2): 112–19.

Saleebey, Dennis. "In Clinical Social Work Practice, Is the Body Politic?" *Social Service Review* (December 1985), 59(4):578–692.

Saltzman, Andrea and Kathleen Proch. *Law and Social Work Practice.* Chicago: Nelson-Hall, 1989.

Sample, Steven. "Message to the University Community." Transcript, 1992.

Sanville, Jean Bovard. "Theories, Therapies, Therapists: Their Transformation." *Smith College Studies in Social Work* (March 1987), 57(2):75–92.

Sarri, Rosemary and Frank Maple, eds. *The School in the Community.* Washington, D.C.: NASW, 1972.

Satir, Virginia M. *Conjoint Family Therapy: A Guide to Theory and Technique.* Palo Alto, Calif.: Science and Behavior Books, 1964.

Schaffer, Stephen and Jerrold Pollak. "Listening to the Adolescent Therapy Group." *Group* (Fall 1987), 11(3):155–164.

Schamess, Gerald. "Boundary Issues in Countertransference: A Developmental Perspective." *Clinical Social Work Journal* (Winter 1981), 9:244–57.

Scheidlinger, Saul. *Focus on Group Psychotherapy: Clinical Essays.* New York: International Universities Press, 1982.

Scheidlinger, Saul. "On Scapegoating in Group Psychotherapy." *International Journal of Group Psychotherapy* (April 1982), 32(2):131–44.

Scheidlinger, Saul. *Psychoanalysis and Group Behavior.* New York: Norton, 1952.

Scheidlinger, Saul and Marjorie A. Holden. "Group Therapy of Women with Severe Character Disorders: The Middle and Final Phases." *International Journal of Group Psychotherapy* (April 1966), 16(2):174–89.

Schiff, Sheldon K. "Termination of Therapy: Problems in a Community Psychiatric Outpatient Clinic." *Archives of General Psychiatry* (January 1962), 6(1):77–82.

Schlosberg, Nancy K. *Counseling Adults in Transition: Linking Practice with Theory.* New York: Springer, 1984.

Schmidt, Julianna. "The Use of Purpose in Casework Practice." *Social Work* (January 1969), 4(1):77–84.

Schon, Donald M. *The Reflective Practitioner: How Professionals Think in Action.* New York: Basic Books, 1983.

Schopler, Janice H. and Maeda J. Galinsky. "When Groups Go Wrong." *Social Work* (September 1981), 26(5):424–29.

Schur, Edwin M. *Labeling Deviant Behavior,* New York: Harper & Row, 1971.

Schutz, William C. *Interpersonal Underworld.* Palo Alto: Science and Behavior Books, 1966.

Schwartz, William. "Between Client and System: The Mediating Function." In Robert W. Roberts and Helen Northen, eds., *Theories of Social Work with Groups,* pp. 171–97. New York: Columbia University Press, 1976.

Schwartz, William. "Private Troubles and Public Issues: One Social Work Job or Two?" In *The Social Welfare Forum, 1969,* pp. 22–43. New York: Columbia University Press, 1969.

Seabury, Brett A. "Arrangement of Physical Space in Social Work Settings." *Social Work* (October 1971), 16(4)"43–49.

Seabury, Brett A. "Communication Problems in Social Work Practice." *Social Work* (January 1980), 25(1):409–44.

Seattle Post Intelligencer. "A Bad Ruling for Child Services." Editorial, April 10, 1991.

Segal, Lynn. "Focused Problem Resolution." In Eleanor Reardon Tolsen and William J. Reid, eds., *Models of Family Treatment,* pp. 199–233. New York: Columbia University Press, 1981.

Selby, Lola G. "Supportive Treatment: The Development of a Concept and a Helping Method." *Social Service Review* (December 1956), 30(4):400–414.

Selby, Lola G. "Support Revisited." *Social Service Review* (December 1979), 53(4):573–85.

Sereno, Kenneth K. and C. David Mortensen. *Foundations of Communication Theory.* New York: Harper & Row, 1970.

Sharfstein, Steven S., O. B. Towery, and Irvin D. Milowe. "Accuracy of Diagnostic Information Submitted to an Insurance Company." *American Journal of Psychiatry* (January 1980), 137(1):70–73.

Shaw, Lulie A. "Impressions of Life in a London Suburb." *Sociological Review* (December 1954), 2(2):177–94.

Shaw, Marvin E. *Group Dynamics: The Psychology of Small Group Behavior.* 3d ed. New York: McGraw-Hill, 1981.

Sherman, Sanford N. "Family Therapy." In Francis J. Turner, ed., *Social Work Treatment: Interlocking Theoretical Approaches,* pp. 457–94. New York: Free Press, 1974.

Sherman, Sanford N. "The Choice of Group Therapy for Casework Clients." In *Social Work Practice, 1962,* pp. 174–86. New York: Columbia University Press, 1962.

Shimer, John A. *This Sculptured Earth: The Landscape of America.* New York: Columbia University Press, 1959.

Shulman, Lawrence. "Scapegoats, Group Workers, and Pre-Emptive Intervention." *Social Work* (1967), 12(2):37–45.

Shulman, Lawrence. *The Skills of Helping Individuals, Families, and Groups.* 3d ed. Itasca, Ill.: Peacock, 1992.

Siegel, Bernie S. *Love, Medicine, and Miracles.* New York: Harper & Row, 1990.

Silberman, Buddy. "A New Strain for Social Work." Paper presented at the Annual Meeting of the Group for the Advancement of Doctoral Education, October 1982.

Silverman, Phyllis. *Mutual Help Groups: Organization and Development.* Beverly Hills: Sage, 1980.

Simmons, June W. "A Philosophical Perspective on Social Work Administration." Unpublished paper, 1986.

Simmons, June W. "Planning for Discharge with the Elderly." *Quality Review Bulletin* (1986), 12(2):68–71.

Siporin, Max. *Introduction to Social Work Practice.* New York: Macmillan, 1975.

Smalley, Ruth Elizabeth. *Theory for Social Work Practice,* New York: Columbia University Press, 1967.

Smolar, Elwyn M. "Schizophrenic Disorders." In Francis Turner, ed., *Adult Psychopathology: A Social Work Perspective,* pp. 119–47. New York: Free Press, 1984.

Solomon, Barbara Bryant. *Black Empowerment: Social Work in Oppressed Communities.* New York: Columbia University Press, 1976.

Somers, Mary Louise. "Group Process Within the Family Unit." In National Association of Social Workers, *The Family Is the Patient: the Group Approach to the Treatment of Family Health Problems,* pp. 22–39. Monograph VII. New York: NASW, 1965.

Somers, Mary Louise. "Problem-Solving in Small Groups." In Robert W. Roberts and Helen Northen, eds., *Theories of Social Work with Groups,* pp. 331–67. New York: Columbia University Press, 1976.

Sotomayor, Marta. "Language, Culture, and Ethnicity in the Developing Self Concept." *Social Casework* (April 1977). 58(4):195–203.

Sotomayor, Marta. "Mexican-American Interaction with Social Systems." *Social Casework* (May 1971), 52(5):316–22.

Spiegel, John P. "An Ecological Model with an Emphasis on Ethnic Families." In Eleanor R. Tolson and William J. Reid, *Models of Family Treatment*, pp. 327–68. New York: Columbia University Press, 1981.

Sprung, Gloria M. "Transferential Issues in Working with Older Adults." *Social Casework* (December 1989), 70(10):597–602.

Startz, Morton R. and Helen F. Cohen. "The Impact of Social Change on the Practitioner." *Social Casework* (September 1980), 61(7)400–406.

Stein, Irma L. *Systems Theory, Science, and Social Work*. Metuchen, N.J.: Scarecrow Press, 1974.

Stein, Irma L. "The Systems Model and Social Systems Theory." In Herbert S. Strean, ed., *Social Casework: Theories in Action*, pp. 123–95. Metuchen, N.J.: Scarecrow Press, 1971.

Stempler, Benjamin. "A Group Work Approach to Family Group Treatment." *Social Casework* (March 1977), 58(3):143–52.

Stewart, Robert. "From the President." *NASW News* (1985), 30:2–3.

Stiles, Evelyn et al. "Hear It Like It Is." *Social Casework* (May 1972), 42(5): 292–99.

Sue, Donald Wing. *Counseling the Culturally Different: Theory and Practice*. 2d ed. New York: Wiley, 1990.

Sundel, Martin, Norma Radin, and Sallie R. Churchill. "Diagnosis in Group Work." In Paul Glasser, Rosemary Sarri, and Robert Vinter, eds., *Individual Change Through Small Groups*, pp. 105–25. New York: Free Press, 1974.

Takaki, Ronald R. *Strangers From a Different Shore. A History of Asian Americans*. Boston: Little Brown 1989.

Taylor, Edward H. "Schizophrenia: Fire in The Brain." *Social Work* (May 1989), 34(3):258–61.

Taylor, Edward H. "The Biological Basis of Schizophrenia." *Social Work* (March/April 1987), 31(2):115–21.

Terkelsen, Kenneth G. "Toward a Theory of the Family Life Cycle." In Elizabeth A. Carter and Monica McGoldrick, eds., *The Family Life Cycle: A Framework for Family Therapy*, pp. 21–52. New York: Gardner Press, 1980.

Thomlinson, Raymond J., ed. *Perspective on Industrial Social Work Practice*. Ottawa: Family Service Canadian Publications, 1983.

Toch, Hans. "The Care and Feeding of Typologies and Labels." *Federal Probation* (September 1970), 34(3):15–19.

Tolson, Eleanor Reardon. "Conclusions Toward a Metamodel for Eclectic Family Practice." In Eleanor Reardon Tolson and William H. Reid, eds., *Models of Family Treatment*. New York: Columbia University Press, 1981.

Tolson, Eleanor Reardon and William J. Reid, eds. *Models of Family Treatment*. New York: Columbia University Press, 1981.

Toseland, Ronald W. and Robert F. Rivas. *An Introduction to Group Work Practice*. New York: Macmillan, 1984.

Toseland, Ronald W. and Lyndan Hacker. "Self-Help Groups and Professional Involvement." *Social Work* (July 1982), 27(4):341–48.

Toseland, Ronald W. and Max Siporin. "When to Recommend Group Treatment: A Review of the Clinical and Research Literature." *International Journal of Group Psychotherapy* (April 1986), 36(2):171–206.

Toth, Robert C. "New Ties to the Old Country." *Los Angeles Times*, May 14, 1991.

Towle, Charlotte. "Social Casework in Modern Society." *Social Service Review* (June 1946), 20(2):65–79.

Tracy, Elizabeth M. and James K. Whittaker. "The Evidence Base for Social Support Interventions in Child and Family Practice: Emerging Issues for Research and Practice." *Children and Youth Services Review* (1987), 9(4): 249–70.

Trefethen, Florence. "Circles of Strength." *Bryn Mawr Alumnae Bulletin* (Fall 1990), 72(1):6–8.

Truax, Charles B. and Robert R. Carkhuff. *Toward Effective Counseling and Psychotherapy: Training and Practice.* Chicago: Aldine, 1967.

Tufts, Edith, *Group Work with Young School Girls.* Los Angeles: Los Angeles Area Council, Camp Fire Girls, 1968.

Turner, Francis J., ed. *Adult Psychopathology: A Social Work Perspective.* New York: Free Press, 1984.

Turner, Francis J. *Psychosocial Therapy: A Social Work Perspective.* New York: Free Press, 1978.

Turner, Francis J., ed. *Social Work Treatment: Interlocking Theoretical Approaches.* 2d ed. New York: Free Press, 1979.

Tyson, Katherine B. "A New Approach to Relevant Scientific Research for Practitioners: The Heuristic Paradigm." *Social Work* (November 1992), 37(6):541–57.

U.S. Code. Congressional and Administrative News. 94th Cong., 1st sess. Public Law 94-942. "Education for All Handicapped Children Act of 1975," pp. 773–96. St. Paul: West Publishing, 1976.

U.S. Code. Congressional and Administrative News. 96th Cong., 2d sess. Public Law 96-272. "Adoption Assistance and Child Welfare Act of 1980," pp. 511–35. St. Paul: West Publishing.

U.S. Department of Labor. *A Report on the Glass Ceiling Initiative.* Washington, D.C.: GPO, 1991.

U.S. Department of Labor. *Pipelines of Progress: An Update on the Glass Ceiling Initiative.* Washington, D.C.: GPO, 1992.

University of Southern California. *Transcript. Faculty Newsletter* (March 1989). Los Angeles: University of Southern California.

Velasquez, Joan et al. "A Framework for Establishing Social Work Relationships Across Racial Ethnic Lines." In Beulah Roberts Compton and Burt Galaway, eds., *Social Work Processes*, pp. 197–203. Homewood, Ill.: Dorsey Press, 1979.

Videka-Sherman, Lynn. "Child Abuse and Neglect." In Alex Gitterman, ed., *Handbook of Social Work Practice with Vulnerable Populations.* New York: Columbia University Press, 1991.

Videka-Sherman, Lynn. *Harriet M. Bartlett Practice Effectiveness Project Final Report.* Silver Spring, Md.: NASW, 1985.

Videka-Sherman, Lynn and William J. Reid, eds. "Symposium: Epistomology for Clinical Social Work." *Advances in Clinical Social Work Research.* Washington, D.C.: NASW Press, 1990.

Vigilante, Florence Wexler and Mildred D. Mailich. "Needs-Resource Evaluation in the Assessment Process." *Social Work* (March/April 1988), 33(2):101–04.

von Bertalanffy, Ludwig. *A General Systems Theory.* New York: Braziller, 1968.

von Bertalanffy, Ludwig. "General Systems Theory and Psychiatry." In Silvano Arieti, ed., *American Handbook of Psychiatry*, pp. 1095–1117. New York: Basic Books, 1976.

Vourlekis, Betsy S. "Cognitive Theory for Social Work Practice." In Roberta R. Greene and Paul H. Ephross, *Human Behavior Theory and Social Work Practice*, pp. 123–50. New York: Aldine DeGruyter, 1991.

Wallace, Stephen R., Richard S. Goldberg, and Andrew Slaby. *Clinical Social Work in Health Care.* New York: Praeger, 1988.

Wallerstein, Judith S. "Transference and Countertransference in Clinical Intervention with Divorcing Families." *American Journal of Orthopsychiatry* (July 1990), 60(3):337–45.

Warner, W. Lloyd. *Life in America: Dream and Reality.* New York: Harper, 1952.

Warner, W. Lloyd. *Social Class in America.* New York: Harper, 1949.

Wasserman, Sidney. "Ego Psychology." In Francis J. Turner, ed., *Social Work Treatment: Interlocking Theoretical Approaches*, pp. 42–83. New York: Free Press, 1974.

Watkins, Sallie A. "Confidentiality and Privileged Communications: Legal Dilemma for Family Therapists." *Social Work* (March 1989), 34(2):133–44.

Watkins, Sallie A. and John C. Watkins. "Negligent Endangerment, Malpractice in The Clinical Context." *Journal of Independent Social Work* (1989), 3(3):35–50.

Wayne, Julianne L. and Barbara B. Feinstein. "Group Work Outreach to Parents by School Social Workers." *Social Casework* (June 1978), 59(6):345–51.

Webb, Allen F. and Patrick V. Riley. "Effectiveness of Casework with Young Female Probationers." *Social Casework* (November 1970), 51(9):566–72.

Webb, Nancy Boyd. "A Crisis Intervention Perspective on the Termination Process." *Clinical Social Work Journal* (Winter 1985), 13(4):329–40.

Weil, Marie and Ernest Sanchez. "The Impact of the Tarasoff Decision on Clinical Social Work Practice." *Social Service Review* (March 1983), 57(1):112–24.

Weil, Marie, James M. Karls, and Associates. *Case Management in Human Service Practice.* San Francisco: Jossey-Bass, 1985.

Wellisch, David K. "On Stabilizing Families with an Unstable Illness: Helping Disturbed Families Cope with Cancer." In M. R. Lasky, ed., *Family Therapy and Major Psychopathology.* New York: Grune and Stratton, 1981, 281–300.

Wells, Richard A. and Alan Dezen. "The Results of Family Treatment Revisited: The Nonverbal Methods." *Family Process* (September 1978), 17(31):251–74.

West, Jane. "Ending or Beginning: A Discussion of the Theory and Practice of Termination Processes in Play Therapy." *Journal of Social Work Practice* (May 1984), 1(2):49–65.

Whittaker, James K. *Caring for Troubled Children.* San Francisco: Jossey-Bass, 1979.

Whittaker, James K. "Causes of Childhood Disorders: New Findings." *Social Work* (March 1976), 21(2):91–96.

Whittaker, James K. *Social Treatment: An Approach to Interpersonal Helping.* Chicago: Aldine, 1974.

Whittaker, James K., James Garborino, and Associates. *Social Support Networks: Informal Helping in the Human Services.* New York: Aldine DeGruyter, 1983.

Whittington, Ronaele. "The New Friendly Visitors: A Rediscovered Role for Independent Social Workers." *Journal of Independent Social Work* (Fall 1986), 1(1):65–78.

Wiener, Norbert. *The Human Use of Human Beings.* 2d ed. New York: Doubleday, 1954.

Williams, Barbara E. "The Salvation of Sara: Treatment History of an Adolescent Girl." *Residential Treatment for Children and Youth* (Fall 1987), 5(1):17–29.

Williams, Janet B. W. "DSM-III: A Comprehensive Approach to Diagnosis." *Social Work* (March 1981), 26(2):101–6.

Williams, Marla. "Taking Charge: Local Tribes Evoke the Spirit of the Past to Shape a New Vision of Independence." *Pacific, Seattle Times–Seattle Post Intelligencer*, September 22, 1991, pp. 16–29.

Wilmott, Peter. *Family and Kinship Ties in East London.* London: Routledge & Kegan Paul, 1957.

Wilson, Gertrude. *Group Work and Casework: Their Relationship and Practice.* New York: Family Welfare Association of America, 1941.

Wilson, William J. *The Truly Disadvantaged: The Inner City, the Underclass, and Public Policy.* Chicago: University of Chicago Press, 1987.

Winett, R. A. "Ecobehavioral Assessment in Health Life Styles: Concepts and Methods." In Paul Koroly, *Measurement Strategies in Health Psychology*, pp. 149–82. New York: Wiley, 1985.

Winnicott, Clare. "Casework Techniques in the Child Care Service." In Eileen Younghusband, ed., *New Developments in Casework*, pp. 135–54. London: Allen & Unwin, 1966.

Winters, Wendy Glasgow and Freda Easton. *The Practice of Social Work in Schools.* New York: Free Press, 1983.

Wood, Katherine. *Families at Risk: Treating the Multiproblem Family.* New York: Human Sciences Press, 1989.

Woods, Mary E. "Personality Disorders." In Francis J. Turner, ed., *Adult Psychopathology: A Social Work Perspective*, pp. 200–249. New York: Free Press, 1984.

Woods, Mary E. and Florence Hollis. *Casework: A Psychosocial Therapy*. 4th ed. New York: McGraw-Hill, 1990.

Yalom, Irvin D. *Inpatient Group Psychotherapy*. New York: Basic Books, 1983.

Yalom, Irvin D. *The Theory and Practice of Group Psychotherapy*. New York: Basic Books, 1970; 2d ed. 1975; 3d ed. 1985.

Younghusband, Eileen, *Social Work and Social Change*. London: Allen and Unwin, 1964.

Zalba, Serapio R. "Discontinuance During Social Service Intake." Ph.D. dissertation, Western Reserve University, 1971.

Index